Words on the Wing

Slang, Aphorisms, Catchphrases and Jargon
of Canadian Military Aviation Since 1914

Compiled and Illustrated by

Tom Langeste

Canadian Cataloguing in Publication Data

Langeste, Thomas, 1954-
  Words on the wing: slang, aphorisms, catchphrases and jargon of Canadian military aviation since 1914

Includes bibliographical references.
ISBN 0-919769-53-5

1. Aeronautics, Military - Canada - Terminology. 2. Aeronautics, Military - Canada - Slang. I. Canadian Institute of Strategic Studies. II. Canada. Canadian Armed Forces. Office of Air Force Heritage & History. III. Title.

UG628.L35 1995   358.4'003   C95-932428-3

This volume was printed and bound in Canada
by Canadian Printco Limited.

Requiem for an Air Gunner

My brief sweet life is over, my eyes no longer see,
No summer walks - no Christmas trees - no pretty girls for me,
I've got the chop, I've had it, my nightly ops are done,
Yet in another hundred years, I'll still be twenty-one.

R. W. Gilbert

TABLE OF CONTENTS

LIST OF ILLUSTRATIONS

ABBREVIATIONS

AC1	Aircraftman 1st Class
AC2	Aircraftman 2nd Class
ASW	Anti- Submarine Warfare
CAF	Canadian Air Force or Canadian Armed Forces
CF	Canadian Forces
CFB ·	Canadian Forces Base
CO	Commanding Officer
Cpl	Corporal
CWO	Chief Warrant Officer
DH	De Havilland
DHC	De Havilland Canada
F/S	Flight Sergeant
HMS	His Majesty's Ship or Her Majesty's Ship
HMCS	His Majesty's Canadian Ship or Her Majesty's Canadian Ship
LAC	Leading Aircraftman
MCpl	Master Corporal
NATO	North Atlantic Treaty Organization
NCO	Non-Commissioned Officer
NCM	Non-Commissioned Member
NORAD	North American Air Defence
POW	Prisoner of War
RAF	Royal Air Force
RCAF	Royal Canadian Air Force
RCEME	Royal Canadian Electrical and Mechanical Engineers
RCN	Royal Canadian Navy
RFC	Royal Flying Corps
RNAS	Royal Naval Air Service
Sgt	Sergeant
USAF	United States Air Force
USN	United States Navy
USMC	United States Marine Corps
WO	Warrant Officer
WWI	World War One
WWII	World War Two

FOREWORD

Through two World Wars and the UN Korean war, many Canadians served their country and lived, while others made the supreme sacrifice. For those of us who survived, we have had the opportunity to read, if not write, about our experiences. With each passing year more appear in print since personal stories will become lost or forgotten with the passage of time if they are not put on paper.

Writing about war is difficult enough and almost impossible to describe so that the reader can understand, without using the colourful language that the stress of war and the fear of dying generate. Some writers choose to ignore this aspect of war while others do not and in so doing use a vocabulary almost unknown to the layman. The idiom of the moment depended on the timing and, in many cases, the location of the war.

I believe it is true to say that many words and expressions came from the tongue of the British Tommy, even before WWI, who did not hesitate to express his dislike, if not hatred, for the life he found himself in and would do so using every cuss or swear word he had ever picked up in the back streets of London. It was colourful language to say the least and has been passed down from war to war but modified to meet the conditions of the current situation.

This book or lexicon of the expressions used by the Canadian military aviation community, past and present, is a valuable addition to military history although it is not a narrative history which one normally expects from a military book. Instead the avid reader of such fare will find this book almost a necessity if much jargon and idiom is used. But even by itself it is a fascinating read for those who spent many years in the military and wondered where certain expressions originated. Now they can find out.

R.J. 'Reg' Lane
LGen (Ret'd) DSO DFC CD

INTRODUCTION

"He wants to get back to that closed language that is Air Force slang"

Richard Hillary,
The Last Enemy

This lexicon had its genesis during my service in the late and much lamented 418 "City of Edmonton" Squadron, where for many years I had been an airframe technician and later an engineering officer. Our Public Affairs Officer was proposing a monthly unit newsletter and asked if I would contribute a cartoon from time to time. I agreed and began to search for a unifying theme for what I thought might become a local cartoon series.

I settled upon the idea of using a cartoon to illustrate a common, everyday phrase heard around the hangar so I set to work, jotting down familiar "air force" words and phrases, drawing first on my experience of two decades or so. After my list had grown to several hundred without discernable effort, I realized there was more here than a cartoon series. Indeed this was a job for a serious lexicographer! However, in the absence of a serious lexicographer, I began to scour reference works myself. I re-read various memoirs for the slang of earlier generations, and I consulted long-suffering friends for current slang. Five years later, the result is this compendium and its illustrations.

At first blush, this book is about words. It is less concerned with formal or technical terminology than with informal, day-to-day vocabulary: slang, jargon, cant, colloquialisms, catchphrases, nicknames, aphorisms, codewords and verbal short-hand. Though the academics may object, I have taken the liberty of describing all of these categories as "slang".

This collection is not a scholarly work in the truest sense of the word, though I have attempted to honour scholarly requirements. Where possible, words and phrases have been researched from primary sources and the bibliographic references cited at the end of the entry. Many entries however, do not list a reference. This means the entry has been included on the basis of my own experience or on that of other contributors.

Also, as is manifestly obvious, this is a collection of English-Canadian slang; I make no claim to be able to catalog the informal usage of French-Canadian airmen and airwomen. Nonetheless, I hope that this work may assist them in comprehending some of the more puzzling speech of their Anglophone *copains*!

This book is about words, but as importantly, it is also about the experiences behind these words. Canadian military aviation boasts an unbroken line of experience, service and tradition dating from 1914, and this specific sub-culture now spans several generations. These experiences found expression in language and in turn, their vocabulary helped to define this unique culture.

In deciding what words and phrases to include I have cast my net widely. This is not just a collection of aircrew slang, though their central role means that much will be familiar to those with wings on their tunic. Still, most airmen and airwomen do not fly for a living, and they are no less "air force" for being pedestrians! Therefore I have tried to collect the slang of the logisticians, the air traffic controllers, the aircraft engineers and technicians, and indeed everyone who supports flying operations. Nor have I distinguished between the peacetime regulars, the wartime "hostilities only" volunteers, or the auxiliaries and reservists. This collection includes slang of administrators and military musicians!

I have also taken liberties with the scope of the words "air force". Canadians have served in many military flying organizations: the Royal Flying Corps, the Royal Naval Air Service, the Royal Air Force, and the Royal Navy's Fleet Air Arm; they have served in the Canadian Air Force and the Royal Canadian Air Force; they have flown as members of the Royal Canadian Navy and the Canadian Army, which amalgamated with the RCAF in 1968 to form the Canadian Armed Forces. I hope I am not too presumptuous when I regard all of these as "Air Force" for the purposes of this book.

Dyed-in-the-wool sailors and soldiers will recognize many of the entries in this collection. Much of the vocabulary of airmen and airwomen is military in the general sense rather than being specifically air force. Life-long civilians will recognize much in these pages also. Indeed many words and phrases common in civilian slang have their origins in military life. Similarly, a lot of air force slang is merely "adopted" civilian slang, and is only "military" because it has lived on in the service after falling into disuse by civilians. This is especially true of British wartime slang picked up by Canadian servicemembers in two world wars.

For the first half of the Twentieth Century, British and Canadian military flying were inextricably linked, and Canadian military aviators served as readily with British units as Canadian. Therefore I have included much of the RNAS, RFC, Fleet Air Arm and RAF slang as was current prior to 1945, and have deemed it "Canadian". The records show that, for the most part, the slang was common, so I do not feel that this is too great a liberty. Similarly, after 1945 very close links were established with the United States armed forces, links which enriched Canadian military vocabulary. Though there isn't a one-to-one correspondence with American military slang, many words and phrases will be familiar to our cousins, the "Yanks", from whom we got them. Indeed, the post-Second World War period saw the Canadian military forge strong links with many military air services through NATO, the UN, NORAD, and the Commonwealth connection. The result has been a rather cosmopolitan vocabulary of international military aviation, much of which is reflected in Canadian Air Force slang.

I make no apologies for the fact that the vocabulary to follow is often off-colour, occasionally obscene and frequently lacks political correctness. I do not believe this lexicon dwells unduly on off-colour subjects, nor is their inclusion gratuitous. However, I will not ignore them. This is, after all, the slang of a military body which trained for, and all too often fought in, the wars. Indeed, even peacetime service is fraught with hazard. Airmen and airwomen serve under terms commonly described as "unlimited liability", and genteel social sensibilities usually pale in importance as a servicemember confronts his own mortality. One's sense of propriety, morality, humour, and proportion all change. Those who are easily offended are advised to read other books.

A lexicon such as this can never be truly accurate, nor truly complete. Still I have done my best to ensure that each entry is as correct and complete as I understand it. Also, I am painfully aware that the slang of several important service branches is under-represented in these pages. I wish there had been more entries from Canadian Army aviation, and from the Air Traffic Controllers, the RCAF Women's Division, the medical and dental folks, etc. However, I acknowledge that incompleteness and inaccuracy are inevitable therefore I invite comment, correction, and corroboration. This book only scratches the surface! It is the nature of slang to be subjective and ever-expanding, and with good luck and good management this will result in further editions of Words on the Wing.

ACKNOWLEDGEMENTS

This book could not have come about without the assistance, encouragement, contribution, comment and correction, and (in several notable cases) the very hard work, of others. This brief space does not permit me to recognize everyone I would have liked, but I must express my sincerest gratitude to the following (listed 'tallest on the right, and shortest on the left' - and alphabetically):

Doreen and Jim Anderson, Wayne and Darlene Bakker, Leonard Birchall, Jock and Sheila Cameron, Iain and Tammy Cameron, Scott Clements, Bill Cottrell, Ray Cryderman, Glenna Dunfield, Jim Hanson, Ron Haskell, Dr Bob Hursey, Reginald Lane, Martin and Debbie Langeste, Mark Larsen, Gil MacCaulay, Ian and Kit McCandie, Joe McGoldrick, Rick Maclagan, Susan McNish, Bill March, Art Maskell, Dr. Carolyn Neal, Pat Parsonage, Don Pearsons, Graham Rosher, Spence Sample, Tom Sand, Tom Stobbs, H.M. "Suds" Sutherland, Bob Thompson, Rick Watson, Robbie Watt, Willy Williams, Roy Woodburn, Marie Wright, and of course, Mum and Dad!

Tom Langeste
Edmonton, Alberta
August, 1995

A LPHA

A.A.A.   See **Triple A**

A.B.   See **Burners**

ABBEVILLE BOYS; ABBEVILLE KIDS (RAF, RCAF; 1940-44) — Second World War RAF and RCAF fighter pilots often referred to the Luftwaffe fighter units stationed at or near, Abbeville, France as the "Abbeville Boys" or the "Abbeville Kids". Located across the English Channel south-east of Dover, the Abbeville Boys were the closest and the most commonly-engaged of the Luftwaffe units faced by Allied fighters in Britain. [Ref: Partridge (8th)]

Some of the Abbeville Boys

The Abbeville Boys jumped us just as we crossed over the French coast.

ABDUL (RCAF; post 1945) — "APDAL" (or perhaps "APDL" - the origins seem lost) was a once-common RCAF abbreviation or acronym. It was a supply code for surplus aircraft or equipment, destined for disposal. Occasionally, clubs on air bases that needed a financial break would seek surplus equipment or furniture "from APDAL". Now and then however, gullible young airmen unfamiliar with the term APDAL were deceived into believing that the term was actually "Abdul", and told that there was an enterprising Arab around with a private source of air force equipment! [Ref: Sutherland]

Do you suppose that we could get some furniture from Abdul?

ab initio (RAF, RCAF, CF; current) — Ab initio is a Latin term meaning "from the beginning", and is commonly used in relation to initial flying training. Therefore, one speaks of an ab initio trainer, or an ab initio pilot trainee, etc.

The Air Force used the Chipmunk aircraft as an ab initio trainer until the Beechcraft Musketeer replaced it.

ABORT (universal, aviation; since at least WWII) — Aviators do not stop an event; instead they abort it. In strict military parlance, the word abort is only used if the task is cancelled for reasons other than enemy action. Therefore, military aviators abort a takeoff, abort the mission, or perform a ground-abort, etc. [Refs: Gentle and Reithmaier; Harvey]

The pilot spotted a deer on the runway ahead and aborted the takeoff.

ACE (since 1914; originally French) — An "ace" is a combat aviator who has destroyed five or more enemy aircraft in aerial combat.

The term ace comes from pre-1914 French slang, where an ace was someone who excelled in sports (in French: *l'as*). The term was first applied to combat aviators in June of 1915. A French newspaper dubbed French aviator Adolphe Pegoud *l'as de notre aviation*, after destroying five German aircraft (he was to ultimately destroy ten). After this, the names of French aviators who had destroyed five or more enemy aircraft were regularly publicized. Borrowing from the sportsman's slang of the day, these airmen became popularly known as aces.

Ace

The custom of designating an aviator as an Ace after five victories, originated in France during the First World War.

In contrast to the French, British Commonwealth air services have never formally recognized ace as a status. The high command believed that glorifying fighter pilots merely caused bad blood between fighter pilots and other airmen whose jobs were as dangerous and demanding, but who could never become an ace. However, despite this lack of official standing, the British public, in search of heroes, soon lionized pilots with over five "kills" as aces. Still, regulations do not recognize the status of ace and though a strong tradition exists, it remains an unofficial tradition.

Though the status of ace is usually associated with fighter pilots, navigators of two-seat fighters and air gunners have also been received as aces. For example, RCAF Flight Sergeant Peter Engbrecht became an ace after shooting down five Luftwaffe aircraft from the top turret of a Lancaster bomber. (For another example, see **Brisfit**)

A "Double Ace" is a person who has shot down ten aircraft, twice the number needed to become an ace; similarly, a "Triple-Ace" has shot down fifteen. An "Ace of Aces" is the ace having the highest final tally of aircraft destroyed. Canada's Ace of Aces is Billy Bishop, with 72 victories during the First World War. The Ace of Aces of the First World War was Baron Manfred Von Richthofen, with 80 victories. Canada's leading ace of the Second World War was Flight Lieutenant George "Screwball" Beurling, with 31 kills. The all-time "Ace of Aces" is Erich Hartmann, a Luftwaffe ME-109 pilot who destroyed 352 aircraft, nearly all on the Eastern Front during the Second World War. [Refs: Longstreet; Partridge (8th)]

ACEY-DEUCEY (RCAF, post WWII) — An "Acey-Deucey" is an Aircraftman 2nd Class, the lowest rank in the RCAF. Acey-Deucey derives from the official abbreviation for the rank: "AC 2". The number 2 becomes "deuce" and the term becomes "AC deuce", then Acey-Deucey. (Acey-Deucey is also the name of a variation of backgammon popular in the navy) (See also **AC Plonk**) [Ref: Collins; Elting]

Acey-Deucy

ACK-ACK (British Commonwealth; 1914-45) — "Ack-Ack" is Anti-Aircraft fire. The term derives from the First World War British phonetic alphabet where the word "ack" denotes the letter "A". Therefore, anti-aircraft fire becomes AA fire, which then becomes ack-ack fire, which is finally abbreviated to ack-ack. (Hence also, ack-ack gun) [Ref: Partridge (8th)]

Gerry's Halifax got nailed by ack-ack north of Frankfurt.

ACK EMMA (RFC; WWI) — "Ack Emma" was a term derived from the First World War phonetic codes for the letters "A" and "M", and could be taken to mean either of:

(1)   "Air Mechanic", the most junior rank in the Royal Flying Corps, as in: *our ack emmas had been very busy.* The short-lived Canadian Air Force (1920-24) also used the "Air Mechanic" rank, and so the nickname ack emma was common in Canada until this rank lapsed into obsolescence in 1924 when the RCAF was established. The rank of Aircraftman supplanted Air Mechanic in both the RAF and the RCAF) (See also **Acey Deucey, AC Plonk, Erk**) [Refs: Partridge (8th); Sutherland; Voss]

(2)   "Ante Meridiem", or A.M., which describes times after midnight and before noon. (For example, ten o'clock ack emma) Until the twenty-four-hour clock became universal in the British Imperial Forces, it was critical to distinguish between times that were A.M. and times which were P.M. Times

that were A.M. were ack emma, as in *9 o'clock ack emma*. (See also **Pip Emma**)

ACK W (RFC; WWI) — During the First World War the Armstrong-Whitworth aircraft company designed and built an artillery observation aircraft designated the FK-7. This aircraft was occasionally known as the "Ack W", another example of the First World War phonetic alphabet being incorporated into common usage. The Armstrong-Whitworth became known by its initials, A.W. Given that ack was the phonetic code for the letter A, it didn't take long for the aircraft to become known as the Ack W. (There was then no codeword for the letter W.)(See also: **Ack Emma, Pip Emma, Emma Toc, O Pip**) [Ref: Voss]

ACKERS (Originally British) — Originally English naval slang, "ackers" is money, as in: *Me?! I haven't any ackers!* [Refs: Harvey; Partridge (FS)]

ACM (ie., "eh-see-emm") — ACM is the abbreviation for either of two common terms:

(1)   *Air Chief Marshal*, the highest rank in the RAF after Marshal of the RAF (generally seen only in print, and not spoken), or

(2)   *Air Combat Manoeuvring*, the tactics, technology, arts and sciences of aerial combat. This has long since supplanted the word dogfight in military aviation, as in: *We spent an hour in ACM training out on the range this morning.*

AC PLONK (RAF since 1920's; RCAF in WWII) — An "AC plonk" is a person holding the rank of Aircraftman 2nd Class, the lowest rank in the RAF and RCAF. The term is derived from the initials AC (for Aircraftman) and plonk. Plonk is said to mean mud, but can also be very cheap white wine (from the French word *blanc*). Either word can mean worthless, a humorous reflection of the low status of the Aircraftman 2nd Class . (See also **Acey-Deucey**) [Ref: Partridge (8th)]

I'm not an AC Plonk! I'm an Aircraftman FIRST Class!

ADJ.; ADJIE — The Adjutant of an air force unit is inevitably called the "adj." or (occasionally, in wartime days), the "adjie". The adj. is the deputy to the Commanding Officer for administrative and disciplinary matters. [Ref: Partridge (8th)]

ADRIFT, TO BE (RCN, RCAF; WWII) — "To be adrift" is naval slang for being lost, or late and may have entered air force use through the Royal Naval Air Service of the First World War. However, the unification of the Canadian Forces in 1968 probably added new life to its usage outside the navy. Former naval and air force aviators began to serve together, and adopted each other's slang. [Refs: Elting; Partridge (8th)]

Is McIntosh adrift again?!

AERIAL COOLIES (Far East Forces, WWII) — "Aerial Coolies" were air transport squadrons tasked with aerial resupply of the British and Indian Army forces in Southeast Asia, primarily in Burma. The RCAF had two such squadrons in the theatre: 435 (Chinthe) Squadron, and 436 (Tusker) Squadron, both of which flew the DC3 Dakota. The term borrows from coolie, the word for an Asian manual labourer. (See **Dak**) [Ref: Partridge (FS)]

AFFIRMATIVE (general military and aviation use) — Affirmative is what an aviator often says instead of "yes". Occasionally "affirmative" is shortened to "affirm", "that's affirm" and is even sometimes pronounced: "eh- firm". Use of the word is mandated by the rules of radio voice procedure. These rules prefer multi-syllabic words to words of one syllable (to reduce loss of clarity when there is static or interference). So, affirmative is preferable to yes in radio speech and the practice has now crept out of the cockpit.

> *Are you guys finished for the day?*
> *...that's affirm' !!*

A.F.P. (RCAF; post WWII) — "A.F.P." is the abbreviation and moniker for the airman's natural enemy, the "Air Force Police", responsible for law enforcement and disciplinary control. As such they were the agents charged with curbing the natural exuberance of young airmen when it began to annoy the taxpayer. During the Second World War they were known as the Service Police. After unification in 1968 the A.F.P.'s were integrated with the army's Provost Corps and the Naval Police to form the CF Security Branch, though they are usually referred to (outside polite company) as the Military Police, or "M.P.'s". (See also **A.P., Gestapo, Meathead, S.P.**)

AGENTS, TO HAVE ONE'S — A person who "has his agents" is well-informed. The term suggests that the speaker is surreptitiously advised by a network of informants or agents. It is also an ironic way of refusing to reveal one's sources of some information or rumour, while suggesting the cloak and dagger world of secret agents. [Ref: Partridge (8th)]

> *How do you know I'm posted to CFB Beaverleavings?!*
> *I have my agents...*

AGONY BAGS — "Agony Bags" are bagpipes (a term considered pejorative by those who love pipe music, and a proper noun by those who don't). [Ref: Partridge (8th)]

A.I. (RCAF since the 1950's, CF; now rare) — "A.I." was the designation and nickname for the air navigator who directed an air intercept from the rear seat of a two-seat interceptor aircraft. The term is shorthand. During the 1950's such an airman was designated "Observer/Air Intercept" or "Observer/A.I." (as distinguished from, say, "Observer/Maritime"). Later, the designation changed to "Navigator/Air Intercept", or "Nav/A.I.". In any event, a Canadian fighter navigator was generally known as an A.I.

The A.I. flew as the second crewman in both CF-100 Canuck and CF-101 Voodoo interceptor aircraft. The A.I. operated the radar, directed the interception of an intruding aircraft, and controlled the weapons release. It is said (more often by navigators than by pilots) that the "pilot rowed the boat, while the A.I. shot the ducks."

However, A.I. was not their only nickname! RCAF navigators were often called "alligators" through to the 1950's, and a host of other terms also applied. There are many such nicknames in the American services. Many USN and USAF fighter and attack aircraft have a pilot and an additional crewmember: an Air Intercept Officer, a Bombardier-Navigator, a Weapons System Officer, an Electronics Warfare Officer, or even a second pilot. These crewmen have a variety of nicknames: "Fightergator", a contraction of the words fighter and navigator; "GIB", for Guy in Back; and "Wizzo" for the W.S.O., or Weapons Systems Officer. In the USN, the Bombardier-Navigator is sometimes called a "Beenie", for the abbreviation "B/N". Some refer to the second crewmember as a "Bear" (for trained bear!). Other common terms are "Front-Seater", for pilot, and "Back-Seater" for the Navigator or Weapons Officer.

The Canadian Forces no longer operates a two-place fighter, so there are no more Canadian A.I.'s. Debate lingers over the need for a second crewmember on fighters, and over the combat survivability of single-seat fighters. Many feel that modern avionics and computers have made the A.I. navigator unnecessary. They add insult to injury by saying: ...*pound for pound, I'd rather have the extra fuel!* Others aren't so sure. Computer systems in modern fighters can create "information overload" and a pilot's senses can be overwhelmed, receiving more information than can be digested to fly the aircraft effectively in combat. There is a catch-phrase in the RAF (whose mainstay fighter is the two-seat Tornado): *Single-seat? Easy meat!* The debate continues.

There was no need for an A.I. after they retired the Voodoo...

AIR, TO LAY ON (1939-45, British Commonwealth) — To "lay on air" is to arrange for close air support of ground forces. To "lay on" is air force slang that means to arrange, procure, or obtain something. Air is just shorthand for "Close Air Support". (See **Lay On**) [Ref: Partridge (8th)]

Call Brigade, and get them to lay on air, at the south end of the bridge!

AIR COMMODE (RAF; RCAF; since at least WWII) — "Air Commode" is an abusive nickname for Air Commodore, an RAF and RCAF officer rank equivalent to an Army Brigadier or a Navy Commodore. (Commode is an occasional term for a toilet, especially a portable toilet.) [Ref: Partridge (8th)]

AIRCREW FLASH (RAF, RCAF to 1960's; now obsolete) — A "flash" is a badge that enables quick identification or recognition. An "aircrew flash" was a white cloth insert placed in the front of a wedge cap which identified the wearer as an aircrew trainee. Later the RCAF decided the white flash would be worn both by aircrew trainees and by officer cadets, whether aircrew candidates or not.

During the Second World War, the white aircrew flash was occasionally referred to as a virginity flash. This was an allusion to the wearer's neophyte status, and because white suggests purity. In stark contrast to the suggestion implicit in the term

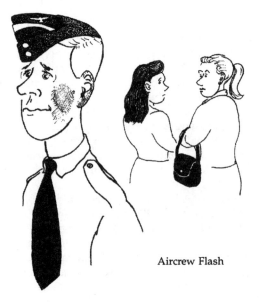

Aircrew Flash

virginity flash, the white aircrew flash was the centre of an ongoing prank perpetrated by RCAF groundcrews, in civilian communities near RCAF Stations.

Often groundcrew spread the rumour among local girls that this white cap flash was an official RCAF badge warning that the wearer was infected with a venereal disease! This of course cut down on the competition for female attention and prompted young single females to avoid the aircrew trainees and their white-flashed caps, and spend their time with the others.

The Aircrew Flash disappeared in the early 1960's when the RCAF ceased issuing the wedge cap. Though the wedge cap returned to the CF, the only flash worn on a blue wedge cap today is a red flash worn by the Military Police. (See also **Wedge Cap**)

AIR DEFENDER (CF, current) — An "Air Defender" is an airman or airwoman serving in the ground control system of the air defence radar network. Alternately, air defender can denote a soldier serving in the Air Defence Artillery.

Ron decided to become an Air Defender.

AIREDALE (RCN; post 1947) — "Airedale" was US Navy slang for a naval airman, and was a term that probably entered RCN slang after the first Canadian aircraft carrier entered service in 1947. The term seems to have been coined because of the first syllable of the word - "aire" - which suggests the air that an aircraft flies in. [Ref: Sutherland]

AIRMAN — In its broadest usage, an "airman" is any male involved in aviation, but in the RAF and RCAF the word Airman also had a very specific legal meaning. The Royal Canadian Air Force Act of 1940 stated:

airman means a person who is liable under this Act or the regulations to perform air force duty otherwise than as an officer.

In otherwords, the noncommissioned members of the RAF and the RCAF were collectively termed airmen. It was common to speak of the air force as consisting of "Commissioned Officers, Warrant Officers, Non-Commissioned Officers and Airmen." Females were of course, Airwomen. The equivalent navy term was Rating and the army used the words Other Ranks, often abbreviated as "O.R.'s". The Canadian Forces adopted much army terminology on unification in 1968, and former Airmen and Airwomen became known as O.R.'s. However, by the late 1980's many felt that the term other ranks was demeaning, so the term Non-Commissioned Member, or NCM, replaced it. [Refs: RCAF Act (1940, 4 George VI); Partridge (FS)]

AIRMAN'S BURN (RCAF and RAF Medical Services; WWII) — "Airman's Burn" was a term coined by Dr. Archibald McIndoe for a particular type of burn often suffered by aircrew in an aircraft fire. Dr. McIndoe was the Plastic Surgeon who ran the RAF's Burn Treatment Unit in Queen Victoria Hospital, at East Grinstead in Sussex, England. This hospital was the home of the famous Guinea Pig Club. The Airman's Burn was a flash burn affecting the hands and face, and was typical of the burns suffered by airmen who had bailed out from burning aircraft. It was particularly severe among those not protected by gloves, helmets, oxygen masks, or goggles. (See also **Guinea Pig Club**) [Ref: Milberry and Halliday]

AIR MOVER (CF) — An "Air Mover" is a person working in Air Movements, that branch of the air force responsible for handling of air cargo and passengers.

AIR POCKET (since WWI) — Anyone who has flown in a light aircraft on a hot, sunny day or in a gusty wind has experienced the light, choppy turbulence that the nonprofessional attributes to "air pockets". The peculiar term "air pocket" was coined early in aviation history to describe the minute, but sudden losses and gains of altitude that occur in turbulence. The term seems to imply that these zones in the atmosphere - air pockets - do not sustain lift as well as the rest of the sky. Actually, such turbulence is caused by columns of air that rise as the sun heats the earth, during the day. A column of rising hot air is called a thermal. A thermal will cause an aircraft to gain altitude - indeed, sailplanes and gliders depend on thermals to stay aloft. The term air pocket was common among early aviators, but today is only heard from the inexperienced layperson. [Ref: Voss]

AIR-TO-MUD (CF, current) — Air attack missions against ground targets are "air-to-mud" missions, as in: *the CF-5 hasn't got the range it needs for the air-to-mud role.* (See also **Mud Moving**)

AIWA! (Arabic; pronounced eye-owe-WA; British, Canadian since 1956) — *"Aiwa"* is Arabic for yes, or alternately, it can be an enthusiastic register of approval. It was an indispensable word for personnel of the Desert Air Force (see also **Scruff**) and, a generation later, for servicemembers posted to the Middle East on peacekeeping duty. [Ref: Partridge (FS)]

> *Check out that blonde!*
> *Aiwa!*

ALBATRI (pronounced "AL-ba-try") (RFC, RNAS; WWI) — "Albatri" was mock Latin for the plural of Albatross, a series of fighters flown by the Imperial German Air Service during the First World War. One assumes that the word Albatrosses insulted the sensibilities of British aviators schooled in Latin at private schools (who had learned for example, that "alumni", "octopi" and "cacti" are each plural for alumnus, octopus, and cactus). So they borrowed from their old Latin Masters and coined the word Albatri. (For another example, see **Argi**)[Ref: Voss]

> *Both Albatri got away...!*

ALBATROSS (RAF, RCAF, CF) — For decades a peculiar but popular debate has raged in Canada's air force over the correct identity of the bird that graces the badges of the RCAF and CF. Is it an Eagle? Or is it an Albatross? According to Wing Commander F.H. Hitchins, the RCAF's Air Historian, the bird is (and has always been) an Eagle. However, the misconception that it is an Albatross has deep roots, and has even been perpetuated in service manuals and training.

This unusual dispute has its origins in the Royal Air Force. The RAF was formed in 1918 from an amalgamation of the Royal Flying Corps (a corps of the British Army) and the Royal Naval Air Service. Members of the RFC, though airmen, had fought the First World War as part of the army. Likewise, the airmen of the RNAS had served in the Royal Navy. Amalgamating the two services brought problems, as the ex-soldiers and sailors in this new air force resented the loss of their former service identities. (Similar problems accompanied formation of the Canadian Forces in 1968 from the RCN, Canadian Army and RCAF.) The new light blue RAF uniforms, strange new ranks, and unfamiliar badges were the source of much culture shock. (For another example of problems, see **Blues**)

The official badge of the new RAF featured a bird with wings outspread, a bird copied from the cap badge of the Royal Naval Air Service. Later the RCAF adopted a similar badge, and this bird became an air force icon, featured on badges of the RAF, RCAF, and Canadian Forces. Indeed most Commonwealth air forces followed suit.

It is beyond doubt that the earliest heraldic records of the Royal Navy and RAF both identify this bird as an eagle. Despite this, naval airmen always called it an albatross - a proper seagoing bird! When the RAF was formed, former naval airmen enthusiastically fostered the misconception that this bird was an albatross, as part of a communal effort to keep the naval origins of the RAF alive and healthy. Their success was enormous and for many airmen in the early RAF it became an article of faith that the bird was an Albatross. Even though the dispute was laid to rest in the RAF before the Second World War, the debate passed into the RCAF.

Until 1943, the RCAF had no official badge of its own. Rather, the RCAF had borrowed the badge of the RAF, and modified it by adding a scroll containing the words "Royal Canadian Air Force". Until the official RCAF badge was approved, artist's renderings of the unofficial RCAF badge varied widely and the bird was depicted differently with every version of the badge. This variance in depiction caused other problems. The shoulder flash worn by airmen and airwomen incorporated the same bird as on the RAF and RCAF badge. Unfortunately, companies that manufactured the shoulder flash often took liberties. Sometimes the bird resembled an eagle and sometimes an albatross - on both the badge and on the shoulder flash. To some, this fostered the notion that while some RCAF badges and flashes depicted an albatross, there were others that depicted an eagle!

In the final analysis, the earliest heraldic records for the RNAS, RAF, RCAF and Canadian Forces identify the bird as an eagle. In 1943 the Chester Herald described the bird in the RCAF badge as *an eagle volant affronte, the head lowered and to the sinister.* Still, even the authority behind this Queen's Herald and Inspector of RCAF Badges is unlikely to convince old sweats who believe what their corporal told them in recruit training. The author is aware of hotly contested albatross-eagle disputes occurring as recently as the late 1980's. [Refs: Russell; Campbell; Hitchins]

Of course it's an Albatross! The Corporal told me so!

ALBERT (RCAF 1950's,60's) — "Albert" was the nickname given to the Grumman Albatross, a twin-engined amphibian aircraft, used by the RCAF for Search and Rescue.

ALL OF A DOO-DAH, TO BE (RFC; WWI) — A First World War pilot who became "all of a doo-dah" was becoming nervous. [Ref: Partridge (8th)]

Dave is all of a doo-dah over night flying.

ALLIED TRADES (RCAF) — The term "Allied Trades" has been used since the First World War to describe a variety of aircraft technical trades. The primary aircraft trades were the airframe and engine mechanics, the "riggers" and "fitters", but it was quickly discovered that they needed the help of other skilled artisans. The term Allied Trades came to refer to technicians other than the Riggers and Fitters.

During the First World War the Allied Trades were tradesmen such as the blacksmiths, tinsmiths, turners, and welders, who worked in workshops and not on aircraft. Another term, Ancillary trades, referred to the technicians (other than engine and airframe technicians), who worked on the aircraft rather than in a shop. Ancillary trades included photographers, instrument techs, and armourers. The term Ancillary trades seems to have faded out early in air force history.

Before the 1950's, the ranks of RCAF technicians were populated by two groups: the riggers and the fitters who were the majority, and by a smaller group of those who supported them, the Allied Trades. By the 1950's however, electronics and instrumentation systems were becoming much more complex and the number of technicians who maintained them was on the rise. By this time the term Allied Trades seemed to imply a second class citizen status, naturally resented by instrument, electrical, and electronics technicians and it faded away. Common usage among Canadian airmen for over a half century, the term Allied Trades no longer exists. (See also **Armament Sister, Fitter, Rigger, Tech, Mech**) [Ref: Sutherland]

ALLIGATOR (RCAF) — "Alligator" is rhymed slang for a navigator, as in: ...*anybody seen that bus full of alligators? It's overdue again!* [Ref: Harvey]

AMERICAN GLOVES (Canadian military, 1950's to the present) — To wear "American Gloves" is to have one's hands in one's pockets while wearing a military uniform, a practice too casual for proper military decorum. The term alludes to the American reputation for having a lower standard of military deportment than Canadians. However, anyone observing a group of Canadian airmen at coffee might dispute this reputation.

> *O'Toole! Take off those American Gloves!*

AMERICAN LUFTWAFFE (Allied Armies, 1944-45) — "American Luftwaffe" was a pejorative Second World War nickname for the U.S. Ninth Air Force. This nickname was derived from the Ninth Air Force's reputation for attacking almost any likely ground target, whether identified as German or not. [Ref: Peden]

AMPLESS   See **Gremlin**

ANCHOR CRANKER; ANCHOR CLANKER (CF; post-war) — A member of the senior service - the navy - could expect to be occasionally called an "anchor cranker" or an "anchor clanker". The terms may be American in origin. (See also **Dory-Plug, Fish-Head, Hairy Ass**)

ANCILLARY TRADES   See **Allied Trades**

ANGEL FACE (RFC,1914-18) — An "Angel Face" was a Provisional Pilot Officer, the

Anklebiter

Many Canadian airmen and airwomen served as cadets in their youth.

First World War term for a student pilot. The term conjures up an image of the stereotyped innocence of a youthful junior officer, someone who knows just enough about flying to be dangerous, but not much more. [Ref: Partridge (8th)]

We've got 10 Angel Faces doing their first solo next week.

ANGELS (WWII, later general, though now dated) — "Angels" was a 1940's radio codeword meaning "One Thousand Feet of Altitude", and was usually used to describe higher altitudes. "Angels Twenty" meant an altitude of 20,000 feet above sea level, "angels twenty-five" meant 25,000 feet above sea level, etc. The term "Flight Level" has long since replaced angels. (see also **Grand**) [Refs: Harvey; Partridge (8th)]

We'll level off at angels ten.

ANKLE-BITER (CF; current) — "Ankle-biter" is a mildly pejorative term for an Air Cadet, though occasionally ankle-biter can refer to children generally. The Royal Canadian Air Cadets were formed in 1941 to provide preliminary aviation and military training to young men of high school age, to prepare them for joining the RCAF. After the end of the Second World War, the focus of Air Cadet training changed slightly to embrace citizenship training. Though individual cadets are not members of the Armed Forces, their training is sponsored in part by the CF and they wear military uniforms and can earn cadet rank. As such, they attend camps and undergo some training at military facilities. Though young women had trained from time to time on an "unofficial" basis with air cadet units, they were not entitled to partake in the full range of cadet training until the early 1970's when the National Defence Act was amended to permit female enrolment.

The presence of these adolescent (and often, miniature) cadets on an air force base often leads to occasional comments about ankle-biters - people so small that they can easily harass their military elders by biting them on the ankle! The term is not so much an insult, as an expression of adult exasperation on trying to cope with teen-agers. In fact, a very large proportion of CF personnel were cadets in their younger days.

ANNIE (RAF, RCAF; WW 2) — Annie was the nickname for the "Anson", a very reliable British twin-engine monoplane used for a variety of roles, including coastal patrol, liaison and training. Officially the Anson was named for George Anson, a British Admiral of the 1700's; however, aviation folklore has it that the name is a pun on Avro and Son, the manufacturers.

The Annie was a twin engine, low wing monoplane that was first designed as a civil aircraft to compete with the Boeing 247. It saw much RAF service as a transport and liaison aircraft, and even as a light bomber. In 1939, the Anson Mark I was selected as the standard twin-engined trainer for the British Commonwealth Air Training Plan (BCATP). When the BCATP selected the Anson, it had instigated what was to become the largest aircraft construction program in wartime Canada. Early Annie's were powered by the Jacobs radial engine (which became known as the "Shaky Jake", for its low 330 horsepower rating). The need to modify the Anson for Canadian use led to the homegrown development of completely new variants, the Anson Mark V and VI. It saw service in the British Commonwealth Air Training Plan in multi-engine pilot training, navigator training, and air gunner training. [Refs: Molson and Taylor; Partridge (8th)]

Annie

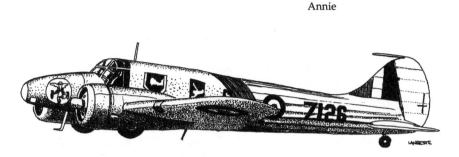

A.O.C.; A.O.C.'s INSPECTION (RAF, RCAF) — "A.O.C." is the abbreviation and shorthand term for "Air Officer Commanding". In the RAF and RCAF, the term "Air Officer" applied to very senior officers, those equal in rank to "General Officers" in the army or "Flag Officers" in the navy.

The Air Officers were Air Commodore, Air Vice Marshal, Air Marshal or Air Chief Marshal. Consequently, the A.O.C. was the officer in charge of an RCAF Group, Command or Air Division - a very, very senior fellow indeed! Another very senior fellow, retired Brigadier-General H.M. Sutherland described the A.O.C.'s Inspections of his early career: The AOC's Inspection was an annual rite where the man himself arrived, reviewed a full-dress parade of all unit personnel and then did a walk-through inspection of every unit and section on the base. Most AOC's seemed to have a nose that would find the places on the station that weren't all that tidy. (It) made sure the base was clean at least once per year. (See also Brass Hat, High-Priced Help) [Ref: Sutherland]

The Flight Sergeant must be really worried about the A.O.C.'s Inspection.

A.P. — Abbreviation for either of:

    (1)   *Air Publication*, a book containing official RAF orders or procedures, as in: *...anyone seen my copy of A.P. thirty-six twelve?* A.P.'s were significant for Canadians because the RCAF tended to adopt RAF procedures wholesale until after the Second World War. (See also **C.A.P.**)

    (2)   *Air Police*; A.P's, or "Air Police" are USAF police and security personnel, a natural enemy of USAF personnel - and also migratory Canadian airmen. (in USAF slang, an "A.P." is generally called an "Ape")

APDAL   See **Abdul**

APESHIT, TO GO — "Going apeshit" is an energetic, awe-inspiring and thoroughly splendid loss of control, orientation or self-possession.

The Base Warrant Officer, hearing the same excuse once too often, went apeshit!

APPLE; GREEN APPLE (Military aviation; general) — A crewmember who bales out of an aircraft at a very high altitude risks passing out from oxygen deprivation. The "apple" (or "green apple") is a small, green coloured ball attached to a tiny portable oxygen bottle located on the parachute harness. The jet crewmember yanks on the green apple to start a flow of oxygen into the oxygen mask after the bailout.

Aircrew in high performance jet aircraft wear an oxygen mask and receive oxygen from a tank mounted in the aircraft structure. However, this flow of oxygen from the aircraft stops if the crewmember bales out. Further, if the bailout occurs at very high altitude, the crewmember risks losing consciousness from oxygen starvation during the slow parachute descent to the ground. To prevent this, a small emergency bottle of high pressure oxygen is attached to the crewman's parachute harness and to the oxygen mask. To start the oxygen flow the crewmember pulls on a small green ball attached to both the parachute harness and the bottle. The colour green is a universal indication for oxygen, so it is unsurprising that this small green ball would suggest a green apple. [Ref: Sutherland]

If you bale out at high altitude, don't forget to pull on your little green apple!
Otherwise, you'll be having a little nap!

APRON (originally RAF, now universal; 1920's to the present) — The "apron" is the concrete or asphalt area around a hangar, used for aircraft movement or parking. [Refs: Gentle and Reithmaier; Partridge (8th)]

ARCHIE (RFC, RNAS; 1914-18) — "Archie" was anti-aircraft fire. The word was originally used by steeplechase riders at the turn of the 20th century to denote a hard ride and was later borrowed by aviators to connote turbulence in the air. Apparently the term was first coined to describe turbulent air encountered over the sewage farm conveniently located on the final approach to landing at the Brooklands aerodrome. It would seem that Archie later connoted turbulence due to anti-aircraft fire, and eventually came to mean the anti-aircraft fire itself. [Ref: Partridge (8th); Voss]

Archie got my wingman as we crossed over the enemy lines.

"ARE YOU HAPPY IN YOUR WORK?" "ARE YOU HAPPY IN THE SERVICE?" (Commonwealth Forces, 1939-45) — "Are you happy in your work?" or "Are you happy in the service?" were sarcastic questions asked of anyone who complained about military life just too damn much. [Ref: Partridge - Catchphrases]

ARGI (pronounced "are-guy") (RCAF, CF) — "Argi" is mock Latin for the plural of Argus. The Argus was a four-engine, piston, ASW patrol aircraft in Canadian service from the 1950's to the 1980's. Pluralizing the word Argus by saying Argusses grated on the tongue so someone coined the word Argi, mimicking Latin grammar.

The Argus was intended to replace the Avro Lancaster 10MR (a modification of the wartime heavy bomber), then the standard RCAF anti-submarine patrol and reconnaissance bomber. (The Lockheed P2V Neptune was an interim Lancaster replacement until the Argus was brought on line.) The Argus was developed by Canadair from the Bristol 175, more commonly called the Britannia. Though the Argus incorporated the Britannia's wings, tail surfaces and undercarriage, in all other respects it was redesigned. First flown in 1957, it was powered by four 3,700 HP Wright piston

A pair of Argi

engines, for high power at low altitudes. It was unpressurized and had two bomb bays. The Argus incorporated a variety of anti-submarine detection systems and carried a flight crew of five, plus a further six sensor operators. The Argus justly earned a reputation as a workhorse and had tremendous endurance. Flights of over twenty hours aloft were common, and the record is a flight of over thirty hours. In the mid-1980's, all Argi in Canadian service were replaced by the Lockheed Aurora, a Canadianized version of the Lockheed P-3 Orion. [Ref: Molson and Taylor; Sutherland]

We're expecting a pair of Argi from Summerside tonight.

ARMAMENT SCREWDRIVER (RCAF; 1950's, 1960's) — An "Armament Screwdriver" is a large ball-peen hammer. This term is merely a joke at the expense of the armourers, technicians responsible for care and maintenance of aircraft weapons and weapons systems. Armourers have a unique approach to military life and discipline which sets them apart from other aircraft technicians - a uniqueness that armourers foster with pride. Others would simply say that finesse is not their strong suit; hence the term: armament screwdriver for a ball-peen hammer. (See also **Gun Plumber, Tech**) [Ref: Sutherland]

Be careful where you swing that Armament Screwdriver, will you!?

ARMAMENT SISTER; SISTER (RCAF; 1950's, 1960's) — "Armament Sister" (sometimes just "sister") was RCAF rhyming slang for a technician in the Armament Systems trade (ie., sister, for systems). The Armament Systems Technician was responsible for maintenance of an aircraft's electronic radar and fire-control systems.

This isn't an electrical snag, this is a fire-control snag! Call over a sister to look at it!

ARRIVAL; TO ARRIVE (RAF, RCAF; 1930's, 1940's) — The word "arrival" described a thoroughly inferior landing. In a proper landing, the pilot causes the aircraft to transition gently from flight, to taxiing down the runway. The word arrival however, implies that the pilot has merely planted the airplane on the ground, somehow. [Ref: Partridge (8th)]

My dear Jim, that wasn't a landing! That was merely an arrival!

ARSE-END CHARLIE (RCAF, RAF; WWII) — "Arse-End Charlie" was the last aircraft in a combat formation, and consequently the most vulnerable to being attacked. (Compare with **Tail-End Charlie**) [Ref: Partridge (8th)]

I could've sworn that arse-end charlie was with us a second ago...

AS YOU WERE! — "As you were" is a command used on a parade square. It is both a recognition that an error has been made, and an order to return to the situation before the error. However, its use has expanded so that "as you were" is also used as a dry observation of another's social error.

I say, Basil! As you were! ...I hope you took your shoes off, first!

ASPIRIN   See **Headaches**

ASSHOLE OF THE WORLD (RCAF, RAF since the 1920's) — "Asshole of the world" is a description of any base or station that one would not want to be sent to, under any conceivable circumstance. It was commonly used to describe the RAF stations in the Persian Gulf area, during the 1920's and 1930's, and lives on to this day. Indeed, in the 1980's one small town outside the gate of a CF Base was often described as a "pimple on the asshole of the armed forces..." [Ref: Partridge-Catchphrases]

What is CFB Beaverleavings like?
...asshole of the world, I'm afraid.

AUGER IN, TO (aviation, current) — To "auger in" is a euphemism for crashing an aircraft. More specifically, to auger in is to strike the ground at high speed - as though the aircraft is trying to burrow into the earth. The term suggests an auger, a common woodworker's tool, entering a piece of wood; the auger, to enter the wood and be effective, must be pressed against the wood very firmly indeed.

If you don't pay attention to the terrain while low flying, you'll auger in!

AUTOVON (US, Canadian Forces; current) — Autovon is the acronym for Automated Voice Network, a military telephone system connecting all U.S. and Canadian military bases, plus many NATO facilities; it is primarily used for calling friends to catch up on rumours and gossip, or for military administrative communications. [Ref: Elting]

Hello Operator? Can I have an Autovon line to Toronto, please...

AVIATE, TO — To "aviate" is to fly, especially, to fly in a showy or ostentatious manner. The implication is that to aviate is one step above merely flying. [Ref: Partridge (8th)]

Wally, that was an impressive display of aviating!

AVIONICS (Aviation; post 1945) — "Avionics", an agglomeration of "aviation" and "electronics", is that branch of electronic technology that embraces aircraft communications, navigation, radar, and fire control systems. Strictly speaking it is not slang, but avionics is extremely common jargon that has gained widespread acceptance.

AWA; AWL (Canadian military) — During the 1950's "AWA" was the acronym for "Absent Without Authority". Later amendments to regulations changed the term to "AWL", for "Absent Without Leave", known in the U.S. as AWOL. [Ref: Sutherland]

B RAVO

BABY, TO HAVE A — To "have a baby" is to become anxious, concerned or upset (though sometimes one "has a Bird", or "has Kittens" instead). [Ref: Partridge (FS)]

> *When both the main gyrocompass and the standby compass failed, I thought*
> *the Navigator would have a baby!*

BACK-END CREW; FRONT-END CREW (Aviation general; current) — Often aircrews on larger aircraft informally divide themselves into two categories; the "Front-End Crew", and the "Back-End Crew".

The front-end crew are those who fly the aircraft from the flight deck, the front-end of the aircraft. Generally, the front-end crew include the pilots, the navigator and the engineer. In contrast, the back-end crew are those whose station is in the rear of the aircraft and who perform other functions in the mission.

On a transport aircraft, the back-end crew are the loadmasters, in charge of the passengers and cargo. On a maritime patrol aircraft, the back-end crew comprise the navigators and sensor operators. Many believe there is higher prestige in being front-end crew, though back-end crewmembers in maritime operations will disagree. In maritime operations the front-end crew fly the aircraft so that the back-end crew can detect and track the enemy, and if necessary, destroy him.

BACK-SEATER   See **A.I.**

BAD ACTOR (CF, Current) — "Bad actor" is a denigrating term for someone who behaves, (ie. acts) badly, in a professional or disciplinary sense. To describe someone as a bad actor is a warning to take care when working with that person.

> *What's the new Flight Engineer like?*
> *I heard he was a really bad actor...*

BADEN (pronounced "Bad-n") (CF, 1950's to 1994) — "Baden" was CFB Baden-Sollingen, near the village of Sollingen in the State of Baden, Germany.

BAG, IN THE — The term "to be in the bag" has had several connotations to Canadian airmen over the years:

> (1)   In the Commonwealth Forces in the Second World War, a person who is "in the bag" has become a prisoner-of-war, as in: *Sandy baled out of his Spitfire over Belgium so he's probably in the bag somewhere.* (For Prisoner-of-War slang, see **Kriegie**) [Ref: Partridge (FS)]

> (2)   In the CF of the 1970's, a servicemember who was "in the bag" was

very, very inebriated. [Ref: Sutherland]

BAG, TO (WWII) — "To bag" an aircraft is to shoot it down, a term probably borrowed from hunting. [Ref: Partridge (8th)]

BAG, THE (RAF, RCAF; 1930's - 40's) — In the 1930's and 1940's one's parachute was often called a "bag", from its shape when packed. Recall that at this time in aviation history, most parachutes were seat packs, that is, the pilot sat on the parachute in the cockpit. [Ref: Partridge (8th)]

> *Where are you going?*
> *The Corporal over at the Safety Equipment section has my new bag.*

BAGS OF (RAF, RCAF, WWII) — During the Second World War, whenever something was abundant or plentiful, there were "bags" of it. Consequently, one spoke of bags of sunshine, bags of altitude, bags of panic, etc.

> *Can you take a few more passengers?*
> *Sure, we've got bags of room!*

BAGTOWN (RCAF, CF; general) — "Bagtown" is the RCAF Station (and later, Canadian Forces Base) at Bagotville, Quebec.

BALE OUT; BAIL OUT — To "bale out" is to exit an aircraft in distress, in flight. The term derives from "baling" water out from a boat. Often the term is spelled "bail" out. [Ref: Partridge (8th)]

BALLISTIC, TO GO — To "go ballistic" is to abruptly lose one's temper. The term suggests a rocket that ignites and flies ballistically until gravity asserts itself, when it lands on whatever happens to be in its way.

> *The Colonel went ballistic when he read his transfer orders!*

BALLS TO THE WALL (military aviation; since at least WWII) — "Balls to the wall" means very fast, or at full throttle. This phrase refers to the fact that a small ball or sphere was placed on the top of an aircraft throttle lever, (to distinguish it from other cockpit controls). Therefore when the throttle lever is advanced all the way forward, to full power, the ball is at the wall (ie. the cockpit firewall). Generally the term applies to aircraft, but balls to the wall can also describe automobiles, and even people, moving rapidly. [Ref: Harvey]

> *...an' there's Jimmy, runnin' past the hangar, balls to the wall, with Flight Sergeant Kuzyk gainin' on 'im!*

BALLS-UP — A "balls up" is a highly confused situation, where nothing has gone according to plan. The term originated as English 19th Century equestrian slang, in which balls referred to flying clumps of mud or turf raised by a galloping horse's hooves, interfering with the horse's gait. The phrase found its way into British military slang and from there, Canadians picked it up. [Ref: Harvey; Partridge (8th)]

There were no spare parts and there was only enough fuel for half the aircraft!
It was a real balls-up, all right!

BANDIT — "Bandit" is the universal radio codeword for a hostile aircraft.[See also **Bogey; Friendly**] [Ref: Partridge (8th)]

Yup, me an' Chuck had 14 bandits cornered before we decided to bugger off...

BANG ON (Commonwealth air forces; since about 1940) — This term, now very common, began as Bomber Command slang for dead accurate, or all right. No doubt this term was originally used to describe bombing accuracy. [Ref: Partridge (8th)]

BANG SEAT (RAF, RCAF; 1950's) — An ejection seat was occasionally called a "bang-seat". (See also **To Punch Out**)

BANG-WATER [Canadian military;1939-45] — Gasoline was occasionally called "bang-water" during the Second World War. [Ref: Partridge (FS)]

BANJO (RCN, 1950's) — "Banjo" was a nickname for the McDonnell F2H Banshee, a carrier-based fleet air defence fighter flown by the RCN from 1955 to 1962. The Banshee was acquired from the United States Navy to replace the RCN's Hawker Sea Fury fighters. Thirty-nine Banjos flew from the Naval Air Station at Shearwater, Nova Scotia and from the aircraft carrier HMCS Bonaventure, a 19,000 ton, light fleet carrier of the British "Majestic" Class. Despite its inability to match its contemporaries in air-fighting, the Banjo remained in service due to its armament. Until the CF-18 came into service, it was the only Canadian military aircraft armed with the deadly "Sidewinder" air-to-air missile. [Refs: Petipas; Snowie]

BARATHEA (pronounced "barra-THEE-ah") (RAF, RCAF) — "Barathea" was the wool fabric from which an RCAF officer's service dress uniform was tailored. Thus, the uniform itself was often called a barathea, though officers who wished to make a real fashion statement also had their battledress tailored from barathea! [Ref: Sutherland]

Damn! I spilled gravy on my barathea!

BARRACK-ROOM LAWYER — A "barrack-room lawyer" is a servicemember who claims an unfounded expertise in military rules and regulations, and who expounds at length on this partial knowledge of military law. [Ref: Partridge (FS)]

BARN — A "barn" is a hangar, from its large dimensions, as in: *After that aircraft is refuelled, tow it into the barn.*

BARON, THE   See **Red Baron**

BASE BUS; BASE BIKE; STATION BUS; STATION BIKE (originally RAF, 1920's, later RCAF; now rare) — "Base bus" or "base bike" was a discreet, unkind reference to a servicewoman who was comparatively indiscriminate about when, where, or upon whom, she bestowed her sexual favours. The term has faded out of usage as times have changed. In the days when the air force lived on stations instead of bases, the term was station bus or station bike. [Ref: Partridge (8th)]

They call her the base bus because everybody on the base rides her...

BASE CONDUCTOR (CF, 1970's) — The Base Commander of a CF Base was occasionally called the "Base Conductor", from that somewhat less auspicious appointment: bus conductor. (See also **Bravo Charlie, Stationmaster**)

BASE LEG   See **Circuits and Bumps**

BASH — Besides its more usual meaning as party, the word "bash" also referred to a particular type of deformation in an airman's wedge cap. A bash occurs only after the cap had been jammed on one's head many, many times. A bash in one's wedge cap resulted naturally only after much wear and was therefore associated with long service. In the 1940's and 1950's having a bash in one's wedge became an affectation that implied wisdom and experience, and status as an Old Sweat. This, of course, invited junior airmen to form a bash artificially, and affect seniority they hadn't yet earned! In any event, the bash was anathema to the SWO or to a "discip". (See also **Discip; Fifty-Mission Cap; Old Sweat; SWO; Wedge Cap**)

BASHER (RAF; RCAF; since WWII, now rare) — "Basher" was at first Second World War air force slang for a mechanic. The word was always used after another word describing the type of mechanic, as in clock-basher (an instrument technician) or metal-basher (a metalworker). Its usage eventually spread so that nearly anyone could be a basher; a supply clerk was a "stores basher", and a person who flew or fixed Halifax aircraft was a Hallybasher. In this sense the word is akin to words like "type", "puke" or "weenie". (See also **type, puke, weenie**) [Ref: Harvey; Partridge (FS)]

BATHTUB (RFC; WWI) — To members of the RFC, the "bathtub" was the nacelle of the FE2 aircraft. This aircraft was a so-called pusher aircraft - its engine and propeller were mounted behind the cockpit, which projected forward, giving the crew an unimpeded view ahead. This forward-projecting nacelle became known as the bathtub, for its resemblance to this bathroom fixture. [Ref: Partridge (8th)]

Bats

Before the advent of modern visual-optical landing aids, naval aviators relied on signals from the deck landing control officer – the Batsman.

BAT-BOAT (RNAS; WWI) — The "Bat-Boat" was a single-engine flying boat built by Sopwith that served in the Royal Naval Air Service during the First World War. It was small and was the first flying boat of all British construction to serve in the RNAS. The origins of the name are unknown. However, it has been suggested that the unusual name Bat-Boat contributed to the nickname of another classic aircraft, the Supermarine Walrus. The Walrus flying boat of the Second World War was universally known as the Shagbat. (See **Shagbat**) [Refs: Phelan; Partridge (8th)]

BATS (Fleet Air Arm; since 1938) — In the aircraft carriers of the Royal Navy and the RCN, the Deck Landing Control Officer (also known as the Landing Signals Officer, or LSO) was often known as "Bats". This referred to the pair of large paddles - one in each hand - with which the LSO guided an aircraft descending to land. [Ref: Partridge (8th)]

BATTLE-BOWLER (British Commonwealth forces; WWII) — A "Battle Bowler" (or sometimes a "Panic Bowler") was a steel helmet, as worn by combat troops. Often airmen had a conceit that wearing a battle-bowler was beneath their dignity. However this notion passed quickly during air raids and among airmen serving near the front lines in Europe after D-Day. [Ref: Partridge (FS)]

BATTLE BREAK (general usage, 1950's to present) — A "battle-break" is a spectacular-looking aerial manoeuvre, used by fighter aircraft slowing to land after returning to base at low altitude and high speed.

The returning aircraft flies down the runway at low altitude and high airspeed. At the far end of the runway, the pilot pulls up and enters a climbing 180-degree turn, bringing the aircraft onto the "downwind" leg. On the downwind leg, the pilot levels the aircraft and flies down to the base leg. The climb forces the aircraft to lose airspeed so that it can safely approach to land. At the appropriate time the pilot again turns 180 degrees, lowers undercarriage and flaps, extends speedbrakes, and lines up on the runway for landing. (See **Circuits and Bumps, Overhead Break**)

BATTLE-DRESS; BATTLE-DRESS BLUES (RCAF to 1968) — The RCAF's number 5A uniform was called "battledress", or "battledress blues". It was patterned on the Second World War battledress uniform worn in combat by Commonwealth armies and was worn by airmen overseas during the Second World War. Modified slightly after the war, it became standard issue in the RCN, RCAF and Canadian Army. (However, used in a more amorous sense, the word battledress referred to pyjamas!) Battledress was a working uniform and consisted of a short "Ike Jacket", shirt and tie, and high-waisted trousers. During the Second World War, Battledress was very functional and popular among airmen:

> *We gleefully exchanged our wrinkled summer uniforms for blue battledress. It cried out "overseas!" because ground crew in Canada never wore it. It also flattered every man's figure. The blouse-tunic with its side buckle at the waist seemed to broaden shoulders and chests and nip emerging bellies. The trousers had a jaunty patch pocket on the left front thigh, for heroes to carry their maps in. And there was not one scrap of despicable brass to polish!*
> [Collins, page 74]

In smaller sizes, it was issued to members of the Royal Canadian Air Cadets, until they too, received CF green uniforms. Battledress disappeared after unification in 1968. (See **Barathea, Blues**. Contrast with **Tee-Dubs, Pinks(2)**)[Ref: Collins; Partridge (8th)]

BEAM, ON THE (RCAF, 1950's) — "On the beam" means absolutely correct, without difficulty, without error. On the beam was a term used by pilots while using the low frequency Radio Range system, an electronic navigation aid used during the 1950's and 1960's. This system broadcasted a narrow electronic signal from one navigation beacon to another. A receiver in the aircraft showed the pilot where the aircraft was, in relation to the beam. The pilot would then simply fly the aircraft along this electronic beam, adjusting left or right as needed, until they had reached the destination. Consequently, to be on the beam is to be proceeding satisfactorily. [Ref: Partridge (8th)]

BEARTRAP (CF) — "Beartrap" is a device that enables a helicopter to land safely on a warship's small flight deck, even in heavy seas. It was developed by the RCN and is standard equipment on many Canadian naval vessels. Properly called the Helicopter Haul-Down and Securing Device, the Beartrap was first installed in HMCS Assiniboine in 1962-3, when the RCN acquired the Sea King helicopter. (See also **Sea Thing**)

In the Beartrap system the helicopter hovers over the flight deck and lowers a probe on a cable. A flight deck crewman then fixes the cable and probe into a winch that is mounted flush with the deck. The crewman departs and the helicopter flies along, keeping station with the ship, its pilot applying just enough engine power to keep the cable taut. On the ship, the Landing Signals Officer winches down the helicopter to exactly the correct spot on deck. Once the helicopter is down on the deck, the probe and winch keep it stationary until the pilot can shut the engines down. Then the winch (itself mounted into a trolley beneath the flight deck) moves the helicopter forward and into the ship's hangar.

> The beartrap, developed by the RCN, permits large helicopters to land on comparatively small warships.

Bear Trap

BEAT UP, TO (general, since at least WWII) — "To beat up" a place is to fly over that place at extremely high speed and at extremely low altitude, for the sole reason of announcing one's presence. [Ref: Partridge (8th)]

BEAU (RAF, RCAF; circa WWII) — The "Beau" was the Bristol Beaufighter, a twin-engined, two-seat attack, anti-shipping bomber and night fighter. The Beau was developed from the Beaufort light bomber (hence the Beau, in the name). The Beau normally carried a crew of two, a pilot and gunner, though night-fighter variants carried a radar operator instead of a gunner. It was an effective aircraft, robust enough to carry weapons and armament, but fast and manoeuvrable enough to survive as an attack aircraft. The Beaufighter, when armed with a torpedo, became known by its Coastal Command aircrews as the "Torbeau". The Beau also saw service in the Far East, where the Japanese gave the Beau its own nickname: "Whispering Death", from the whispering sound of its engines. [Ref: Partridge (8th)]

Beau

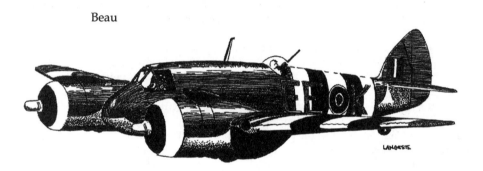

Though its crews simply called it the 'Beau', the Beaufighter was known as 'Whispering Death' to the Japanese.

BEAVER (CF; current) — "Beaver" is the occasional nickname for a technician from Construction Engineering, or as it is more commonly known: C.E. The Construction Engineering technicians are responsible for repair and maintenance of military buildings, hangars and facilities, and are members of the Military Engineering branch. As such, their badge has a beaver at the centre - therefore the nickname. (See also **Works and Bricks**)

BECOME UNSTUCK, TO — "To become unstuck" has two connotations among Canadian military aviators:

> (1)   To become unstuck is to commence flying after a take-off roll. It is the exact end of a take-off roll, when an aircraft's wings generate enough lift to sustain flight and the wheels leave - or become unstuck - from the runway. The phrase to become unglued is also current.

> (2)   To become unstuck is also used to describe a senior who gets upset, as in: *The Commanding Officer got real unstuck over the problem in the mess.* [Ref: Sutherland]

BEE-GEN (CF) — "Bee-gen" is the nickname for the rank of Brigadier-General, derived from the CF abbreviation for that rank: BGen.

Did you hear that Hanson is a Bee-Gen now?

BEEHIVE (RAF, RCAF; 1940-42) — "Beehive" was a Second World War British codename for a daylight bomber operation with a fighter escort. The bomber was the "Bee" and the escort, the "Hive". This code faded out of use as British doctrine shifted away from daylight raids due to very heavy losses. [Ref: Partridge (FS)]

BEER-LEVER (British Commonwealth; WWII) — A "beer-lever" is an aircraft control column. The term derives from its similarity to a beer tap in a pub, ie. a vertical handle. [Ref: Partridge (8th)]

BEETLE-JUICE (RAF, RCAF; since 1920's?) — "Beetle-Juice" was what Air Navigators often wrote and said, when they referred to the star Betelgeuse, a star often relied on for a sextant fix in astral navigation. [Refs: Partridge (8th); Sutherland]

Get a fix from Beetle-Juice if you can.

BEETLE OFF, TO (RFC WWI) — During the First World War, to "beetle off" was to take off in an aircraft and depart the area without turning. Later, however, to beetle off simply came to mean to depart or to leave, in a general sense. [Ref: Partridge (8th)]

Where's Willie? It's his turn to buy!
He beetled off an hour ago...

BEHIND THE POWER CURVE, TO BE — Being "behind the power curve" is a technical phrase from aerodynamics that has acquired an additional, informal meaning. A person who is behind the power curve is weary, fatigued, or lacks energy. To be behind the power curve is to have insufficient power to carry on.

This term is borrowed from aerodynamic science, where a Power Curve depicts the mathematical relationship between thrust and velocity for any given aircraft type. The Power Curve is based on the following observations. In normal steady-state flight, thrust must equal drag. However, as an aircraft slows, induced drag increases. To offset this increase in drag, the pilot must apply more power to the engine. If the aircraft slows even further, the induced drag increases at an ever greater rate. This slows the aircraft even further, and to continue flight, even more engine power is needed. This vicious cycle continues until even all the power the engines can produce is insufficient to maintain flight. At extremely low airspeeds, drag becomes mathematically infinite, and there comes a point at which even maximum engine power cannot keep the aircraft flying. The airplane then stalls, and falls out of the sky. Mathematically, this point is plotted on a graph outside the Power Curve.

BELGIQUES (NATO Europe) — Canadian airmen and airwomen stationed in Europe came to refer to Belgians in the same way that Belgians refer to themselves in the French language: *Belgiques*.

Jeez! I didn't know the Belgiques flew "Clunks" too!

BELLY; BELLY-IN, TO; TO BELLY-LAND — Since the mid-1920's, "belly" has referred to the bottom of an aircraft. Thus, to "belly in" is to land an aircraft with the landing gear retracted, ie. the aircraft lands on its belly. Generally this occurs when the aircraft's landing gear is damaged or when it would be dangerous to land with the wheels lowered. (For example, in a forced landing on rough ground, lowering the wheels increases the risk that the aircraft will flip over on its nose). [Ref: Partridge (8th)]

BELLY UP (CF; current) — Anything described as "belly up" has ceased existence or has died. Thus, a crashed aircraft is belly up. Similarly a person who has died is belly up. Presumably the term is an allusion to a dead fish, floating belly up in the water.

BELTS AND BOARDS (RCAF; 1950's and 1960's) — "Belts and Boards" were accoutrements worn on an RCAF officer's dress blue tunic on formal ceremonial occasions. Unlike the army, the RCAF never had a ceremonial uniform, per se. Instead, accoutrements were added to the standard dress uniform tunic. Belts and Boards comprised stiff epaulettes in blue and gold, and a gold ceremonial cloth belt. Therefore, situations calling for their wear were "Belts and Boards occasions". (see also **Instant Dictator Kit**)

What's the dress for this affair?
Belts and Boards...

Beware of the Hun in the Sun

BEND THE AIRPLANE, TO — To "bend an airplane" is to severely damage it in a crash (though usually short of complete destruction).

BENNIES (CF, current) — "Bennies" are financial benefits, such as for example, overseas allowances. [Ref: Elting]

There are some really good bennies that go along with an overseas posting.

"BEWARE OF THE HUN IN THE SUN!" (British Commonwealth; WWI and WWII) — "Beware of the Hun in the sun!" was an aphorism (current in both world wars) which warned aviators to watch out for German aircraft attacking them by surprise, especially from the direction of the sun. An aircraft attacking with the sun behind it enjoys an advantage. The defending aviator must look directly into the bright sun to detect the attacker and evade it. A bright sun of course, makes spotting the attacker very difficult, so the up-sun position was the ideal place to watch for attack from. "Hun" was the common British epithet for Germans, hence the warning: *Beware of the Hun in the Sun!* Apparently this phrase was borrowed from a piece of doggerel often heard in early operational flying training: *Beware of the Hun in the Sun - Beware of the Goon in the Moon!* [Ref: Williams]

> *If you want to live longer, remember: BEWARE OF THE HUN IN THE SUN!*

BIFF   see **Brisfit**

BIG CITY, THE (WWII, RAF Bomber Command) — During the Second World War, the "Big City" was Berlin, a major target of the Allied Bomber Offensive. The term alludes to going out on the town. (See also **Chopburg**) [Refs: Harvey; Partridge (8th)]

> *Where are you going tonight?*
> *We're going to the Big City.*

BIG SMOKE (RAF, RCAF; WWII) — To an airman in England during the Second World War, the Big Smoke was the great city of London, as in: *I'm going to the Big Smoke for my 72-hour leave!* [Ref: Harvey]

BIG STUFF (RAF, RCAF; WWII) — In the Second World War, "Big Stuff" generally meant heavy bombs. Heavy bombs weighed from 500 pounds up to the massive 22,000 pound Grand Slam. The Grand Slam was so heavy that a standard Lancaster bomber had to be stripped down to allow it to carry just one. (See also **Blockbuster, Clapper, Cookie, Grand Slam, Tallboy**) [Ref: Partridge (FS)]

BIG X   See **Kriegie**

BIND; TO BIND (RCAF; WWII) — "To bind" is to complain. Likewise, a situation which prompts complaining is described as a "bind". [Ref: Collins]

> *This bad weather sure is a bind.*
> *You'd still be binding even if the weather was great!*

BINGO — "Bingo" is a radio codeword that, when used by a pilot, means "I have only enough fuel remaining on the aircraft to return to base". When the codeword is used by a ground controller to an aircraft, it means proceed to your alternate destination. Bingo therefore usually implies urgency.

> *What is your fuel state?*
> *I'm almost at bingo fuel.*

BIN RAT (RCAF, CF; since at least WWII) — "Bin Rat" is one of several nicknames for a Supply Clerk. The term was coined because supply personnel spend much of their time around the bins containing the equipment and materiel, in a supply depot. (See also **Blanket-Stacker, Box Kicker**)[Ref: Harvey]

BIRD BATH (Maritime Aviation; current) — A "Bird Bath" is the apparatus used to rinse sea salt from the surface of a maritime patrol aircraft following its return from a patrol out over the ocean. Maritime patrol aircraft, such as the Aurora and its predecessor, the Argus, spend their operational lives flying through the salt sea air over the ocean. As such, inevitably they accumulate sea salt on their fuselages and in their engines. This sea salt damages the aircraft by facilitating corrosion of its metal components and so must be removed. The Bird Bath helps to get rid of salt which has accumulated on the fuselage on a patrol.

A Bird Bath is as near to an automatic car wash as one will find in aviation. Typically, a Bird Bath consists of many pipes and nozzles embedded beneath the surface of an air base taxiway which direct several large, powerful large jets of fresh water upward from the taxiway surface. After landing, the pilot taxis the large aircraft over the Bird Bath and through the massive wall of water sprayed upward from the ground. This helps to remove much of the salt and makes life easier for the ground crew striving to prevent corrosion damage to the aircraft.

Bird Dog

BIRD DOG (U.S. Army, Canadian Army; 1950's to 1970's) — "Bird Dog" was the name given to the Cessna L-19, a single-engine, two-place army scout aircraft, used for artillery spotting, liaison, and forward air control. Though a simple aircraft, the Bird Dog was robust and its role was demanding. Army L-19 pilots flew extremely low, often below the visible horizon, to avoid detection by enemy troops.

The Canadian Army acquired a number of L-19's during the 1950's from the U.S. Army. The Royal Canadian Horse Artillery used Bird Dogs as air observation posts, to spot the fall of shells from its guns and self-propelled howitzers, and to direct fighter-bombers. Ultimately, the Bell Kiowa helicopter replaced the Bird Dog, and the army's Bird Dogs went into storage. However shortly after that, the Royal Canadian Air Cadets acquired a number of L-19 Bird Dogs that are still flying as towplanes in the air cadet gliding program. (See also **Butane Budgie, LOH**)

The Bird Dog may not be fast. But when you always fly at about three feet off the ground you feel like you're going supersonic!

BITCHIN' BETTY (CF, current usage) — "Bitchin' Betty" is an automatic warning system that provides a verbal warning to a pilot when a potentially hazardous situation is encountered while flying. Bitchin' Betty is incorporated in several advanced aircraft, including the CF-18 Hornet.

Bitchin' Betty exists to provide a spoken warning system. Extensive research has shown that people respond more quickly to emergencies if audible warnings (such as horns or buzzers) augment visual warnings (such as warning lights). Moreover, it has been found that a spoken warning is more effective than a horn or siren alone. Accordingly, certain aircraft have pre-recorded warnings that "speak" to the pilot, just as the visual warning appears. For example, when a CF18 Hornet is flown too low to the ground, a pre-recorded voice is heard over the pilot's headset: "Altitude! Altitude!"

The pre-recorded voice is female. This is because the higher-pitched female voice is more easily distinguished from background noises, and because male aircrews (unsurprisingly) respond more readily to a female voice. Therefore, the term Bitchin' Betty.

BLACK BOX (military aviation; since at least WWII) — "Black Box" is a euphemism for any of an aircraft's avionics or airborne computer components. Such systems might control the aircraft's navigation, communications, auto-pilot, fire control, etc. The term derives from the fact that the wiring, switches, circuitry, and other parts of each such systems are contained in a portable metal box, mounted within the airframe. The practice in the electronics industry was originally to paint such boxes black (hence the term black box). However, today these boxes are just as likely to be painted grey.

Despite this, the media often uses the term Black Box to refer specifically to an aircraft's Flight Data Recorder. This special item of electronic equipment creates a continuous record of that aircraft's airspeed, altitude, engine performance, etc. In the event of a crash, this black box is recovered and its record is examined by investigators to help to determine the cause of the crash. The term black box seems to have caught on, although Flight Data Recorders are typically painted bright orange, to be easily spotted among wreckage. (See also **PFM, PFM Box**) [Ref: Harvey]

Admit it! You Comm Techs don't know how it works! You just change Black Boxes!

BLACK FLIGHT (RNAS; WWI) — "The Black Flight" was the nickname for the all-Canadian "B" Flight of No. 10 Squadron, Royal Naval Air Service, which destroyed 87 enemy aircraft during the weeks between May and July, 1917. The Black Flight was so-named because of the black cowlings and wheel spinners on its four Sopwith Triplanes [See **Tripehound**], and because of the nicknames of these aircraft: "Black Maria", "Black Sheep", "Black Roger", and "Black Death". The accomplishments of the Black Flight are the more laudable because of the limits of their aircraft, the Sopwith Triplane; though it had a sound airframe, was considered by many to be under-powered and under-gunned.

"B" Flight was comprised of four Canadians whose leader was Flight Lieutenant Raymond Collishaw, of Nanaimo B.C. Collishaw went on to become the leading RNAS ace, with 60 victories, and he ranked only after Billy Bishop among Canadians. He remained in the RAF and went on to become an Air Vice-Marshal.

BLACK FRIDAY — Though there have been many "black" days in history, "Black Friday" in Canadian aviation was February 20th, 1959. This was the day that the federal government of Prime Minister John Diefenbaker cancelled the Avro Arrow program.

The Arrow was a highly advanced supersonic, delta-wing interceptor of entirely Canadian design and construction. Its cancellation put 15,000 people out of work and led to the collapse of Avro Aviation. The cancellation resulted from fiscal and political considerations, but thus far no satisfactory explanation exists about why the government ordered the engineering data to be destroyed, or the completed Arrows reduced to scrap.

BLACK OUT, THE — "The Black Out" is the mandatory extinguishing of outside lights at night during wartime. During wartime, outdoor lights are extinguished to deny a target to enemy bombers. However, this also makes it risky to walk around at night!

> *If you're going out tonight, take care! Last week the CO was nearly run down in the blackout!*

BLACK OUT, TO — Aviators "black out" when they temporarily lose their vision after experiencing too many "gees" while flying in an aircraft. Excessive gee causes a variety of ills. These include grey-out, tunnel vision, black-out, and G-LOC (pronounced jee-lock, for gee-induced loss-of-consciousness). Another, less common ailment is red-out. All these hinder an aviator's ability to fly safely. (See **Gee**)

One gee (ie. 1g) is the normal earthward force exerted on the body by gravity; most people go through life never experiencing more than one gee. However, aircraft manoeuvres can impose punishing forces on the body, forces that can exceed human tolerance. One increases the apparent effect of gravity by continually pulling back on the aircraft control column, and soon the crew begin to feel two gees (ie. 2g's or twice their normal weight), three gees (ie. 3g's or three times their normal weight), etc. This effect is identical to that felt on a roller-coaster, at the bottom of a valley.

At about 3.5 to 4 gees, most people begin to experience a dimming of their vision; this loss of visual acuity is termed a grey-out. This greying begins at the periphery of one's vision and progresses towards the centre, so that one's only clear vision is straight ahead; this progressive loss of peripheral vision is called tunnel vision.

At about 4 to 6 gees (ie. four to six times their normal body weight), even a relatively fit person will begin to completely lose the ability to see. This is the black out. Strictly speaking, a person remains conscious while experiencing a blackout. Their vision is lost, not their awareness. If the excessively high gee is maintained, the aviator will lose consciousness - a state known as G-Induced Loss of Consciousness or G-LOC. However many still refer to this loss of consciousness as a black out.

This progressive loss of vision and loss of consciousness is caused by oxygen starvation. The high gee drains blood away from the head and the upper body; this in turn starves the eyes and brain of the oxygen they need to function.

"Red out" is caused by excessive negative gee. Negative gee is like the normal force of gravity, but experienced in the opposite direction from normal. In otherwords the blood, rather than being forced to drain away from the head, is forced towards the head! This is normally the result of the pilot pushing the control column forward. The aviator will experience a very flushed, unpleasant, full feeling in the head. There may be hemorrhaging of blood vessels of the head and eyes. At high levels of negative gee, major hemmorhaging of ocular blood vessels can result in loss of sight. This last extreme is the red out.

All these are a serious hazard, especially in air combat manoeuvring. In air combat, to lose one's vision or to lose consciousness is fatal. It is possible to counter the effects of excessive positive gee by wearing an Anti-G Suit while flying. However, there is no effective way to counter excessive negative gee. (See **G-Suit**). [Ref: Partridge (8th)]

BLACK TROOPS (RAF, British generally) — "Black Troops", originally a British Army administrative term for non-white colonial soldiers, later became a sarcastic term among some Britons for personnel from the colonies and dominions, including Canadians. [Ref: Partridge (FS)]

BLADE, TO (CF; current) — "To blade" is to betray a friend or comrade. The allusion to a knife is very clear, and the inference is sinister.

BLANKET-STACKERS (RCAF, CF; current) — "Blanket-Stacker" is the mildly derogatory nickname for a member of the supply branch, because their job consists ostensibly of stacking and arranging things. (See also **Bin Rat, Box-Kicker**)

BLENBURGER (Allied Air Forces; WWII) — "Blenburger" was the nickname for the Bristol "Blenheim", an RAF light bomber used early in the Second World War. The word is a combination of Blenheim and Hamburger, though why this contraction should be formed, is a mystery. (See also **Boly**) [Ref: Partridge (8th); Berrey and Van Den Bark]

BLISTER (RCAF, CF; Current) — A "blister" is an extrusion or fairing on the surface of an aircraft's fuselage or canopy, usually used to cover a projecting component. A clear plexiglass blister is used to allow a better view to the crewmember inside. Perhaps the most prominent aircraft blisters ever were those found on the Consolidated Catalina, built in Canada as the Canso.

As well, the word blister can refer to an extension built on the side of a hangar that usually houses an aircraft servicing section. The blister extends slightly onto the ramp or tarmac area. Those within can easily observe ramp activity and monitor the approaching and taxiing aircraft. [Refs: Partridge (8th); Sutherland]

The Aircraft Servicing Officer is in the #1 hangar blister.

BLOCKBUSTER (RAF, RCAF; 1944-45) — A "blockbuster" is any of a series of large aerial bombs used by Bomber Command during the Second World War. These bombs weighed 4,000, 8,000, 12,000, and 24,000 pounds! Blockbusters earned their name from the ability to flatten, or bust, a city block. After a half-century, blockbuster's meaning has changed. It is now synonymous with big. (See also **Clapper, Cookie, Grand Slam, Tallboy**)

BLOOD CHIT   See **Goolie Chit**

BLOODY (British Commonwealth) — "Bloody" is an intensifier of near universal use and application. It is not, strictly speaking, air force slang. However, to exclude it from these pages would be to ignore much of the casual conversation of Canadian airmen and airwomen.

BLOODY APRIL (RFC; WWI) — Bloody April was April of 1917, a month in which the RFC suffered very heavy aircraft losses to the German Air Service. Spring was traditionally when major land offensives could begin, because the battlefield had become sufficiently dry for troops to move. In the spring of 1917, in preparation for such an offensive, the RFC began a heavy program of artillery-spotting and reconnaissance flights over German lines.

However, by spring of 1917, the Imperial German Air Service had introduced two radical changes to the way it fought the air war. First, the German air force redesigned their ad hoc fighting establishment. They reorganized their fighter forces into squadrons of 14 to 18 aircraft, each called a *Jagdstaffel* (commonly shortened to *Jasta*). This reorganization, along with improved command and control, multiplied the effectiveness of their fighter forces.

The second change was the appearance of the Albatros, a fast, new and highly manoeuvrable German fighter. The Albatros made mincemeat of the RFC's slow and ungainly Be2 and RE-8 observation aircraft. Until more advanced allied fighters appeared, the Albatros remained the scourge of the RFC. The changes wrought by the Germans inflicted devastating losses on the Allies, losses that became so great that April of 1917 became known as Bloody April in the Royal Flying Corps. [Ref: Phelan]

BLOWER — The word "blower" can refer to a telephone, as in: *Wing Commander Price! The Station Commander is on the Blower!* Occasionally blower referred to a loudspeaker. [Ref: Partridge (8th)]

BLUE BARK — "Blue Bark" is a term describing the travel entitlement given to persons travelling home because of a death in the family. When transportation is scarce, Blue Bark passengers rank behind persons travelling on duty, but ahead of persons travelling on leave. The origins of the term are obscure, though it has been suggested that the word "Bark" derives from the word "embark". [Ref: Russell]

> *They're flying Kurt home Blue Bark.*

BLUE JOB (originally British) — A "blue job" was a member of the Navy or of the Air Force, depending on the context. The term derives from the blue colour of the naval or air force uniforms, and is always a means of distinguishing the wearer from brown jobs, that is, members of the army. The word job was often used to describe a particular type or category of aircraft or person. (See also **Brown, Brown Job; Job**)

> *Angie's brother is a Blue Job*

BLUE SHEETS (RCAF, CF current) — "Blue Sheets" are an aircraft maintenance form used to record an aircrafts' "minor" unserviceabilities, ie. technical faults which do not affect its ability to fly safely. They are so-called for their colour. (See also **L-14, Major(2), Minor, Pink Sheets, Snag**)

BLUES (RAF, RCAF, CF; current) — "Blues" referred to the RCAF winter uniform (as distinct from the khaki summer uniform). However, blues could also refer to the CF air force blue Distinctive Environmental Uniform (which replaced the CF green uniform worn from 1970 to 1987).

The use of the colour blue to distinguish the air force uniform dates from 1918 and the formation of the RAF, when it introduced its slate blue-gray uniform. Members of the short-lived Canadian Air Force (1919 to 1924) wore a distinctive, dark navy-blue uniform. However, when the RCAF was created in 1924 it adopted RAF uniforms and badges and throughout its history, the colour of the RCAF uniform was identical to that of the RAF. Thus, the blue-grey RCAF uniform dates back to 1918.

Initially, the decision to issue a blue uniform was not popular among RAF officers. The RAF was a new, untried and very junior service and many members had earned their spurs as naval officers in the Royal Naval Air Service or army officers in the Royal Flying Corps. There was significant grumbling, and many would have preferred it had the naval and army air services not amalgamated. Indeed so many RAF officers continued to wear their old navy and army uniforms, that special measures became necessary. RAF commanders had to decree that promotions would only be effective for people who could prove they had a blue uniform to put the new rank badges on!

Air force folklore abounds with stories of how the specific shade of blue was chosen. The following excerpt from *Behind the Hangar Door* (page 29) seems to be the authoritative story:

> *"...how the blue uniform arrived is something of a mystery. Apparently the Tsar's government ordered vast quantities of light Ruritanian blue material in 1915 to clothe a Cossack cavalry regiment. By 1917 the order had been completed and was ready for shipment, but the demise of the Tsar in 1917 left the material on the manufacturer's hands. What was he to do with this cloth? It proved impossible to dye. Then, in 1918, the sudden announcement of the formation of a Royal Air Force seemed a heaven-sent opportunity to get rid of the now surplus cloth in the manufacture of new uniforms! The records are unclear. Part and parcel of the light blue uniform were gold wire badges and brevets. Legend attributes this innovation to a Lily Elsie, who thought it rather dashing and suggested it to one of the senior members of the Air Council. However, the serving officers of the time did not share either the textile manufacturer's or Lily Elsie's enthusiasm for the light blue uniform and in due course it was abandoned under Air Ministry Order (AMO) 617 published in July 1918. Instead a more sober blue-grey material was selected, sanctioned as the official uniform colour and authorized as such in AMO 1049 published on 15 September 1919. The present RAF blue-grey colour dates from that time."*

In 1924 the RCAF adopted this same RAF blue and it was proudly worn by Canadian airmen and airwomen until unification in 1968. In 1968 the RCAF disappeared, along with its two sister services, when the Canadian Armed Forces was created. The Canadian Armed Forces uniform was dark rifle-green and was worn by all members, regardless of element. However, in the late 1980's distinctive environmental uniforms returned and Canadian airmen and airwomen again wore a distinctive air force blue. The decision was made, however, not to return to the RAF blue-grey colour worn by the RCAF before 1968. The shade chosen is reminiscent of the earlier RAF blue, but is unique in that no other air force in the world uses it. (See also **Barathea, Battledress, Tee-Dubs, Pinks**) [Refs: Partridge (FS); Congdon]

BLUE TICKET   See **Green Ticket**

BLUIE (Allied Air Forces; 1940's-50's) — "Bluie" was the short form of the code word, "Bluie West 1", an allied air base located on a fjord on the west coast of Greenland. Bluie's proper name is Narssarsuarq. It was as a refuelling stop for aircraft flying from Canada to Europe via Gander or Goose Bay. Its importance declined as non-stop transatlantic flight became practical. However, for short-range aircraft crossing the Atlantic in stages, Bluie became a common stop-over.

BOAT PERSON; BOAT PEOPLE (CF, current) — To most of the world, the "boat people" were refugees who escaped Viet Nam after the fall of the Saigon government, often in crowded, unseaworthy vessels. The word is associated with desperate people in dire straits.

However, to the non-naval elements of the Canadian Forces, the words boat people refers to the Canadian Navy and a boat person is a member of it! It is an oblique, teasing insult. It also refers to the fact that sailors cringe whenever a ship is called a boat! Airmen and airwomen are advised to use this term only with discretion when visiting either Halifax or Esquimalt, Canada's principal naval bases.

I hear you're going to pay a visit to the Boat People in Halifax!

BODY; BOD; BODIES — "Body", "bodies" and "bod" are all off-hand terms for a person and people, respectively. (The term always refers to living, breathing bodies and not to deceased ones) Occasionally, the term used will be warm bodies. An extra person is sometimes known as an "odd bod". [Ref: Partridge (8th)]

How many bods will 405 Sqn send to England?

BOEING, THE — "The Boeing" always referred to the Boeing 707 aircraft used by the CF for passenger transport and aerial refuelling. Although the Boeing Corporation has made many aircraft, in the Canadian Forces the Boeing always referred to the 707.

How are they getting you to Comox?
I'm taking the Boeing...

BOFFIN — "Boffin" is a word with two meanings:

(1)   (Britain and Commonwealth; WWII) A "Boffin" was a scientist or technologist working on a specialized military project, invariably under conditions of secrecy, to improve air force operational capability. [Ref: Harvey; Partridge (8th)]

(2)   (CF to late 1980's) The word "Boffin" was also the name of a 1940's vintage anti-aircraft gun used to defend the two Canadian air bases in Germany from air attack, until the late 1980's. Boffin Guns never fooled anybody; their fire-control system was simply too slow to track a fighter aircraft flying at high speed and low level. The guns had been originally mounted in HMCS Bonaventure - and put into storage once the "Bonnie" was scrapped in 1969. However, in the early 1970's they were uncrated and moved

to the CF Bases at Lahr and Baden-Sollingen, in Germany. The origin of the term Boffin as applied to these guns is uncertain, though it has been suggested that it may have been a variation on "Bofors", the Swedish gun manufacturer. It has also been suggested that it is the name of a town. In any event, the Boffin has been replaced by the ADATS (Air Defence, Anti-Tank System) and the 35 millimetre Oerlikon gun. ADATS is so deadly to intruding aircraft that the watchword of the Air Defence Artillery has become: *If it flies, it dies!*

BOGEY (sometimes "Bogie") — "Bogey" is the standard codeword for an aircraft that is unidentified but assumed to be hostile. An aircraft not presumed to be hostile is merely referred to as "unidentified". (Compare with **Bandit**) [Refs: Partridge (8th); Gentle and Reithmaier]

BOLTER, TO (RCN until 1969; still current USN) — "Bolter" is naval aviation terminology and radio code for a missed approach to landing on an aircraft carrier. If an aircraft approaching to land on the deck of a carrier is not situated to land safely, the pilot must pull up and try again, calling "BOLTER! BOLTER!" on the radio. Likewise, if the Landing Signals Officer on the carrier feels that the landing is unsafe, he will order the pilot to try again, by calling "BOLTER! BOLTER!" on the radio.

BOLY (pronounced "BOW-lee") (RCAF WWII) — "Boly" was the nickname for the Bolingbroke aircraft. The Boly was developed in parallel with the Bristol Blenheim (see **Blenburgher**), and was to have been a general reconnaissance aircraft to replace the Anson (see **Annie**). The RAF Boley development program would have been scrapped but for RCAF insistence. The RCAF had evaluated both the Blenheim and the Bolingbroke, and had judged the Bolingbroke to be the superior aircraft. Ultimately the RAF agreed and the Blenheim was redesigned, incorporating Bolingbroke features. 628 Boleys were produced in Canada. They were primarily used within the British Commonwealth Air Training Plan where they saw extensive service as bombing and gunnery trainers. [Ref: Partridge (8th); Molson and Taylor]

BOMB-SIGHT BUGLET   See **Gremlin**

BOMB UP, TO (RAF,RCAF; WWII) — To "bomb up" is the process of loading an aircraft with bombs, as in *the squadron was bombed-up by 1700 hours.* (See also **Upload**) [Ref: Partridge (8th)]

BONE DOME (RAF, RCAF; since mid-1930's) — A "Bone Dome" was an aviator's hard flying helmet. In the RCAF of the 1950's (and up to 1963) it specifically referred to the hard shell of the outer helmet, as opposed to the soft fabric inner helmet, worn beneath. Another common nickname for a flying helmet was brain bucket. [Refs: Partridge (8th); Sutherland]

BONNIE (RCN; CF) — "Bonnie" was the affectionate nickname for Canada's last aircraft carrier, HMCS Bonaventure, a 19,000 ton light fleet carrier of the British Majestic Class. Commissioned in 1956, it replaced HMCS Magnificent, known as the "Maggie". The Bonaventure was an improvement over the Magnificent in that it incorporated an angled flight deck, mirror landing aids, and a steam catapult. Furthermore it was capable of Arctic operations. While commissioned, the Bonaventure carried Banshee and Tracker aircraft and H04S and Sea King helicopters. (See **Banjo, Bolter, Club 22, Stoof,**

35

Horse, Cat, Jesus Wire, Goofing Stations) [Ref: Snowie]

BOOGER (CF; late 1980's to early 1990's) — A "Booger" is an avionics technician, though the origins of this nickname are highly uncertain. However, given that booger is American slang for a piece of nasal excreta, it is not surprising that this nickname has not caught on with the avionics techs themselves! (See also **Boomatron, Fraggle**) [Ref: Sutherland]

BOOMATRON (CF current) — A "Boomatron" is an avionics technician. (See also **Booger**)

BOOMER (Navy and Maritime air forces; current) — Arguably the most sinister threat to peace is a nuclear-powered submarine that is capable of launching its nuclear-armed ballistic missiles at shore targets, while itself remaining undetected. NATO naval and maritime air forces devote great efforts to tracking hostile or potentially hostile missile submarines which, over the years, have come to be known as "boomers"

BOOSTER (RCN to 1968) — "Booster" was naval slang for the catapult used to launch naval aircraft from the relatively short deck of an aircraft carrier.

BOREDOM — "Boredom" is an occasional rhyming nickname for CFB Borden, near Barrie, Ontario - in terms of population, the largest training base in the CF. The origins of the nickname are apparent to anyone who has spent a weekend there without a car.

BOREX (CF, current) — A "Borex" is a boring activity. The term derives from the military practice of creating a catchphrase for an exercise, by adding the suffix "ex" (for "exercise"), to a word describing the nature of the exercise. Therefore, a Torpedo Exercise is a "Torpex", a Field Exercise is a "Fieldex", etc.

> *Well, how was your visit with your in-laws?*
> *A real borex...*

BOSS (RCAF, CF; 1960's to the present) — One's "boss" is one's superior officer, and more specifically, one's Commanding Officer. On flying units it is not unusual for junior officers and senior NCO's to address their C.O. by the civilian term boss - to the amazement of army or navy types, for whom such familiarity would be scandalous.

BOTCH (CF current) — "Botch" is the occasional nickname for "Basic Officer Training Course", from its abbreviation: BOTC.

BOTTLE TO THROTTLE (RCAF, CF; current) — "Bottle to Throttle" refers to the time that must elapse between when a crewmember of an aircraft last has an alcoholic drink, and when that person can legally fly again as crew. The rule is that twelve hours must elapse, and further, the rule extends not only to aircrew, but to anyone who works on aircraft or who supports flying. This includes air traffic controllers, aircraft technicians, and even the cooks who prepare in-flight meals.

> *Let's see... is it twelve hours from bottle to throttle? ...or from throttle to bottle?*

BOUNCE (Military Aviation; since at least WWII) — To "bounce" is to attack, or to simulate an attack, on an aircraft flying at a lower altitude. (See also **On the Perch**) [Ref: Partridge (FS)]

> *Did you see how I bounced that T-Bird?*
> *Yeah. Did you notice it was the Wing Commander flying it?*

BOWLER, TO GET ONE'S (RAF, RCAF; WWII) — "To get one's bowler" was RAF slang that meant to retire from the air force. Presumably the phrase referred to the fact that the well-dressed English gentleman-about-town wore a bowler hat rather than an air force cap. [Ref: Harvey]

> *After I get my bowler, I think I'll buy a pub!*

BOWSER — A "bowser" is a tank truck, usually a fuel truck. The word bowser is common usage in Great Britain (where it may have originally been a trade name), but in Canada it is virtually unknown outside the military. Its most common air force usage is in describing fuel trucks - fuel bowsers - though in the Army one occasionally hears of bowsers, as well. One RCAF aircraft, the Argus, consumed engine oil in such copious quantities that it became necessary to have an oil bowser at each Argus base! (See also **Argi**) [Refs: Harvey; Sutherland]

BOX — The "box" is a flight simulator, from the fact that early simulators (such as the venerable Link Trainer) were but a small, closed replica of an aircraft cockpit.

> *Well Harry, you're going into the box for an hour this morning.*

BOXCAR (RCAF 1950's) — "Boxcar" was the usual nickname for the Fairchild C-119 "Flying Boxcar", a twin piston-engined long-range transport flown by RCAF squadrons during the 1950's. It was easily recognized by its twin-boom tail. In the early 1960's the Boxcar was replaced by the C-130 Hercules. (See **Dollar-19**)

Box-Kicker

About three-quarters full, I'd say...

BOXHEAD (CF Europe; 1970's to 1990's) — A "Boxhead" is a German. Once exclusively a pejorative term, it is now used quite colloquially by CF personnel stationed overseas. However, no one ever asked the Germans whether they think its merely "colloquial!" (Interestingly, the same term in French, "tete carre", refers to English Canadians!) (See also **Deutscher**)

BOX-KICKER (CF, current; probably American in origin) — A "box-kicker" is a member of the CF supply branch. The term derives from the supposed habit of performing an inventory count by merely kicking storage boxes to determine how much is inside. (See also **Bin Rat, Blanket-Stacker**)

BRAIN BUCKET   See **Bone Dome**

BRASSARD — A "brassard" is an armband, or armlet worn about the upper sleeve, indicating the wearer's rank, or that he has some particular (often temporary) status, such as Duty Officer, Security Guard, or Military Police, etc.

BRASS HAT — A "Brass-Hat" is a senior officer, from the gold braid embroidered on the visor of the senior officer's dress cap, to distinguish them from lesser mortals. [Ref: Partridge (8th)]

BRAVO CHARLIE (CF; current) — "Bravo Charlie" refers to the Base Commander. The term is derived from the military phonetic alphabet and the initials "B.C." for Base Commander. (See also **Base Conductor, Stationmaster**)

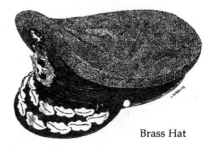

Brass Hat

Jim, the Bravo Charlie wants to see you.

BREEZE UP (RFC; WWI) — A "breeze up" is a feeling of panic, concern or uneasiness. The origins of the term are uncertain. However, it might derive from the surprise a woman in a skirt (or a kilted highlander) experiences on feeling an unexpected updraft. [Ref: Voss]

Barney always gets a vertical breeze-up about crossing the front lines...

BREVET (RAF, RCAF; since 1914) — In the RAF (and to a lesser extent, the RCAF) the flying badge, or wings, worn by aircrew were often called a "brevet". The term brevet actually applies to a type of rank, similar to acting rank. In brevet rank an officer is entitled to exercise the authority, and wear the rank badges of a higher rank than one's own, but receives no additional pay. According to Whitehouse, the RAF practice of referring to aircrew wings as a brevet comes from the First World War. The RFC gave newly-graduated pilots a brevet promotion along with their wings. After a time, graduation from aircrew training became known as receiving one's brevet and the word brevet became associated with the flying badge, not the promotion. (See **Wings**) [Ref: Whitehouse]

BRIGSHIFF   See **Gremlin**

BRISFIT (RFC, RAF; circa 1919) — "Brisfit" was the post-1918 nickname for the F2b Bristol Fighter, the outstanding two-seat fighter of the First World War. Brisfit is a contraction of the words Bristol and Fighter. However, during the First World War itself, the aircraft was commonly called the "Biff" (presumably an attempt to pronounce the letters "BF", for Bristol Fighter).

The Brisfit, designed as a reconnaissance fighter, first saw action in April of 1917 and remained in RAF service until 1932. In combat it proved highly effective because it combined the agility of a single-seat fighter with the advantage of having a rear gunner to protect the tail. Indeed, Sergeant (later, Captain) L.F. Powell, a rear gunner on the Biff, achieved the rare distinction of becoming an Ace by shooting down eight enemy aircraft. (Powell and his Canadian pilot, Captain A. E. McKeever, together destroyed four enemy aircraft in one patrol; each downing two) [Refs: Partridge (8th); Phelan; Bowyer/Turner]

BRISTOL — Almost any aircraft built by the Bristol aircraft company could be termed a "Bristol". However, in the RCAF of the 1950's and 1960's the Bristol always referred to the Bristol Freighter. The Bristol was a basic but highly effective twin-engine, piston-powered transport aircraft characterized by its large "clamshell" nose cargo door. The entire nose of the aircraft opened to admit large bulky cargo, such as an entire F-86 Sabre aircraft (minus the wings), or large vehicles. The RCAF used the awkward-looking Bristol during the late 1950's and the early 1960's for intra-theatre airlift in Europe.

Bristol

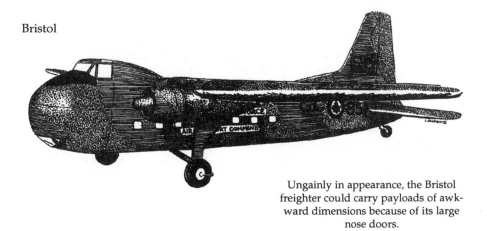

Ungainly in appearance, the Bristol freighter could carry payloads of awkward dimensions because of its large nose doors.

BRIT — "Brit" is a term which can mean either of:

(1)   A person or thing from Britain, as in: *A Brit Hercules will be arriving any time*, or

(2)   The Bristol Britannia, a four-turbo-prop engine airliner of the 1960's and 1970's, used by the RAF as a passenger aircraft. The Britannia airframe was the basis of Canadair's Argus and Yukon aircraft. (See also **Argi, Yuke**)

BROWN; BROWN JOB (originally RAF circa 1920's, with Navy use by 1939; still current) — "Brown" was usually a reference to the army, and a "brown job" was a member of the army. Brown refers to the dark khaki colour of the British Army uniform, essentially identical to that of the pre-unification Canadian Army. The word "job" was RAF slang for any specific aircraft type and later the word applied to categories of anything, not just aircraft. The term brown job was always used in distinction to a blue job. [See **Blue Job, Job, Purple**] [Ref: Partridge (FS)]

BROWNED OFF, TO BE (Commonwealth Forces; WWII) — To be "browned-off" is to be disgruntled. The origin of this term is obscure, but Partridge suggests that it could either refer to the brown colour of unpolished brass air force buttons, or (perhaps more likely) it could have a scatological origin. [Ref: Partridge (8th)]

Doug looks really browned-off today; what's the matter?

BRUTE (RCAF, CF; to early 1980's) — At Canadian air bases operating the Argus anti-submarine patrol bomber, a "Brute" was a large, towed electrical power unit which was used to provide electrical power to an Argus aircraft on the ground. Normally aircraft produce their own electrical power from engine-mounted generators; however, when an aircraft is undergoing maintenance it is not advisable to run the aircraft engines simply to provide electrical power. The "brute" provided this power on the ground, using a caterpillar diesel engine that ran a 400-Hz generator. (See also **Comstock**) [Ref: Sutherland]

BRYLCREEM BOYS (Great Britain; WWII) — "Brylcreem Boys" was a sarcastic Second World War nickname for members of the air force. The nickname Brylcreem Boys came from a Second World War newspaper advertisement for hair cream, published in Britain in the early months of WWII. This ad featured a handsome, exquisitely well-coiffed airman. Thus, soldiers or sailors who wished to vent their spleen at the Air Force would refer to those in light blue as Brylcreem Boys. [Ref: Partridge (FS)]

BUCKET (aviation; general) — A "Bucket" is a thrust-reverser. A thrust-reverser is a shield mechanically lowered over the exhaust of a jet engine after the aircraft has landed and while it rolls down the runway. The buckets deflect the jet blast sideways. The effect of a thrust-reverser is to act as a brake. Buckets are usually found on multi-engine passenger aircraft.

BUCKSHEE (since the late 1700's; commonwealth military) — To a Canadian airman or airwoman, "buckshee" is an adjective meaning worthless, slipshod, or makeshift. Alternately, it can mean surreptitious, unofficial, additional or unexpected.

It derives from *backsheesh*, a word used in any of several Middle-Eastern languages to mean a present, a gift, or a bribe. The word became buckshee in the British Indian Army, where it came to mean a tip or gratuity, though it ultimately came to mean costing nothing or free. It has also come to mean free, in the sense of being available. These are still the accepted meanings of buckshee in most places, though in the RCAF and the air element of the CF, its meaning has developed one step further. From "costing nothing", the meaning of buckshee has come to mean worth nothing, or worthless. Thus one can speak of a buckshee repair, or a buckshee plan. As well, it can mean surreptitious or unofficial as in: *we got this computer on the buckshee!*. [Ref: Partridge (8th)]

Buff

BUFF (CF, current usage) — "Buff" is the nickname for the De Havilland Canada DHC-5 Buffalo, a twin turbo-prop medium transport with excellent Short Take-off and Landing (STOL) performance. The Buffalo was originally intended to be a straightforward improvement on De Havilland's earlier success, the Caribou. However, a 1962 U.S. Army requirement for a STOL tactical transport spurred further development. The Buff differed from the Caribou by having General Electric turbo-prop engines and an increased payload. It was designated the CV-7A by the U.S. Army and the CC-115 by the CF. In Canadian service the Buff was initially employed as a tactical transport aircraft, but later most were converted to Search and Rescue. Several Buffs also flew in the Middle East as part of Canada's United Nations commitment. The Buffalo airframe was also used in several test programs. These included the joint Canadian Government-NASA Augmentor Wing, super STOL tests, and a Bell Aerospace Co. program to evaluate the utility of an air cushion landing system, similar to a hovercraft. (The Canadian meaning of Buff should not be confused with the USAF meaning of Buff. In the USAF, Buff always refers to the B-52 bomber, for Big Ugly Fat Fucker) [Refs: Elting; Molson and Taylor]

BUG-OUT (since Korean War) — To "Bug-Out" is to pack up and evacuate as fast as humanly possible, to avoid being overrun by advancing enemy forces. During the cold war the massive superiority of Warsaw Pact forces gave the term bug-out a particular poignancy for CF personnel in Europe with NATO forces. After all, during the Second World War, the inability to either defend their bases on the ground or bug-out cost the RAF 14,000 ground personnel killed at air bases in France, Crete, Greece, North Africa, and Burma were overrun. [Ref: Partridge (8th)]

BUGSMASHER (American, adopted in Canada) — "Bugsmasher" was an affectionate nickname for the Beech C-45 Expeditor. The Expeditor was a light twin-engined, piston transport aircraft used by the RCAF and the RCN in a variety of roles including pilot and navigator training, utility transport, search and rescue, aerial photo work, etc. (See also **Exploder**)

BULKED OUT   See **Grossed Out**

BULLETPROOF (RAF, RCAF, CF; current) — To be "bulletproof" is to be able to escape accountability, or arduous or unpleasant duty through reliance on rank, seniority, or influence. Occasionally the term "fireproof" is used instead. (See also **Per Ardua Ad Asbestos**) [Ref: Partridge (FS)]

BULLSHIT TOWERS (WWII) — During the Second World War "Bullshit Towers" referred to the control tower of an aerodrome. This resulted from the fact that the tower normally housed the Station, or Wing, Headquarters, as well. (See also **Chateau, Castle Dismal, Disneyland on the Rideau, Fort Fumble, Fraggle Rock, Glass Menagerie; Glass Palace, Petrified Forest**) [Ref: Partridge (8th)]

BUMF (British Commonwealth; WWII) — "Bumf" is paperwork, especially useless paperwork. Strictly speaking, bumf is short for "bumfodder", British slang for toilet paper since the 1600's.

Though bumf refers to paperwork, in the early days of the Second World War it attained another very specific meaning. The Air Ministry deemed it in the interests of the war effort for Bomber Command to drop leaflets on enemy cities - to undermine the morale of the German population. These were codenamed "Nickel" operations. Of course, the only ones whose morale suffered were the bomber crews who risked being shot down to deliver useless leaflets to unsympathetic Germans. Indeed, Air Chief Marshal Harris, later to become commander of Bomber Command agreed, saying *the only thing (that dropping leaflets achieved) was largely to supply the continent's requirements for toilet paper for the five long years of the war.* Bomber crewmen began to refer to the loads of leaflets as bumf and to themselves, as "Bumfleteers" (ie. from "pamphleteer") [Refs: Harvey; Messenger; Partridge (8th)]

BUNFIGHT (CF; current) — A "Bunfight" is a petty or minor dispute. The term seems to be derived from a unique feature of some air force officer's mess dinners: the pitching of buns (sometimes with great accuracy) at fellow diners.

The mess dinner is an old military tradition. A mess dinner is a formal banquet for members of the mess. Mess dress uniform is worn and diners observe specific protocols and decorum that reflect the traditions and morale of the unit. In contrast to the propriety and mature fellowship of a senior NCOs' mess dinner, an officers' mess dinner can be a raucus affair. Indeed, many air force officers enjoy making a point at a mess dinner by throwing buns at one another, or at long-winded speakers! Occasionally the phrase *visibility was ten feet in flying buns* was heard to describe the melee. (Meteorologists describe visibility at an aerodrome in similar terms, like: *visibility is half a mile in light rain.*). Since the early 1980's however, a concerted effort has been made by commanders to stifle such displays, and where there is a risk of a bunfight, bread is served in lieu. Folklore has it that this policy resulted, not so much because the Commander of Air Command was "nailed" by a bun, as by the fact that he was hit by three at once! Shortly thereafter, the powers-that-be issued all Air Command officers with CFACM 1-900, a small (just the right size for a Mess Dress jacket pocket), official manual entitled "Mess Dinner Procedures"!

The Engineering Officer and the Operations Officer got into a Bunfight again!

BURNERS — "Burners" is short-hand for afterburners, a thrust augmentation system

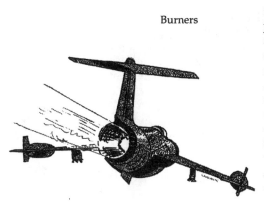

Burners

incorporated in many, though not all, jet engines. When a pilot selects the afterburner, raw fuel sprays into the hot exhaust. The exhaust flame ignites this fuel and produces added thrust. Afterburners are used sparingly, as added heat breaks down the metal of the exhaust and because engine fuel consumption becomes astronomical. It is also known by its abbreviation: "A.B.'s", as in: *The Pilot kicked in the A.B.'s right after take-off.* (In Britain, afterburners are known as re-heat)

Once I lit the burners the aircraft's fuel consumption tripled!

BURTON   See **Gone for a Burton**

BUS (RNAS, RFC; WWI) — During the First World War, a "bus" was an airplane. The term may have originated with a First World War fighter, the Vickers Gunbus. In later years, the word bus referred to heavy, multi-engine aircraft, as opposed to smaller aircraft such as fighters. This nickname suggests that large aircraft are sometimes denigrated as being no more manoeuvrable than a bus. (See also **Bus Driver, Kite**) [Refs: Partridge (FS); Voss]

BUS DRIVER (WWII) — During the Second World War, a "bus driver" was a bomber pilot, as distinguished from a fighter pilot. Bombers were much less manoeuvrable than fighters, just as a bus is less manouvrable than a sports car. Also, like buses, bombers flew well-travelled routes. [Ref: Partridge (8th)]

BUSTER — "Buster" has two different meanings in the Air Force.

(1)   See **Gremlin**

(2)   **buster** (RAF WWII, now universal) — "Buster" is a radio codeword which means *proceed as fast as possible.* (See **Angels, Bandits**)

Bandits at Angels Twelve over Dover. Your code is buster!

BUTANE BUDGIE (CF; current) — "Butane Budgie" is an occasional nickname for the Bell CH139 Kiowa Helicopter. It was coined by the Air Reservists of No. 2 Wing in Toronto because the Kiowa is rather small and stubby in appearance and, as helicopters go, fairly basic. The word butane alludes to jet fuel, as a jet engine provides the Kiowa's power.

BUTT CAN — Canadian servicemembers become quite familiar with the "Butt Can". A butt can is a bright red can with a lid, resembling a waste paper basket. Unlike a waste paper basket though, a butt can is reserved for refuse capable of producing a spark, such as matches and cigarette butts. Military institutional wisdom recognizes the serious fire hazard which results when matches and cigarette butts are disposed of with ordinary garbage. Woe betide the young airman or airwoman who throws paper, or other combustibles into a Butt Can instead of a normal garbage can. Woe betide the person who empties an ashtray (perhaps with smouldering matches in it) into a normal garbage can!

BUTTON (Canadian aviation, general) — The "button" is the approach end of a runway, ie. , the end that aircraft first touches down on when landing. Hence one hears of the button-end of the runway, or putting it down "on the button".

> *Why are the fire trucks out at the button of runway 31?*
> *Pat's on final approach...*
> *Wise precaution.*

BUTTON UP, TO (aviation general) — To "button up" something is to close it, fasten it, or latch it. Alternately it can mean that a situation, a plan, or a task is in hand and ready to proceed. Presumably this term derives from the design of certain locking devices used to fasten metal aircraft panels (such as "Dzus Fasteners"), which resemble metal buttons against an aircraft skin. Buttoning up the panel is the last thing done in any given maintenance task, Therefore, to button up can mean to finish a task, or to have it in hand and be ready. [Ref: Partridge (8th)]

> *When you're finished buttoning up that panel, meet me inside the hangar.*

BUTTONSTICK (British Commonwealth) — A "buttonstick" was an article of kit issued to all RCAF personnel in the days when the bright shine on one's buttons or badges resulted only after strenuous polishing. It was a brass (or card) plate, with a groove cut down its centre. The plate was inserted behind the brass buttons or cap badge on one's uniform. Liquid polish could then be applied to the brass button or badge without staining the uniform cloth behind. (The polish of choice was, of course, Brasso) [Refs: Collins; Sutherland]

BUY IT, TO (since at least WWII) — To "buy it" is to die. The term is probably derived from the euphemism to buy the farm, which refers not to a real estate transaction, but rather to the acquisition of a funeral plot. (See also **Gone for a Burton; Chop, to get the; Gone West, to have a bad day**) [Ref: Partridge (8th)]

> *He bought it while buzzing an abandoned airfield.*

BUZZ — "Buzz" is a word which can mean either:

(1)   A rumour, as in *What's the latest buzz?*, [Ref: Partridge (8th)] or

(2)   To fly low over the ground, or over an object on the ground, usually for "recreational" purposes (see also **Beat Up**), as in *He was spotted buzzing the abandoned airfield.* Canada's leading ace of the Second World War, Squadron Leader George Beurling was nicknamed "Buzz" for his love of low flying. [Refs: Carlson; Partridge (8th)]

BUZZ BOMB   See **Diver**

BY (THE) NUMBERS (military; general) — To do something "by numbers" means to do it in stages, or according to the authorized procedure.

The term derives from parade-square drill. When a drill instructor demands that his charges execute their manoeuvres by numbers, he is ordering them to perform each movement in sequential steps. This enables the instructor to check closely for correct posture and procedure. Therefore, to do something by numbers is to do it carefully, in correct stages.

> *Today we will learn to strip the Browning .303 machine gun; let's take it by numbers.*

HARLIE

CAB (RCN; still used in 1990's in CF Maritime Air Group) — To a Canadian naval aviator, his aircraft was his "cab".

CABBAGE (RAF; WWII) — In Bomber Command of the Second World War, the word "cabbage" was code for bombs, part of an RAF policy of deriving codenames from the names of vegetables and foodstuffs. (See also **Cookie, Lay Eggs, Gardening, Groceries**) [Ref: Partridge (8th)]

CAB RANK (RAF, RCAF; WWII) — The term "cab rank" referred to aircraft neatly lined up in order - whether on the ground or flying.

Air Force use of this phrase came from common English slang. A file of taxis waiting for fares at a taxi stand is a cab rank. When a passenger hails a cab, the first cab in the "rank" has priority for the fare. After the first taxicab drives away with its fare, the remaining cabs move up and priority for the next passenger passes to the cab now first in line. This common everyday usage passed into the air force so that several aircraft parked in a neat line could be termed a cab rank. (See also **Gyppo Line**)

Airmen used the term cab rank in a slightly different way after the Normandy invasion of June, 1944. The Allied armies relied heavily on fighter-bomber aircraft for close-air support as they fought to establish a hold in nazi-occupied Europe. Allied armies and tactical air forces had pioneered a highly effective system of coordinating these fighter-bombers with ground forces. This was called Air Support Control and is the basis for today's complex close air support systems. Rather than assigning aircraft to targets back at their home bases in England, the responsibility for control of tactical fighters was given to those who best knew how it was to be employed in a fluid battle, the fighting troops at the front. The air force detached a Forward Air Controller (FAC), himself a fighter pilot, to a mobile visual control post with the leading army elements. The FAC called down the fighters as they were needed and directed them in. (This was not a popular posting for the fighter pilots, nor has its popularity increased in a half-century.)

A "Cab Rank" was a section (or several sections) of fighter-bombers which flew on a standing patrol near the land battle. They stood by, waiting until the FAC called them down to attack the ground targets he had designated. When a section of fighter-bombers received a request for air support, one or two aircraft detached themselves from the formation to attack the target with rockets, bombs, or guns. After the attack was finished, they returned to the formation if fuel remained. If fuel was short they returned to base. The rest of the fighter-bombers patrolled until they received another call for fighter support. The next aircraft then detached themselves and entered the fray. This rotation continued until the ground battle ended, or the surviving fighter-bombers had to return to base. This cycle functioned in much the same way that taxis at a cab rank await their turn for a customer. The cab rank patrols were innovative because it put the control of fighter-bombers into the hands of those best able to direct them, the front-line troops.

(See also **FAC, Winkling Out**) [Refs: Partridge (FS); Rawlings]

C.A.M. (WWII)   See **Hurricat**

CAM UP, TO (CF, current) — To "cam up" is to camouflage something - anything - including aircraft, vehicles, buildings, faces.... Consequently, camouflage paint is cam paint, camouflage clothing is cam gear, etc....

When did they "cam up" the Hercules fleet?

CANADA FLASH (CF current, since WWII) — A "flash" is a badge that enables quick identification. A "Canada flash", or a shoulder flash, is a cloth shoulder badge used as the national, or service identifier on Canadian military uniforms. As this excerpt describes, those who wore it thought highly of the Canada Flash:

> *I rushed back to my bunk and sewed the white-lettered "Canada" patches onto my blue shoulders. It was my proudest moment in the RCAF. For the rest of my service I would be entitled to wear them. To the home folks it meant that the wearer had served overseas. To people abroad the Canada patch instantly identified us as natives of that most favoured and popular of countries.* [Collins, p.74-5]

Up to and during the Second World War Canadian military uniforms appeared, for all intents and purposes, identical to those of Britain. Army uniforms identified the wearer as Canadian only by the wording on its regimental or corps badges. Canadian sailors, airmen and airwomen were indistinguishable from members of Britain's navy and air force. This caused identification problems and hurt morale and it became necessary to distinguish Canadians from Britons and other Commonwealth troops. The Canada Flash was one such distinguishing mark.

Soldiers, sailors and RCAF officers wore a shoulder flash simply bearing the word CANADA. However, the flash worn by noncommissioned air force personnel bore a prominent "air force eagle" over which was embroidered the title: CANADA. (The eagle was again inherited from the RAF uniform; however, see also **Albatross**.) Custom

dictates that when these eagle shoulder badges are worn, the head and eyes of each eagle face to the rear of the wearer, presumably to "check his six". Consequently the eagle shoulder flashes come in pairs, left and right. (See also **Check Six**) The eagle shoulder badge disappeared on the unified, green Canadian Forces uniform introduced about 1970 (and in 1973 the eagle shoulder badge disappeared from the RAF uniform also). However, the eagle reappeared on the "blue" CF air element uniform first seen in 1988.

The Canada Flash has become the national identifier for Canadian military personnel and has become a proud tradition. [Ref: Collins]

CAN DEAD MEN VOTE TWICE?   See **True Virgins Make Dull Company**

CANNIBALIZE, TO — Cannibalization occurs when usable parts and components are removed from a seriously damaged aircraft and are used to repair other aircraft. It is generally accepted that the cannibalized aircraft will never fly again. Interestingly, even in modern times there are lingering taboos against cannibalizing aircraft involved in a fatal crash. (Compare with **to Rob**)

CAN OPENER (WWII) — An aircraft employed to attack tanks was a "can-opener", an obvious allusion to the tool used to open a metal container. Such aircraft were generally armed with very heavy rapid-fire cannon (e.g. 40 millimetre), or with rockets. Normally the term can-opener was used with the proper name of the aircraft, such as for example a "Hurricane Can-Opener". [Ref: Partridge (8th)]

CANOPY — A "canopy" is the covering over an aircraft cockpit; it must both protect the crewmember from the elements, and afford visibility. An aircraft without a canopy is said to have an open cockpit. (Note that a "cockpit" differs from a flight deck in that one walks onto a flight deck, whereas one climbs into a cockpit. Aircraft with a flight deck, such as large cargo aircraft, do not have a canopy).

Broadly speaking, there are three types of canopy: the Bubble Canopy, the Greenhouse Canopy, and the Razorback Canopy. The canopy most often seen on modern aircraft is the Bubble Canopy, a clear, teardrop shaped plexiglass covering so-called because it suggests a bubble blown from clear plastic. A Greenhouse Canopy comprises many flat plates of plexiglass, each plate being fitted into a metal framework of ribs and longerons. This framework is called a greenhouse for its resemblance to the framework and glass panes of a garden greenhouse.

Initially the term Razorback Canopy referred to a canopy fitted on an aircraft with a razorback fuselage. Razorback fuselage is an American aviation term that describes an aircraft with a sharp, pronounced ridge along its top surface, aft of the cockpit to the tail. (An apparent reference to the Razorback Hog, a wild pig native to the United States characterized by a ridge of stiff, vertical bristles along its spine.) A razorback canopy is faired into this ridge-like frame behind the cockpit. Perhaps the best example of the razorback design is the Republic P-47B, designated the Thunderbolt Mk.I in the Commonwealth. However, the term Razorback Canopy is also commonly applied to any canopy faired into the aft fuselage, whether or not there is a sharp vertical ridge on the fuselage.

Canteen Cowboy

Airwomen were on guard
in the presence of a
canteen cowboy.

Often mistaken for the Razorback Canopy is the Turtle Deck. In this pattern, a prominent canopy set above the upper surface of the fuselage has a solid fairing behind it, going downwards to the fuselage. The Hawker Hurricane is an example of a Turtle Deck.

Modern canopies usually incorporate a rubber seal, permitting partial pressurization of the cockpit. Early canopies were opened and closed by hand, but today the tendency is to hydraulically raise and lower the canopy. Modern high performance aircraft usually have explosive charges that blow the canopy clear of the aircraft to enable an emergency exit or ejection. If these charges fail, the top of the ejection seat usually has a canopy cutter, a hard, sharp ridge of steel at the top of the seat. As the ejection seat fires the occupant out of the cockpit, this steel edge shatters the canopy overhead, like an egg, enabling the crewmember to clear the cockpit.

CANTEEN COWBOY (WWII) — A "Canteen Cowboy" is an aggressively heterosexual airman who goes out of his way to provide airwomen with his company, whether welcome or not. The term derives from "Drugstore Cowboy" - the civilian prewar counterpart. Before the Second World War every self-respecting drugstore had a soda fountain which usually became a favourite place for young males and females to observe each other (while studiously pretending not to). In the slang of the day, a Drugstore Cowboy was a young man particularly persistent in his pursuit of female company. On an RCAF Station the Dry Canteen, a snack bar for all ranks, was the social equivalent of the drugstore soda fountain and became a place for socializing. On stations with airwomen on establishment, it was the home of highly heterosexual canteen cowboys, wearing air force blue. [Ref: Partridge (8th)]

CANUCK — Canuck is a term that by now has three meanings appropriate to air force slang:

> (1)   The original usage of the word **Canuck** was as a nickname for Canadians, (particularly French-Canadians in the 1800's). It derives from an archaic Canadian French word, "*Canocq*", a tree used for collecting syrup. By the early 1900's, newspaper cartoons were depicting the character of "Johnny

Canuck (1)

Canuck" as a symbol of the Canadian nationality. For a while Johnny Canuck was to Canadians as Uncle Sam was to Americans or John Bull was to Englishmen.

(2)   The name **Canuck** was first applied to an aircraft during the First World War. The Canadian-made variant of the Curtiss JN-4 Jenny, a popular and reliable First World War biplane trainer, became unofficially known as the "Canuck". In 1916, a British proposal to train aircrew in Canada was approved and the first of the 20 RFC flying training schools was established. To ease transatlantic shipping problems, the training aircraft were to be obtained in Canada. Almost simultaneously, Canadian Aeroplanes Ltd. was founded in Canada, a company that owned the rights to produce the American-designed Curtiss JN-3 biplane. The basic JN-3 aircraft was modified and became known as the Curtiss JN-4 (Canadian) to distinguish itself from a slightly different American aircraft, the Curtiss JN-4 Jenny. As a result, the Canadian version became known as the Canuck JN-4 as opposed to the American JN-4. The name stuck and the Canadian variant has been the Canuck ever since.

Canuck (2)

Flying Training started at Camp Borden in February 1917, and later, the RFC (Canada) included gunnery training and photo-reconnaissance training. A few Canucks were fitted out as air ambulances. The Canuck saw service in both the RFC (Canada) and in the U.S. Aero Service, and in the postwar Canadian Air Force. Canucks were used in the first aerial survey in Canada and in the first flight through the Rocky Mountains. About twelve hundred complete Canuck aircraft were built. [Ref: Molson and Taylor]

(3)   In the latter half of the 20th Century the name **Canuck** referred to the Avro CF-100. The Canuck was a twin-engined, two-seat, all-weather jet interceptor and was the first fighter aircraft designed and built entirely in Canada. The Canuck was born out of a 1945 agreement between the Canadian Government and the as-yet unformed Avro Canada corporation, to develop a jet fighter aircraft in Canada. The official name Canuck was chosen in honour

Canuck (3)

of the biplane trainer of the First World War, though this name never really stuck; airmen and airwomen generally referred to it by one of its many nicknames: CF-Zilch, Clunk, Kerosene Canso, Lead Sled.

The Canuck first flew on January 19th, 1950. During tests at Wright Field, the USAF test pilot Lieutenant Colonel Moon remarked: *This is the first aircraft I have flown for a long time that I wouldn't mind going to war in.* The wing tips were cut straight to mount rocket pods, and the twin engine nacelle design was based on wartime German research. The Canuck became the first straight-wing aircraft to exceed Mach 1 without rocket power. The CF-100 equipped Canadian all-weather interceptor squadrons up to the early 1960's and later was used for electronic warfare in NORAD. The Belgian Air Force purchased the Canuck in preference to the American Northrop F-89 Scorpion, the only nation to do so. (Other nations were restricted from purchasing the CF-100 because it incorporated an American Hughes Fire-Control Radar system on which the US government had placed export restrictions).

The Canuck was an interceptor, as opposed to a fighter. It lacked the daylight air-fighting capability of its contemporary, the Canadair Sabre, a fact that Sabre pilots took advantage of at every opportunity. However, the CF-100 crews generally got their own back on the Sabre pilots in foul weather or at extremely high altitude. Its construction was robust, to put it mildly; as a result, the CF-100 remained in service over a decade longer than the Sabre. (See **Clunk, Kerosene Canso, Lead Sled**) [Ref: Molson and Taylor]

C.A.P. (usually pronounced "see-eh-pee", but occasionally "kap") (RCAF to 1968) — "C.A.P." invariably meant *Canadian Air Publication*, the designation for official RCAF books, orders, regulations, instructions, etc. For example, C.A.P. 6 was RCAF Dress Regulation, C.A.P. 100 was RCAF Flying Orders, C.A.P. 90 was the RCAF Manual of Drill and Ceremonial, etc. (See also **A.P.**)

CAP (pronounced "kap") — "CAP" is an acronym for Combat Air Patrol, a fighter mission to escort or protect surface forces or other aircraft. Occasionally a prefix is added for greater clarity; for example, a SAR CAP is a fighter escort for Search and Rescue operations in hostile terrain, MiG CAP is fighter protection against MiG aircraft, etc. (See **MiG**)

CAREER MANGLER (CF, current) — A Career Manager is often called a "Career Mangler".

A Career Manager (or mangler) is the person at National Defence Headquarters who controls the personnel within a given military occupation. The career manager assigns servicemembers to the various air bases and jobs where people of that occupation are needed. In selecting where a servicemember is to be posted, the Career Manager must first meet air force staffing requirements. However, within this broad constraint, a Career Mangler has some degree of discretion. So it pays to maintain a good relationship with one's career manager. The career manager plays a big role in deciding where you will be posted for the next couple of years, what training courses you need for your next job, and why you will (or will not) be promoted. Career managers reportedly consider personal preferences and it is rumoured that from time to time they are forced to admit that a person's posting preferences actually coincide with air force needs!

CARPET   See **On the Carpet**

CARQUAL (Naval Aviation, general; RCN to 1968) — "Carqual" is an acronym for Carrier Qualification. A naval pilot who has completed a Carqual has proved competence in landing an aircraft on an aircraft carrier. [Ref: Snowie]

You're no good to the navy unless you complete your carquals!

CARRY THE CAN, TO (military general, since at least WWII) — To "carry the can" is to take the initiative for completing a task. Alternately, it may mean to be left holding the responsibility (usually for something that one would rather not be responsible for). [Ref: Partridge (8th)]

C.A.S.; C.D.S. — "CAS" (since the 1930's in the RAF and often pronounced: "kaz") is the "Chief of the Air Staff", the title of the senior RAF officer, and also the senior RCAF officer (at least up to 1965 when the Canadian Army, Navy and RCAF integrated their headquarters). In 1965, the Canadian Forces command structure changed and a single officer was placed over all three services; the title was the "Chief of the Defence Staff", or "C.D.S." (See **Chief (1)**) [Ref: Partridge (8th)]

CASTLE DISMAL (WWII; RCAF) — "Castle Dismal" was the Second World War nickname for the Headquarters of 6 Bomber Group, RCAF. This headquarters was at Allerton Hall, a stately home in Britain. (See also **Bullshit Towers, Chateau, Disneyland on the Rideau, Fort Fumble, Fraggle Rock, Glass Menagerie; Glass Palace, Petrified Forest**)

CAT — A short form for either of:

(1) **Catapult**, that is, the steam catapult used to launch naval aircraft from the Flight Deck of an aircraft carrier. Following the Second World War, Naval aircraft became heavier and required a faster speed for takeoff. Turning the aircraft carrier into the wind (to increase airflow over the wing) was not enough to guarantee that heavier postwar carrier aircraft would take off. A catapult was needed. The British Admiralty began experiments with a deck-mounted steam catapult (a technique then only used to launch small floatplanes from battleships and cruisers). Today a catapult is standard in carrier design (though helicopters and vertical takeoff and landing aircraft like the Harrier survive quite nicely without them). Therefore, a "cat shot" is a catapult launch.

(2) **Category**, that is, any use of the word category is inevitably shortened to "cat", as in a "Cat B accident" or in one's "Med Cat" (ie., Medical category).

(3) **Catalina**, a high wing, twin-engined flying boat flown by the RCAF from 1940 to 1963. The "Cat" was designed and built by Consolidated Aircraft though a number were also manufactured under licence in Canada using the name Canso. Originally the Canadian-built variant was to have been named the Convoy. However this notion was abandoned due to the potential for confusion in signals between a convoy of ships and an aircraft called a Convoy. [Ref: Molson and Taylor; Partridge (FS)]

CATERPILLAR CLUB — The "Caterpillar Club" is an association comprised exclusively of people who have escaped by parachute from an aircraft in distress.

The club was formed in Ohio in the 1920's. It is sponsored independently by two United States parachute firms, the Irvin Air Chute Corporation and the Switlik Parachute Company. Today, membership exceeds 375,000 members. Membership is open to anyone, provided they have baled out of an aircraft in distress, and sent proof thereof to either of these corporations. Upon confirmation of eligibility, they will send you a membership card and a gold "Caterpillar" lapel pin. The caterpillar motif derives from the fact that early parachutes were not made of nylon, as today. They were made of silk, the product of the silkworm, a type of caterpillar. A similar, Britain-based club exists, known as the "GQ Club" (See also **G.Q. Club**)[Ref: Hampson]

C.B. (pronounced "see-bee") (Commonwealth Forces since early 1900's; CF, current) — "C.B." is the acronym for Confined to Barracks - a minor punishment for petty, disciplinary offences. Therefore, one can C.B. a trainee or be C.B.'d. [Ref: Partridge (8th)]

Cb (pronounced "see-bee") — "Cb" is the meteorologists' written shorthand for the Cumulonimbus cloud - colloquially known as a "thunderhead". This written shorthand is now verbal shorthand as well and this type of cloud is called a Cb.

The Cb at its worst is characterized by hail, rain, and turbulence capable of causing an aircraft to break up. It is easily the most dangerous type of cloud formation for aircraft in flight, and as such has attracted nicknames such as Thunderbumper or Cumulo-Concrete.

C.D.F. (ie., "see-dee-eff") — "C.D.F." are the initials for "common dog fuck", an earthy phrase incapable of precise definition but which equates roughly to horse sense, that is, the most common possible type of common sense. A person without C.D.F. is unable to comprehend something so plainly obvious that even a common dog knows it. In all likelihood this is merely the Canadian variant of "common dry fuck", a phrase common in the Royal Navy having the same meaning, but borrowing from another Canadianism "fucking the dog". [Ref: Partridge (8th)]

The trouble with Corporal Miles is that he has absolutely no C.D.F.!

C.D.S.   See **C.A.S.**

CFR (ie., "see-eff-are") — "C.F.R." is the acronym for "Commissioning from the Ranks". This is a program under which qualified noncommissioned officers become commissioned officers in their area of military expertise. For example, a sergeant who is an Airframe Technician might be commissioned from the ranks and become an engineering officer. Therefore, one is CFR'd, and such an officer is called a CFR.

CHAFF (since WWII) — "Chaff" (once a secret codename) is a type of electronic countermeasure that confuses and deceives radar. Chaff consists of bundles that contain millions of small thin metallic strips (the strips are not unlike the tinsel used to decorate a Christmas tree). These bundles drop from an aircraft in flight and break open, spilling these millions and millions of tiny strips into the air. These strips form a metallic cloud in the sky which reflects a radar echo back to the enemy radar as they slowly float down. This large echo camouflages and obscures the real radar echo produced by the aircraft itself.

CHALK (Military Aviation; since WWII) — "Chalk" is air transport slang which means *one aircraft cargo delivered to the destination*. It is analogous to a sortie. For example, if it will take ten separate flights to fly passengers or cargo to a destination, it is said to take ten chalks. The term derives from early U.S. Army Air Corps practice. The code number for a specific load of cargo was written in chalk on the cargo packaging, and also on the fuselage of the aircraft in which the cargo was to be carried. Often this term is misspelled as chock. (See **Sortie**) [Ref: Krisinger]

CHARM SCHOOL (CF, current) — The term "Charm School" could refer to several types of training course offered to Canadian airmen and airwomen.

The term Charm School could refer to the Royal Military College at Kingston, where officer cadets receive subsidized university education and military training through the Regular Officer Training Plan. Charm School also refers to the Senior Leaders Course, attended by all Sergeants who aspire to the rank of Warrant Officer. The Senior Leaders' Course is a finishing school intended to give newly-promoted Sergeants the supervisory knowledge and military bearing expected of a Senior NCO. As such, it is quite demanding and tremendous emphasis is placed on personal appearance and spit and polish. On return to their unit, new Charm School graduates typically embark on an offensive. They seek to eradicate sloppy uniforms, non-regulation haircuts, and unshined shoes, so as to generally improve the dress and deportment of their subordinates - much to the latters' discomfiture. Hence, the ironic title: Charm School.

Before unification in 1968, Charm School often referred to the RCAF's special Officer's Training Course for NCO's who were commissioned from the ranks. (See **CFR**) This course, having been designed for veteran NCO's, tended to skip much of the more basic subject-matter taught to those officer candidates without previous air force service. Thus it was called the Charm School, a finishing school where the NCO learned to become an officer and a gentleman. It was also known as the "Knife, Fork and Spoon Course". [Ref: Sutherland]

> *Sgt. Jones is coming back from 'Charm School' next week...*
> *Then I'm asking for a week's Leave!*

CHATEAU, THE (RCAF; 1950's, 1960's) — "The Chateau" referred to Chateau de Mercie, a beautiful chateau near Metz, France. The chateau served as the headquarters of the RCAF's No. 1 Air Division from April, 1953 until April, 1967. No. 1 Air Division comprised all RCAF fighter units in Europe and at its peak the Air Division had twelve fighter squadrons under its command. The Air Division was headquartered at Metz from its inception until 1967, when France's defence policy changed and foreign units armed with nuclear weapons had to leave. The RCAF's fighter squadrons were armed with American tactical nuclear bombs at the time, so the Air Division Headquarters moved to Lahr, Germany. (See also **Bullshit Towers, Castle Dismal, Disneyland on the Rideau, Fort Fumble, Fraggle Rock, Glass Menagerie; Glass Palace, Petrified Forest**) [Ref: Sutherland]

> *Did you hear that Claude's in trouble with the Wing Commander?*
> *How come?*
> *He buzzed the Chateau at dawn last Tuesday.*

CHECK SIX! — The phrase "Check Six" has two meanings, the second derived from the first:

(1)   First, **Check Six** is a radio warning given to a friendly aircraft to watch for a threat immediately behind them. "Six" refers to the six o'clock position in the Clock System. This system is used to describe the location of another aircraft relative to one's own. (See also **Clock-Code**)

(2)   Also, **Check Six!** can be a warning to protect one's personal or professional interests from unseen threats and intrigues. It is derived from the meaning above. Just as a combat pilot should check six for hostile aircraft, one

should look behind one's back for threats on the ground.

CHICKEN IN A BASKET — The "chicken in a basket" was the metal Air Command Badge worn on the CF Air Force tunic until 1992. The small, circular badge depicts an eagle arising in flight from within a Crown. Chicken in a Basket - pieces of fried chicken served in a small wicker basket - is a common restaurant menu item. The eagle in the badge is, of course, the chicken, and the crown is the basket!

CHICKENSHIT (general; probably American in origin) — "Chickenshit" is a noun or adjective meaning exasperatingly petty. It is usually used with reference to formal rules or requirements. [Ref: Elting]

CHIEF (CF) — In the CF, the word "Chief" has two possible meanings:

(1)   **Chief** can refer to the Chief of the Defence Staff, the senior officer in the Canadian Forces; this usage is common among persons serving out a posting at National Defence Headquarters.

(2)   **Chief** is also the near-universal, though incorrect, short form of address for a Chief Warrant Officer. Properly, only a Chief Petty Officer in the navy is addressed as Chief, but everyone in the CF seems to favour the term Chief to refer to a Chief Warrant Officer. It remains to be seen whether the regulations will yield to this usage. (See also **Chiefy**)

CHIEFY; CHIEFIE (WWII RAF, RCAF) — For many decades, "Chiefy" was the casual form of address for (or reference to) a Flight Sergeant, the RAF and RCAF rank immediately superior to Sergeant. Flight Sergeant is equivalent to today's CF Warrant Officer. The origins of Chiefy go back to 1918, when the RAF was formed by amalgamating the army's RFC and the navy's RNAS. Former naval airmen started addressing Flight Sergeants as Chief or Chiefy, which was the sailor's popular mode of address for a Chief Petty Officer, the naval rank then equivalent to a Flight Sergeant. The usage stuck, and though it passed out of Canadian slang after the Second World War, it remains current in the RAF. [Ref: Partridge (8th)]

Chiefy

...has anyone seen Chiefy Barlow?

CHIT (originally British Indian Army; now general) — A chit is an official receipt or memo issued in lieu of a more formal document. [Ref: Partridge (8th)]

Brown! You're late!
Uh, I was at Sick Parade, sarge...
Then, lets see your Medical Chit!

CHOCK — A "chock" is simply a steel, wooden, or rubber block, wedged under the wheel of an aircraft to prevent it from rolling as it sits on the ground. Consequently, placing them beneath the aircraft wheels is to chock the aircraft. An aircraft that is chocked and chained has chocks beneath the wheels and is further secured to the ground by steel chains; this is usually necessary on fighter aircraft when a full-power engine ground run is necessary. Aircraft on board a ship are always chocked and chained so they will not roll around on a rolling and pitching carrier deck, in the swell. (But see also **Chalk**)

CHOCKS AWAY! (Aviation; general) — "Chocks away" is the shouted instruction from a pilot to the ground crew to remove the wheel chocks, so the pilot can apply power and taxi the aircraft away. Thus it is the last step before the flight properly begins.

However, this aviation phrase crept into use in non-aviation situations. Since the 1930's, chocks away! has been an admonition to get on with it! Just as the phrase is used to remove the wheel chocks, the last obstacle to flight, it is also used to remove other obstacles. [Ref: Partridge (8th)]

CHOPBURG (RAF, RCAF; WWII) — Hamburg became known as "Chopburg" among Bomber Command aircrews, because of its fierce anti-aircraft defences. (See **To get the chop, Big City**) [Ref: Partridge (8th)]

CHOPPER (probably American in origin) — A "chopper" is a helicopter, from the chopping sound of the rotors. [Ref: Partridge (8th)]

CHOP, TO GET THE (RAF, RCAF; WWII) — "To get the chop" was Bomber Command slang for being shot down. It particularly implied a loss over the target, with no survivors. (See also **Chopburg**)[Ref: Partridge (8th)]

CHUGALUG, TO (RCAF since at least WWII, CF current) — "The Chugalug" is a form of drinking celebration common in air force messes, on occasions such as birthdays, promotions, retirement, or postings, etc. Generally, only those esteemed by their peers are subjected to this ancient ritual. Protocol demands that the drinker be given a tankard filled with some alcoholic beverage. The drinker stands silent while his or her peers chant *The Chugalug Song*, the words of which are:

> *Here's to (person's name), he's true blue!*
> *He's a drunkard, through and through!"*
> *He's a drunkard so they say,*
> *Tried to go to heaven, but he went the other way!*

The victim then drinks the tankard without pause, while everyone else chants:

> *So DRINK! chugalug! chugalug! chugalug!*
> *So DRINK! chugalug! chugalug! chugalug!*
> etc., etc.,

To ensure that the tankard truly is empty, custom dictates that the person tip it over their head. That way, if there is anything left unconsumed, the victim wears it! [Ref: Harvey]

CIRCUIT (general aviation usage) — The "circuit" is a rectangular path flown around a runway by slow-flying aircraft when approaching an airport to land, or when taking off and departing.

When the aircraft takes off and climbs it is on the "departure" leg. To remain in the circuit, the pilot turns the aircraft 90 degrees (left or right as decreed by air traffic control), and continues for a set distance on the "crosswind" leg. By this time the aircraft should be at circuit altitude, generally 1000 feet above ground. The pilot then turns the aircraft until it is flying parallel to the runway, and is heading in the opposite direction to that used on landing. This is termed the "downwind" leg. Then, to bring the aircraft back down for a landing, the pilot turns the aircraft another 90 degrees toward the runway. It is now on the "base leg", and the descent begins. Finally, at the appropriate point, the aircraft is turned another 90 degrees, onto "final approach" to a landing. (For a more pedestrian application of the word "circuit", see **Kriegie**) [Ref: Partridge (8th)]

CIRCUITS AND BUMPS (general aviation usage) — "Circuits and Bumps" is a sarcastic variation of "circuits and landings", a familiar training exercise for student pilots, in which the trainee pilot practices approaches and landings. However, instead of stopping after landing, the aircraft continues rolling and takes off again, to repeat the circuit. Given that novice pilots are prone to performing bumpy landings, this manoeuvre literally and figuratively becomes circuits and bumps rather than circuits and landings. [Ref: Partridge(FS)]

CIRCUS (RAF; WWII) — "Circus" was the Second World War RAF codename for an offensive fighter sweep involving several wings of fighter aircraft, all flying in search of Luftwaffe fighters. Circuses were conducted during the first half of 1941. The operation was nominally a fighter escort of a few bombers, often Blenheims or Stirlings, but in fact the bombers were there as bait to attract the enemy. A similar operation where the bombers were more than bait, but were actually hitting important targets was codenamed Ramrod. These operations began in a new spirit of aggressiveness after the Battle of Britain; unfortunately the results were disappointing. RAF fighters suffered precisely the same tactical disadvantages over Europe that the Luftwaffe had over England during the Battle of Britain: a lack of surprise and short endurance over enemy territory. After suffering mounting losses without significant effect on the enemy, they were ended. (See also **Flying Circus, Ranger, Rodeo; Rhubarb**) [Refs: Rawlings; Spick, Terraine]

Both our wing and the Biggin Hill wing are on a circus tomorrow.

CIVVY; CIVVY STREET (Commonwealth services; since at least WWII) — "Civvy" means civilian, as opposed to military. As a noun referring to an individual civilian, it is often shortened further to "civ". "Civvies" are civilian clothing and civvy street is civilian life. [Ref: Partridge (8th)]

You just can't get food like this on civvy street!
Of course not. Would you pay for it?

CLAG (originally RAF, 1930's; current) — "Clag" is a thick layer of overcast cloud (usually associated with rain) which reduces or eliminates visibility when flown through. [Refs: Partridge (8th); Harvey]

*We descended through the clag, but didn't see the ground until we were a
mile back from the runway.*

CLAM-GUN (CF, present) — The "clam-gun" is the weapon used to hunt the wily clam,
that is, a shovel.

CLAMPERS (Aviation general; since at least 1920's) — When the weather goes
"clampers", it has deteriorated to the extent that flying is not possible. In otherwords,
bad weather has "clamped" down on flying. (See also **Clag; Shit (Piss) and Corruption**)
[Ref: Harvey; Partridge (8th)]

We were set to take off at dawn, but the weather went clampers.

CLAPPED OUT — An aircraft long past its serviceable prime is "clapped out", though
this term can also describe a person who is weary. However, given that the clap is also
vernacular for venereal disease, this latter usage has become less common. [Ref:
Partridge (8th)]

CLAPPER (Bomber Command WWII) — A "Clapper" was a Lancaster bomber specially
modified to carry the massive 22,000 pound "Grand Slam" bomb, the largest
conventional bomb used during the Second World War. To carry this massive bomb, the
standard Lancaster bomber was refitted with a special, larger bomb bay, and all possible
weight was removed including the crew positions for the mid-upper turret gunner and
the wireless operator. It was fitted with more powerful 1280 HP engines, and the
undercarriage was strengthened. After the 11-ton bombload was released, the modified
Lancaster flew very fast indeed, and was very manoeuvrable! It was known by its crew
as a "Clapper" because "after dropping the bomb, one would go like the clappers!" (*To
go like the clappers on the bells of hell!* is a British euphemism for speed and was common
in the RAF of the 1930's) (See also **Grand Slam, Tallboy**) [Refs: Cooper; Partridge (8th)]

CLASSIFIED (general military usage) — Information is "classified" when it would be
harmful to the national interest to release it. Therefore it is protected and kept secret.
Such information falls into one of three security classifications: Confidential, Secret, and
Top Secret.

CLEAN; DIRTY (general aviation usage) — An aircraft is "clean" when parasite drag
has been reduced to a minimum. Consequently, an aircraft is "dirty" when there is lots
of parasite drag.

Parasite drag is produced by equipment protruding from an aircraft, such as
undercarriage, flaps and spoilers, external fuel tanks, bombs, or rockets. Every aircraft
will experience some parasite drag; however, the aircraft can fly faster if the sources of
parasite drag are minimized. Thus, to clean up the aircraft is to eliminate sources of drag,
by retracting the undercarriage, flaps and brakes, or by dropping the external stores and
fuel tanks. (Of course, the word clean has an entirely different connotation for apprentice
technicians when their sergeant says: *clean up the aircraft!*)

CLEARANCES — In the air force, the word "clearances" can have either of two
meanings:

(1)   **Clearances** can be Air Traffic Control instructions specifying an aircraft's altitude, heading, communications instructions, procedures, etc.

(2)   However, the term **clearances** can also mean administrative notations on an airman's records showing that the airman has severed connections with his base, or unit (ie., paid debts, returned air force property, etc.). This becomes necessary on transfer to a new unit, or on leaving the military. Therefore, to obtain such acknowledgements is to clear the base.

CLEARED, TO BE (military; general) — A person who "is cleared" is deemed sufficiently trustworthy to have access to highly sensitive information. (See also **Cleared to Rumour**)

CLEARED TO RUMOUR (CF Current) — A person who is "cleared to rumour" is aware of an open secret.

This phrase alludes to one's security clearance, ie. the extent to which one is permitted access to classified information. Hence, a servicemember could be cleared to confidential, cleared to secret, etc. However, when a juicy piece of gossip is circulating, one need merely be cleared to rumour to hear it. (See also **Classified**)

CLICK   See **Klick**

CLOCK (RAF, RCAF to 1950's) — The "clock" is an aircraft instrument, especially the airspeed indicator or altimeter. Therefore, "nothing on the clock" suggests either zero altitude, or zero airspeed. The term alludes to the appearance of either of these instruments - a circular face with numbers and hands reminiscent of a timepiece. (See also **Clock-Basher**) [Refs: Partridge (8th); Harvey]

There I was: a full bomb load, and nothin' on the clock!

CLOCK-BASHER (RAF, RCAF to 1950's) — A "clock-basher" was an Instrument Technician. Clock refers to aircraft instruments, and basher denoted a technician or mechanic. (See **Basher, Clock**) [Ref: Partridge (8th)]

CLOCK-CODE (originally RFC, WWI; now universal) — The "Clock Code" is the method used by aircrew to quickly describe the position of another aircraft, relative to their own.

To understand this code, it is necessary to visualize one's own aircraft positioned flat at the centre of a large clock-face, with the nose pointing towards twelve o'clock. The location of another aircraft is described as at whatever clock number corresponds to its bearing from one's own aircraft, at the centre of the imaginary clock-face. For example, an aircraft directly ahead of one's own aircraft, would be at twelve o'clock. An aircraft directly behind would be at six o'clock. An aircraft to the right, and behind one's own, would be at four-thirty, etc.

Likewise, if the aircraft is at an altitude above one's own, it is described as "high". If below one's own aircraft, it is stated to be "low". Thus an aircraft high and directly to the front of one's own is described as being at "twelve o'clock high". Similarly, an aircraft behind one's own and flying at a lower altitude is at "six o'clock low".

This system may have been adapted from the clock code used during the First World War by RFC observation aircraft to describe the fall of artillery bursts on enemy positions. In this system, the target was at the centre of an imaginary clock, with the twelve pointed towards north. Thus the fall of artillery shells was described by its distance in miles and its direction from the target in terms of the clock code. [Refs: Phelan; Spick]

> *Bandits! Eleven o'clock high!*

CLOSE ENOUGH FOR GOVERNMENT WORK! (CF current) — "Close enough for government work" is an oath, usually heard after a task is completed, suggesting that the speaker won't waste any more effort on that job. Denoting a barely acceptable quality of work, the phrase is an indirect insult to the quality of government programs.

CLOSE PATTERN (General, Military Aviation) — Instead of joining the circuit, fast military jet aircraft returning to base to land often execute a "close pattern".

Jet aircraft arc too fast to execute a conventional circuit when returning to an air base to land. Further, if many jet aircraft are using the runways simultaneously, the multiplicity of approach patterns in a conventional "circuit" increases the chance of a collision. Therefore the close pattern was developed. In a close pattern, returning aircraft fly over the runway in the direction of landing, at an altitude of about 1000 feet. The pilot then executes a steep 180 degree turn, to straighten out on downwind leg". At this point, the aircraft is slowed to a safe speed and the flaps, speed brakes, and undercarriage are extended. At the appropriate point, the pilot executes another 180-degree turn while descending, lines up on final approach, and lands. (See **Circuit**)

CLOSE THE HANGAR DOORS! (RAF, RCAF, CF though now dated) — Since the 1930's, "close the hangar doors!!" has been a favourite admonition to stop talking shop! [Ref: Partridge (8th)]

> *Anyway, I don't know why they haven't amended Form 378...*
> *Will you 'Close the Hangar Doors'!?*

CLOUDY JOE (RAF, RCAF WWII) — "Cloudy Joe" was the Base, or Station, Meteorologist. [Ref: Partridge (8th)]

CLUB (RAF, RCAF; WWII) — On occasion, an aircraft propeller blade was termed a "club" - presumably for its appearance and for the mortal danger that a spinning propeller poses to a frail human body. [Ref: Partridge (8th)]

CLUB ED (CF; current) — "Club Ed" is current slang for the Canadian Forces military prison and detention facility at CFB Edmonton. The word is a play on the famous Club Med chain of resorts where the fortunate can spend several enjoyable weeks in the sun. In contrast, Club Ed is a place for the not-so-fortunate. (See also **D.B.'s, Digger, Jankers**)

> *Wayne spent a couple of weeks double-timing and polishing garbage cans in*
> *Club Ed after he threw a punch at an M.P.*

CLUB 22 (RCN; 1959-69) — "Club 22" was an ironic jocular allusion to the aircraft carrier HMCS Bonaventure as a night spot. The number 22 was Bonaventure's pennant number. The degree of good cheer in a sailor's use of the phrase Club 22 depended entirely on the availability of alternate entertainment. If the ship was at anchor in Rio de Janeiro, returning to Club 22 was a dour prospect. On the other hand, during a "Banyan" (a shipboard party during calm seas) Club 22 was a good place to be. (See **Bonnie**) [Ref: Snowie]

Chief, when's the last liberty boat to Club 22?

CLUNK (RCAF, CF, 1950's to 80's) — The Avro CF-100 Canuck was universally known as the "Clunk" in the RCAF and the CF. (See also **Canuck (3)**)

The origins of the nickname are uncertain, though various explanations exist. For example, the aircraft was - to put it mildly - ungainly and "clunky" looking. Another possible explanation was that when the undercarriage was retracted, a solid CLUNK was heard and felt throughout the airframe.

CLUTCHING HAND   See **Skyhook (1)**

CLUTTER — "Clutter" on a radar screen is a display of radar echoes of natural origin (e.g. geographic features, weather). Clutter interferes with the tracking of an aircraft or other target. (See also **Grass**) [Ref: Gentle and Reithmaier]

COCKED AND LOADED (CF current) — A military aircraft that is fully armed and mechanically ready for a combat mission is "cocked and loaded". The term is an allusion is to a pistol that, when ready to be fired, is also cocked and loaded.

COCKPIT (universal; naval in origin) — The "cockpit" is the small compartment that contains the pilot's seat and flight controls. To properly be a cockpit, one must enter it directly from outside the aircraft (as opposed to a flight deck, which one enters from within the aircraft). (See also **Canopy, Flight Deck**)

COCOON, TO — "To cocoon" an aircraft is to place it in storage and completely cover it with an airtight rubber or plasticized coating to protect it from the elements and from moisture. Cocooning is usually done to an aircraft destined for long-term storage. (See also **in Mothballs**) [Ref: Gentle and Reithmaier]

COFFIN (RCAF from 1950's, CF; still current) — A "coffin" is the metal or fibreglass shipping case in which one stores and transports an aircraft missile. In Canadian usage it especially referred to the bright yellow shipping cases for the Falcon missile, standard armament for the CF-101 Voodoo aircraft. The origin of the term is clear: the missile's shipping case closely resembled a coffin in size and dimensions. (See **One-o-one; One-o-wonder**)

Crack open those two coffins and we'll arm this aircraft.

CO-JOE (Since WWII) — A "co-joe" is a co-pilot. It is rhymed slang, where "joe" is a synonym for the word "guy". [Ref: Partridge (8th)]

I'm not the captain. I'm the co-joe.

COKE-BOTTLE FUSELAGE — An aircraft with a "coke-bottle fuselage" has a fuselage designed in accordance with the "area rule" principle of aerodynamics. The area rule is a design principle that describes how an aircraft can more easily accelerate through Mach 1 (the speed of sound). A so-designed fuselage is easily recognized by its pinched-waist planform. The centre section of the fuselage is narrower than the forward and aft sections, rather like the shape of a coke-bottle.

However, the term coke-bottle fuselage can occasionally refer to curvaceous women, who also have a "pinched-waist planform".

COLLAR-DOG (CF) — A "collar-dog" is a metal collar badge, worn on the collar of a shirt, or the lapels of a tunic.

The term collar dog may be naval in origin. The RCN, alone among the three services before unification in 1968, issued metal rank badges to be worn on a shirt collar (by officers on their khaki summer shirt). As well, "to dog", is naval slang meaning to secure, as in *to dog a hatch*. However, the term is also current in the British Army, so the term may have other origins.

RCAF uniforms were without collar dogs, except for those of certain specialty occupations such as medical officers and chaplains. However, the CF green uniforms that came into use in 1968 had a distinctive collar dog on the lapel, showing the wearer's service branch, corps or regiment (ie., Administration, Air Operations, Logistics, etc). Noncommissioned personnel also wore collar dogs showing their rank, on the shirt collar. The introduction of the CF Air Force uniform in 1988, saw the rejection of collar dogs for the revived air force-blue uniform. Quite apart from the return to RCAF tradition, it was feared that a broken metal collar dog that had fallen on a tarmac or a hangar floor created a FOD Hazard. (See **FOD**)

COLLEGE, THE (CF current) — Royal Military College of Canada, at Kingston, is called "The College" by its students and alumni. (See also **Charm School**)

COMIC CUTS (RAF; WWI) — RAF communiques during the First World War were commonly known as the "comic cuts". These were brief messages routinely distributed to all RAF squadrons on the western front. Each comic cut contained a general account of all aerial action on the Western Front, and contained more specific accounts of individual combat. [Ref: Voss]

Have you read the latest comic cuts?

COMING UNGLUED (CF current) — A person is said to be "coming unglued" when he or she has become angry and has lost their self-control. However, the term can also refer to the beginning of flight after a takeoff roll, when the wheels of an aircraft leave the runway (ie., the wheels become "unglued" from the runway). (See **Coming Unstuck, to go Apeshit, to go Ballistic**)

COMING UNSTUCK (CF, current) — An aircraft "comes unstuck" at that moment on its takeoff roll when the force of lift exceeds its weight, and the undercarriage leaves the runway surface. It is often used with an airspeed or a distance, as in: *We came unstuck at 67 knots.*

COMSTOCK (RCAF; CF to early 1980's) — A "Comstock" was a towed portable electrical power unit used to provide auxiliary power to an aircraft on the ground. This permitted an aircraft to start its engine without depleting the battery on board. Essentially a Comstock was a six-cylinder auto engine linked to an electrical generator, within a housing and all on wheels. It was produced in great number by the Comstock corporation and entered Canadian service along with the T-33, F-86 and CF-100 aircraft in the early 1950's. [Ref: Sutherland]

Hook a Comstock to that mule and get ready to go on start crew.

CON, TO　　　See **Contrail**

CONED, TO BE (RAF, RCAF; WWII) — An aircraft was "coned" when it was lit up by two or more searchlights, at night. RAF and RCAF bombers, attacking German cities at night, relied on darkness for cover from enemy fighters and flak. However, to bomb accurately they had to slow over the target. Worse, they had to do so while ground-based searchlights tried to spot the bombers for the anti-aircraft guns. The more searchlights that caught a bomber in its glare, the more difficult it was to break off before the anti-aircraft crews got the range. Thus a bomber caught by two or more searchlights was at the apex of several beams of light, creating a triangular, or cone-like appearance. [Ref: Bowyer]

CONEHEAD (CF, current) — "Conehead" was a disparaging nickname for either of two groups of aircrew during the 1980's, depending on location,:

(1)　　　An Air Navigator in maritime anti-submarine squadrons, and

(2)　　　A student pilot at number 2 Canadian Forces Flying Training School, CFB Moose Jaw, where advanced flying training is conducted on the Tutor jet trainer.

The origin of the title is clear: *The Coneheads* were a rather obtuse species of alien, featured in the early 1980's on the *Saturday Night Live* television program and which reappeared in a 1993 movie. Sometimes the term was shortened to "cone", as in *has that cone figured out the answer yet?*

CONTRAIL; TO CON (military aviation, general) — "Contrail" is short for condensation trail, a brilliant white cloud streak created by an aircraft in flight in certain atmospheric conditions. Often mistaken for engine exhaust, it is mere water vapour, so sometimes the term vapour trail is used instead. Contrails form when air, flowing over the wing or around a hot engine, changes pressure. This change of pressure causes moisture in the air to vaporize and form a cloud which trails the aircraft.

In air combat, contrails are to be avoided because the white streak in the sky acts like an arrow pointing out the presence of your aircraft to the enemy. Consequently, the verb "to con" describes the process of creating a contrail, as in: *We were at angels 30 and conning when we were bounced a Belgique '104.* [Ref: Sutherland]

COOKIE (originally RAF; still current) — During the Second World War, "cookie" was slang for the large, 4000 lb. high explosive, high capacity bomb used by RAF Bomber

Command. Later it came to mean any bomb larger than normal. Unsurprisingly, this term was applied to atomic and nuclear bombs carried after the Second World War. Until the early 1980's, Canadian CF104 Starfighter aircraft based in Germany were armed with U.S.-controlled tactical nuclear weapons. Therefore, one spoke of "having to drop the cookie". (See also **Blockbuster, Grand Slam, Groceries; Tallboy**) [Refs: Bowyer; Partridge (FS)]

COOKIE-CUTTER (CF current) — The cap badge worn by officers of the Cadet Instructors Cadre (CIC) is occasionally referred to as the "cookie-cutter". (The Cadet Instructors Cadre is the branch of the Reserve Force that trains and administers the Royal Canadian Air Cadets, together with its Naval and Army counterparts.) The CIC cap badge is brass and maple leaf-shaped. As such, its irregular edges are reminiscent of the serrated edge of a kitchen Cookie-Cutter.

COOL POOL (CF current) — "Cool Pool" is the occasional nickname for CFB Cold Lake.

COPACETIC (pronounced "cope-ess-set-tik") (RCAF; late 1950's to Unification) — "Copacetic" is an adjective that suggests that all is well, organized and going according to plan. It would appear that the term was coined from the verb to cope and from antiseptic. Thus, if things are copacetic, it is easy to cope. [Refs: Sutherland; Partridge (8th)]

> *How's that repair coming along?*
> *Everything's copacetic, boss...*

COPROLITE (CF; current) — The term "coprolite" attained currency for a time among students at the Canadian Forces Command and Staff College to describe a less-than-inspiring guest lecturer. At Staff College, promising officers of the rank of Major spend nearly a year studying to acquire the skills and knowledge needed to prepare them for success at higher ranks. Some of their lecturers are better than others, which of course implies that some of their lecturers are worse than others. Uninspiring lecturers became known as "coprolites". Coprolite is the technical term used by paleontologists for fossilized dung.

> *What was the Colonel's presentation like?*
> *He was another bloody coprolite...*

CORNFLAKE (CF current) — The "cornflake" is the cap badge worn by CF recruits.

When the Navy, Army and RCAF unified in 1968, policy decreed that all military personnel would wear a common style of uniform. Only the cap badge denoted distinctions between service branches. This caused certain complications for recruits who had not yet been assigned to a specific branch. From the 1970's to the early 1990's CF recruits did not wear the badge of a specific service, branch or element until selected for such service. Until so selected, the raw recruit wore a special cap badge: a tiny, nondescript brass miniature of the Canadian Forces badge. At a distance, the badge resembles a cornflake because of its yellow-brown colour and irregular oval shape. It was also termed a "pinecone".

COSMO (RCAF, CF) — "Cosmo" is the nickname for the CC-109 Cosmopolitan, a twin turboprop transport based on the Convair 440 Metropolitan that was built by Canadair under licence from Convair. The Cosmo was in CF service as a general utility and VIP transport until the early 1990's.

In the late 1950's, General Dynamics (then the parent company of both Canadair and Convair) decided to cease production of its Convair 440 Metropolitan in favour of larger jet airliners. The Convair 440 was a successful medium commuter airliner, powered by two piston engines. Canadair elected to obtain the jigs for the Convair 440 and build and sell them in Canada, though with turboprop engines. The aircraft was renamed the Cosmopolitan. The only purchaser of the production Cosmo proved to be the Canadian government, which purchased ten for the RCAF. [Ref: Molson and Taylor]

COUNTER-AIR — "Counter-Air" Operations are air attacks against enemy air forces, including its aircraft, facilities, supplies, runways, people, etc. The term is inevitably shortened to counter-air.

COUNT THE HOOKS! COUNT THE HOOPS! (CF, current) — "Count the hooks!" and "Count the hoops!" are each a rebuke to a subordinate, to the effect that he or she is a subordinate and should do as ordered. Hooks are the chevrons worn by NCO's, and hoops are officer's rank braid. Consequently, to be invited to count them is to be told to compare your (junior) rank with their (senior) rank.

COVENTRATE, TO (Bomber Command WWII) — To "coventrate" is to utterly destroy a city through aerial bombardment.

The term derives from the English city of Coventry, which was largely demolished by the Luftwaffe, early in the Second World War. The emotional impact of its being destroyed did much to accelerate widespread acceptance of the bombing - or coventration - of German cities.

CRAB (RAF, RCAF 1920's) — This term has two possible meanings.

> (1)   **Crab** was the affectionate nickname for the Avro 504K, a widely-used biplane trainer of the First World War and the 1920's (though it has also been applied to the De Havilland DH6). It is said that the name derives from the Avro 504K's slow speed and its wide, spindly, well-braced undercarriage, reminiscent of the legs of a crab.
>
> The Crab was designed by A.V. Roe (the principal behind Avro Aviation). Indeed, the first aircraft was designed and completed within 12 weeks. It first saw service in the RFC and the RNAS in April 1913. The Avro 504 was ordered as a standard service fighter, and it saw combat against Zeppelins. However, its true avocation was as a trainer. Used in the RFC's new flying training system and equipped with the Gosport Tube, the Avro 504 was to First World War aviators what the Harvard trainer became to subsequent generations. It was well-suited for service as a trainer because, although it could be flown safely with ease, care was required to fly it accurately. Thus, good pilots stood out. The aircraft, powered by a 110-HP Rotary piston engine, earned a reputation for being unforgiving of slipshod maintenance. Following the First World War, the CAF and the RCAF took delivery of 63 Crabs for use as trainers. It was

Crab

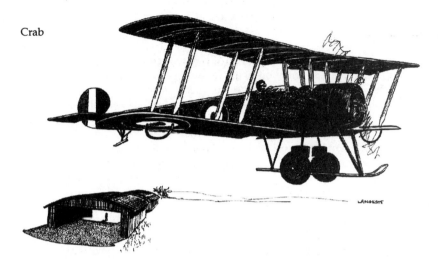

preferred to the Curtiss Canuck as a trainer because, unlike the Canuck, the Avro 504 had a rotary engine. Most service types of the day had rotary engines. (see: **Canuck (2); Gosport System; Gosport Tube**) [Refs: Molson and Taylor; Allez-Fernandez, Cacutt; Voss; Winter; Partridge (8th)]

(2)   **To crab** is to fly an aircraft such that its nose points in a different direction from the aircraft's actual path over the ground. This is necessary when a crosswind blows the aircraft from its intended track; the solution is to point the aircraft slightly into the crosswind, to offset the tendency to drift. This use of the word probably developed because the aircraft seems to be flying slightly sideways, the same way that some crabs walk. [Ref: Partridge (FS)]

CRABFAT (RN, RCN) — "Crabfat" is naval slang for a member of the Air Force. The term is an excellent example of how the meanings of slang evolve over time; indeed the origins of crabfat date from a time long before air forces even existed.

Crabfat, to a Royal Navy sailor at the turn of the 20th Century, was blue unction; a blue-gray ointment prescribed by naval surgeons as a treatment for body lice, or crabs. This was the accepted meaning of crabfat as the Royal Navy re-equipped with modern steel warships.

The steel warships of the Royal Navy were painted Admiralty grey. It was perhaps inevitable that, as sailors applied this dull grey paint to the steel plates of their ships, it would suggest that grey-coloured ointment that the ship's surgeon gave you when you had acquired a dose of the crabs. After a time, the original medical meaning was lost. By the 1930's, the word crabfat meant the colour grey, specifically Admiralty Grey, to sailors.

By the 1930's the first large aircraft carriers had entered Royal Navy service and like other warships they too were painted Admiralty Grey. However, unlike the US Navy, the Royal Navy had no naval air arm. The Fleet Air Arm, which operated from the decks of

British aircraft carriers and included naval aircrew, was actually a branch of the RAF and was controlled not by the Admiralty, but by the Air Ministry! (It remained so until 1938, when the Admiralty assumed total control of the Fleet Air Arm and the sea-going RAF types went ashore.) The aircrews and the groundcrews on Royal Navy carriers in the 1930's were a cosmopolitan mix of sailors wearing dark blue and airmen wearing RAF blue. This made for interesting times, as the following quote reveals:

> *"The relationship between RAF and Royal Navy personnel aboard the carriers was, to commence with it seemed, a joke, especially when the 'boys in light blue' went ashore dressed in riding breeches, puttees and Glengary-type hats; plus their complete ignorance of all things Naval. Eventually the RAF groundcrews became as much a part of the ship's company as the naval ratings."*

After awhile these boys in blue became known as crabfats, an allusion to the blue-grey tone of the RAF uniform and its closeness to the grey colour of the steel warship.

This meaning of crabfat passed on to sailors of the Royal Canadian Navy and since the Second World War, Canadian sailors have referred to Canadian airmen as "crabfats", though few in either service really knew why! The term is lapsing out of Canadian usage ("zoomie" seems to be supplanting it), but it remains a strong part of British service slang. It is said that a bumper sticker was available in the U.K. that read: *Airmen Walk Sideways!* [Refs: Beaver; Partridge (8th)]

CRACK OF CROW (RCAF; 1960's) — "Crack of crow" is a euphemism for very, very early in the morning, as in: *...get some sleep; we have to get up at crack of crow!* (See also **Crow Fart, O-Christ-Thirty, O-Dark-Thirty, Sparrow Fart, Wakey-Wakey**) [Ref: Sutherland]

CRAFT (CF, current) — "CRAFT" is an acronym for "Can't Remember a Fucking Thing", a phrase which probably needs little elaboration.

> *My Captain occasionally suffers from CRAFT syndrome*

CRASH; CRASH AND BURN; CRASH OUT (CF current) — To "crash" (or to use any of its above variations) is to fall asleep from pure exhaustion. Of course, these allude to an aircraft impacting the ground - just as a tired person's body might impact on one's bed. (See **Flame Out**)

CRASH WAGON — A "Crash Wagon" is a fire truck specially designed to fight aircraft fires and to conduct crash rescue. (See also **Hungry Liz**)

CRATE — A "crate" is an obsolete or dilapidated aircraft. (origins unknown) [Ref: Partridge (8th)]

CREEPER   See **Gremlin**

CREW UP, TO (WWII) — To "crew up" was Second World War slang that meant to form a specific aircraft crew. It could also mean to join such a crew already in existence. [Ref: Carlson; Partridge (8th)]

Bob and I crewed up in training, and we've been together ever since.

CROOKER   See **Gremlin**

CROSSWIND; CROSSWIND LEG   See **Circuit**

CROW FART (since WWII) — "Crow Fart" is very, very early in the morning as in: "Go to sleep early, because we're getting up at crow fart." This term seems to suggest a time of day that is so still that if one listens very closely, one can hear a flatulent crow. Sometimes one hears the term "Sparrow Fart" instead. (See also **Crack of Crow, O-Christ-Thirty, Sparrow Fart, Wakey-Wakey**)

CROWNS (RAF, RCAF, CF; current) — "Crown" or "crowns" usually refers to the rank of Flight Sergeant (in the RAF or RCAF) or Warrant Officer (the equivalent rank in the CF). The term is derived from the badge for those ranks. A Flight Sergeant wore three sergeant's chevrons with a crown in the vee. A CF Warrant Officer wears a crown on each tunic sleeve, low on the cuff. Therefore one speaks of "getting one's crowns", or the classic: *...give a guy a crown and he thinks he's a King!* (See also **Chiefy, Dodo Club, Mini-Warrant**) [Ref: Partridge (8th)]

CRUD — The word "crud" originally meant shit, but now implies poor. However, it has three quite specific meanings among airmen and airwomen:

> (1)   **Crud** can be bad weather, characterized by low cloud, rain, and poor visibility, or

> (2)   **Crud** can also be an illness, and has been applied to a nagging cough, cold or ache, diarrhea, or the flu. It can refer to various intestinal disorders requiring fleetness of foot and proximity to a toilet.

> (3)   **Crud** is also a unique indoor sport popular throughout the CF. It is said to have been invented in RCAF officers messes in Europe during the 1950's, and its popularity has gradually spread. It is common throughout the Canadian Forces, and is slowly spreading into the American and British services!

Crud is played at a pool table, using one red ball and one white ball, but no cues. Any number of players can play (though groups of more than a dozen or so become unwieldy) and appointing an umpire or referee is advisable. There are no rules against either players or umpire imbibing alcohol. Military rank has no place in a Crud match.

Players sort themselves into a batting order, not unlike in baseball. The umpire places the red ball at a point at one end of the table. The white ball is placed at the other. The first player, using one hand, rolls the white ball at the red. Immediately on the two balls colliding and rolling away, the next player must grab the moving white ball from wherever it is on the table, and roll it at the now moving red ball. The aim is to sink the red ball and gain a point, though it is enough if the player merely strikes the red ball with the white before the red ball stops moving. If the player fails to hit the red ball before it stops rolling,

Crud

that player is out, and plays no more. If he "sinks" the red ball, he gains a point. If he succeeds and hits the red ball (causing it to keep moving), the play switches to the next player. The new player must now grab the white ball, roll it at the red, and hit it before it stops - seeking to sink it. If he hits it without sinking it, the play shifts to the next player on the other team, and so on.

To further complicate things, the white ball can only be launched from the ends of the pool table, and never from the sides. Apart from this restriction players may move around the table at will, though they are forbidden from crawling over the table.

Crud is fast-moving and demands good hand and eye coordination. (A variation for the more robust is Combat Crud, where opposing players feel free to hip-check another player racing around the table to catch the White Ball. Combat Crud isn't for everyone...)

CRUMP　　　　See **Crump Dump**

CRUMP DUMP (WWII Bomber Command) — The "Crump Dump" was the Ruhr Valley, Germany's industrial heartland, which bore much of the onslaught of Allied aerial bombing. The term is rhymed slang, derived from the word crump (First World War slang for a bomb shell, from the sound made on detonation). [Ref: Partridge (8th)]

C.T. (RCAF, CF) — "C.T." is the abbreviation for Ceased Training, an annotation on a military trainee's records that indicates he's off the training course - for whatever reason. C.T. has since become a verb, as in: *he was C.T.'d.*

Cu (pronounced "kew") — "Cu" is meteorologist's shorthand for Cumulus - a type of cloud characterized by its "puffiness". This written shorthand has now become verbal shorthand as well, so since the mid-1920's it has been common to hear aviators and meteorologists speaking of: scattered Cu, towering Cu, etc. [Ref: Partridge (8th)]

CUMULO-CONCRETE   See **Cb**

CUMULO-GRANITUS (CF current, especially among SAR units) — "Cumulo-Granitus" is mock Latin for a cloud that hides a mountain within it. Latin is used to describe various cloud types (e.g. Cirrus, Cumulus, Nimbus, Cumulo-Nimbus, etc.). The term Cumulo-Granitus alludes to this Latin usage while also humorously describing the hazards inherent to mountain flying in bad weather. Mountains shrouded by cloud are a deadly hazard to aircraft flying through mountainous terrain.

CUSHY (Commonwealth military, since before WWI) — "Cushy" means easy, or safe. It was British Indian Army slang from before the First World War and may be borrowed from the Hindustani word *khush*, which means pleasure. [Ref: Partridge (8th)]

That's a rather cushy job you've got...

CUSTOMER (WWII) — "Customer" was Second World War radio code for an enemy aircraft attempting to enter allied airspace. It was used by ground-based radar controllers directing fighters to intercept, as in "I have a customer for you, twelve o'clock low, at three miles". From this came other, similar terms, such as "custom", or "trade", to describe groups of many enemy aircraft. These radio codewords were intended to fool German electronic eavesdroppers, but postwar research showed they fooled no one. (See also **Lay Eggs; Gardening; Groceries**) [Refs: Jones, W.E.; Partridge (8th)]

CUVVIES (CF current) — To air force technicians, "cuvvies" are coveralls.

C.Y.A. (current, probably American in origin) — C.Y.A. is an abbreviation for "Cover Your Ass", a warning to take steps to protect oneself from hidden threats to one's personal or professional interests. The term is also used in relation to bureaucracy, to describe excessive aversion to risk. (See also **Check Six (2)**)

ELTA

DAISY CUTTER (RAF, RCAF; since 1930'S) — In the pre-war air force, a "daisy cutter" was a perfect landing. Apparently the term is derived from cricket, where a daisy cutter also described a low bowl. [Ref: Partridge (8th)]

DAK (British Commonwealth, since the 1940's) — "Dak" is shorthand for Dakota. Dakota is the name adopted by Commonwealth air forces for the Douglas DC-3, perhaps the most successful aircraft ever. To the U.S. Army and Air Force this aircraft was officially known as the C-47 Skytrain and in the US Navy and US Marines it was the "R4D". Unofficially (and universally) though, American servicemen called it the Gooney Bird. To men and women in Commonwealth military forces this classic aircraft was the Dakota, or Dak.

The Dak, which first flew in 1935, remains in service in many smaller airlines and air forces well into the 1990's! The RCAF acquired its first Dakotas in the Second World War and did not retire the aircraft until 1988. In Canadian service the Dak performed well in a variety of roles: towing gliders, dropping cargo or paratroopers, hauling freight and passengers, searching for downed aircraft, training aircrew and even teaching CF-104 Starfighter pilots to navigate!

D AND D (CF current) — "D and D" means delegate and disappear, a term denoting non-leadership, or a desire to escape responsibility. It is also a play on the initials DND, for Department of National Defence.

When in doubt, D and D!

DASH-ONES, (DASH TWOS, THREES, FOURS) (RCAF, to 1970) — "Dash-ones", etc., were shorthand for the individual parts of the RCAF Engineering Order for a specific aircraft type. Engineering Orders (E.O.'s) are the technical bible for any given aircraft and are consulted frequently by both groundcrews and aircrews in the course of their duties. Each part of the E.O.'s described a different aspect of the aircraft, its operation, and its repair and maintenance procedures. The Engineering Orders for each aircraft had a unique number, and individual parts were identified by adding "-1", "-2", "-3", (the dash-ones, dash-twos, dash-threes) etc. The various chapters were:

Dash-1's	Aircraft Operating Instructions (A.O.I.'s);
Dash-2's	Description and Maintenance Instructions;
Dash-3's	Structural Repair Manual;
Dash-4's	Parts List;
Dash-5's	Special Information;
Dash-6A's	Field Modifications;
Dash-6B's	Overhaul Modifications;
Dash-7's	Special Inspections;
Dash-8's	Weight and Balance Data;

| Dash-9's | Storage and Preservation Instructions; |
| Dash-10's | Quick Engine Change and Powerplant Build-Up Instructions. |

It became common to refer to refer to specific volumes of an aircraft's E.O.'s as the dash-ones, dash twos, and so on. [Ref: Sutherland]

You'd better look it up in the Dash-Ones ...

D.B.'s (British Commonwealth military.) — "D.B.'s" are the initials for Detention Barracks, the formal title for a military jail. No one in the armed forces goes to jail, they go to the DB's, which differ somewhat from civilian jails. D.B.'s exist to reinforce one required military behaviour: obedience to orders. Thus, the regime is akin to recruit training, but infinitely more demanding. There are other nicknames for DB's, including: the "Digger" (said to come from the letters DGR, for Damned Guard Room) and the Glasshouse (apparently from the notorious British Army jail in Aldershot, England). (See also **Club Ed, Jankers**) [Ref: Partridge (FS)]

I spent the longest two weeks of my life in the D.B.'s...

DDH (NATO, CF; current) — DDH is the standard naval designation for a Helicopter-Destroyer. A Helicopter-Destroyer, despite the title, does not destroy helicopters. A DDH is a destroyer that carries one or two helicopters. These anti-submarine helicopters extend the effective combat reach of the warship and allow a coordinated search for submarines many miles beyond the range of the ship's own sensors.

The NATO alliance has adopted the USN system of designating warship types. In this system the letters "DD" designate a Destroyer. The letter "H" is added to indicate that the destroyer carries helicopters. Individual ships are identified within this system by using the code and adding the pendant number of the individual ship. For example, the Canadian helicopter-destroyer HMCS Iroquois is identified as DDH 280.

Dead Air Gunner

The new class of DDH can carry two helicopters.

DEAD AIR-GUNNER (WWII) — Dead Air-Gunner is slang for "Spam", a processed meat food developed to meet dietary requirements during the austere conditions of the Second World War. Spam's unique consistency, appearance and taste aroused a certain black humour among airmen who found it on

their mess menu. [Ref: Partridge (8th)]

> *What's for dinner?*
> *Dead Air-Gunner.*

DEAD ANTS! (RCAF; 1950's, 60's) — "Dead Ants" was a game, popular in RCAF officers' messes of the 1950's and 1960's. Its proper name was never spoken aloud, due to the grave risks involved, risks that become obvious only upon learning the rules.

Often at officers' mess dinners an officer was appointed to be the Antmaster. It was the duty and privilege of the Antmaster to shout, at random intervals during the evening: DEAD ANTS! Upon hearing this cry, all persons within earshot were required to drop to the floor on their backs, raise their arms and legs, and twitch - mimicking an ant in the last throes of death from insecticide! The last person to drop to the ground had to buy a round of drinks.

Generally, Dead Ants was played at stag functions, though skirt-wearing female officers and visitors were often grudgingly exempted. Should someone other than the Antmaster utter the fatal words Dead Ants, whether in jest or error, this person had to buy the round of drinks.

People reacted very quickly on hearing these words; after all, junior officers weren't paid very much, and a round of drinks - even at low mess prices - was costly. Therefore one did not hesitate to drop to the floor, nor did one utter the magic words Dead Ants

Dead Ants

Dead Ants was one of the more
unorthodox mess activities.

LANGESTE

lightly,   hence the safe codewords: Deceased Insects. One may wonder why such a game existed. There do not seem to be any reasons except that RCAF officers were thirsty, not well paid, and often had to make their own fun. Any excuse would do to cadge a free drink.

> *I wonder if someone will call "Dead Ants!" tonight?*
> *QUIET! Please use the words 'Deceased Insects' unless you're the*
> *Antmaster!*

DEAD RECKONING; D.R. (pronounced "dee-are") — "Dead Reckoning", or "D.R." is synonymous with deduced reckoning. Dead Reckoning, the basis of all navigation, is the method of determining where the aircraft is (or will be) by computing the wind's effect on the aircraft's heading, and applying the true airspeed of the aircraft to the aircraft's last known position. D.R. requires the pilot or navigator to do many things. The course must be plotted and measured. Flight instruments must be monitored to determine airspeed, heading, and altitude. The forecast winds must be accounted for, and heading adjusted in flight as winds change. Heading, airspeed and altitude must be adjusted as necessary to arrive at the destination on time. [Ref: Welch]

> *The winds have changed. How good are you at dead reckoning?*

DEADSTICK (RAF, since at least 1925) — An aircraft is flown "deadstick" when it has no engine power. Presumably, stick refers to the throttle, which would be useless (ie., dead) in these circumstances. Therefore, a deadstick landing is a landing without engine power, so the pilot has minimal control over the aircraft's rate of descent.

A deadstick landing is very challenging even at the best of times. The handling characteristics of aircraft without power vary according to design. Of course every landing in a glider is a deadstick landing and they are typically designed to have very respectable handling characteristics. In stark contrast, a fighter aircraft flown deadstick tends to glide like a brick. (see **Flame out, Hang a Rat**) [Ref: Partridge (FS)]

> *He landed the aircraft deadstick, on the grass.*

DEBRIEF; TO DEBRIEF — "Debrief" has two common meanings, the first leading naturally into the second.

> (1)   The verb to **debrief** is the obverse of the verb to brief. To brief is to formally issue instructions and information to mission participants, before a flight or operation. Therefore, a debriefing occurs after the mission. During the debriefing, participants discuss mission results, problems encountered and how they might improve matters for the next time. Lord Trenchard, who commanded the Royal Flying Corps in the First World War, introduced the practice of debriefing into the Air Force and made it a matter of doctrine.

> (2)   A **debriefing** is also a post-operation party or a round of drinks, in the company of operation participants.

DECI (pronounced "det-chee") (RCAF, CF, NATO Europe; 1950's to present) — "Deci" is a shorthand slang name for Decimomannu, an air base on the island of Sardinia where

NATO fighter units deploy for air gunnery exercises and training.

The squadron is going on a six-week Gun Camp to Deci.

DECK, ON THE (general aviation usage; since WWI) — The "deck" is the earth's surface, whether covered by land or water. To be on the deck is to fly very low over the ground. The phrase dates back to Royal Naval Air Service slang of the First World War where it meant to fly at deck height, that is, the deck of a ship, or very low. [Ref: Partridge (8th)]

I got down on the deck and flew out of the area as fast as I could!

DECK APE (RCN; to 1969) — "Deck Ape" was the nickname for naval airmen who worked on the flight deck of an aircraft carrier, handling and servicing aircraft. This was a very specialized task, due to the limited space and dangerous working conditions on an aircraft carrier's flight deck. In the navy, technicians *per se* usually remained below on the hangar deck where they repaired aircraft, leaving the Deck Apes to run the Flight Deck.

Naval airmen wore jerseys of different colours while working on the noisy, cramped and dangerous flight deck. Each colour identified the activity performed, as follows:

Yellow	- the "Deck Apes", ie, the Flight Deck Officer and Aircraft Boatswains
Blue	- Chockmen and Drivers
White	- Engineers and Electricians responsible for catapult, arrestor cables, and ship's landing aids.
Green	- Aircraft Maintainers
Red	- Armourers
Red with Black Stripe	- Fire-Fighters

[Ref: Snowie; Sutherland]

Those Deck Apes have a tough job; they can be blown off the deck into the sea, chopped into pieces by a propeller or rotor blade, or they can be run over by a pilot!

DEFAULTERS (Commonwealth military general; current) — In the commonwealth military forces, "defaulters" was an informal, non-judicial punishment parade for airmen whose conduct has dissatisfied their superiors, ie. , who have defaulted against the rules. This included airmen under open arrest, those confined to barracks, or given extra duties by the Station Warrant Officer. Presumably the term is short for Defaulters Parade. Such miscreants were typically assigned extra duties that usually involved cleaning, polishing, sweeping up, painting, dusting, mopping, shining, buffing... (See also **Hatless Tap-Dance, CB**) [Ref: Sutherland]

Roberts! You're on Defaulters!

DE-LOCALIZE, TO (CF; current) — To "de-localize" is a euphemism, occasionally used by crews of anti-submarine warfare (ASW) aircraft, for losing contact with a hitherto confirmed submarine. It is the height of professional embarrassment among anti-submarine air crews, once having located a submerged submarine, to lose contact with it.

The sequence of events in sinking a submarine is:

1. Detect: the presence of a submarine is sensed,
2. Acquire: the aircraft crew locks on to the submarine
3. Localize: the submarine's exact position, track, speed, and depth are plotted,
4. Attack: the aircraft is brought to close quarters and the submerged submarine is attacked with torpedoes or depth bombs.

To avoid embarrassment, a crew never admits to losing a submarine, rather, they have de-localized. Of course, this ironic term never fools anyone but the layman.

We'd tracked the submarine for eight hours or so, when we, uh.. - de- localized.. - and had to come home....

DELOUSE, TO (RAF, RCAF; WWII) — "De-lousing" was a term used by RAF and RCAF fighter crews during the Second World War. It described their efforts to stop the Luftwaffe fighters that harassed American bombers returning to Britain after raiding Germany.

In the early days of the American daylight bomber campaign against Germany, bombers lacked their own fighter escort. As well, it was several years before any allied fighters could escort the bombers all the way to their targets and back again. Until the U.S. Army Air Corps built up their own fighter forces, RAF and RCAF fighters provided this vital escort service for the Americans. This meant that after a mission, U.S. bombers were harassed by Luftwaffe fighters all the way back to Britain. So Spitfires were sent out from England at the greatest extent of their range to meet the returning Americans and protect them from Luftwaffe fighters. This became known in Fighter Command as de-lousing the bombers that had been "infested" with German fighters. [Ref: Partridge (FS)]

The Spitfires spotted the returning American bombers over France, and began de-lousing them.

DEPTH CHARGES (universal 'military; WWII) — During the Second World War, prunes were occasionally known as "depth charges" because of the explosive effect that they can have on the digestive system if consumed in quantity. [Ref: Partridge (FS)]

Don't eat too many depth charges before flying; you'll regret it!

DET — "Det" can be shorthand for either of two words. A det can be a detonator, a device needed to cause explosives to function as advertised. Alternately, it can mean detachment, a military sub-unit geographically separated from its parent military unit. [Ref: Partridge (8th)]

DEUCE; DEUCE-AND-A-HALF (Canadian Army and CF; originally American) — "Deuce-and-a-half" was the nickname for the standard GMC 2 1/2 ton army troop truck. The term derives from its cargo capacity (ie., deuce for two). The Deuce-and-a-half was the standard troop truck in the Canadian Army, and entered the lives of many airmen after Unification in 1968. A variety of air force field units, such as Tactical Helicopter Squadrons and Aircraft Field Maintenance Squadrons, used the Deuce-and- a-half. The Deuce-and-a-Half remained in service until the late 1980's. It was replaced by a newer vehicle that bears the ungainly title of MLVW (Medium Logistics Vehicle - Wheeled, pronounced T - R - U - C - K).

DEUTSCHER (pronounced: "doyt-chur") (CF; current) — "Deutscher" is the (masculine) German word for a German. As a consequence, Canadian servicemembers stationed in Europe with the NATO forces tended to refer to anything German as Deutscher. Thus a Luftwaffe Sabre aircraft was a Deutscher Sabre, German beer was Deutscher beer, the Germans themselves were the Deutschers, etc.

A Deutscher captain wants to talk to you, Sarge!

DIAMOND — "Diamond" is a formation in which four or more aircraft fly coordinated manoeuvres, while maintaining station in a diamond-shape.

DICEY; DICER; TO DICE (British Commonwealth; since WWII) — "Dicey" means risky, or hazardous. Therefore a dicer was a dangerous operation and to dice was to take risks. They are derived from the roll of the dice, as evocative of risks taken. However, air force usage was also sometimes derisive, a sarcastic reference to sensationalistic language often used by wartime journalists, like dicing with death. [Ref: Harvey]

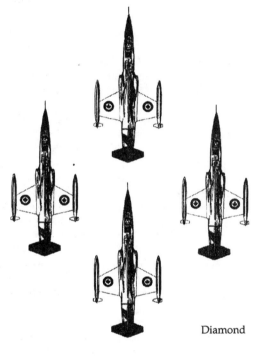

Diamond

Tonight's trip could be dicey.

DICKEE (CF, 1970's, 80's) — A "dickee" is a neckpiece, similar to an ascot, once worn with the now-obsolete CF green work-dress uniform to identify the wearer's service branch, regiment or element. After unification in 1968, all CF personnel, whatever service or branch, wore essentially the same uniform. Though wear of a dickee was an old army custom, a resurgent air force identity caused many airmen and airwomen to wear a dickee of RCAF Tartan with their green Canadian Forces working uniform.

DIEFENBUNKER (CF, general; since late 1950s) The "Diefenbunker" was the self-contained underground fallout shelter and command and control complex built at Carp, Ontario, to house essential federal government facilities in the event of a nuclear attack on Canada. Should the unthinkable happen, the federal cabinet and much of the senior echelon of the executive branch of government would repair to the Diefenbunker and try to put the country back together. Each of the provincial governments has a similar shelter facility and they too are often refered to as Diefenbunkers. The word is clearly borrowed from the name of the Prime Minister of the day, John Diefenbaker, whose government was in power during the construction of the shelters.

DIGGER (Commonwealth military; since early 20th Century) — A "digger" is a military jail. "Digger" is said to derive from D.G.R., the initials for Damned Guard Room. It originated in the British Army and dates from the early 20th century. (See also **Club Ed, D.B.'s, Jankers, Glasshouse**)[Ref: Partridge (8th)]

> *Andy popped the corporal one in the mouth, and later the C.O. sentenced him*
> *to 30 days in the Digger*

DILBERT DUNKER — The "Dilbert Dunker" is a device used to train aviators how to escape from an aircraft submerged in water. The Dilbert Dunker gives trainees a brief taste of the disorientation that can occur when trapped underwater.

They have been constructed in several variations, but in essence, the Dilbert Dunker is an aircraft pilot's seat fixed on a slide, next to a body of water. The seat - in which a trainee is strapped - slides into the water until the trainee and the seat are both completely immersed. The seat then rotates automatically and the trainee (still strapped into the seat) hangs upside down, underwater. The dizzy trainee must immediately escape the seat harness, decide which way is up, and swim to the surface. The usual advice to the trainee is to watch the bubbles and follow them to the surface, even if you are so disoriented that all your instincts tell you to swim in another direction.

Though the origin of the nickname is not clear, it might just honour the mythical Sub-Lieutenant Dilbert Swingit. (See also **Dilbert Swingit, R.N., Sub-Lieutenant**)

> *The Dilbert Dunker isn't difficult to cope with - provided you remember that*
> *bubbles float upwards!*

DILBERT SWINGIT, R.N., SUB-LIEUTENANT (RN, RCN; since WWII) — Sub-Lieutenant Dilbert Swingit, Royal Navy, was a cartoon character epitomizing the thoroughly unsafe naval aviator, developed during the Second World War by the publishers of the Royal Navy Flight Safety magazine. ("Swingit!" is older naval slang, a warning to a malingerer to get on with his work and is said to be short form for swing the lead!)

Sub-Lieutenant Dilbert Swingit was the naval counterpart to the RAF's own cartoon pilot, "Pilot Officer Percy Prune". Therefore, a naval aviator who was accident-prone or plainly dangerous was a Dilbert. (see **Prunery; Prunism**) [Ref: Partridge (FS)]

> *Don't be a Dilbert!*

DIRTY　　　　See **Clean**

DISCIP (pronounced: "dis-sip") (RAF; RCAF to 1968) — "Discip" is the shortened form of Disciplinarian, the title given to Drill Instructors in the RCAF. Most often encountered in recruit training, Discips were selected for their excellent dress and deportment and for their ability to impart the skills and knowledge of military service to raw recruits. This noble aim was lost, of course, on the recruits themselves, who often associated the Discip with the Spanish Inquisition. The term Disciplinarian still lives on in the CF, but its meaning has changed. Today a Disciplinarian is a staff NCO at a Military Jail. [Ref: Partridge (8th)]

Those discips have no sense of humour!

DISNEYLAND-ON-THE-RIDEAU (CF, current) — "Disneyland-on-the-Rideau" is National Defence Headquarters (NDHQ), located on the Rideau Canal in Ottawa. The term alludes to the fact that at NDHQ, just as at Disneyland, things happen which are mysterious and inexplicable and which cause amazement and wonder to all. (See also **Bullshit Towers, Chateau, Castle Dismal, Fort Fumble, Fraggle Rock, Glass Menagerie, Glass Palace, Petrified Forest**)

Where are they posting you?
Disneyland-on-the-Rideau!

DISPERSAL — A "dispersal" is an aircraft parking area intentionally located some distance from normal base facilities. This disperses the aircraft and makes an air attack more difficult. Often these dispersed aircraft parking spots offer some measure of protection, such as walls made of sandbags, or enclosed concrete shelters. Canadian air bases in Europe typically had three large circular dispersals. Each was rather like a large traffic circle, around which were placed many smaller aircraft parking spots. For some unknown reason, these large dispersals were often called a Marguerite, as in: *tow that aircraft to the north marguerite.* By the 1970's, each aircraft parking spot contained a hardened aircraft shelter or H.A.S. (generally called a "haz"). A H.A.S. was a reinforced concrete bunker that housed one fighter aircraft and protected it from rockets and bombs. (See also **Gyppo Line, H.A.S.**)[Ref: Sutherland]

Taxi to the central dispersal for parking.

DITCH, TO (originally Naval, circa 1870) — To "ditch" an aircraft is to make a controlled emergency landing into water. The term is borrowed from 19th century sailor's slang, where to toss away an object into the water was to ditch it. Thus, to put an aircraft into the sea, was to ditch it. [Ref: Partridge (FS)]

We think the aircraft ditched off the harbour mouth.

DIVER (WWII; Allied Air Forces) — "Diver" was the allied codename for the V-1, a German flying bomb first used in 1944. The V-1 (for *Vergeltungswaffe 1*, or terror weapon number one) was basically a crude cruise missile powered by a pulse-jet. Each V-1 was launched from a fixed, inclined ramp using a small rocket booster to provide the initial thrust. Once the V-1 cleared the ramp, the rocket booster fell away, the pulse-jet ignited and the missile began flying to its target. The launch ramp was just a long, narrow inclined plane which prompted allied photographic intelligence analysts to refer to them as ski-jumps, though their code-name was "No-Ball sites".

Diver

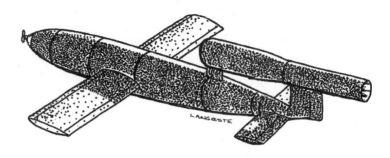

V-1's first appeared in June 1944 and by the end of the war, the Germans had launched about 1200 flying bombs at England, the majority aimed at London. The V-1, which carried hundreds of kilograms of high explosive, was very difficult to shoot down due to its high speed and small size.

Only very fast fighters, such as the Spitfire, Tempest, Mosquito, or the new jet- propelled Meteor, had any hope of destroying a V-1. Only two techniques existed for destroying them. First, the fighter aircraft dived down on the V-1, caught up, and opened fire for the brief moment that the fighter could keep up; this technique was perilous, as the resulting explosion often damaged the intercepting fighter. The alternate method wasn't much safer; the aircraft had to catch up to the V-1 and the pilot would tip the V-1's wing with his own. This knocked the V-1's inertial guidance system off-balance and sent it out of control!

The V-1 also attracted several other nicknames. It was known as the "Doodle Bug", common English slang for an unusual machine, much like the words gadget, or contraption. It was also known as the "Buzz Bomb", a reference to the peculiar rumbling sound produced by the V-1's Pulse Jet. (See also **No-Ball**) [Ref: Partridge (FS)]

> *If you fly too close to a Diver when you open fire, you'll blow yourself up, along with the Diver!*

DND PICKLE (CF, 60's to 80's) — A "DND Pickle" was a Department of National Defence passenger bus, particularly of the sort used during the 1960's, which was rather bulbous in appearance. Canadian Forces depot vehicles such as passenger buses were painted forest-green in colour. The combination of the green colour and the stubby lines of the buses resulted in the term DND Pickle, alluding to pickled gherkins, of course. Occasionally DND passenger vans, also stubby in appearance and painted forest-green, were called a DND pickle.

> *Get ready to leave, a DND Pickle is coming to pick us up.*

DOC — "Doc" has two meanings relevant to military aviators:

(1)   **Doc** can be the short form of address for a Medical Officer, as in: *Hi Doc! What are those rubber gloves for?*

(2)   **Doc** can also be short for document, as in *Did you bring your Finance docs?*

DODO CLUB — The "Dodo Club" is a convivial association of former RCAF airmen who held the now obsolete rank of Flight Sergeant. In the mid-1960's, the RCAF eliminated this rank and replaced it with the rank of Warrant Officer. Consequently, the Dodo Club was formed to perpetuate the memory of this rank, and its members celebrate themselves as the last of an extinct breed, like the Dodo Bird. Their motto is: *Distinction to Extinction.* (See also **Chiefy, Flight, Mini-Warrant**)[Ref: Hampson]

DOG AND PONY SHOW (CF, current) — A "Dog and Pony Show" is a travelling briefing team, usually from a headquarters. From time to time, it is necessary for headquarters staff to visit field units, and advise them of the "big picture" as seen from HQ or to brief them on some new policy. However, line air force personnel generally view a Dog and Pony Show as a mere subterfuge by which deskbound headquarters staff escape the office to go on a "swan".

Typically, those delivering a Dog and Pony Show use slides, videos or charts to illustrate the points in its briefing. In Britain and Europe of the 1800's it was common for Dog and Pony Shows to travel from town to town, performing animal tricks and entertainments for the local gentry. Often billed as world-class entertainment, they were usually rather humble little groups. Coincidentally, this mirrors the attitude in most military units when a headquarters Dog and Pony Show arrives. [Ref: Elting]

The Dog and Pony Show from headquarters will arrive tomorrow.

Dog and Pony Show

DOGFIGHT (WWI to present) — A "dogfight" is an ongoing aerial battle between two or more fighter aircraft. The pilot of each aircraft tries to destroy their opponent using altitude, manoeuvre, surprise, deception, and marksmanship.

Up to 1916, aircraft usually patrolled alone or in very small groups, and air fights involving more than four aircraft were rare. Then formations of aircraft appeared and air battles became a matter of outfighting a unit of aircraft. The term dogfight first appeared in official RFC communiques in November 1916. Whereas today, combat between two aircraft can be considered a dogfight, in the First World War only a large, freewheeling, multi-aircraft melee was properly considered a dogfight. British Ace James McCudden always reckoned that thirty machines had to be involved to justify the word. An American who served in the RFC, Arch Whitehouse, felt 50 aircraft were needed before it could be considered a dogfight. [Refs: Spick, Whitehouse, Winter]

A typical dogfight, even in jet fighters, occurs at subsonic speeds.

DOGTAG (military general; current) — "Dogtag" is slang for the metal identity tag worn by all servicemembers when flying, or on operations. Dogtags, used to identify one's remains in case of death, contain one's name, branch of service, religion, blood type and service number. The term alludes to the identity tags that dog-owners typically obtain for their pets. Military identity tags come in pairs. Upon death, one tag is sent to National Defence Headquarters, and the other stays with the body as identification. [Ref: Partridge (8th)]

Gentlemen, whatever you do, don't split your dogtags and give one half to your girlfriend as a souvenir!

DOLLAR 19 (RCAF, 1950's) — "Dollar 19" was a nickname for the C-119 Flying Boxcar. The nickname comes from its numerical code: 119, and its allusion to the price: $1.19, often seen in stores (at least, that is, back in the days when a dollar was a dollar).

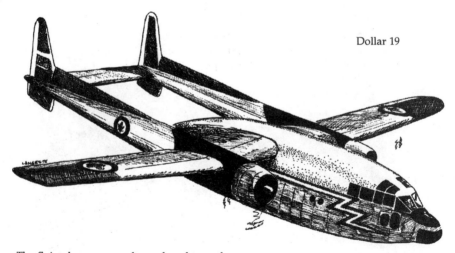

Dollar 19

The flying boxcar was often referred to as the
Dollar 19 because of its designation C-119

The high twin-boom tail characterized the Flying Boxcar. Primarily intended to airlift the Canadian Army's airborne strike force, the Flying Boxcar was a noisy airplane to fly in. (See also **Boxcar**)

Crossing the country in the back of a Dollar 19 can ruin your hearing for life!

DON'T CALL ME SIR! MY PARENTS WERE MARRIED! (CF, current, though probably American in origin) — When a junior servicemember mistakenly addresses a noncommissioned officer as sir, a common response is "Don't call me sir! My parents were married!" Another typical response is "Don't call me sir! I work for a living!"

Only Commissioned Officers and Warrant Officers are addressed as "Sir", whereas Sergeants and Corporals are addressed by their rank. However, nervous new recruits, unaware of this, tend to address everyone as sir. This reply reminds recruits that NCO's are not addressed as sir, while simultaneously commenting on the character of the commissioned officers who are addressed as sir.

> Recruit: *Excuse me, sir...*
> Sergeant: *Don't call me "sir"! My parents were married!*

DOODLE-BUG   See **Diver**

DOOZER (CF Europe; 1990's) — "Doozer" is slang for either of the mechanically-oriented aircraft technician trades: Aero-Engine Technicians, and Airframe Technicians. Doozer was borrowed from the popular CBC television of the 1980's, "Fraggle Rock", in which Doozers were small, industrious creatures who lived underground, constantly building and fixing things. One suspects that an airframe or aero-engine technician coined the term Doozer, because avionics technicians became known as Fraggles, idle characters in the TV series who were the antithesis of the hardworking Doozers. (See also **Fitter, Rigger, Fraggle**)

You'd better call a Doozer! This strut is leaking hydraulic fluid.

DORY PLUG (Army and RCAF; since WWII) — "Dory Plug" was an unkind nickname for a member of the Royal Canadian Navy. It is an allusion to the removable plug at the bottom of a boat, used to drain bilge water while on land.

Aw jeez, Bill! You don't really wanna become a Dory Plug, do you!?

DOWNLOAD   See **Upload**

DOWNWIND; DOWNWIND LEG   See **Circuit**

DRINK, THE (universal, RAF since 1920's) — The "drink" is a large body of water such as the sea, or ocean, as in: *There's an aircraft down in the drink!* [Ref: Partridge (8th)]

DRINKING FOR EFFECT (Originally army, CF; current) — "Drinking for Effect" is heavy drinking. The term is borrowed from the Artillery. Artillery fire can be of several types: e.g., ranging fire, harassing fire, counter-battery fire, etc. "Firing for Effect" is to fire all available guns as fast as possible on a specific target, and is the most devastating fire. Therefore, drinking for effect is the most devastating type of alcohol consumption.

Ken is hung over; he was drinking for effect last night.

DRIVER (originally pre-WWI Naval, now universal) — A "driver" is a pilot. It is said that this slightly mocking nickname arose in the Royal Naval Air Service during the First World War. These naval aviators had in turn borrowed it from the surface navy where "driver" was slang for a warship's captain. Thus, to fly an aircraft is to drive the airplane.

Since then, other similar mock titles have been coined. Just as a military driver was titled a *Driver (Vehicle)*, a pilot was said to be a *Driver (Airframe)*! [Ref: Partridge (FS)]

Steve's a Boeing driver in Trenton.

'DROME (RAF, RCAF; to WWII) —"'Drome" is merely shorthand for Aerodrome. [Ref: Partridge (8th)]

DRUNKEX   See **Borex**

DRY   See **Wet(1)**

DRY CANTEEN — "Canteen" is British and Commonwealth argot for a coffee shop, commissary, lounge, or a kiosk where goods or confections can be purchased. However, there are two types of Canteen, a wet canteen and a dry canteen. The difference between the two is critical. A wet canteen sells alcoholic beverages; a dry canteen doesn't. (See **Canteen Cowboy, Wet(2)**)

The dry canteen is open until 1530 Hours.

D.S. (ie., "dee-ess")(originally British Army) — "D.S." is the moniker for a member of the "Directing Staff", the faculty of a military training or educational establishment. The D.S. is an instructor who has the additional duty of being a facilitator and advisor for students. This position is especially necessary where tutoring of individuals or small groups occurs, such as at leadership courses, staff training, staff school, instructional courses, etc. (See also **School Solution**)

Doherty was my D.S. back in Borden.

DUFF (originally Scots; still current) — "Duff" is an adjective synonymous with the words bad or unreliable. Its origins are obscure, though it is most commonly associated with the terms duff weather (poor weather) or duff gen (incorrect or unreliable information). The word also survives in duffer, a golfer of indifferent talent. (See **Gen**) [Ref: Harvey]

We can expect some duff weather for the next few days.

DUMB BOMB   See **Iron Bomb**

DUSTBIN (RAF, RCAF; WWII) — The "Dustbin" (ie., garbage can) was a gun turret on a bomber aircraft. The term may have derived from the fact that early turrets on RAF bombers were configured as a rotating vertical cylinder, which may have invited comparison to a garbage can, or dustbin. (See also **Tail-End Charlie**) [Ref: Partridge (FS)]

If you like privacy, you'll like flying around in the dustbin!

DUTICALLATUS PRANGIFEROUS   See **Gremlin**

DUTY WATCH (RCAF; to 1960's) — "Duty Watch" was an extra duty crew of airmen and airwomen who formed a labour gang after duty hours. They were available to do jobs for the Station Warrant Officer or the Duty NCO. Sometimes the term applies to an aircraft servicing crew that was called in to service aircraft outside usual flying hours. [Ref: Sutherland]

Hey Brian! Are you coming to the mess?
I can't! I've been joe'd for the Duty Watch...

CHO

E.A. (WWI, WWII) — "E.A." was the common wartime abbreviation for enemy aircraft.

EAGLESHIT (American) — "Eagleshit" is American money. Though a depression-era American term, eagleshit found its way into Canadian, and Canadian military slang.

Have you got any spare eagleshit? We're flying into Tinker Air Force Base
tomorrow and the banks have already closed.

EATING IRONS (RAF, RCAF; WWII) — "Eating Irons" are a knife, fork and spoon, as in: *pass me the eating irons...* (See also **Tools**) [Ref: Partridge (8th)]

E-BUILDING (RCAF; 1940's to 1960's) — Among personnel stationed at RCAF Headquarters in Ottawa during the 1940's, 50's and 60's, the "E-Building" referred to the Lord Elgin Hotel. More specifically, it referred to its beer parlour. RCAF Headquarters of the day was housed in three large wooden wartime temporary buildings known respectively as the "A", "B", and "C" Buildings. The Lord Elgin was the nearest drinking establishment to Air Force Headquarters and perhaps unsurprisingly, became known as the E Building. [Ref: Sutherland]

There's a committee meeting at the E-Building at 4:30 on Friday. Be there!

ECONOMY, ON THE   See **On the Economy**

"EFF ALL"; "EFFING" — "F" (ie., eff) is occasionally used as a means of pronouncing F***ing, a euphemism for fucking. Therefore, "eff all" is fuck all and "effing" is fucking. [Ref: Partridge (8th)]

Where's my effing flying jacket?!

EGG IN THE HOLE (RCAF, CF; still current) — "Egg in the Hole" is the customary dish served during a "TacEval", an unannounced visit to a friend's home after a particularly convivial evening at the mess. Egg in the hole, apparently a naval dish, is merely a slice of bread with a hole cut out of the middle. This slice of bread is then placed in a frying pan, and an egg is cracked into the hole, where it is fried. It is said that this was a dish created for the difficult conditions aboard a ship; the real purpose of the bread is to prevent the egg from slipping and sliding on the hot plate as the ship pitches and rolls in heavy seas. Whatever its origins, many an airman and airwoman has consumed egg in the hole in a friend's kitchen, early in the morning.

Let's drop in on Woody and see if we can get some egg in the hole!

ELECTRIC HAT (CF; current) — An "electric hat" is an aircrew flying helmet, from the built-in microphone and headset needed for radio communications.

The microphone in my electric hat isn't working!

ELECTRIC JET (aviation general; current) — An "electric jet" is an aircraft that incorporates a fly-by-wire flight control system, a radical departure from conventional control systems. In a fly-by-wire system there is no direct mechanical link between the cockpit controls and the flying control surfaces, the rudder, elevators and ailerons. Instead, moving the cockpit controls merely provides input to onboard computers. In turn, the computers control hydraulic actuators that physically move the rudder, ailerons, elevators and flaps. The computers process the input from the pilot's controls, determine the optimum deflection of the flying control surfaces and move them. This allows the flight controls to respond much more quickly than would be possible if there were only a mechanical linkage from the cockpit to the control surfaces. Indeed these rapidly-reacting computers stabilize an aircraft that would otherwise be highly unstable. This rapid response makes it possible to easily control aircraft designed to be so manoeuvrable that human response time is inadequate.

The first electric jet in Canadian service was the CF-18 Hornet, followed by the Airbus A310.

In an Electric Jet, if you lose all your computers, there is nothing you can do but bail out...

EMMA TOC (British Army and RFC; WWI) — The words "emma" and "toc" were the British Army phonetic codewords for the letters M and T during the First World War. Thus the words "emma toc" represented the initials M.T., for motor transport. An aerial Observer might spot an enemy road convoy and would report having seen German "emma toc". [Ref: Voss]

The German aircraft crashed straight down into some of his own emma toc on the road.

Empire

EMPIRE (Since WWII) — An "Empire" is an organization whose size and complexity exceeds that actually needed do its job. There is always the implication that the organization has grown primarily for the aggrandizement of its leaders. However, the term is also used to describe any large organization, generally, as in the Maintenance Empire, the Training Empire, etc. [Ref: Partridge (FS)]

> *That's quite an empire they've built for themselves up at Group*
> *Headquarters, eh?*

ENGINE BAY (Originally RAF, still current in CF) — In an air force hangar, the "Engine Bay" is the area reserved for inspection and maintenance of aircraft engines and propellers.

ENGINES (RAF, RCAF; since at least WWII) — "Engines" is wartime aircrew slang for the unit Engineering Officer. [Ref: Partridge (FS)]

> *You'd better tell 'Engines' that five of his technicians are being posted away.*

ENSIGN — Strictly speaking, an ensign is a flag bearing a specific service badge. As such, the word "ensign" can refer to any of several flags flown over the years at air force establishments. The RAF Ensign, first flown in 1918, has been used as the basic pattern for all Canadian air ensigns. This flag was light blue, with a Union Jack in the "canton", and the RAF roundel in the "fly". The Royal Canadian Navy in turn had adopted the Royal Navy's "White Ensign" and flew it from its warships, shore establishments and air stations until Unification in 1968.

The Canadian Air Force adopted the RAF Ensign in 1920 to symbolize the Canadian contribution to the RAF during the First World War. When the RCAF was formed in 1924, it also adopted the RAF Ensign. By the Second World War, a rising Canadian nationalism was manifested in changes to RCAF markings and flags. Soon a red Canadian maple leaf replaced the red disc in the centre of the RAF roundel on the ensign and on RCAF aircraft. The RCAF Ensign with its new maple leaf roundel was approved in June 1940, and flew until 1968, when unification saw the demise of the RCAF. The new Canadian Armed Forces flew a smart white ensign with the red Canadian flag in the fly and the Canadian Forces badge in the fly. But there was no uniquely "air force" flag until 1985. Then the "Air Command Ensign" was created which stands in the same place as did the RCAF Ensign earlier. It too, is light blue, with a red-and-white Canadian flag in the canton, and the Canadian Forces roundel in the fly. (See also **Roundel**)

> *Hoist the Ensign at either sunrise, or at 0800 hours, whichever is earlier.*

ENVELOPE; "OUTSIDE THE ENVELOPE"; "PUSH THE ENVELOPE" (current; aviation engineering) — The "envelope" is the engineering limit of an aircraft's performance capability, as displayed in a two-dimensional geometrical chart. This chart is published in the aircraft's engineering orders, for the benefit of pilots and engineers. An aircraft flying "within the envelope" is performing within its normal operating limits. Similarly, to be "outside the envelope" is to fly the aircraft beyond its normal operating limits, where it may respond unpredictably or unsafely.

Aeronautical engineers establish the performance limits of aircraft and their components

Ensign

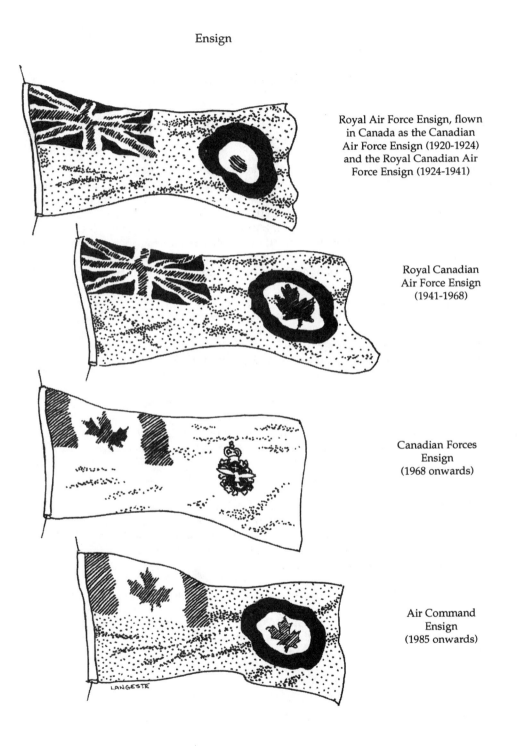

Royal Air Force Ensign, flown
in Canada as the Canadian
Air Force Ensign (1920-1924)
and the Royal Canadian Air
Force Ensign (1924-1941)

Royal Canadian
Air Force Ensign
(1941-1968)

Canadian Forces
Ensign
(1968 onwards)

Air Command
Ensign
(1985 onwards)

LANGESTE

through theoretical calculation, and test pilots confirm them through flight testing. When a test pilot determines the actual design limits in flight, he "pushes the envelope", ie., he stretches it out of its expected shape as displayed on the geometric chart.

Even though he ejected outside the envelope, the pilot succeeded in getting out of his burning aircraft.

E.O. (pronounced "eeh-owe") (RAF, RCAF) — "EO" was a common RCAF abbreviation that could mean either Engineering Order, or Engineering Officer.

ERK (RAF; since WWI) — "Erk" is RAF slang for the lowest form of RAF life: the Aircraftman 2nd Class, or AC2. Though erk has been accepted RAF usage from its earliest days, its origins are extremely vague. It has been suggested that erk is a variant of "erg". In physics, erg is a mathematical unit of work, and was also a turn-of-the-century nickname for sailors of the rank of Ordinary Seamen, the lowest navy rank, presumably because it is they who do all the work! Another suggestion is that erk was a corruption of "AirC" (ie., pronounced "ayrk"), which was once proposed (but rejected) as the official RAF abbreviation for "Aircraftman". [Refs: Collins; Partridge (FS); Partridge (8th)]

I'm getting tired of telling erks to shine their shoes...

EUCHRED, TO BE (CF; current since 1950's) — "To be euchred" is to be defeated, broken, or in a bad way. The term is drawn from the card game Euchre, popular in Canada's air force, wherein a player who is euchred is out of the game.

The hydraulic system is leaking; it looks like the aircraft is euchred...

EXCREMENTUM VINCIT CEREBELLUM (WWII) — This mock Latin phrase may be roughly translated as "bullshit baffles brains!" It attained a certain currency during the Second World War in all services. (for other mock Latin, see also **Argi; Albatri; Illigitemus Non Carborundum; Per Ardua Asbestos**) [Ref: Partridge-Catchphrases]

EXPLODER (RCAF; 1950's) — "Exploder" is a humorous nickname for the Beechcraft C-45 Expeditor. The Exploder was a twin-engine light transport aircraft, in RCAF and RCN service from the Second World War until the 1960's. Variously used for training and utility duties, the Exploder was a reliable airplane notwithstanding its nickname. It was also known as the Bugsmasher.

There's an Exploder leaving for Cold Lake at 1900 hours.

EYE-TIES (originally British; since at least WWI) — "Eye-tie" is slang for an Italian. It derives from the common, though incorrect, pronunciation of Italian in which the "I" rhymes with "eye". [Ref: Partridge (8th)]

A pair of Eye-tie aircraft will arrive at 1300 hours.

F OXTROT

FAARP; FAARPING; TO FAARP (CF; current) — "FAARP" is the acronym and abbreviation for "Forward Area Arming and Refuelling Point", a mobile fuel and armament cache used by tactical helicopter units in a land battle. An army division will ordinarily have its own tactical aviation wing, which bivouacs and moves with the division in the land battle. In a fluid land battle there is no guarantee that the helicopter's home base will still be there when the helicopters return from a mission. The enemy may have located it and attacked it, or the base may have advanced with the division. To ensure operational flexibility, a mobile servicing and refuelling unit deploys into the field; this is the FAARP. Consequently for a tactical helicopter to use this facility is to faarp, the aircraft sets down at the faarp, and spends some time faarping.

We'll set down and faarp in about three minutes!

FAC (pronounced "fack") — A "FAC" is a Forward Air Controller. A FAC was a pilot sent to the front lines to coordinate air strikes against enemy ground targets. The job takes an airman away from flying and puts him in the front lines with the army. There the FAC, equipped with binoculars, map and radios, directs his fellow aviators overhead to attack the appropriate targets. Since the 1950's, however, the trend has been for the FAC to fly a light, manoeuvrable aircraft equipped with smoke rockets. The smoke rockets are used to "mark" the target for the fighters. (See also **Bird Dog, Butane Budgie, LOH**)

For a pilot, being sent to the front lines as a FAC with the army was a fate worse than death!

FALCON CODES (CF; current, naval in origin) — "Falcon Codes" are semi-official radio and signal codes used by sailors, and by naval and maritime air forces. Falcon Codes convey sarcastic or humorous messages that might be inappropriate if transmitted in clear voice. Regulations do not allow anyone to transmit an impolite radio message, no matter how badly they may want to. To fill this communications gap, Falcon Codes were invented. A Falcon Code is simply a number that corresponds to an irreverent and mutually agreed-upon meaning. Tables of Falcon Codes are unofficially distributed throughout naval and maritime air forces, and enjoy tacit approval of senior staff. Though these codes are naval in origin, shipboard helicopter crews and land-based maritime aircrews also use Falcon Codes. (The 1st Canadian Submarine Squadron in Halifax uses a similar set of signals called Dolphin Codes).

For example, imagine a maritime patrol aircraft far out over the ocean, training with a navy destroyer. Now imagine that for some reason the actions of the naval vessel excite consternation to the crew of the maritime patrol aircraft. Thus the crew of the patrol aircraft expresses its dissatisfaction, and the ship responds, through use of Falcon Codes, as follows:

	Falcon Code:	Meaning:
Aircraft to Ship:	FALCON 1	*You should at least try to give the impression that you know what you're doing!*
Ship to Aircraft:	FALCON 34	*Let go of my ears, I know my job!*
Aircraft to Ship:	FALCON 169	*If you think your next evolution is going to be equally disastrous please give me advance warning!*

(For a full list of Falcon Codes, see **Appendix B**)

FAN (since WWI, though rare by WWII) — A "fan" is a propeller, from its similar appearance and function. (See also **Prop, Club**)[Ref: Partridge (FS)]

> *The fans stopped without warning, and it suddenly became very quiet in the cockpit...*

FAST CAT   See **Quick Pussy**

FAST MOVER (military aviation; current) — A "fast mover" is a fighter or attack aircraft, that is, a high-speed aircraft. The term is common among ground troops, air traffic controllers, and other non-fighter aircrew.

> *We need air support immediately; any fast movers available?*

FAT PILLS (CF; current) — A doughnut, cookie, slice of pie, cupcake, brownie, or any other sweet confection is a Fat Pill. The allusion, of course, is to a pharmaceutical though the effect of this particular pill is to gain weight.

> *I do believe that I'll have a Fat Pill with my coffee.*

F-BOAT (RAF, RCAF; WWII) — "F-Boat" means Flak Boat, a small German warship armed almost exclusively with anti-aircraft guns. An F-Boat delivered concentrated anti-aircraft fire to defend harbour facilities or ships from air attack. They were a serious threat to low-flying aircraft, and were to be avoided. Occasionally however, Allied pilots mistook such vessels for normal patrol boats, which carried far fewer Flak guns. This error was rarely made twice. (See **Flak**)

> *Don't confuse an F-Boat with an ordinary trawler or you'll be swimming home!*

F.E. (ie., "eff-eeh") (RCAF; CF; current) — "F.E." is both abbreviation and shorthand for Flight Engineer. A Flight Engineer is an aircrew specialist, responsible for in-flight monitoring of an aircraft's flight, power and electronic systems. The Flight Engineer repairs mechanical or electrical unserviceabilities when no ground crew are available and performs aircraft servicing away from base. In the RCAF and the CF, Flight Engineers are selected from the ranks of qualified groundcrew technicians. (See also **Flight Magician**)

The F.E. noticed the problem before the rest of the crew.

FEARNAUGHT SUIT (Aircraft Firefighters) — A "fearnaught suit" is a protective suit worn by air base or shipboard firefighters. This suit protects them from heat and flame while they fight an aircraft fire and rescue the victims. "Fear naught" is obsolete English usage meaning fear nothing! or don't be afraid! The term is apt because the firefighter can wear the suit into the flames, confident of not being incinerated - at least not immediately! These suits permit the wearer to quickly attempt a rescue of trapped crew or passengers only. Even a fearnaught suit will not protect the wearer for very long. Early Fearnaught Suits were made of asbestos but latter-day Fearnaught Suits are covered with a shiny reflective material that reflects heat away from the wearer. This works well unless the fire begins to deposit soot and carbon on the suit; this ruins the reflective quality of the suit and the wearer's temperature rises rapidly! [Ref: Snowie]

FEATHERED ARSEHOLE　　　　　See **Flying Arsehole**

FEE (RFC; WWI) — "Fee" is the nickname for the FE2b, an early fighter flown by the RFC during the First World War, from the designation: FE (for "Fighter Experimental").

FEELING NO PAIN (CF current; general Canadian usage) — To "feel no pain" is to be very, very drunk, as in: *After spending about fifty dollars in the Mess, Joe was feeling no pain.*

FIDO (Allied Air Forces; WWII) — "Fido" was both acronym and slang for equipment used to temporarily disperse fog from runways. Used on Allied airfields in Britain during the Second World War, Fido was developed to enable bombers to land safely if fog developed on the airfield while away from base.

The acronym Fido was coined while the system was undergoing trials. It stood for: "Fog Investigative Dispersal Operations". Later, after being introduced operationally, its definition changed (keeping the accepted term Fido) to: "Fog, Intensive Disposal of".

Its principles of operation were very simple. Fido was based on the principle that fog is water vapour, and will condense into liquid water when heat is applied. Fido consisted of a system of pipes running along the length of a runway; the pipes conducted aviation gasoline to ports at intervals along the tubing, where it was burned. This heated the fog, condensed the water vapour, and cleared the air over the runway. However, the fog would disperse only while the burning continued, and if there was any wind, the clear patch would drift off the runway. Usually, the fog cleared enough that an aircraft in distress could land. [Ref: Partridge (FS)]

The fog is building, and we've got a shot-up Lancaster coming in to land. We'd better get Fido ready.

FIFINELLA　　　　　See **Gremlin**

FIFTY DOLLAR SWITCH (RCAF, CF; 1963 to 1980's) — The "Fifty Dollar Switch" was the cockpit switch in a CF-104 aircraft that fired the Emergency Nozzle Closure System, or ENCS. It was said that a clumsy technician who accidentally fired this system on the ground could expect a charge and a fifty-dollar fine.

The ENCS was intended to help a Starfighter pilot with perhaps the worst problem that he could face: an engine failure in flight. The CF-104 flew on its engine; if the engine lost power - even partially - the CF-104 could not glide. It fell like a stone!

In case of engine power loss, the Emergency Nozzle Closure System closed the diameter of the engine's circular tailpipe to a tiny fraction of its normal size. This kept the pressure of the exhaust gas that remained inside the engine as high as possible, and helped conserve engine thrust. Of course, in a complete engine failure, this thrust would only last for only a few seconds. But these seconds could make the difference between crashing and ejecting safely. The ENCS was activated by a small explosive charge and once activated, could not be reset except after a costly overhaul. In a real emergency, this did not matter, but if activated by accident on the ground, an expensive and unnecessary engine repair resulted. Therefore, the fifty-dollar fine.

You see this red button? That's a fifty-dollar switch; if you push it, it'll cost you fifty dollars!

FIFTY-MISSION CAP; FIFTY-MISSION CRUSH (originally USAF WWII; now general) — The "fifty-mission cap" or "fifty mission crush" was a U.S. Army Air Corps affectation that crossed the border into Canada. This was a permanent deformation of one's dress cap caused by wearing radio headsets over it until the sides of the cap were permanently bent down. This gave the cap a very rakish aspect, much in vogue among well-heeled aviators in the 1940's and 1950's. It symbolized operational status or long flying experience.

Fifty-Mission Hat

The term implies that it took fifty missions (twice the wartime American requirement for rotation home) for the look to become permanent. Of course, one didn't need to be operational, or experienced, to affect a fifty mission crush, and many simply deformed the cap with string, at home. This fashion entered the RCAF during the Second World War, when pilots of multi-engine aircraft often wore their dress cap while flying. The style seems to have faded out in the mid-1960's. (Compare with **Bash**)

You have to work awfully hard to put a fifty-mission crush in one of these new air force hats!

FIFTY-p.s.i. FINGER (CF; current) — The "fifty p.s.i. finger" refers to an index finger that is jabbed angrily into another's chest - to punctuate points in an argument. The finger is said to be poked into the other's chest at a pressure of about 50 psi, or 50 pounds per square inch.

96

Fifty p.s.i. Finger

> *I'm gonna go over to the Orderly Room and give that Corporal a fifty p.s.i.*
> *Finger!!*

FIGHTER COP (RCAF; 1950's) — "Fighter Cop" is the nickname for a Fighter Controller. A Fighter Controller was an airman or airwoman at a ground radar site who monitored the air battle on radar and directed friendly fighters by radio. The term arose because in a sense, Fighter Controllers were like traffic cops, and told fighter pilots where to go. Their name changed in the 1960's to Air Weapons Controller. Plans now exist for the Air Weapons Controller occupation to amalgamate with that of the Air Traffic Controllers. (See also **Scope Dope**)

FIGHTERGATOR   See **A.I.**

FIGMO (CF, 1970's 1980's; originally American) — The acronym "FIGMO" describes a person who has lost all interest in a job they are about to leave. FIGMO, an acronym for "Fuck it, got my orders!", was apparently coined in the American military during the Korean War but attained real popularity during the Viet Nam War. The orders referred to are the travel orders sending a serviceman back to the U.S. from Viet Nam. American soldiers in Viet Nam knew the date of their scheduled return home months in advance. Consequently, when a service member was about to return to the United States and noticeably lost their enthusiasm for their job, they were described as being FIGMO. The close contacts that existed between the United States military and the Canadian Forces led to this phrase entering Canadian military slang in the 1970's and 1980's. Most people are FIGMO prior to being posted away or before going on leave. Mind you, it seems some people are always FIGMO. [Ref: Elting]

FILL YOUR BOOTS (CF; current) — "Fill your boots!" is an invitation, or comment, which roughly corresponds to: *do whatever you want* or *go ahead* The origins are unknown though the phrase was used as far back as the Second World War. [Ref: Partridge (FS)]

> *Do you mind if I read your magazine?*
> *Fill yer boots...*

FIN FLASH (CF current, though originally RAF) — A "flash" is a badge that enables fast identification. A "Fin Flash" is a badge painted on the fin (or vertical stabilizer) of a military aircraft to identify service or nationality.

Canadian military aircraft bore the red, white, and blue fin flash of the RAF until the early 1960's. This three-colour flash was replaced by the Red Ensign, then Canada's national flag, though the Royal Canadian Navy painted the Navy's "White Ensign" on certain of its aircraft instead. In 1965 Canada adopted its distinctive red and white maple leaf flag, which then became the Canadian military fin flash.

FINGER FOUR (military aviation; since 1940's) — Finger Four is a combat formation flown by four fighter aircraft, so-called because the placement of the four aircraft closely resembles the relative location of one's fingertips.

The Finger-Four was used by the Luftwaffe in 1939, which quickly proved its superiority over the three-aircraft "Vic", in vogue with the RAF before the Second World War. The Finger Four comprises two pairs of fighters, each pair consisting of a Lead, who sought

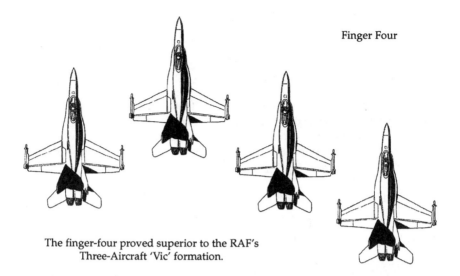

Finger Four

The finger-four proved superior to the RAF's
Three-Aircraft 'Vic' formation.

out the enemy, and a Wingman who protected the Lead. In a Finger Four, one of the two Leads is the formation lead, and directs all four aircraft into battle, while the other three watch for bandits. The Finger Four can, if necessary, then be divided into two pairs, which complement each other tactically. The RAF's three-aircraft Vic was less flexible. The formation leader couldn't split the formation without leaving one aircraft all alone. The RAF adopted the Finger Four in 1939-40 after suffering serious losses. (See also **Vic, Wingman**) [Ref: Spick]

FINGERTIGHT (universal among technicians) — A bolt, screw or nut that is "fingertight" is tightened only as far as is possible using bare hands, ie., without a wrench or screwdriver. Often non-critical components, or components intended to be fastened and re-fastened in succession, are left fingertight for ease of removal. (See also **Torque it tight, then back it half a turn**) [Ref: Partridge (8th)]

> *How tight should I turn this bolt, Al?*
> *Fingertight will do fine...*

FINGERTROUBLE (CF, current) — "Fingertrouble" is a generic category of blunder, which includes any fumbling of switches. This could mean mistakenly pulling, rather than pushing, a control. It could mean accidentally turning on a system that should have remained off, or leaving on something that should have been turned off. All these may be considered fingertrouble. The term seems to suggest that the person's insubordinate fingers caused the problem, not the person himself.

However, British usage suggests a slightly different application. In British slang, a dawdling, or blundering person is said to be sitting on his finger (ie., to have his finger inserted in his anal orifice!) Thus, in telling such a person to get on with things, one tells him to remove his finger (a process occasionally termed "exdigitation"). A failure to remove one's finger and get on with things has also been known as fingertrouble. (See **Switchology**) [Ref: Partridge (FS)]

Jones!! Why did you advance the propeller lever instead of the throttle, like you were supposed to?!
Fingertrouble, sir...

FIREPROOF   See **Bulletproof**

FIRE'S GONE OUT, THE (Fleet Air Arm; since 1930's) — "The fire's gone out" is a cute way of saying that the aircraft's engines have stopped. Apparently the term originated in the Royal Navy Fleet Air Arm during the 1930's, doubtless a reference borrowed from the surface navy, whose ships once ran on coal. The use of this phrase later spread into the air force. [Ref: Partridge-Catchphrases]

Uh-oh! Have you got your parachute? The fire's gone out.

FIREWORKS (Allied Air Forces; WWII) — "Fireworks" is severe anti-aircraft fire. (See also **Flak**) [Ref: Partridge (FS)]

FISH-HEAD (RN, RAF, RCAF, CF; still current) — To a member of the Air Force or Army, a "fish-head" is anyone who serves in the Navy. Therefore it may seem surprising that this pejorative term actually originated in the navy's own Fleet Air Arm. During the Second World War, naval aviators (including many RCN personnel) referred to their cousins in the Seaman Branch (the seagoing navy) as fish-heads. Presumably this epithet was picked up by soldiers and airmen, to whom anyone in a navy uniform is a fish-head, whether a sailor or a naval aviator. (See also **Anchor-Cranker, Dory-Plug**)

Fish-head

Airmen and airwomen refer to all sailors as fish-heads, though naval aviators coined the term to describe non-flying members of the navy.

Lieutenant-Commander Flotsam is a good guy, for a Fish-head, that is...

FITTER (RCAF, CF; current) — A "Fitter" is an Aero-Engine Technician. Though slang in Canada, in Britain, the word Fitter has a more formal meaning as a technician who is qualified to fine-tune and adjust machinery. Therefore, in the RAF one spoke of an Airframe Fitter, or an Electrical Fitter, whereas in Canada these would each be a *non sequitur*. By the early 1990's plans were in place to amalgamate the Aero-Engine and Airframe Technician trades into a single, unified trade. It remains to be seen whether members of this new Canadian Forces occupation will become known as "Friggers". (See also **Doozer; Greasy Paw; Rigger**)

Without us fitters, you'd all be glider pilots!

FIVE HUNDRED GOLDEN HANDSHAKES, THE (RCAF; early 1960's) — In the early 1960's, several years after the cancellation of the Avro Arrow project RCAF Headquarters concluded that the Air Force had too many pilots and navigators. So it was decided to reduce their numbers by several hundred. Not enough aircrew left voluntarily, so RCAF Headquarters deemed it necessary to summarily dismiss several hundred junior pilots and navigators *en masse*. This was the "Golden Handshake", a summary farewell. This layoff generated much ill-will, as many did not want to leave the RCAF. Resentment grew stronger when, only short time later, the RCAF realized that it was short of trained aircrew! Many who received a Golden Handshake were asked to re-enrol in the RCAF at no loss of seniority or pay; quite a few, their lives seriously disrupted, declined the invitation. (See **Black Friday**)

After I got one of the Five Hundred Golden Handshakes I joined the airlines

FIX, GET A — In navigation, to "get a fix", is to ascertain one's location on a map. A fix on one's own position is obtained by measuring the compass bearing to each of several visible landmarks. If the position of these landmarks is known on a map, one can derive one's own map location. However, getting a fix now has another, more colloquial meaning, developed from the original navigational usage. It can mean to ascertain, as in *have you got a fix on when they'll finish painting my office?* [Ref: Partridge (FS)]

FLAK (Since WWI; universal) — "Flak" is the explosion of a round from an anti-aircraft gun, particularly one set to explode at a predetermined altitude, or in close proximity to an aircraft. The term Flak is a German acronym for *Flugzeug Abwehr Kanone*, or aircraft defence gun. The meaning of the word Flak has now broadened to include verbal abuse, as in *Did you get any flak from your wife?* (Interestingly, acronyms are as common in the German language as in English. After the acronym Flak was coined, German troops began to speak of a Chaplain as a Sak, for *Sunde Abwehr Kanone*, or anti-sin gun!) [Ref: Phelan]

The Flak over the target was so heavy that you could get out of the aircraft and walk on it!

FLAME OUT, TO (universal aviation; since late 1940's) — Strictly speaking, a "flame out" describes the situation when a jet engine stops burning fuel and therefore ceases producing thrust. (Hence the verb "to flame out") A flame out can be caused by fuel starvation or a poor fuel-air mixture. In a more colloquial sense, however, to flame out is to fall asleep. A tired person, like a flamed-out engine, lacks the power to carry on. (See also **Behind the Power Curve**)

I've got to go home and flame out; I only got about two hours sleep last night!

FLAMER (RFC, RNAS, RAF, RCAF; WWI, WWII) — A "flamer" is an aircraft which, in being shot down, bursts into flames. [Ref: Partridge (FS)]

I fired at least a hundred rounds into him, and he went down, a flamer...

FLAMING COFFIN; FLAMING FOUR (RAF; 1920's) — The "Flaming Coffin" and the "Flaming Four" were rueful nicknames for the De Havilland DH-4. The DH-4, a two-place bomber, was introduced in the latter part of the First World War and remained in

Canadian service until the late 1920's. Many DH-4's served in the CAF and the RCAF after the First World War. There was nothing wrong with the performance, capability, or serviceability of the DH-4; unfortunately, its designers had placed the fuel tank between the pilot's cockpit, and the observer's cockpit. Thus, both the pilot and observer faced the very real possibility of cremation if the fuel tank was hit by enemy fire. Hence, the nicknames. [Ref: Partridge (8th); Allez-Fernandez, Cacutt]

FLAMING DATUM (RCAF, CF; still current) — Among aircrews in anti-submarine patrol squadrons, "flaming datum" describes an aircraft or vessel which is damaged or destroyed. In maritime air warfare, sophisticated electronic and acoustic detection systems are used to detect and engage targets. These systems all acquire data which is processed by machines and interpreted by aircrews. The term flaming datum aptly describes a target which has been successfully engaged. [Ref: Sutherland]

The most constructive thing which that destroyer could do in this exercise is provide us with flaming datum!

FLAMING ONIONS (RFC, RNAS; WWI) — "Flaming Onions" was the allied pilot's term for a particularly dangerous type of German anti-aircraft weapon used during the First World War. They have been described as being ... *fired from rocket guns to become glowing balls which twisted about like live things and seemed to chase an aeroplane, turning over end on end in a leisurely way...* Very little has been recorded about this weapon, but they seem to have comprised ten fireballs connected together on a single, long chain (reminiscent of onions often sold by street merchants by the dozen, on a string). The idea was that the long chain would wrap about an aircraft and the flames from the fireball would ignite it. When fired, Flaming Onions attained great speed. Indeed, Canadian ace Billy Bishop remarked that flaming onions were particularly terrifying because they moved too fast for evasive action. [Refs: Elting; Partridge (8th); Voss; Winter]

FLAP (RAF, RCAF; to 1940's) — The word "flap" implies a commotion, panic, disturbance or excitement. One source suggests that the term is army in origin, and alludes to the furore and commotion among a flock of chickens in panic. The term seems to have its origins in the Royal Navy of the turn of the 20th century, where it described the activity during shipboard evolutions, especially emergency drills. However, a competing explanation has been offered to the author. It has been suggested that RAF use of the term began when retractable wing flaps were introduced in the 1920s. Flaps, most commonly extended on an approach to landing, simultaneously increase both lift and drag during this critical climax to a flight. Their use would probably have caused something of a commotion in the cockpit for a generation of airman unschooled in their use, a situation begging to be described as a flap.[Partridge (8th)]

What's the flap at headquarters all about?

FLASH — A "flash" is a badge that enables fast identification. There are several uses of the word that are in common air force usage. (see **Aircrew Flash; Canada Flash; Fin Flash**)

FLAT SPIN (Aviation general, though becoming dated) — To go into a "flat spin" is to go into panic, or to reach the limit of one's nerve or patience. The term is borrowed from aerodynamic science, where a flat spin is a spin in which the aircraft remains fully stalled as it rotates. In otherwords it rotates in a flat attitude, like a falling leaf. Though most modern aircraft are spin-resistant, this was not the case in the early days of aviation and a flat spin was to be avoided at all costs. The term connotes a complete loss of control. (See also **Flap**) [Ref: Harvey; Partridge (8th)]

Andy went into a flat spin when he realized he'd forgot his room key in the cab.

FLAT TOP (since 1930's) — Since the 1930's, an aircraft carrier has been known as a "flat top". [Ref: Partridge (8th)]

FLIGHT (universal air force usage; since 1912) — A "flight" is the largest subunit within an air force squadron. Originally a flight was any group of aircraft smaller than a squadron, though its meaning has since expanded. A flight may consist of several aircraft, together with their crews, or it may comprise service support personnel, as in a maintenance flight or an administrative flight. Interestingly, Winston Churchill claims credit for coining this usage of the word flight.

The unique nature of Air Force organization makes it difficult to make cross-service comparisons. On a ceremonial parade, a flight corresponds to an army platoon. But in raw firepower, a flight of the right type of aircraft could easily equal an artillery regiment!

The RCAF adopted the RAF rank system in 1924, a system that maintained a correspondence between the rank title and the level of command. Thus, a flight would be commanded by a "Flight Lieutenant" who was assisted by an NCO with the rank of Flight Sergeant. Air force practice of the day permitted Flight Sergeants to be addressed by the abbreviated title "Flight" and an airman might be heard to say: *Yes Flight! No Flight! No excuse, Flight!* (See also **Flight Lustre**)

Growing operational complexity inflated command of a flight to the next higher rank: Squadron Leader. Today, using Army or Canadian Forces parlance, a flight might be commanded by either a Captain or a Major. [Ref: Coote and Batchelor]

FLIGHT DECK — In military aviation, the term "Flight Deck" has two possible meanings:

(1) **Flight Deck** (Naval Aviation since 1914): The deck on an aircraft carrier or other warship from which aircraft or helicopters land and take off. In American Navy parlance, the Flight Deck is sometimes termed the "roof", because of its broad expanse, and because most other ships' activities occur beneath it.

(2) **Flight Deck** (aviation general since 1920's): On a large aircraft, the Flight Deck is the cabin that contains the crew positions for the pilot, co-pilot, flight engineer, and navigator. A Flight Deck differs from a cockpit in that one walks onto a Flight Deck, whereas one climbs into a cockpit. (See also **Cockpit**)

FLIGHT LINE; HANGAR LINE (air force, general) — Properly speaking, a "flight line" or a "hangar line" is that area of an air base where the hangars are sited. Given that hangars are usually arrayed along the edge of the tarmac in a line, it has always been termed the hangar, or flight, "line".

However, the terms hangar line or flight line have another, slightly more humorous meaning. In the context of practical jokes, these terms suggest an apparently useful but mythical material, a substance that has been the source of much embarrassment for apprentice technicians. The unaware apprentice is typically sent on a simple errand: *To go get a hundred-yard roll of flight line.* The hapless young man proceeds hither and yon in search of this ostensibly plausible item (perhaps visualizing wire or string), later discovering to his embarrassment that neither flight line nor hangar line exist except as several miles of concrete and buildings. The game requires the willing complicity of more senior airmen who assist the victim by offering suggestions about where the hundred-yard roll of flight line might be located! (*Flight Line? We're all out of it, but try over at Avionics, they might have some...*) Recruits seem more sophisticated these days, so hardly anyone falls for it anymore but, now and then... (For other mythical but useful substances see also **Flight Lustre, Long Weight, Propwash, Radar Contacts, Relative Bearing Grease, Skyhook; Tartan Paint; Tacan Gate**)

> *You called, Sarge?*
> *Yeah. Collins, go get a hundred-yard roll of hanger line!*

FLIGHT LOOIE; FLIGHT LOOT; FLUTE LOOT (RAF; RCAF to 1968) — A "Flight Looie" is an officer of the rank of Flight Lieutenant. The term draws on the fact that in the U.S. military, "looie" is slang for Lieutenant. Flight Looie alludes to this American army slang.

This makes sense on remembering that Commonwealth personnel tend to pronounce the word lieutenant as LEF-tenant, whereas in American usage it is pronounced: LOO-tenant. Thus an RCAF Flight Lieutenant would be addressed as Flight Lef-tenant, except of course by an American who would likely say "Flight Loo-tenant". "Flute Loot" was rhymed slang for this rank. These terms probably originated in the Second World War, when Americans served in England alongside British and Commonwealth Forces. They had to cope with unfamiliar ranks, such as Flight Lieutenant, and the unique pronunciation that went with it. [Ref: Partridge (FS)]

> *Where's the new Flight Looie from?*

FLIGHT LUSTRE (RCAF, 1950's and 60's) — "Flight Lustre" is one of many useful but mythical substances that have caused embarrassment to apprentices. Junior airmen have often been sent in search of Flight Lustre as a practical joke by their more experienced comrades. The actual description, composition and nature of Flight Lustre were apparently left to the victim's imagination, though the implication was made that Flight Lustre was some sort of aircraft polish. So the wild-goose chase was on! Of course the apprentice generally never admitted that he had no idea of what Flight Lustre was. Occasionally the apprentice was sent in search of a mythical person named Flight Lustre. In the RCAF, NCO's of the rank of Flight Sergeant were often addressed by the shortened term "Flight", so the implication was that the apprentice was to locate a certain Flight Sergeant Lustre.

The use of the term Flight Lustre to embarrass junior technicians seems to have died out when, reportedly, an enterprising merchant began to market an aircraft polish actually called Flight Lustre. (For other mythical but useful substances see also **Flight Line; Hangar Line, Long Weight, Propwash, Radar Contacts, Relative Bearing Grease, Skyhook, Tartan Paint; Tacan Gate**)

Ed, go to 4 Hangar supply section right away and get some Flight Lustre!

FLIGHT MAGICIAN (RAF; WWII) — "Flight Magician" was RAF slang for Flight Mechanic, a ground crew technician who flew as part of an aircraft crew to rectify mechanical problems that may occur away from base. In the RCAF, this function was performed by the Technical Crewman. Generally they flew on smaller aircraft that did not normally carry a Flight Engineer, or certain transport aircraft. The nickname Flight Magician is a play on the title Flight Mechanic, and also suggests the magic sometimes needed to repair an aircraft away from base, when needed tools and parts were unavailable. Following the Second World War, the RCAF continued the tradition with the Technical Crewman specialty which ultimately disappeared when it merged into the Flight Engineer trade. [Ref: Partridge (FS)]

Sergeant Frederick is the best Flight Magician on the squadron!

FLING-WING (common usage since the 1950's) — "Fling-wing" refers to helicopters, from the fact that a helicopter's wings (ie., the rotors) are flung about in a circle. Thus, one can belong to a fling-wing squadron, where all the pilots are fling-wing pilots. (See also **Chopper, Rotorhead**)

I still don't understand how those fling-wing contraptions stay in the air!

FLIP (general aviation usage, since 1914) — A "flip" is a short flight. The term was used as early as the First World War. [Ref: Partridge (FS); Voss]

I've never been a fighter pilot, though I did go on several flips in a Starfighter.

FLOATING COFFIN (RN, RCN; WWII) — "Floating Coffin" was the rueful nickname for HMS Puncher, an escort aircraft carrier of the Royal Navy manned by sailors of the Royal Canadian Navy. (See **Woolworth Carrier**) [Ref: Snowie]

FLOOR, THE (CF, current) — In an air force hangar, "the floor" refers to the hangar floor, the domain of aircraft maintenance, because that is where aircraft are parked, and consequently, where engineering activity is centred.

Well, if it isn't the maintenance officer! How are things down on the floor?

FLOWER (WWII; RAF, RCAF) — "Flower" was a codename for a fighter patrol against Luftwaffe aerodromes to divert German fighters while a Bomber Command raid was on.

FLUTE LOOT   See **Flight Looie**.

FLY A DESK, TO (since WWII) — "To fly a desk" is to be employed in static, administrative duties. (Ironically, Second World War air navigators, who perform their duties at a plotting table, occasionally inverted the term and called navigating an aircraft in combat, a desk-job.) (See **Mahogany Bomber**) [Ref: Partridge (8th)]

What do you do in the air force?
I fly a desk...

FLYAWAY KIT (CF; current) — A "Flyaway Kit" is an assembly of vital equipment (such as tools, personal effects, or operations stores), prepacked and ready to be loaded on an aircraft at short notice. When operating away from base, the Flight Engineer or Technical Crewman must bring the tools needed to repair the aircraft, if necessary. These would have been prepacked in a Flyaway Tool Kit.

> *We won't return until next Tuesday, so remind maintenance that we'll need a flyaway kit.*

FLYCO (RCN; 1950's to 1969) — "Flyco" was the codeword and nickname for the Flying Control Officer aboard Her Majesty's Canadian aircraft carriers. When carrier flying operations are underway, the Flyco is in charge. (the analogous American term is Air Boss) [Ref: Snowie]

> *Don't worry, the Flyco is a decent fellow - unless you break one of his airplanes, that is...*

FLY IN EVER DECREASING CIRCLES, TO — The phrase "to fly in ever-decreasing circles" describes a person who is overcome with indecision and worry, but who expresses it through unfocussed, though vigorous, activity. The phrase is generally completed by adding: ...*until he disappears up his own asshole.*

> *How's the new Colonel handling the job?*
> *He is flying in ever-decreasing circles...*

FLYING ARSEHOLE (Commonwealth air forces; 1914 to the 1950's) — A "Flying Arsehole" was the denigrating - but usually good natured - nickname for the Observer's Wing, the flying badge worn by Observers. (Note that the term applied to the badge and not necessarily the wearer!) The origin of the term becomes clear on appreciating the design of the Observer's badge: an embroidered letter "O", to which a single upswept wing is added. (Occasionally, the term "Feathered Arsehole" was used instead.) The Flying Arsehole nickname faded out of use by the 1940's, after the badge became obsolete. (See also **Wings**) [Partridge (8th)]

Flying
Arsehole

FLYING BANANA (U.S. Army, RCAF; 1950's)
— The Vertol/Piasecki H-21, nicknamed the "Flying Banana", was one of the first twin-rotor transport helicopters. It served in both the U.S. Army and the RCAF during the 1950's. The RCAF used it for Search and Rescue, until it was replaced by the Boeing CH113 Labrador. The Flying Banana was aptly named, as it had a very prominent upward bend in the tail section, creating a profile not unlike a banana. This nickname achieved perfection in the U.S. Army, some of whose H-21's were painted overall yellow, to indicate that they were training aircraft. (See **Lab**) [Partridge (8th)]

Flying Banana

FLYING CIGAR (RAF, RCAF; WWII) — "Flying Cigar" was an occasional nickname for the Vickers Wellington bomber, more commonly known as the "Wimpey". The term alludes to the shape of its fuselage, seen from the profile view. (See **Wimpey**) [Ref: Partridge (FS)]

FLYING CIRCUS (originally Allied Air Forces, WWI) — The word circus is often used to describe a peculiar collection of aircraft or people. The nickname "Flying Circus" is most commonly associated with the squadron led by the Baron von Richthofen during the First World War, known as Richthofen's Flying Circus. However, it can also describe a peculiar collection of aircraft or people.

Few realize that the nickname Flying Circus was coined by German ground troops to describe their own air force squadrons generally, as the squadrons were moved from place to place. The German Army, of which the air service was a part, relied upon a well-developed transportation system, even to the extent that flying units, aircraft and all, were shifted from place to place by road or train! This was done to cut down on the loss of life away from the battle zone. Thus, ground troops often had a close-up view of their air force on the move.

By the middle of the First World War, many German Air Service units had elected to paint their aircraft in vivid markings. The most extreme example of this was of course, the squadron commanded by Baron Rittmeister von Richthofen, who became known as the Red Baron for the bright red colour of his aircraft. Thus, when soldiers saw a train load of brightly-painted aircraft, each with the wings removed and folded back, it suggested comparison to a circus train coming to town! The visual effect was astounding, especially for the brightly-painted aircraft of von Richthofen's unit. They, especially, became known as Richthofen's Flying Circus, and the term has been their nickname ever since. (See also **Red Baron**) [Ref: Phelan; Winter]

FLYING GASWORKS (Britain; WWII — The world's first armed ballistic missile, the German V-2, became known as the "Flying Gasworks" for a brief period in 1944.

Though Allied intelligence had known the Germans were developing the V-2, the War Ministry feared that panic would follow if the British public knew the whole story behind this new terror weapon. It was a weapon against which there is no defence. Therefore, the War Ministry deemed it necessary to invent a cover story to explain V-2 detonations. Thus, when the first V-2 exploded on a British city, (Epping, in Essex) the War Ministry explained it away by announcing that an accidental explosion had occurred at a gasworks!

This of course did not fool anyone for long, least of all the local residents who knew there was no gasworks located anywhere near the explosion! Therefore, the sarcastic nickname: Flying Gasworks. (The V-2 proved to be a much less devastating weapon than had been feared. It was determined that 5000 V-2's, five months' production, could have delivered a total of only about 3750 tons of high explosive, less than half the high explosive dropped on Germany in one day by RAF Bomber Command and the U.S. 8th Air Force.) [Refs: Partridge (8th); Jones; Middlebrook]

FLYING PENCIL (Allied and Axis; WWII — The Dornier DO-17 acquired the nickname of "Flying Pencil" from its civilian predecessor, a fast twin-engine civil transport. It had been ostensibly designed as an airliner while the Treaty of Versailles prevented Germany from developing combat aircraft. This civil transport was so long and narrow that the press began to call it the Flying Pencil. Ultimately this airliner (which could carry only six passengers) was the forerunner of the DO-17 medium bomber. The DO-17 bomber retained the civil transport's long, narrow tail section, so the "Flying Pencil" nickname remained. [Ref: Allez-Fernandez, Cacutt]

Flying Pencil

FLYING PIG (RAF, RCAF; WWII) — The Lockheed Ventura, a twin-engined coastal patrol bomber developed in 1941 from the Lodestar transport, was occasionally called the "Flying Pig" by its crews. The epithet Flying Pig likely arose during 1942, early in its operational history, when the RAF used Venturas in bomber operations into France and the Low Countries with disastrous results. Venturas were neither fast nor manoeuvrable enough, and fared badly against the intercepting Luftwaffe Focke Wulf 190's. Soon the RAF replaced the Ventura with the Douglas Boston, and reassigned them to Coastal Command where they did yeoman service. The RCAF operated Venturas primarily on the West Coast. [Ref: Partridge (FS); Allez-Fernandez, Cacutt]

FLYING PORCUPINE (Allied and Axis; WWII) — The Short Sunderland was a large flying boat used by RAF Coastal Command for long-range maritime patrol. The Luftwaffe christened it the "Flying Porcupine", because of the large number of machine

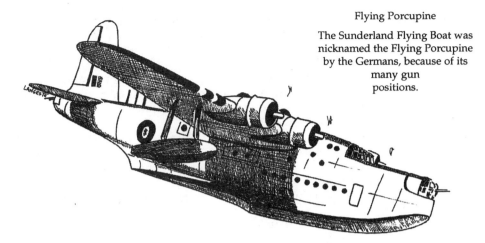

Flying Porcupine

The Sunderland Flying Boat was nicknamed the Flying Porcupine by the Germans, because of its many gun positions.

guns it carried in for self-defence. Besides a tail turret, a nose turret, and a top turret, there were many firing points designed into the airframe to be used as needed. Three RCAF squadrons flew the Sunderland during the Second World War.

FLYING SUITCASE (RAF, RCAF; WWII) — The Handley-Page Hampden was a British light twin-engined bomber that saw service in the first several years of the Second World War. It earned the nickname "Flying Suitcase" because of its dimensions; the fuselage was high and narrow and side-by-side seating was out of the question! The effect was that the Hampden's fuselage resembled a long, tall, narrow box - a suitcase with wings! [Ref: Partridge (FS)]

FLYPAST (RAF, RCAF, CF) — A "flypast" is an aerial salute usually comprising several aircraft flying low, in formation over the person or thing to receive the salute. The aircraft performing a flypast need not adopt any particular type of formation, provided the formation is maintained; thus, flypast aircraft can form up in any of the typical air display formations, such as finger-four, diamond, line astern, or echelon. On the other hand, aircraft in a flypast can take up quite unconventional formations. It was common during the 1950's to see Air Force aircraft fly overhead at an airshow, spelling out the letters "RCAF". In an overseas RCAF salute to France's Bastille Day in the 1950's, a formation of CF-100 fighters formed the shape of the Cross of Lorraine.

FM   See **PFM**

FOD; FOD PLOD; TO FOD (aviation; general) — "FOD" is the abbreviation for "foreign object damage", and has become a very common acronym in military aviation. Aircraft components, particularly engines, are engineered to very close tolerances and must be kept free of objects that do not belong, be they animal, mechanical or mineral. Otherwise movement of components will be impeded, and the aircraft or its engine will suffer damage. The term for this destruction is Foreign Object Damage, or FOD. However, the use of this term has broadened substantially. FOD now describes the intruding materiel itself, so throughout an air force hangar one will see red garbage cans with FOD stencilled on them. These are FOD Buckets. A shoulder-to-shoulder sweep of the ground for debris capable of damaging an aircraft is a "FOD Plod". An aircraft or engine which has been damaged by such debris is said to be "fodded".

Before you go for coffee, sweep up under the engine and do a FOD check.

FOOTBALL (RCAF; 1940's, 50's) — A "football" was the housing for an early ADF antenna (ADF is Aerial Direction Finding, a system that detects the direction from which a ground radio station transmits). It was called a football for the streamlined, teardrop shape of the fairing that housed the antenna.

FORE-AND-AFT HAT (Army, RCAF; to WWII) — A "fore-and-aft hat" was the occasional nickname for a wedge cap, coined because of its orientation, ie., the peak runs in a straight line, front to back. Fore-and-Aft is borrowed from nautical terminology and naval slang (where it describes a type of 19th Century cap, and a type of uniform). [Ref: Partridge (8th)]

FORT FUMBLE (CF; current) — "Fort Fumble" is but one of many disparaging titles used by Canadian servicemembers to refer to National Defence Headquarters (NDHQ) in Ottawa. More particularly, Fort Fumble came to refer to NDHQ's Building 155, the home of the Director-General of Aerospace Engineering and Maintenance (DGAEM), the senior aircraft engineering authority in the air force. DGAEM is the occupational headquarters for all aircraft engineering officers and maintenance technicians, and like all headquarters, is often the source of both amazement and consternation for personnel in the field. The term Fort Fumble may have been borrowed from the U.S. Army (whose installations are each known as a Fort) where it refers to the Pentagon. (See also **Bullshit Towers, Chateau, Castle Dismal, Disneyland-on-the-Rideau, Fraggle Rock, Glass Menagerie; Glass Palace, Petrified Forest**) [Ref: Sutherland]

Have you heard the latest idiocy to come out of Fort Fumble?!

FOUR HUNDRED SERIES, THE (RCAF; since WWII) — Since 1941, nearly all RCAF and Canadian Forces flying squadrons have been assigned numbers between 400 and 450. These are the so-called "400 series squadrons", and their description derives from Article XV of the British Empire Air Training Scheme. Under this agreement Canada, Australia and New Zealand committed themselves to providing flying squadrons to the allied war effort overseas. These squadrons would be integrated into the overall allied effort which was, in 1941, run by Britain. This caused practical problems, because the RCAF, RAAF, and RNZAF like most air forces, had numbered their flying squadrons rather conventionally, ie., No. 1 Squadron, No. 2 Squadron, No. 3 Squadron, etc. How did one distinguish between the RCAF's No. 1 Squadron and No. 1 Squadron of the RAF? (Or of the RAAF and the RNZAF, for that matter?) There was great potential for confusion. Indeed, there was confusion; the RCAF's No. 1 (Fighter) Squadron and RAF No. 1 (Fighter) Squadron both fought in the Battle of Britain, both flying the Hawker Hurricane! To prevent problems, overseas RCAF, RAAF and RNZAF squadrons were renumbered to fit in the British system of squadron numbering. This system was as follows:

Squadron Numbers allocated	Organization
1 - 299	Royal Air Force regular squadrons
300 - 399	Allied air forces-in-exile (Poland, Czechoslovakia, Free

	French, Norwegian, Greek, Belgian, Yugoslav)
400 - 445	Article XV - Royal Canadian Air Force
450 - 467	Article XV - Royal Australian Air Force
485 - 490	Article XV - Royal New Zealand Air Force
500 - 599	Originally intended for RAF Special Reserve Squadrons, but later numbers were allocated to wartime units.
600 - 699	Royal Auxiliary Air Force, but later were numbers allocated to wartime units.
700 - 799	Royal Navy Fleet Air Arm second-line and catapult squadrons.
800 - 899	Royal Navy Fleet Air Arm front-line squadrons
900 - 999	Barrage Balloon squadrons.

At the time of this agreement, there were three RCAF squadrons overseas, No. 110 Squadron, No. 1 (Fighter) Sqn, and No. 112 Sqn (redesignated No. 2 (Fighter) Squadron shortly afterward). These squadrons were renumbered as 400, 401 and 402 Squadrons, respectively. RCAF squadrons which were later transferred overseas or that were directly formed overseas, were numbered in the 400-Series.

In the post-war RCAF, the 400-series tradition was perpetuated, even to the extent of deviating from the Article XV model. Although the wartime RCAF had been allocated the numbers 400 to 445, this did not stop the post-war RCAF from creating squadrons numbered 446, 447, 448, 449 and 450! Indeed, a purist might suggest that the creation of 450 Squadron (as the CF's first heavy-lift helicopter unit) was poaching, because there had already been an Australian bomber squadron numbered 450! The Aussies didn't seem to mind, though...

Wartime RCAF squadrons based in Canada were numbered conventionally, though this is not to say that only the overseas 400-series squadrons saw combat. Canada-based RCAF squadrons saw combat in the Aleutians against the Japanese and east coast squadrons sank 6 German U-boats. The 400-Series tradition was perpetuated in the post-war RCAF but there seemed to be little interest in maintaining the lineage of these Canada-based, "non-400" series squadrons, despite their battle honours.

The RCN formed its first flying squadrons in the dying days of the Second World War, and largely kept the tradition of numbering its squadrons in the naval 800-Series. This naval tradition gradually faded after unification and the last RCN squadron designation, 880 Squadron, disappeared when the Tracker aircraft was retired. Even the ASW helicopter squadrons which deploy to sea aboard warships, directly descended from the RCN, were renumbered into the RCAF 400-Series. [Refs: Halley; Kostenuk and Griffin]

FOUR-STRIPER — A "four-striper" is an officer who wears four rank stripes; in the RCAF this would have been a Group Captain, in today's CF, this is a Colonel, and in the Navy, it is a Captain. (See also **Count the Hooks; Hoops; Two-Striper**)

> *Who's the new four-striper?*
> *That's Group Captain Campbell.*

FOX 1; FOX 2 (NATO; current) — "Fox 1" is radio code for a radar-guided air-to-air missile, and "Fox 2" is code for a heat-seeking air-to-air missile.

FRAGGLE (CF; current) — A "fraggle" is an avionics technician. The term is borrowed from the very popular CBC television series of the 1980's, "Fraggle Rock". In this program, Fraggles were creatures of uncommon idleness, who lived in their own, most unusual world. Presumably avionics technicians became known as Fraggles because they, like their television counterparts, seem to live in a world apart from engine and airframe technicians. (See also **Doozer; Fraggle Rock**)

This aircraft has a radar problem; we'd better call a Fraggle.

FRAGGLE ROCK (CF; current) — "Fraggle Rock" is Air Command Headquarters in Winnipeg. Airmen and airwomen in line units inevitably view Air Command Headquarters, like all headquarters, as a place where all sorts of amazing and inexplicable things occur. Like the term "Fraggle", the use of the term Fraggle Rock for Air Command Headquarters is borrowed from the very popular CBC television series of the same name. (For an explanation of Fraggle Rock, see **Fraggle**) (See also **Bullshit Towers, Chateau, Castle Dismal, Disneyland-on-the-Rideau, Fort Fumble, Glass Menagerie; Glass Palace, Petrified Forest**)

I hear that you'll be spending the next three years at Fraggle Rock!

FREQ (pronounced "freak")(CF; current) — A "freq" is a radio frequency, as in: *What freq are they transmitting on?* [Ref: Gentle and Reithmaier]

FRIENDLY; FRIENDLY FIRE (universal military) — "Friendly" is code, or shorthand, for an ally, the opposite of a hostile, ie., someone from whom no hostilities are expected. Note that the noun is friendly, not friend. Thus, fire inadvertently directed by an ally, ie. a friendly, is friendly fire - not because it is any friendlier than any other fire, but because it comes from a friendly. (See also **Bandit; Bogey**)

Is there a friendly in the area?

FRONT-END CREW See **Back-End Crew**

FRONT-SEATER See **A.I.**

FRUIT SALAD — "Fruit salad" is a vividly-coloured collection of medal ribbons, worn on a military dress tunic. Therefore, someone with lots of medals has lots of fruit salad. (See also **Gong, Brass Hat, Scrambled Eggs**) [Ref: Partridge (FS)]

Who's the guy with all the fruit salad?
Major Bishop...V.C., D.S.O., M.C. and D.F.C.!

FUBAR (universal, though probably American in origin) — "FUBAR" is an acronym for "Fucked Up Beyond All Recognition", a situation that requires little explanation.

FUG BOOTS (RFC, RNAS, RAF; WWI) — "Fug Boots" were leather boots and leggings that were fur-trimmed and lined, for warmth. First World War aviators wore Fug Boots instead of the service issue leather riding boots that afforded little warmth at high altitude, or in cold weather. They were long, rising well above the knees and were often held up by suspenders or braces. Fug Boots were invented by RFC ace Major Lanoe

Hawker to ward off the cold in his DH2 fighter. The origin of the term is unclear. (See also **Sidcot**) [Ref: Greer, Harold]

FUNCTION AS ADVERTISED, TO (Military Aviation; general) — Something that works or operates correctly is said to "function as advertised". The term is used as a way of understating a dramatic event, as in: "the ejection seat functioned as advertised" to describe a bailout, or "the bomb functioned as advertised" to describe an explosion.

I pulled the ripcord and the parachute functioned as advertised

GOLF

GAGGLE — A "gaggle" is a group of aircraft - or sometimes people - of indeterminate organization, formation, and number. It is derived from "a gaggle of geese". [Ref: Partridge (FS)]

GARDENING (RAF, RCAF; WWII) — The use of heavy bombers to lay mines in the ocean was codenamed "gardening", presumably because the floating mines are "sowed" in rows, as the aircraft flies back and forth. (See also **to Lay Eggs**) [Ref: Partridge (8th)]

GARLIC HIT (RCAF, CF Europe; 1950's to 1980's) — To airmen and women stationed at the Canadian NATO air bases in France and Germany, a "garlic hit" was a meal consumed at a local dining establishment. [Ref: Sutherland]

After beer call, let's go to that bistro in Hemmering for a Garlic Hit!

GAS FACTOR (CF, current) — "Gas Factor" is a mythical, but nonetheless useful gauge for describing one's interest or devotion to the task at hand. The term is a spurious acronym that means "Give-A- Shit Factor". Therefore a person with a low Gas Factor, or Give-A-Shit Factor, doesn't care. They don't "give-a-shit."

Tony's gas factor is really low on Fridays.

GCA (aviation general) — "GCA" is a "ground controlled approach", a method of assisting an aircraft to land in poor weather or visibility. In a GCA, a pilot flying on instruments is assisted in landing by an Air Traffic Controller who tracks the aircraft on special "GCA Radar"; this radar shows the controller how the aircraft is deviating from the optimum glide path and heading. The controller observes the radar and continuously advises the pilot by radio how to correct the aircraft's descent so it goes on to land along this optimum glidepath.

G.D. (general RAF, RCAF; since WWI) — "G.D." is an abbreviation that has two potential air force meanings:

(1)   **God-Damned**, as in: "where's that G.D. map?!"

(2)   **General Duties**, which is a service term with different meanings depending on whether it applies to an officer, or to a noncommissioned airman or airwoman. In the RAF, and the RCAF until 1968, to be a "General Duties Officer" was to be an aircrew officer. On the other hand, an airman who was listed as on General Duties, was an untrained (and occasionally untrainable) individual who was only employed as a general labourer, in the mess, mowing lawns, cleaning barracks, etc.

GEE — "Gee" has two potential meanings in military aviation:

(1)   Gee, or "g", is shorthand for "gravity". While at rest on the earth's surface, people experience "One Gee" or, one times the force of gravity (ie., "1g"). However, aircraft can manoeuvre so that each occupant feels more, or less, than One Gee. Too much Gee, whether negative or positive, has adverse effects on aviators and aircraft, and many aircraft and people have been lost as a result. (See: **Black Out; G-Suit; Red Out**)

(2)   Gee was also the codename for an early radio navigation aid, developed during the Second World War to help Bomber Command aircraft reach their targets at night. The term was simply coined from the letter "G", the first letter of the word: "grid". However, a competing explanation suggests that was derived from "Gen Box", a complicated instrument that gave you "gen", or information.

"Gee" allowed a bomber to ascertain its position by "triangulation" on a grid map of Europe. That is, the bomber would receive two coded radio transmissions from two separate locations in England; the navigator would then compute the range and distance of these signals, and plot the aircraft's location on the grid. (See **Gen**) [Ref: Jones; Partridge (8th)]

GEN (pronounced "jenn")(RAF, RCAF; since 1930's) — "Gen" is information. "Straight gen" is accurate information, as is "pukka gen". ("Pukka" is British military slang of Indian origin meaning "correct", or "proper") On the other hand, "duff gen" is false or unreliable information. Consequently, the verb "to gen-up" means "to become informed", as in: *I have to gen-up on radar navigation!*

There are several theories for the origin of this term. One explanation is that it derives from the word "intelligence". Another common explanation is that "gen" is derived from a phrase once found at the beginning of every official RAF publication: *For the general Information of all ranks.* [Ref: Partridge (FS)]

I tell you, the straight gen is that we're going to Bermuda!
That's duff gen. I know we're going to Resolute Bay!

GEN MAN (pronounced "jenn man") (RAF, RCAF; WWII) — A "Gen Man" is an acknowledged expert on some topic, someone sought out for advice. "Gen" is air force slang for information or knowledge. (See also **Gen**; contrast with **Gen Merchant**) [Ref: Partridge (8th)]

Ask Guy, he's the Gen Man on that subject...

GEN MERCHANT (RAF, RCAF; WWII) — In the Second World War, the "Gen Merchant" was the Intelligence Officer, because he had all the "gen", or information. (See also **Spook, Spy**) [Ref: Harvey]

GENTLEMAN'S COURSE (RCAF, CF; current) — A "Gentleman's Course" is a military training course where it is generally accepted that if you show up, do what they ask, and pay attention, you will pass. A Gentleman's Course must be contrasted with the more common "real course", where you have to study hard to pass exams, or complete exercises to graduate. Another term for a Gentleman's Course is a "Snooze and Booze Course".

GENTLEMEN OF THE AIR FORCE (general usage; WWII and 1950`s?) — This phrase (nothing if not ironic) is part of a somewhat longer catchphrase that was common during the Second World War and for some years thereafter: *There's the boys of the navy, the men of the army and the gentlemen of the air force.* This catchphrase was meant to encapsulate the respective temperaments and demeanor of sailors, soldiers and airmen. To anyone familiar with them however, the descriptions implied in this phrase are accurate only in the very broadest and coarsest sense!

GEORGE (RAF, RCAF; WWII) — Aviators have christened an aircraft's auto-pilot "George", reportedly to give a reasonable answer to the question: "who's flying the airplane?" [Refs: Partridge (FS); Berrey and Van Den bark]

> *If you're the pilot, and you're back here with us passengers, then who is flying the airplane?!*
> *Why, George is, of course.*

GESTAPO (RAF, RCAF; WWII) — In contrast to the usual meaning of "Gestapo" (ie., the dreaded Nazi secret police), in wartime Britain the Gestapo were the Air Force Police! Young airmen have a natural resistance to military discipline. Therefore it was perhaps inevitable that the Air Force Police, who were largely the instruments of that discipline, would not be regarded kindly. (See also **AFP, AP, Meathead, SP**) [Ref: Partridge (FS)]

> *Don't be late getting back to the camp. Otherwise the Gestapo will be after you!*

GET SOME IN, TO (Military general; since at least WWII) — "To get some in" is to get some "time" in, that is, time in military service or on operations. This term does not merely allude to seniority, but rather it implies participation in meaningful or arduous duty. (See also **T.I.**)[Ref: Harvey]

> *After you get some in, then we'll see about some leave.*

GET-THERE-ITIS (RCAF, CF) — "Get-there-itis" is a pilot's single-minded determination to reach a destination in the face of obvious hazards, even though safer alternatives are still available. It is self-deception, an unsafe state of mind that causes a pilot to ignore safe alternatives and belittle obvious hazards, all to arrive at the destination. The suffix "itis" bolsters the idea that it is an affliction (as in Bronchitis, Neuritis, etc), albeit an affliction of the mind. Sometimes it is known as "Press-on-itis".

> *What was the cause of the accident?*
> *...the pilot had a bad case of get-there-itis, and took risks he shouldn't have.*

GHOST　　　　See **Kriegie**

GIBSON GIRL (RCAF; 1940's to 1960's) — The "Gibson Girl" was an early emergency radio transmitter equipping large RCAF aircraft from the 1940's, and which was part of the aircraft survival kit. It was used to transmit a distress signal in case of a crash or forced landing. In contrast with the tiny, hand-held solid state radios that entered use in the late 1960's, the Gibson Girl was huge! It incorporated a generator operated manually by a handcrank, a transmitter-receiver, and a long wire antenna held aloft by a box kite that was included in the kit!

The term Gibson Girl was no doubt an allusion to a series of cartoons drawn by Charles Dana Gibson at the turn of the twentieth century. These cartoons featured statuesque young women possessed of an "hourglass figure", who became known as the Gibson Girls. The Gibson Girl radio was housed in a large box that had indentations on either side where the person operating the crank could place his knees, for stability. These indentations also gave the radio a distinctive "hourglass figure". Therefore the name! The Gibson Girl remained part of the survival gear on Canadian Aurora aircraft until 1994!

GIRLS, THE (RCAF, RCN; 1950's and 1960's) — "The Girls" was the collective nickname for two airborne anti-submarine detection systems incorporated in Canadian patrol aircraft; these two systems were themselves codenamed "Julie" and "Jezebel" - hence the nickname "the girls".

"Julie" was a system developed by the RCAF's 404 (Maritime Patrol) Squadron during the 1950's and used by both the RCAF and the RCN. Essentially it involved detecting the presence of a submerged submarine by explosive echo-ranging. The aircraft would drop several sonobuoys into the water in the area where the submarine is suspected. These sonobuoys are floating hydrophones; they detect noises in the water and automatically transmit them back up to the aircraft overhead. The aircraft then drops explosive charges into the water, and the sonobuoy detects any echoes of the explosive charges that have "bounced" off the hull of the submarine. Apparently Julie was quite effective against conventional submarines, but was less useful against nuclear-powered submarines. The system was christened Julie in honour of a Baltimore stripper renowned for being the owner of spectacular body parts that also "bounced" around.

"Jezebel" was the second of "the girls"; it was a passive sonar system developed by Bell Laboratories in New Jersey. Despite the fact that this system was developed in the United States, Bell Laboratories asked the RCAF to do the initial "proof of concept" flying, rather than the USN. The USN was reportedly not impressed. [Ref: Sutherland]

The destroyer to the east reports a possible submarine contact, so get ready with the girls!

GLASS COCKPIT (aviation general; current) — An aircraft that has a "Glass Cockpit" uses Cathode Ray Tubes (ie., CRT's, or computer monitors) to display cockpit information, rather than rows of conventional aircraft instruments. In a glass cockpit one will not find the familiar rows of circular instruments. Instead, one or more glass computer screens display the information. Hence, the term glass cockpit. The glass cockpit is only found where central computers process the engine, flight, weapons and navigation information; usually a glass cockpit is used together with a "Heads Up Display" or "HUD". At date of writing, the only aircraft in the CF with glass cockpits were the CF-18 Hornet and the A310 Airbus. (See also **HUD**)

GLASS HOUSE   See **Club Ed, D.B.'s; Digger, Jankers**

GLASS MENAGERIE; GLASS PALACE (CF; current) — The "Glass Menagerie" and the "Glass Palace" are both nicknames for Air Command Headquarters in Winnipeg. These nicknames were coined because this new edifice, built in the late 1980's, is a modern "open-office" structure that features a broad, clear glass front. Its proper name is "The Billy Bishop Building", named for Canada's leading air ace. However, many airmen and airwomen call it the Glass Palace or the Glass Menagerie (unconsciously borrowing from Tennesee William's play *The Glass Menagerie*). Use of the word "menagerie" suggests that Air Command Headquarters, like most headquarters, exhibits certain circus-like tendencies. (See also **Bullshit Towers, Chateau, Castle Dismal, Disneyland-on-the-Rideau, Fort Fumble, Fraggle Rock, Petrified Forest**)

> *Rick, I hear you're being posted to the Glass Palace!*
> *Yup, I'm spending the next four years in Winnipeg.*

GLASS SHINE   See **Spitshine**

G-LOC   See **to Black Out; G-Suit**

GO/NO-GO (aviation; general) — A "go/no-go" point, or a "go/no-go" time, is a critical decision threshold where the crew must decide whether to proceed (ie, to "go") or whether to stop (ie, "no-go"). This term is used in conjunction with many activities. For example, the go/no-go point on a runway is a specified distance down the runway, where the crew must abort a takeoff if the aircraft wheels have not left the ground. If they do not abort the takeoff by the time they reach the go/no-go point, they will most likely go off the end of the runway into the gravel.

Similarly, a go/no-go time is a threshold decision-making time. It is a deadline, after which changing circumstances will make only one choice possible. For example, if an aircraft is on a search for a ship missing at sea, the maximum time it can spend searching is determined by the amount of fuel carried. The aircraft can search until it has enough fuel to safely return to its base, otherwise it will be lost itself. The time when only this amount of fuel is left is the go/no-go time.

> *Navigator, how long until we reach the Go/No-Go point?*

GO FOR A BURTON, TO (RAF; WWII) — To "go for a burton" is a euphemism, a phrase that means: killed on operations. It seems that "Burton" refers to a type of dark beer brewed at Burton-on-Trent, in England. Hence, to go for a Burton was "to step out for a beer". The term is a euphemism, a phrase that cushions the speaker or listener from the real emotional meaning of the words. It is a verbal anaesthetic. To the uninformed listener, stepping out for a beer might be a plausible explanation for someone's absence, but among aircrews it was universally accepted that the absent person had been killed.

There is anecdotal evidence to suggest that Gone for a Burton was an advertising slogan to promote Bass Ale (*Where's George? Gone for a Burton!*), and that this is where the phrase was picked up by airmen. However, there is a competing theory. It seems that Burton 's was also the name of a tailor shop near an RAF training establishment, often frequented by airmen. The phrase "gone for a Burton" is usually associated with early fighter operations in wartime England. (See also **Gone West, to Buy It**) [Refs: Partridge (FS); Rees; Williams]

> *Where's Andy?*
> *He's gone for a burton...*
> *Bloody hell...*

GOLDFISH CLUB (Commonwealth Air Forces, WWII) — The Goldfish Club is an informal association whose membership is limited to persons who have been rescued from the sea after ditching, or baling out from, an aircraft.

Goldfish Club

LANGASTE

Credit for forming the club goes to Mr. C.A. Robertson, chief draftsman of Messrs. P.B. Cow and Company, manufacturers of Air-Sea Rescue Equipment in Farnborough, England, during the Second World War. Customarily, airmen who had "ditched" were invited by this company to visit their facilities. There they shared their experiences at sea while awaiting rescue, and offered suggestions on how to improve the equipment. Out of such meetings was born the Goldfish Club. Members received a membership card that was "heat-sealed, and waterproofed" (of course!) and were entitled to a badge depicting a silver-winged Goldfish, often worn on a member's flying jacket or battledress tunic. However, naval aviators, displaying the reserve associated with the senior service, generally sewed the badge beneath the tunic lapel, hidden, lifting it to reveal membership discreetly. (See **to Ditch**)[Ref: Hampson]

GONE WEST, TO BE (WWI) — To have "gone west" is a First World War euphemism for being killed while on operations. It appears to have been common English usage even before the First World War. (See also **Go for a Burton**)[Ref: Partridge (8th); Voss]

GONG (Since at least WWI) — A "Gong" is a medal or decoration. The term alludes to the similarity in shape between a circular medal and a musical gong. [Ref: Partridge (8th)]

> *I see they gave you another gong, Roy!*

GONZO (CF; current) — The nickname "Gonzo", borrowed from television's "Muppet Show", refers to the Dash 8 navigation trainer flown by the Canadian Forces. In the late 1980's the De Havilland Dash 8 commuter airliner, after major modification, became the standard navigation trainer in the Canadian Forces. The passenger seats and amenities were replaced by several crew positions for trainee Air Navigators and their instructors, complete with instruments, plotting tables, and computer and radar screens. From the outside the aircraft is virtually indistinguishable from the commercial Dash 8, with one very prominent exception: a very large nose radome. This radome houses the navigation radar used by the neophyte navigators within. The nickname Gonzo derives from this large nose, because the Dash 8 Nav trainer, like the Muppets character of the same name, has a rather large, prominent proboscis.

GOOD SHOW (RCAF, CF; since 1950's) — A "Good Show" is an award given by the RCAF and CF for an outstanding contribution to Flight Safety, or for excellence in airmanship that prevents an accident. The term was originally a standard verbal register of approval, but it has also acquired its own life in Canadian aviator's terminology.

I hear that Brian won a Good Show.

GOOFING STATIONS (RCN; traditional) — "Goofing Stations" is an old naval term for the time, or place, that off-watch sailors could legitimately idle their time away, just watching the world go by. When some unusual sight became visible at sea, it was not unknown for the ship's loudspeaker to blare: *Off-watch Hands, to Goofing Stations!* In naval aviation, Goofing Stations referred to the row of casual spectators on the "island"

Goofing Stations

Off-watch goofers watch from
their goofing stations as a Seafire
waves off.

who gathered - like seagulls on a power line - to impassively watch the landings and takeoffs on the carrier flight deck below. [Ref: Partridge (8th)]

> *From time to time, a Seafire would collide with the carrier's "island" while landing. Still, despite the risks, you had to be there early to get a good spot at the Goofing Stations!*

GOOLIE CHIT; BLOOD CHIT (Commonwealth Air Forces; since at least WWII) — "Goolie Chit" and "Blood Chit" were both nicknames for a printed emergency message carried by aircrew flying in the Middle East and the Far East during the Second World War. The Blood Chit, or Goolie Chit was printed on a piece of handkerchief-sized silk. It was used to convey a message to locals in case the airman carrying it was forced down in unfamiliar territory, and could not speak the local language. For example, the blood chit used during the Second World War in the South-east Asia theatre of war carried a prominent Union Jack, and its text read:

> *Dear Friend,*
>
> > *I am an Allied fighter. I did not come to do any harm to you who are my friends. I only want to do harm to the Japanese and chase them away from this country as quickly as possible.*
> >
> > *If you will assist me, my Government will sufficiently reward you when the Japanese are driven away.*

The same message was repeated in French, Annamite (ie., Vietnamese), Haka, Kachin, Laizo, Karen, Burmese, Malay, Sumatra, Tamil, Chinese, Jawi, Thai, West Shan, East Shan and North Thai, and Bengali.

"Chit" is common military slang for a semi-official voucher, memo, or receipt, used instead of a more formal document. The terms "Blood Chit" and "Goolie Chit" may have developed in the Royal Air Force of the 1920's. The RAF had been tasked by the British government to police Mesopotamia (now Iraq) under the terms of a League of Nations mandate. Airmen forced down in the area occasionally ran afoul of hostile tribesmen, who would often kill or mutilate the unfortunate aviators. As a result, the RAF put the word out to the people of the tribes and villages that the air force would provide a cash reward to the locals for any airman returned to the RAF in a healthy state. This offer was formalized in a printed message carried by every airman flying over the territory.

Airmen referred to this written message as a Blood Chit or a Goolie Chit ("goolies", British vernacular for testicles, is a corruption of the Urdu word for ball!), likening it to a receipt (without which, one might be deprived of one's blood - or goolies.) The practice of issuing printed emergency messages to airmen continued into the Second World War, especially in the Middle East and the Far East theatres of war. Canadian airmen flew in RAF units formations in both the Middle East and the Far East, and carried a blood chit in case they were forced down. These terms fell out of Canadian usage, but the term goolie chit was current RAF usage as late as during the Gulf War of 1991. [Refs: Partridge (8th)]; Neal/Rosher]

GOON   See **Kriegie**

GOON SUIT   See **Poopy Suit (1)**

GOOSE (military aviation; general) — "Goose" was shorthand for Goose Bay, the Labrador airport that served as a stop for aircraft going on across the Atlantic. It remains in use today as the home of a NATO air combat training range. (See also **Bluie**)

We'll stop for fuel at Goose, and then go on to Bluie.

GOSPORT SYSTEM, THE (RFC, RAF; WWI) — Before 1917, military flying training was ad hoc, and learning to fly depended more on the instructor's temperament than on a proper syllabus or standards. In 1917, Lord Trenchard, commander of the RFC, realized the inadequacies of such a scheme and ordered that the School of Special Flying be established at Gosport. Its job was to train flying instructors and to develop a flying training system. The philosophy was that the trainee pilot was airborne as soon as possible with an instructor and should assume control immediately. Each flight was preceded by a half hour of theory with the instructor, and was followed by a half an hour of discussion on the lessons learned. The syllabus was carefully designed and was strictly adhered to; manoeuvres were discussed by student and instructor in flight (through the "Gosport Tubes") and the student was encouraged to solve problems on his own before the instructor would intervene. This system, developed by an airman named Smith-Barry, was the foundation of all flying training to follow.

The Gosport System proved highly successful and was exported, via the RFC training camps in Canada, to the U.S. Army, which incorporated its principles in its flying training. (See also **Gosport Tubes; Crab**) [Ref: Winter]

GOSPORT TUBES (RFC, RAF, RCAF; 1917 to 1945); — Gosport tubes were a basic, though effective, method by which a student pilot and flying instructor could talk in flight, before the era of the electronic intercom. They were named after the RFC School of special flying at Gosport, where they were invented in 1917. At Gosport, it was considered desirable that the instructor actually talk to the student in flight, a hitherto impossible task because the student pilot and instructor sat in tandem, in open cockpits, before the days of the radio intercom!

Gosport Tubes were an ingenious and simple solution to the problem. They are a pair of flexible rubber tubes, each with a mouthpiece at one end and diaphragm earphones at the other. The mouthpiece end of one of the tubes is placed in an available spot in each cockpit. The earphone end of the long tube is attached to earpieces worn by the occupant of the other cockpit. The instructor talked into the mouthpiece, and the rubber tubes carried the sound waves to the earphones of the student, and vice versa.

An RFC pilot named Major Parker developed the Gosport Tubes; apparently they were *modelled on the device popularized by continental waiters in Soho.* It is also said that the Gosport Tube was useful for instructors who wished to get the attention of an inattentive student. They merely had to place the mouthpiece end of the Gosport Tube into the slipstream, which would direct a blast of air directly at the student's ear! [Ref: Winter]

The beauty of Gosport Tubes is that they need no maintenance.

G.Q. CLUB (since 1930's) — The "G.Q. Club" is an informal association whose membership is restricted to people who have made an emergency parachute descent from an aircraft in distress, using a Quilter parachute. The letters "G.Q." are the initials of the British parachute makers, Gerald Quilter Parachute Co. of Stadium Works in Surrey. The G.Q. Club is the British equivalent of the U.S.-based "Caterpillar Club" and is sponsored by this company. In the 1930's, parachute designers James Gregory and Gerald Quilter initiated several advances in parachute design, such as packing parachute shroud lines in vanes, and a cup-shaped canopy. The first member of the G.Q. Club was Leading Aircraftman H. Law, RAF, who bailed out of a Magister aircraft in 1940; the first Canadian was Flying Officer G. W. Hunter who ejected from a CF-100 in 1953. (See **Caterpillar Club**)[Ref: Hampson]

G.R.A. (RCAF since 1961, CF; still current) — The initials "G.R.A." were a very common part of the vocabulary of Canadians stationed at air bases in Europe. G.R.A. is the abbreviation for "General Restricted Area", the flight line and hangar area on a Canadian NATO air base. The G.R.A. was kept very secure by checkpoints, sentries and detection devices and was separated from the domestic and administrative areas of the base by barbed wire. Only personnel who actually worked in the G.R.A. were allowed entry, and even they had to prove that they were authorized by showing their G.R.A. Pass - a special identity card - to the guard at the G.R.A. gate. The term entered the airman's vocabulary when the RCAF deployed the CF-104 Starfighter aircraft to its European bases. The Starfighters were part of NATO's tactical nuclear strike force, so security around Canadian CF-104 bases was extremely high. Though this term applied to European bases, it was occasionally used at Canadian air bases - especially fighter bases like Cold Lake. [Ref: Sutherland]

Don't forget your G.R.A. Pass this time, OK?

GRAND — A "grand" is an increment of 1000 feet of altitude, and is borrowed from popular American slang where a "grand" is a monetary increment of $1000.00. (See also **Angels**) [Ref: Partridge (FS)]

What is your altitude?
Right now we're at six grand and climbing!

GRAND SLAM (RAF Bomber Command; WWII) — "Grand Slam" was both nickname and codeword for the RAF's 22,000 pound bomb, the largest conventional bomb used operationally during the Second World War. The Grand Slam was a further development of the 12,000 pound "Tallboy" bomb. Also known as the "earthquake bomb" and the "Ten-Ton Tessie", the Grand Slam was so heavy that it took a specially modified Lancaster bomber (nicknamed a "Clapper"), stripped of all extra weight, to carry it. Each bomb contained 9500 pounds of Torpex explosive.

After it was dropped, the Grand Slam gained phenomenal speed and penetrated deep into the ground. Its delayed fuse caused it to explode after it entered the earth, often to a depth of fifty feet! This shifted the ground, as in an earthquake. A test drop of a Grand Slam in February 1945 resulted in a crater 30 feet deep and 124 feet in diameter. It was intended for use against specially-hardened targets such as concrete U-Boat Pens and V-1 launch sites, and against targets that were susceptible to damage from shock waves transmitted through the earth, such as bridges and viaducts. (See also **Clapper, Tallboy**) [Ref: Cooper]

Grand Slam

GRASS (since early 1940's) — "Grass" is a type of electronic interference or "clutter", which plays havoc with early radar screens, oscilloscopes and other electronic devices. This type of interference became known as "grass" because of its appearance on the screen, a dense series of vertical strokes at the bottom of the screen, which resembled vertical blades of grass.

However, in very early radar sets, grass describes the normal "picture" on the radar set's cathode ray tube. These tubes were like an oscilliscope, and it was the presence of an aircraft which upset the normal grass of the screen. (See also **Clutter**)[Ref: Partridge (8th)]

> *I'm not getting a very good return on this radar screen, there's too much grass!*

GREASER   See **Squeaker**

GREASY PAW (CF; current) — To an avionics technician, a "greasy paw" is an Airframe or Aero-Engine Technician. Maintenance of airframes and aero-engines is generally more dirty and physical when compared with maintaining electronic components, which usually occurs in more pristine surroundings. Therefore avionics technicians often look askance at their mechanical counterparts, whose hands (ie., "paws") can often be covered in grease or oil. (See also **Rigger, Fitter**)

> *Don't ever trust a greasy paw with a soldering iron!*

GREAT RATE OF KNOTS (CF; current) — "Great Rate of Knots" denotes rapid movement. The term is part rhyming slang, and part allusion to the fact that a "knot" is a "rate" (ie., one nautical mile per hour) and not a distance. The term is probably naval in origin, though it can apply to anything, or anyone, going at high speed.

> *The CF-18 proceeded towards its target at a great rate of knots!*

GREENS, THE   See **School Solution**

GREEN APPLE   See **Apple**

GREENHOUSE CANOPY   See **Canopy**

GREEN TICKET (RCAF, CF; since 1950's) — A "Green Ticket" is a green-coloured card that identifies the bearer as an instrument-rated military pilot. Though today all CF pilots are required to be instrument-qualified, this was not always the case, and in the early 1950's, possessing a "Green Ticket" marked the owner as one of those who had achieved this difficult qualification. Also, during the 1950's there was an even higher mark of distinction: the "Blue Ticket", issued to those pilots who had earned the "Master Instrument Pilot" rating. [Ref: Sutherland]

GREMLIN (1930's to 1950's; now rare) — A "Gremlin" is a Sprite or Elf whose sole reason for existence is to cause aircraft accidents or unserviceabilities. Of course, aviators can make mistakes and airplanes can break; the Gremlin is blamed only for problems where no other explanation can be found, or for which no one will assume responsibility! The Gremlin (in contrast to recent Hollywood depictions) is mischievous but not malevolent.

The Gremlin's origins are highly uncertain and explanations abound, though the stories may date back to the 1920's. One suggestion is that the Gremlins are a variant on the "Linclonshire Imp", an English folk character. It is also said the name Gremlin derives from a mixture of "Goblin" and "Greme" (an Old English verb meaning "to vex"), though some explanations relate it to "Fremlin", a brand of English beer. Yet another explanation says that Gremlin is derived from "Grimlin", a contraction of "Grinning Goblin". Newsweek Magazine (Sept 7th, 1942) attributes the word to a pre-Second World War British naval pilot who was fished out of the sea after a faulty carrier takeoff. Apparently he was hung over and blamed the mishap on "goblins" in the Fremlin beer - goblins that he promptly christened Gremlins. One can only speculate where the whole truth lies.

Aviators of the 1930's found Gremlins to be a useful and humorous way of explaining the inexplicable or dodging responsibility for error. After all, if an aircraft did something not intended by the pilot, or broke down for no apparent reason, it must have been a Gremlin! They were illustrated in comics, and whole families and species of Gremlins were invented, each type presumably being responsible for a different type of mishap! For example:

- a Gremlin who drains electrical batteries of water, is the **Ampless**;

- a Gremlin who breaks control wires is a **Brigshiff**;

- a **Bomb-Sight Buglet** is the Gremlin who interferes with the bombardier's bombsight, by shining bright lights and reflections into the bomb-aimer's eyes;

- the Gremlin responsible for breaking things is a **Buster** (which is coincidentally the codeword meaning "use maximum speed");

- a **Creeper** is the Gremlin that tampers with instrument needles, causing them to creep ahead or lag behind in flight;

- a **Crooker** is the Gremlin that causes a pilot, flying on instruments, to ignore his instrument readings and to believe his senses, which are telling him that he is flying inverted; this causes the pilot to roll the aircraft over, upon which the "Crooker" drinks the gasoline from the fuel tanks;

- the **Duticallatus Prangiferous** is a sharp-nosed Gremlin responsible for rips in the skin of an aircraft;

- a female Gremlin is a **Fifinella**;

- a **Ground Walloper** (also known as the "Grand Walloper") is the Gremlin in charge of lift, if he falls asleep on the job, the aircraft hits the ground!

- **Lowbold** (one of the rare Gremlins who does not live exclusively on aircraft) is the Gremlin responsible for suddenly changing the water temperature in the barracks shower;

- a **Petrol Boozer** (perhaps derived from "bowser", a tank truck) is a Gremlin who causes fuel problems;

- **Shorty** is the Gremlin that creates short-circuits in an electrical system;

- a **Spandule** enjoys being tangled up in the props, but (for some unknown reason) this is only possible at the altitude of 9,999 feet, ie., one foot short of the 10,000 foot mark;

- a **Spanjer** is a Gremlin that only lives above 20,000 feet, where it latches on to passing high-altitude aircraft and causes those problems that only occur at high altitude;

- a baby Gremlin is a **Widget**;

- a **Yehudi** is a type of Gremlin similar to a "Petrol-Boozer", presumably responsible for unaccountable or unpredicted fuel shortages;

- **Zero** is the name of the Gremlin that ices over wings and controls, or which freezes water.

[Refs: Dickson; Partridge (FS); Berrey and Van Den Bark]

GREY-OUT   See **To Black Out**

GREY FUNNEL AIRLINES (RCN to 1969) — "Grey Funnel Airlines" was the RCN nickname for the "Carrier On-Board Delivery" aircraft, a Tracker aircraft especially converted to perform carrier onboard air transport. Most transport aircraft were incapable of carrier operations, so it became necessary for the aircraft carrier to have its own light utility air transport capability. This took the form of the Carrier On-Board Delivery aircraft, known simply as the "COD".

Grey Funnel Airlines, was merely a variation on another navy nickname, the Grey Funnel Line. Among its members, the RCN itself was sometimes called the Grey Funnel Line, mimicking steamship liner companies that often decorated the funnels of their ships with their corporate symbol (e.g. "The White Star Line", or "The Blue Funnel Line"). When one sailed with the RCN, one sailed on Grey Funnel Lines, so it wasn't much of a leap to refer to naval air transport as Grey Funnel Airlines. [Refs: Partridge (8th); Snowie]

> *Those guys in Grey Funnel Airlines don't treat their passengers very well -*
> *but then again, they're the only airline that will fly you to an aircraft carrier!*

Grey Funnel Airlines

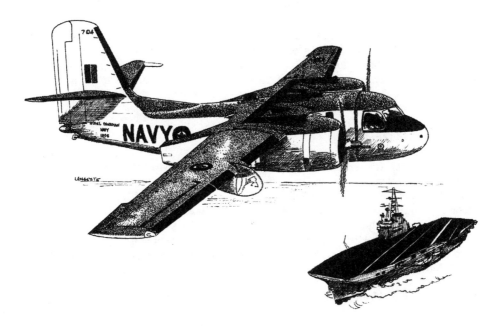

GROCERIES (RAF, RCAF; WWII) — During the Second World, bombs were sometimes called "groceries", as in: *last night we were over Berlin, delivering groceries.* This term developed because the names of various fish and vegetables were used as Bomber Command codewords for different types of air weapons. [Ref: Partridge (8th)]

GROSSED OUT, TO BE (CF; current) — An aircraft that is "grossed out" has been loaded with so heavy a load of cargo or passengers that it is unsafe to carry any more. This term, especially common among air transport units, means that the aircraft has reached its "maximum gross weight for takeoff". Note that an aircraft that is grossed out may not necessarily be "full" (ie., there may be unused space), because not all cargo has the same weight per cubic foot. An aircraft carrying, say, lead bars will gross out long before all the cargo space is used.

On the other hand, an aircraft that is being loaded with ping-pong balls will be full long before the load becomes too heavy for the aircraft to take off. Such an aircraft is said to be "bulked out"; that is, the very bulk of the cargo prevents more from being loaded, rather than its weight.

> We've got extra space, can we take another crate of supplies on this flight?
> Sorry boss, we're grossed out.

GROUNDED, TO BE (aviation general) — "Grounded" is slang, which, when applied to an aircraft or aviator, means that they are no longer permitted to fly. Though this word no longer has official standing and is not used in service records, it remains the common usage.

> What's wrong?
> The Flight Surgeon grounded me...

GROUND POUNDER (general usage) — Strictly speaking, a "ground pounder" is an artilleryman, because the gunner's job is to fire shells that "pound" the ground. Ground pounders are to be distinguished from the other major species of artilleryman, the "air defender". However, to members of the Air Force, unaccustomed to such nice distinctions, ground pounder can be used to refer to anyone in the Army. Alternately it can refer to a non-flying member of the Air Force.

GROUND WALLOPER   See **Gremlin**

GROUND ZERO (general military usage; since 1950's) — "Ground Zero" is the epicentre of a nuclear explosion. To perform the mathematical calculations needed to predict the downwind effects of fallout, it is necessary that civil defence authorities ascertain ground zero immediately - by no means easy after such awful destruction and disruption. During the early 1960's, the RCAF Auxiliary, (ie., the air reserve) was removed from its role as a combat reserve and given the job of helping Canada survive should a nuclear attack occur. One task they trained for was "locating Ground Zero", a job that demanded considerable suspension of disbelief.

> We've identified the most likely location for Ground Zero!
> Where?
> The Base Commander's office...

GROUPER; GROUPY (ie., "grooper", "groopy") (RAF, RCAF; general) — A "Grouper" or "Groupy" is an RAF or RCAF officer of the rank of Group Captain, equivalent to a full Colonel or a naval Captain. Also, occasionally in the postwar RCAF in Europe, the wartime German rank *Gruppenführer* was wryly used to refer to this rank, from its literal translation: "Group Leader". *Gruppenführer* was a rank of the notorious German SS. So there was small wonder that local Germans gave a sideways glance when a Canadian airman referred to his RCAF station commanding officer as *Gruppenfuhrer*! [Refs: Partridge (FS); Sutherland]

GROWLIES (CF; current) — "Growlies" is a generic term for food. One suspects that the term growlies originally meant "a state of hunger", a reference to the growling of an empty stomach, but that it changed over time to mean food.

>*I'm hungry! Let's go for growlies.*

GROWN-UPS (CF; current) — Senior Canadian Forces officers - usually of the rank of Colonel or higher - are occasionally referred to by their juniors as "the grown-ups". This mildly ironic term seems to imply that more junior personnel are treated like children, or perhaps the implication is that senior officers often - like parents - harbour the illusion that they are actually in control. (See also **High-Priced Help**)

>*When are we getting underway?*
>*We don't know yet. The grown-ups haven't made up their minds!*

GRUNT (general military usage; originally American) — To anyone not in the army, a "grunt" is a soldier, though to soldiers a "grunt" is more specifically an infantryman. The term was coined by American forces in Viet Nam War, and is said to originate in the distinctive noise made by a soldier struggling to stand up while wearing a heavy field pack. Between airmen and sailors there is an amusing, if spurious, explanation for this word; it is said that Grunt is merely the acronym for: *General Recruit, Unfit for Normal Training!*

>*The trouble with grunts is they think a helicopter is no more complex than a rifle!*

GRUPPENFUHRER   See **Grouper; Groupy**

G-SUIT (Military Aviation; general) — A "G-Suit" is an article of aircrew life support equipment. The G-Suit protects the wearer from loss of sight or consciousness due to excessive "g", or "gee", while flying. It is generally known as the G-Suit, though its proper name is the Anti-G Suit.

"Gee" (or "g") is the common scientific term for the force of gravity, and is simply the first letter of the word "gravity". A person who is subjected to too many gees will lose consciousness. This happens because the high "gee" causes the oxygen-carrying blood to flow downwards in the body, away from the brain. The brain becomes starved for oxygen and even after normal gravity returns, it can take minutes for a person to regain consciousness.

Military flying inevitably imposes high gee loads on aviators, especially in air combat manoeuvring. (See also **ACM**) In combat, the ability to withstand high gee can make the difference between life and death; a pilot must "out-turn" his opponent without blacking out. A relatively fit person can withstand two, or even three, "gees" with little medical risk (beyond feeling heavy and uncomfortable). However, at about four gees even fit persons begin to lose their vision. This loss of vision is called a "black-out". If gee loads remain high, the aviator can experience "Gee-Induced Loss of Consciousness" (abbreviated "G-LOC"). Some trained aircrew, using the right techniques, can withstand up to five or six gees without a G-Suit, but this is difficult and there is not always a guarantee of success. Many aircraft and aviators have been lost after the pilot blacked out due to excessive gee, especially in the early days of aviation. Consequently air forces have always been interested in overcoming the effects of excessive gee.

Research began in the 1930's when it was discovered that artificially constricting the blood vessels in the lower part of the body was the key to overcoming G-LOC. This is accomplished by applying outside pressure on the lower body, using a tight, constricting garment. This outside pressure constricts the blood vessels in the lower body, making it difficult for blood to flow downward. Inflatable bladders in the tight G-Suit provide this external pressure. As the bladders expand, they compress the body beneath. This in turn constricts blood vessels. This early research gradually slowed to a halt, but the Second World War revived it. The RAF, having learned that the Luftwaffe was also investigating methods of overcoming excessive gee in aerial combat, did not want to suffer a disadvantage. So the research began anew.

Canadians were involved in G-Suit trials from the beginning. In 1941, Squadron Leader Franks, an RCAF Medical Officer, arrived at Farnborough, England with a trial, two-layered, water-filled G-Suit which he had designed in Toronto. The idea was that, as "gee-loading" increased, the water trapped between the two layers would be forced into the lower portions of the suit, exerting pressure on the major leg arteries and restricting blood flow. The Fleet Air Arm conducted operational trials of this suit during the invasion of North Africa in 1943, with good results. As far as the navy was concerned, an additional benefit was that the suit also offered 2 gallons of fresh drinking water which increased the survival chances of a pilot forced to ditch at sea. Research continued, and after the Second World War, water-filled suits yielded to G- Suits that used air-inflated rubber bladders. (See also **Gee; to Black Out**) [Ref: Greer and Harold]

GUARD — The word "guard" has two meanings relevant to military aviation:

(1)   **Guard** (aviation general) refers to either of two radio frequencies reserved by international agreement for distress calls. These frequencies are 121.5 Khz (VHF) and 243 Mhz (UHF), and are called "Guard Frequencies" because aviators and mariners are required to maintain a radio watch (ie., to "guard") these frequencies and to report any persons, aircraft or vessels in distress.

> *Did you hear that Mayday?*
> *No, but we'll monitor Guard Frequency more closely.*

(2)   **Guard** (chiefly American, though much CF usage) is short for either of two elements of the United States reserve forces: the Army National Guard, or the Air National Guard. In contrast to the benign neglect shown Canadian air reserve forces since 1960, the United States has overcome the inherent time limits placed on reservists and built its air reserves into effective combat forces. The Air National Guard is one element of U.S. air reserve forces, and its units operate aircraft as demanding as the F-16, and as large and complex as the C5B Galaxy. Additionally, Army Guard aviation units fly the same range of

helicopters flown by the regular U.S. Army, including Chinooks and Apache gunships. Air National Guard units contribute most of the manned interceptors controlled by NORAD, and as such, cooperate closely with the regular Canadian fighter squadrons performing the same task. "Guard" flying units flew in combat both in Viet Nam and in the Gulf War.

You could fit all Canadian air force reservists in two Air Guard C-5A's!

GUINEA PIG CLUB (Commonwealth Air Forces; WWII) — The Guinea Pig Club is a very exclusive fraternity. Membership is limited to Second World War allied aircrew who were seriously disfigured by fire in an aircraft crash or bail-out and who were treated at the Plastic Surgery Unit, at Queen Victoria Hospital, at East Grinstead in Sussex, England. This hospital was headed by Dr. Archibald McIndoe.

The club is formally constituted, still active, and its name was chosen by its members. It has three categories of membership: the "Guinea Pigs" themselves, the "Scientists" (medical, nursing, and therapy staff), and the "Royal Society for the Prevention of Cruelty to Guinea Pigs" (friends and benefactors of the Guinea Pigs).

The Guinea Pig Club has its origins in a Sunday morning hangover. In the morning of Sunday July 20th, 1941, most of Ward III at the East Grinstead hospital was suffering from a hangover earned on the Saturday night prior. While enduring the headaches on Sunday morning, the patients - young, aggressive, intelligent, and otherwise fit airmen - decided to form a *Grogging Club called The Maxillonian Club, whose members call themselves Guinea Pigs.*

Guinea Pig Club badge

The "Guinea Pigs" numbered 590, of whom 170 were Canadian. The high proportion of Canadians, a tragic aspect of the magnitude of Canada's participation in wartime flying, led to the establishment of a Canadian Wing in the hospital, run by an RCAF surgeon, Wing Commander Ross Tilley.

That the club still exists 50 years after the end of the Second World War is testimony to the efforts of the medical team, led by Dr. McIndoe. Many advances in burn treatment technique were pioneered at the Plastic Surgery Unit. Dr. McIndoe judged that repairing and restoring severely burned tissue could best be accomplished in a hospital regimen that restored the self-esteem and confidence of the patients, usually fit, intelligent young men in their twenties. That his goal was attained is borne out by the "anthem" of The Guinea Pig Club.

(tune: *The Church's One Foundation*)

We are McIndoe's Army,
We are his Guinea Pigs,
With dermatomes and pedicles,

We'll shout with all our might:
"Per Ardua ad Astra!"
We'd rather drink than fight!

John Hunter runs the Gasworks,
Ross Tilley wields the Knife,
And if they are not careful,
They'll have your flaming life,
So Guinea Pigs stand steady,
For all your Surgeon's calls;
And if their hands aren't steady
They'll whip off your _____!

We've had some mad Australians,
Some French, some Czech, some Poles.
We've even had some Yankees,
God Bless their precious souls.
While as for Canadians
Ah, that's a different thing.
They couldn't stand our accent
And built a separate Wing!

(See also **Airman's Burns**) [Ref: Bishop]

GUN, TO GIVE IT THE (WWI) — Since the First World War, the phrase "to give it the gun" has meant "to advance the throttle", and implies flying faster.

GUN PLUMBER — "Gun Plumber" is slang for an "armourer", the groundcrew technician responsible for maintaining aircraft guns and cannon, and for the care and custody of munitions. Of all the ground crew trades, armourers have perhaps the most liberal attitude towards military discipline - thus explaining why they need their own Patron Saint: St. Barbara, the Patron Saint of Gunners and Armourers. (In the Army, a Gun Plumber was the RCEME technician who took care of large artillery pieces, as opposed to the armourers who cared for small arms) (See also **Plumber**)

GUPPY (RCAF; WWII) — "Guppy" was occasional slang for a member of the CWAAF, the Canadian Women's Auxiliary Air Force. The CWAAF was established in 1940, but was soon re-titled the RCAF Women's Division. The origin of the nickname is unknown. (See **WAAF, W.D.**) [Ref: Berrey and Van Den Bark]

GYPPO (pronounced "jip-owe") (British Commonwealth military since 1900's) — A "Gyppo" is an Egyptian. [Ref: Partridge (FS)]

GYPPO LINE (CF Europe; since 1967) — A "Gyppo Line" was a group of aircraft lined up neatly, wingtip to wingtip. The phrase was common among airmen and airwomen on the CF-104 or CF-18 squadrons based at CFB Baden-Sollingen, in Germany, even though parking aircraft this way was the exception rather than the rule at European NATO bases.

Most aircraft were dispersed, or stored in a maintenance hangar or within hardened elements. However at Baden-Soellingen, whenever it became necessary to park aircraft outside, in a row, they were said to be in a Gyppo Line.

The term Gyppo Line was apparently coined after the 1967 "Seven-Day War", in which the Israeli Air Force destroyed the Egyptian Air Force on the ground. The Egyptians - nicknamed "Gyppos" in the Commonwealth - had made the mistake of not dispersing their aircraft; instead Egyptian aircraft were parked in neat rows, making an easy target for the marauding Israelis. Therefore the term Gyppo Line described a group of aircraft neatly lined up, wingtip to wingtip. (See also **Dispersal; H.A.S.**)

421 Squadron has three aircraft out on the Gyppo Line.

Gun Plumber

Armourers, or Gun Plumbers,
remain a breed apart.

OTEL

H2S (RAF, RCAF; WW2) — H2S was a radar navigation system developed by the RAF to guide bombers to their targets during the Second World War. The success of Bomber Command's night bombing operations depended on accurate navigation. However, the blackout, and the need to maintain radio silence made visual long-range navigation at night very difficult. At the direction of Air Chief Marshal "Bomber" Harris, Air Ministry scientific advisors began to develop long-range navigation systems. H2S was one such system.

H2S, a precursor of today's terrain-mapping radar, comprised a radar transmitter and receiver mounted in the bottom of the aircraft, both aimed downwards which provided the navigator with a radar "map" of the ground below. In an H2S-equipped bomber, there were two navigators, the customary "Routine Navigator" and a new "Radar Navigator". The Radar Navigator used the H2S and cross-checked the "radar map" that it produced against the course plotted by the routine navigator. By today's standards H2S was very crude, but it was the precursor of later, more sophisticated systems.

Two competing explanations exist for the origins of the "H2S" codename. One explanation suggests it was coined from the phrase: "Height to Surface" (ie., Height- 2-Surface, or H-2-S). Another suggests that it came from the phrase "Home, Sweet Home", whose initials contain two of the letters "H", and one letter "S", for "H2S". Either way, "H2S" became the official code word. Coincidentally, H2S is the chemical symbol for Hydrogen Sulfide (or "sour gas"), a chemical remarkable for its foul smell. So the H2S system also came to be known as "Stinky", and bombers equipped with H2S were referred to by ground radar controllers as "stinky bombers". Therefore, the resulting nickname: "Stinky". [Ref: Messenger]

Navigator, What's our position?
...according to the H2S, we're just approaching the Rhine river.

HACK — The word hack has three meanings relevant to military aviation:

(1) **Hack** (Noun) (since WW2) A "hack" is an aircraft used for liaison, or training. When resources allowed, squadrons and bases were given a light transport or training aircraft to allow the unit to conduct its own routine transport, or training. For example, a Sabre squadron of the 1950's might have a T-33 trainer on its establishment. A Second World War RCAF bomber squadron might have an "Oxford" twin engine transport assigned to it. After RCAF Squadrons began to deploy to Europe after D-Day in 1944, an amazing variety of aircraft were unofficially "acquired" for use as a squadron "hack". Perhaps the most outrageous case was the RCAF squadron that appropriated, repaired and operated its own Junkers 52 transport formerly owned by the Luftwaffe (after prudently applying Allied insignia, of course!) [Ref: Milberry]

(2)   **Hack, to** (verb) (current): to be able to cope, endure or prevail.

(3)   **Hack, to** (verb) (current): To set or adjust an instrument. For example, "to hack" a watch, is to set it so that it precisely matches another timepiece (ie., this is a "time hack"). Similarly, a "compass hack" is to adjust an aircraft's directional gyroscope so that it is aligned precisely with the aircraft compass.

HACK DOWN, TO (RAF; WW2) — During the Second World War, to hack down an aircraft was to shoot it down. The term borrowed from Rugby football slang of the day, where to tackle an opponent was "to hack" him down. [Ref: Partridge (8th)]

Squadron Leader Hauser hacked down another '109 this morning!

HAD IT, TO HAVE (originally RAF; now common usage) — "To have had it" means "to have met one's demise", either literally or figuratively. Now common usage, this phrase had its origins in the RAF. [Ref: Partridge (FS)]

HALLY; HALLYBAG (RAF, RCAF; WW2) — "Hally" and "Hallybag" were both nicknames for the "Halifax" a four-engine heavy bomber that, along with the Lancaster, was a principal weapon in Bomber Command's night campaign against Germany. Fifteen RCAF Squadrons flew the "Hally". The nickname "Hallybag" may have been adapted from "Stringbag", the nickname for the Swordfish Torpedo-Bomber.

Built by Handley-Page, the Halifax suffered from a poor reputation early in its operational history, the result of difficulty in maintaining service altitude. However, after receiving modifications and new radial engines, the Halifax earned an honourable place in Bomber Command history. Though designed as a heavy bomber, the Hally was also used in maritime patrol. It was also employed in a variety of other less-known roles, such as surreptitiously dropping allied secret agents into Europe and towing gliders into France on D-Day. (See **Stringbag**) [Refs: Harvey; Partridge (8th)]

The Hally developed into a great airplane, even if it didn't have the mystique of the Lancaster.

HALLYBASHER (RAF, RCAF; WW2) — A "Hallybasher" was a member of a squadron that flew the "Halifax" bomber, during the Second World War. The term is a conjunction of the word "Hally", nickname for the Halifax, and "basher", a generic term for a technician. It would appear though, that the term "Hallybasher" was not limited to groundcrew. (See **Basher**)

What kind of aircraft do you fly, then?
Me? I'm a Hallybasher!

HANDRAULICS (CF; current since WW2) — "Handraulics" is a conjunction of the words "hand" and "hydraulics". It alludes to getting things done "by hand" and, by implication, in a more difficult way than need be. The suggestion is that one uses one's hands rather than labour-saving devices such as, for example, hydraulics. [Ref: Partridge (FS)]

Well, we've lost our computer, so I guess we'll have to do things by handraulics...

HANG A RAT, TO (RCAF, CF; to early 1980's) — Among CF-104 Starfighter pilots and groundcrew "to hang a rat" was vernacular for deploying the "Ram Air Turbine" (abbreviated "RAT"). The Ram Air Turbine was a small generator that provided emergency electricity on the CF-104 should it suffer a total loss of electrical power in flight. The generator was located on a small mount, normally stowed within the airframe, but which was deployed into the slipstream during emergencies. The slipstream rotated a tiny propeller mounted on the generator, which in turn caused the generator to create electrical current.

This use of the phrase "to hang a rat" is not to be confused with its other current usage (ie., a male urinating is said to be "hanging a rat").

The Starfighter lost its electrical system, so the pilot had to hang a rat!

HANGAR QUEEN (general aviation usage; probably American in origin) — A "Hangar Queen" is an aircraft that spends most, if not all, of its time, in a hangar being worked on by technicians, either because it is extremely prone to breakdown, or because it is being used as a permanent source of spare parts. A Hangar Queen "reigns" over the hangar - that is, it never leaves.

HANGARETTE   See **H.A.S.**

HANGAR LINE   See **Flight Line**

HANG-UP, TO (military aviation; general) — Whenever an aircraft-mounted rocket, bomb, or missile has failed to clear the aircraft after the crew has released it or launched it, it is said to be "hung-up". The term suggests that the weapon is not safely attached to the airframe, it just hangs there. If this occurs, the aircraft must land and is parked far away from other facilities. Then the armourers and explosive ordnance disposal (EOD) people render the munition safe.

A '104 is landing with a hung-up 500-pounder.

HAPPY VALLEY (RAF Bomber Command; WW2) — Among Bomber Command crews during the Second World War, "Happy Valley" was Germany's Ruhr River valley. Many of Germany's great industrial cities were located in the Ruhr valley, and consequently were subject to heavy Allied bomber raids. Unsurprisingly, cities in the Happy Valley were very well-defended by the German flak batteries that accounted for so many allied bombers. So, the term Happy Valley was nothing if not darkly ironic. [Refs: Harvey; Partridge (FS)]

Gentlemen, our target for tonight once again is Happy Valley!

HARLEY BUCKLE (RCAF, CF; still current) — The "Harley Buckle" was one of thousands of anonymous aircraft parts and it would have remained anonymous - except that it was occasionally the cause of a very embarrassing moment for fighter aircrew. So, it achieved a prominence that it would not have otherwise had. The Harley Buckle was a fitting on an aircraft's ejection seat to which the occupant's parachute release lanyard remained fastened during flight. The idea was that the person would not have to worry about opening the parachute himself during an ejection from the aircraft. The ripcord

Harley Buckle

Forgetting to release the
Harley Buckle could be
embarrassing.

would be pulled automatically when the ejection seat and the occupant parted ways in the air!

However, when the flight was over, you had to remember to unhook the Harley Buckle before standing up to leave the cockpit! If one stood up in the cockpit without first unhooking the parachute lanyard from the Harley Buckle, *there is a short pause, followed by a "POP!", followed by an armful of laundry* as the parachute opens in the cockpit. This blunder is extraordinarily difficult to shrug off, particularly if the forgetful one is a veteran airman who should have known better! Forgetting to uncouple the Harley Buckle was usually good for a mandatory donation to the Safety Equipment Section's "Rumble Fund", because the Safety Equipment Section now had to re-pack the parachute for no good reason. (See also **T-Bird**) [Ref: Sutherland]

> *Now Craig, this time don't forget to undo your Harley Buckle before you get out of the cockpit!*

HARRY TATE; 'ARRY TATE (RFC, WW1) — Harry Tate is Cockney "rhyming slang" for the "RE-8" (ie., "Harry Tate", or "'arry Tate") an aircraft formally known as the "Reconnaissance Experimental No. 8". The aircraft was christened the Harry Tate (or 'arry Tate) after the rising fame of a London music hall entertainer named Harry Tate.

The 'arry Tate was a slow, two-seat biplane reconnaissance aircraft used by the Royal Flying Corps during the First World War. The primary purpose of the RFC was to provide reconnaissance for the ground troops. The well-chronicled exploits of the fighter pilots all served only to protect aircraft like the RE-8, so they could continue their photography, artillery-spotting, and low-level contact missions with the army. It took great courage to be the pilot or observer of the Harry Tate, as the following passage illustrates:

> *"Plodding in performance and sluggish in manoeuvrability, the RE-8 was no real match for the sleek Fokkers and Albatros Scouts of 1917-18, and its crews suffered high casualty rates. Yet one of the commonest sights of the aerial war in 1918 was of lone RE-8's doggedly flying monotonous figures-of-eight paths through a flurry of anti-aircraft shell-bursts as their courageous crews maintained faith with the earthbound infantry they were supporting."*

The Harry Tate was unusual in that it had both a longitudinal and a lateral dihedral, which led to its other nickname: "the Rigger's Nightmare". (See **Rigger**) [Ref: Bowyer/Turner, p. 16]

H.A.S. (pronounced "haz")(NATO general) — "H.A.S." is a "Hardened Aircraft Shelter", a small reinforced concrete hangar, designed to protect a single aircraft from attack. Occasionally, a H.A.S. was called a "hangarette".

> *Normally we put one Starfighter into a H.A.S., but in an emergency, we could get two inside!*

HASSLE; HASSLE, TO (NATO general; originally US) — Among military aviators, "to hassle" is to engage in air combat; Therefore, an air fight is "a hassle".

> *We hassled with a section of CF-5's this morning.*

HATLESS TAP-DANCE (CF; probably Army in origin) — The "Hatless Tap-Dance" is a

Hatless Tap-dance

"charge parade", that is, the process of formally "marching in" a servicemember, charged with a service offence, to a hearing before the Commanding Officer.

Though legally informal, in terms of military protocol, this "Charge Parade" is very formal indeed! The miscreant, between two escorts, marches into the office of the Commanding Officer, under the command of a Warrant Officer. Traditionally, the Warrant Officer shouts his drill commands as loudly as if he were outside on parade, no matter how small the office. Within his office, the Commanding Officer is seated at a desk, rather like a magistrate. All present wear dress uniform with caps (except the accused who wears no cap at all; hence the word "hatless").

The unlucky fellow and his escorts march to a position in front of the Commanding Officer's desk, and "mark time" (ie., they march in place; hence the reference to the "tap dance"). Once halted, the Warrant Officer, acting now as a Court Clerk, reads the Charge, and a small hearing occurs. A "Charge Parade" is normally used to deal with petty, disciplinary offences, with the aim of promoting and enforcing discipline. More serious offences are dealt with in a court-martial.

HAVING ONE'S EARS LOWERED (CF; current) — To "have one's ears lowered" is to have a haircut. (See also **I'm Going To Get My Head Sharpened**)

HEAD SHED (RCAF, CF; since at least WW2) — "Head Shed" is generic air force slang for a headquarters, as in: *Tracy has been posted up to the head shed.* [Ref: Harvey]

HEADACHES (RAF; WW2) — To an RAF radar controller of the Second World War, "headaches" was a codeword for to two types of radio signals generated by the Luftwaffe. These signals, called the "knickebein" system and the "X-Beam" system, guided German bombers to targets in Britain. The Allied jamming systems used to counteract headaches were, perhaps unsurprisingly, codenamed "Aspirin" and "Bromide". These German signals and their British equivalents, were the predecessors of modern ground-based air navigation beacons. [Ref: Jones]

HEADS UP, A (CF; current) — A "heads-up" is a warning, or advance notice of a future issue or problem.

Headquarters just sent us this heads-up!

HEATSEEKER (military aviation; since 1950's) — "Heatseeker" is the common term for an air-to-air missile that senses the heat generated by the target itself, and uses this to guide itself to the target. Heat sources, such as a jet engine exhaust, generate infrared energy. The heatseeker is designed to manoeuvre towards an intense source of infrared energy.

HEAVY (aviation general) — A "heavy" is a large aircraft. For example, during the Second World War, the term heavy referred to four-engine bombers such as the Avro Lancaster, with a gross weight of 63,000 pounds. Today, in air traffic control parlance, a heavy is an aircraft weighing over 300,000 pounds, a far cry from a Second World War heavy.

It isn't as easy to fly a heavy as you might think!

"HE'LL TAKE OFF ANY MINUTE NOW!" (RAF; since 1938) — This stock catch-phrase is the response of an impassive observer to a person "in a flap". In air force slang a "flap" is a situation of great concern, or loss of control. (See **Flap; to Fly In Ever Decreasing Circles**) [Ref: Partridge-Catchphrases]

Look at Flight Sergeant Lamarche get angry! He'll take off any minute now!

HELLYER'S CORPORAL (CF; 1969 to late 1970's) — A "Hellyer's Corporal" was a person promoted to Corporal after the promotion pre-requisites were lowered on October 1st 1966, by order of the Minister of National Defence, Paul Hellyer. In the mid-1960's, a Minister's Manpower Study, chaired by Commodore Ralph Hennessy, had concluded that military pay rates had fallen seriously behind inflation and recommended that they be raised, especially for junior ranks. However, the Treasury Board did not approve. Thus, it was decided within the Department of National Defence that the only way to raise the pay of the junior ranks was to promote them, and plans were laid to lower the promotion pre-requisites for the rank of Corporal in the army and RCAF (and its naval equivalent).

The army did not immediately agree however, and insisted that a new level be created in the chain of command - the "Master Corporal" - before its support was given. The government could not arbitrarily create a new Master Corporal rank; this required an amendment to the National Defence Act and Parliament would have to approve. Parliamentary approval was made unnecessary when it was decided that the Master Corporal would not be a "rank", rather it would be an "appointment", the creation of which was within ministerial authority. The army got their Master Corporals - and all the privates, ordinary seamen and Leading Aircraftmen were promoted to Corporal in 1966 so they could receive higher Corporal's pay.

For a time, confusion reigned supreme in the lower end of the military chain of command. Before this, an RCAF Corporal was a skilled supervisor; afterward, a Corporal was just another journeyman. All this severely diminished a Corporal's authority. It was a particularly bitter pill for those who were already Corporals (who referred to themselves as "real" Corporals or "Queen's" Corporals, as distinct from "Hellyer's" Corporals).

As if this were not enough, the rules regarding this new Master Corporal appointment were inconsistent; the army got the Master Corporal appointment almost immediately, while the RCAF and the Navy waited for two years to nominate people to this rank. Even when air force Master Corporals appeared, the eligibility and selection were delegated to individual bases which, unfortunately used different criteria! Some bases selected its Master Corporals on seniority, others on merit, and still others rotated the appointment between all Corporals!

Though not part of the unification of the Canadian Forces, the creation of Hellyer's Corporals took place at the same time. Consequently Hellyer's Corporals have been identified with the turmoil and loss of morale during and after unification. Indeed some believed that creation of all these new Hellyer's Corporals was merely a subterfuge intended to prevent an exodus of Junior Ranks disaffected by unification.

Ultimately the selection of Master Corporals became a matter for service-wide promotion boards, and the mess was cleared up. The rank of Master Corporal has been in the chain of command for nearly thirty years and though it has been the subject of debate, its future appears secure. Today, a CF Master Corporal performs the duties once performed by an RCAF Corporal. (See **M-Slash**) [Ref: Sutherland]

> *...and when were you promoted to Corporal?*
> *1967*
> *...ahhh, you're just a bloody Hellyer's Corporal, then!*

HELMET FIRE (CF, current) — A pilot who has a "helmet fire" is experiencing serious concern, or panic. The term alludes to the various other types of fire that an aviator might expect, such as an "electrical fire", "engine fire", "oxygen fire", etc. It evokes an image of heat generated by the brain as the pilot tries to cope with an emergency.

Helmet Fire

> *When I saw that bird flying straight towards the cockpit, I had a helmet fire! Luckily the bird missed us!*

HENHOUSE   See **Waffery**

HERBIE (CF to 1960's; originally Army) — A "Herbie" was a recruit, or alternately, an unusually slovenly and dim-witted servicemember. This nickname derived from *Herbie*, a very popular cartoon character published in *The Maple Leaf*, the Canadian Army newspaper of the Second World War.

HERC; HERK; HERKY BIRD (universal aviation usage; current) — "Herc", "Herk", and "Herky Bird" are nicknames for the Lockheed C-130 Hercules, perhaps the most successful transport aircraft designed in the latter half of the Twentieth Century. During the 1950's, when most air forces still relied on the Douglas DC-3 for airlift, the USAF announced a requirement for a fast, heavy transport, capable of carrying cargo or passengers over distances as far as 4700 miles, and which could also operate from rough, unprepared airfields. Lockheed conceived the Herk in 1951 to satisfy these needs: its four engines are mounted on a high wing to keep the propellers and intakes above rocks and gravel; it has a tail ramp, which allows cargo to be driven directly on or off; and it has ample power. The Herk entered USAF service in 1956, and the RCAF first obtained C-130 Hercules aircraft in the early 1960's. The type will remain in service well into the 21st Century.

HERO SHOT (CF; current) — A "Hero Shot" is a portrait photograph of an airman (subjects are invariably post-adolescent male pilots) in front of his aircraft. The pose usually suggests an aviator who is humbly aware that he is irresistibly handsome and has the "right stuff". (See also **I-love-me-wall**)

H-HUT (CF since WW2) — An "H-Hut" is any building that is laid out like the letter "H". The H-Hut has been common in Canadian military architecture since the Second World War, and it is amazing how many "temporary" Second World War H-Huts remain in use a half-century later.

Our new quarters are in the H-Huts across the road.

HIGH-PRICED HELP (CF; current) — The "high-priced help" are senior officers, as in: *Get your feet off the desk, I hear the high-priced help coming down the hall!*

HOLE, THE (RCAF, CF; since 1950's) — Undoubtedly, airmen and airwomen will have seen many "holes" during their military service. Still, only one place seems to have earned the honour of being known as "The Hole". This is the underground air defence command and control complex at North Bay, Ontario.

The Hole is a series of large manmade caverns carved from the pre-cambrian rock of the Canadian Shield near North Bay, Ontario. It was created in the 1950's to shelter a regional North American Air Defence (NORAD) command and control centre. From the Hole, senior NORAD commanders would direct the air battle in case of attack on North America by air. Today, it contains the command and control elements of all Canadian elements of the NORAD system. The Hole was carved from solid rock to ensure its surviveability in case of even a nuclear attack. Thankfully, this has not been tested.

I work in the Hole...
Well, that explains why you don't have a sun tan!

HOLY COW, THE (CF; current) — "Holy Cow" was the occasional nickname for the Boeing 707 transport aircraft, as flown by the CF since 1970. The term probably arose because a 707 arriving at a CF base during a scheduled passenger run generally enjoys priority for maintenance and fuel over other aircraft. Thus, like a cow in Hindu-dominated India, it enjoys the ability to go anywhere and do anything it wants! As applied to aircraft, the term was probably borrowed from the United States. "Holy Cow" was the nickname of an aircraft used to fly the President of the U.S. (before the codeword "Air Force One" was adopted).

We can forget about getting fuel while the Holy Cow is refuelling.

HONK BAG (aviation general) — A "honk bag" is an airsick bag, from the fact that "to vomit" is "to honk". Though many people (including aircrew) get airsick, there are proprieties to be observed - the most important is to not foul the airplane. Consequently one uses a honk bag if one has to. Failing this, one uses one's hat, gloves, etc., - anything but fouling the airplane. Honk bags are distributed liberally throughout aircraft, and are handy for a variety of other uses, such as refuse containers, notepaper for calculating weight and balance data, or for jotting down one's will.

God help you, if you get sick in my aircraft and don't use a honk bag!

HOOKS (CF current) — A "hook" is a chevron, as worn by Corporals and Sergeants to show rank. The term derives from the appearance of the chevron, which roughly resembles a hook. (See also **Count the Hooks**)

Congratulations on getting your second hook, Corporal!

HOOPS (CF current) — A "hoop" is to officers what a "hook" is to a sergeant or a corporal, that is, a single stripe of officer's rank braid. It is called a hoop because a stripe of rank braid is, effectively, a loop of fabric sewn around the lower sleeve, roughly a "hoop". (See also **Count the Hooks**)

Congratulations on getting your second hoop, Captain!

HOP THE TWIG, TO (RCAF; WW2) — In the Flying Training Schools of the British Commonwealth Air Training Plan, to have "hopped the twig" was a euphemism for suffering a fatal aircraft accident. The origins of this phrase are obscure, though it has been a synonym for sudden departure as far back as 1800. It certainly seems to suggest a baby bird falling off a branch. (See also **Go for a Burton; Gone West; Buy it; Auger in**) [Ref: Partridge (8th)]

It looks like we're all going to another funeral parade. Ted hopped the twig yesterday...

HORSE (RCN; 1950's and 60's) — "Horse" was the nickname for the navy helicopter designated the HO4S. The nickname Horse was adapted from its designation: "H-O-four-S".

Built by Sikorsky, the Horse was operated from the aircraft carriers Magnificent and Bonaventure. Its most important role was as "plane guard", the rescue of sailors or aviators in the water. In this role it became known by its radio codename: "Pedro". In its land-based rescue role, operating from the Naval Air Station at Shearwater, it was known as "Angel", and achieved a great prestige among East Coast mariners, whether RCN, merchant marine, fishermen or yachtsmen. Later the Horse was used in anti-submarine warfare, until replaced by the Sikorsky Sea King. (See also **Sea Thing**)

HOT MIKE (aviation, general) — A "hot mike" is an intercom microphone that is continuously turned on, that is, the crewmember does not need to manually push a "transmit" button before speaking. This is very convenient, though unfortunately, it also means that other crewmembers must continuously hear each other breathing and burping through their earphones.

HOUSEWIFE (RCAF; to 1960's) — Every airman in the RCAF was issued with a "housewife", that is, a small sewing kit used to effect minor repairs to one's uniform. [Ref: Peden]

My sock needs darning. Pass over my Housewife, will you?

HUD (military aviation; general) — "HUD" is the acronym for "Heads Up Display", a unique electro-optical system that enables a pilot to read vital aircraft instruments while still maintaining a watch outside the aircraft. The HUD projects aircraft instrument readings, gunsights, or bombsights onto a clear glass plate in front of the pilot. This enables the pilot to keep an eye out on events outside the aircraft while still obtaining critical aircraft information. Without the HUD, a pilot would have to continuously shift his gaze from outside the aircraft, to within, and outside again, shifting eye focus each time and losing precious seconds of time.

In the early 1990's however, the nickname "the Hud" was also used by personnel serving in Air Command Headquarters to refer to Lieutenant General D. Huddleston, Commander of Air Command from 1991 to 1993.

HUG AND SLUG (CF; current) — "Hug and Slug" is a generic term for any bar where "action" is to be found, be it amorous or pugilistic. However, in the CF, if there is any one Hug and Slug, it is the Army, Navy and Air Force Veteran's Club in Barrie, Ontario, just down the highway from CFB Borden. It is a gentle establishment, popular among predatory females "out on the town". Senior NCO's temporarily stationed at Borden seem to be their favourite prey.

If you haven't been to the Hug and Slug, you haven't been to Borden!

HULK (general usage) — In aviation, as in marine shipping, a "hulk" is an aircraft reduced to little more than its frame by damage, age or cannibalization.

Even in its sorry state, a hulk can be useful in training firefighters in aircraft crash rescue techniques. A dummy is placed inside the hulk, the fuselage is set afire, and the Firefighters, wearing their "Fearnaught Suits", fight the fire and rescue the dummy as fast as possible. Generally a hulk can stand repeated torchings, which is useful, as Firefighters regularly train in this hazardous operation. (The unofficial motto of the CF Fire Academy is: *Lurn or Burn*) (See also **Fearnaught Suit**)

HUN (British Commonwealth; WW1 and WW2) — "Hun" was the common, bitter epithet for Germans, and was commonly used by Allied personnel in both World Wars. The word Hun suggests invaders from the east.

I hear the Hun has a new version of the Messerschmitt 109 in service.

HUNGRY LIZ (RFC; WW1) — "Hungry Liz" was First World War aviator's slang for the ambulance which was invariably called to the scene of a crash. The origins of the term are unclear; one wonders whether it had anything to do with "tin lizzie", early automotive slang. The word "hungry" seems to imply that the ambulance is hungry for more occupants. (See also **Meatwagon**) [Ref: Voss]

HURRICAT (RAF; Merchant Navy; WW2)

A "Hurricat" is a Hawker "Hurricane" fighter aircraft, launched by a rocket catapult from a "Catapult-Armed Merchantman" for convoy air defence. The Catapult-Armed Merchantman was a merchant ship specially modified early during the Second World War, to carry a single Hurricane fighter aircraft launched by rocket catapult. The word Hurricat is a conjunction of "Hurricane" and "Catapult".

Allied convoys sailing from Britain to the Soviet port of Murmansk and back suffered

Hungry Liz

Hungry Liz sat waiting
beside the airfield.

great losses to the Luftwaffe Focke-Wulf 200 "Condor" aircraft, based in Norway. The Condor, a four-engine patrol bomber with long endurance, struck Allied convoys well beyond the protection of land-based Allied fighters. Due to the shortage of aircraft carriers to provide defensive fighter cover, the Catapult Armed Merchantman was developed as a stopgap. These ships mounted a rocket catapult to launch a modified Hawker Hurricane fighter, nicknamed a Hurricat, on a one-way trip. When a Focke-Wulf 200 was sighted, the lone pilot climbed into the Hurricane, started the engine, and was rocketed off the ship into flight. The Hurricat then engaged the bomber and returned to the convoy.

However, there was no place for the Hurricat to land, so every flight ended with the pilot "ditching" into the sea! After ditching, an escort vessel would fish the Hurricat pilot from the water, though realistically, in the cold arctic seas, survival chances were slim. It was felt that even if only one ship was saved, it was worth the loss of the aircraft. The Hurricat and the C.A.M. were phased out - to no ones' disappointment - when escort carriers became available. (See also **Cat (1), Hurry, Woolworth Carrier**)

The only good thing about being a Hurricat pilot is that you don't have to
worry about lowering the undercarriage...

HURRY; HURRYBACK; HURRIBIRD; HURRIBUSTER (RAF; WW2) — "Hurry", "Hurryback", "Hurribird" and "Hurribuster" are all nicknames for the Hawker Hurricane, the mainstay of RAF Fighter Command for the first two years of the Second World War. The Hurricane first flew in 1935 and was a product of the superb Hawker

Hurry

LANGESTE

design team led by Sidney Camm. It was the RAF's first modern monoplane fighter, and was the first to carry eight guns. The Hurricane was slightly slower and less manoeuvrable than its more glamourous partner, the Spitfire, but was very sturdy and could absorb much damage. Indeed, in the Battle of Britain, Hurricanes accounted for 80% of the RAF's victories over the Luftwaffe. At the outbreak of the Second World War, the RCAF's No. 1 (Fighter) Squadron was equipped with Hurricanes, which it flew in the Battle of Britain. (No. 1 Squadron was the only RCAF Squadron to fight in the Battle of Britain, though many other Canadians fought in RAF squadrons, most notably in Douglas Bader's 242 Squadron.) Gradually supplanted by the Spitfire, the "Hurry" was relegated to second-line units, though it did make a fine name for itself in the North African campaign as a tank destroyer. It equipped several Royal Navy squadrons as well.

Approximately 14,000 Hurricanes were built, about ten percent of which were constructed in Canada. [Ref: Harvey, Partridge (8th)]

Brian flies a Hurry with 402 Squadron.

HURRYBOY (RAF, RCAF; WW2) — "Hurryboy" was the nickname for a pilot who flew the Hawker Hurricane, which occasionally bore the nickname: "Hurry". [Ref: Partridge (FS)]

HUSH-HUSH (since WW2) — Something is "Hush-Hush" if it is an official secret.

NDIA

IC (pronounced "eye-see")(CF, general) — An IC is the aircraft intercom, as in: *The IC is busted!*

i/c (pronounced "eye-see")(CF, current) — "i/c" is the abbreviation for: "in command" or "in charge". From this comes the following:

O i/c (ie., "owe eye-see"):	Officer in Command
NCO i/c:	Non-Commissioned Officer in Charge
2 i/c:	Second in Command
3 i/c:	Third in Command

Who's i/c around here?
He's on leave, sir.
Well then, who's the 2 i/c?!

"I COULD TELL YOU, BUT THEN I'D HAVE TO SHOOT YOU!" (CF, current) — *I could tell you, but then I'd have to shoot you!* is the blithely evasive reply to a question that one is not inclined to answer for reasons of confidentiality or security. Occasionally such a question is asked innocently, and the answer cannot be revealed for security reasons. So, rather than be impolite or evasive, a person faced with such a question will often jokingly reply *I could tell you, but then I'd have to shoot you!* It is an "off the wall" reply that alludes to security, though with humour.

However, this reply used as frequently in situations where the question isn't sensitive at all; the person replying simply has no idea of the answer.

Where did that Aurora go on patrol?
I could tell you, but then I'd have to shoot you!

IDIOT LIGHT (aviation; current) — "Idiot Light" is aviation vernacular for an "annunciator light", or "warning light". The origins of the term are lost, though it seems to suggest that the aircraft is saying: *Hey, idiot! Pay attention! I'm broken!*

Aircraft, like automobiles, have warning lights that visually signal a technical malfunction. For example, if the electrical generator fails, the words GENERATOR FAILURE would illuminate on a small panel. Such a light may be accompanied by a warning buzzer or horn. As well, in modern aircraft, the pilot may hear a prerecorded voice, advising of the system failure. (See also **Bitchin' Betty**)

If the Idiot Light illuminates, you've got a problem.

IFF (pronounced "eye-eff-eff") (military aviation; universal) — IFF means "Identification - Friend or Foe". Military aircraft are equipped with an electronic system called IFF that distinguishes them from enemy aircraft on radar, in combat.

It is very difficult, if not impossible, to use radar alone to distinguish friendly aircraft from enemy aircraft. Therefore in combat, each friendly aircraft will have an IFF set on board. When this aircraft is tracked by friendly radar, its IFF automatically transmits a secret coded signal displayed on the radar screen. This signal identifies the aircraft to the radar operator as friendly. If the aircraft has no IFF, or if the wrong coded signal is sent, that aircraft is assumed to be an enemy aircraft. IFF is very similar to the "transponder" used by civil aircraft to distinguish one aircraft from another on a crowded Air Traffic Controller's radar screen.

These IFF codes can be changed on the ground by Radar Technicians and are a closely guarded secret. An enemy that had discovered our own IFF codes could enter friendly airspace, without anyone realizing they were hostile until the bombs began to fall!

"IF I STICK A BROOM UP MY ARSE, I CAN SWEEP THE HANGAR AT THE SAME TIME!" (RAF since circa 1925) — This phrase was apparently a stock catch-phrase once common in the RAF. It was the favourite oath of airmen who had been assigned a never-ending series of menial tasks around the hangar. The implication is that the poor airman must cross the hangar floor so often that he could clean the floor simply by taking the advice offered by the phrase! (Ref: Partridge - Catchphrases)

IFR (pronounced "eye-eff-are") (aviation, general) — IFR is the abbreviation for "Instrument Flight Rules", standard procedures used when flying without visual reference to the ground. The term is also used as an adjective, to describe the weather conditions requiring reliance on instruments, as in: *We were flying in IFR conditions...* A spurious definition was once coined; IFR was said to be the abbreviation for "I Fly Railroads". "Flying a Railroad" was the early practice of navigating, not with a map, but by following well-known railroad lines. (See also **Iron Compass**)

"IF YOU CAN'T TAKE A JOKE, YOU SHOULDN'T HAVE JOINED!" (since at least WWII; current CF) — *If you can't take a joke, you shouldn't have joined!* is a fairly common response to anyone complaining about military life. It is also a reflective comment about any military absurdity that one happens to be encountering. So, if the military transport aircraft stops at Trenton when it should have gone on to Halifax, a passenger might comment: *Well, if you can't take a joke, you shouldn't have joined.* (See also **It's all pensionable time**) [Ref: Partridge (8th)]

> *This exercise sounds like it'll be really tough!*
> *Well, if you can't take a joke, you shouldn't have joined, I guess!*

ILLEGITIMUS NON CARBORUNDUM (Since WWII) — *Illegitimus non carborundum* is mock Latin for "don't let the bastards grind you down!" This phrase was apparently coined in British military intelligence during the Second World War and spread throughout the allied forces. The phrase attained a popularity during the Second World War, a popularity that has diminished little. [Ref: Partridge - Catchphrases]

> *The unofficial motto of this squadron is: Illegitimus non carborundum!*

I-LOVE-ME WALL (CF; current) — An "I-Love-Me Wall" is a feature wall, usually in an airman's office or den, devoted exclusively to celebrating the career, life, and times of the wall's owner. An I-Love-Me Wall" typically displays the owner's squadron or unit plaques, framed "Hero Shots", Certificates of Military Achievement, and other mementos. The term suggests that the wall exists for the benefit of the owner, and not necessarily to improve on the decor. (Just ask the owner's wife.) (See also **Hero Shot**)

I notice that Ian has a new plaque on his I-Love-Me Wall

I-Love-Me Wall

"I'M EASY" — "I'm easy" corresponds to "I'm accommodating" or "I'm agreeable", and seems to have been service slang since the Second World War. Lately however, to be "easy" is also taken to mean "sexually available". Consequently the words "I'm easy" are not commonly heard from female servicemembers. [Ref: Partridge (8th)]

Do you prefer your eggs scrambled? or Poached?
I'm easy...

"I'M FROM NDHQ, AND I'M HERE TO HELP YOU!" (CF; current) — This phrase is widely regarded to be a lie. It is a wry commentary on a universal military theme: namely, that most personnel believe headquarters staff (especially those in National Defence Headquarters, or "NDHQ") are thoroughly disinterested in helping them get on with the job. Of course, this is a biased perspective, but it is widely held nonetheless. Interestingly, this phrase became popular after the size of NDHQ ballooned to employ more personnel than an army division. (See also **Bullshit Towers, Castle Dismal, Chateau, Disneyland-on-the-Rideau, Fort Fumble, Glass Menagerie; Glass Palace, Petrified Forest**)

"I'M GOING TO GET MY HEAD SHARPENED" — An airman who has gone to get his "head sharpened" has gone for a haircut. The allusion to a pencil-sharpener is clear. [Ref: Partridge - Catchphrases]

IMMELMANN (aviation general; since WWI) — "Immelmann" is short for "Immelmann Turn", an aerobatic manoeuvre developed by the great German ace of the First World War, Max Immelmann. The manoeuvre allows an aircraft to change direction 180 degrees within a small lateral area. However, there is confusion as to just what sort of manoeuvre makes up an Immelmann.

It appears that the turn developed by Max Immelmann during the First World War was in fact a "stall-turn", described as a manoeuvre that followed a diving attack on an enemy aircraft, when the "...*nose was pulled up vertically. The aeroplane was then ruddered over sideways, leaving it well placed for a further attack.*" First World War aircraft using this manoeuvre could turn 180 degrees within a lateral distance of 30 feet! However, in recent times the term Immelmann is used to describe a turn whereby the aircraft commences a loop. At the top of the loop, the aircraft is rolled level and flight is continued in the opposite direction. [Ref: Spick, Welch]

INFANTEER (CF; current) — An "infanteer" is an infantryman. (See also **Grunt**)

INFIELD (General Aviation; current) — The infield is the area of the airport that lies between the runways, or between the runways and the ramp (see Ramp). It is usually a grassy area, uncluttered by anything except the occasional light or radar transmitter, possibly a road, and millions of smug, secure gophers. The term may have its origins in the analogous area of baseball diamond, also called the Infield.

IN ROUTINE; OUT ROUTINE (CF; current) — Whenever a member of the Air Force is posted to a unit, or formally leaves the unit, a variety of administrative requirements must be completed. Records must be transferred, accommodations assigned, equipment must be issued or returned, etc. Thus, in joining a unit, one goes through one's "In-Routine", and in leaving, one goes through one's "Out-Routine". The term may be naval in origin. [Ref: Sutherland]

Welcome to the squadron! Have you completed your in-routine yet?

INSTANT DICTATOR KIT (RCAF Bands; since WW2) — The "Instant Dictator Kit" consists of all the various articles of brass and braid that, when added to an airman's uniform, transformed it from fairly standard appearance, to bandsmans' ceremonial regalia. Unlike the army's bands, which were kitted out with traditional full-dress ceremonial uniforms, air force bands wore standard dress trousers, tunic, and cap. However these were polished up by adding extra ceremonial accoutrements, such as gold wire epaulettes, a ceremonial belt, gold trouser stripes, and fancy embroidery on the sleeves. The term "Instant Dictator Kit" suggests that the ceremonial uniform, when worn, was reminiscent of a Third-World dictator's regalia. The term has also been applied to "Belts and Boards", ceremonial accoutrements for an RCAF officer's dress uniform. (See also **Belts and Boards**)

IN THE GREEN (general aviation; current) — "In the green" is a term meaning that "all is well", or "everything is normal". Its origin in aviation is to be found in aircraft's

Instant
Dictator
Kit

Before

After

cockpit instruments which, like auto instruments, use the colour green to indicate the "safe" range of performance. For example, when the needle of an airspeed indicator is in the green, the aircraft is flying within its safe speed range. Consequently, when there are no problems with the aircraft, everything is in the green. Similarly, when an aircraft has safely lowered its undercarriage, the pilot will often report "three in the green", meaning that the nose wheel, and each of the main wheel assemblies have successfully been lowered. Of course, this usage soon left the cockpit, and can be heard in many contexts as a way of saying all is well.

> *How's everything goin'?*
> *Everything's in the green.*

INTERROGATE (Aviation general; current) — To "interrogate" is jargon for an electronic procedure where the operator of one electronic system demands information from another electronic system, as in an IFF system. (See also **IFF**)

> *Interrogate that aircraft's IFF...*

I.O.R. (ie., "eye-owe-are") (CF; current) — "I.O.R." is the abbreviation for "Immediate Operational Requirement", the designation for highest priority that can be given to an article of equipment ordered through the CF supply system. Supplies ordered with an I.O.R. designation are required immediately! However, occasionally someone orders materiel on an I.O.R. basis not because of need, but convenience. Many airmen tend to resent the term I.O.R. as an army and navy intrusion on a well-working aviation system. In civil aviation and in the RCAF before unification, urgently needed aircraft parts were designated "A.O.G." (for "aircraft on ground"). Civilian freight handlers are familiar with the A.O.G. designation, but sometimes have no idea what I.O.R. means. Occasionally airmen - rightly or wrongly - believe that vital aircraft parts are treated no differently from bootlaces or paint! [Ref: Sutherland]

I.P. (General military aviation; current since WW2) — The "IP" is the "Initial Point". Many aircraft manoeuvres are preplanned, such as an approach to landing, or a bomb run to a target. In any preplanned manoeuvre, it is always assumed that the manoeuvre will begin at a precise position. This position is called the I.P. The manoeuvre will be carried out in a standard, practised fashion, presuming the enemy has no contrary intentions, of course.

> *Make sure you're over the IP at precisely the right time; then do your bomb run, just as we've briefed it.*

IRON BOMB (general military aviation; since 1960's) — What most people think of when they think of a bomb, is an "Iron Bomb". An iron bomb is an unguided, non-precision weapon whose likelihood of hitting the target depends on the skill of the Bomb-Aimer or Pilot who releases it. In contrast, a "Smart Bomb" is guided to its target by some tracking mechanism, such as reflected laser energy, Low-Light Television, etc. (See also **Smart Bomb**)

> *Have they got any Smart Bombs in the Bunkers?*
> *Nope. Just Iron Bombs.*

IRON COMPASS (general aviation; since WW1) — The "Iron Compass" is a set of railway tracks observed from the air, used by disoriented aviators to provide a bearing or reference. (See also **I.F.R.**) [Ref: Harvey]

> *How did you find your way without a map?*
> *Simple! I just followed the Iron Compass.*

IRON PIG (RCAF; 1960's) — "The Iron Pig" was the very first computer purchased by the RCAF to manage its supply system, an IBM 705, in 1960. The term was current in Air Materiel Command. [Ref: Sutherland]

IT'S ALL PENSIONABLE TIME (CF; current) — "It's all pensionable time" is the fatalistic observation often expressed by someone engaged in a military activity that is a thorough waste of time. It advises that one shouldn't get too upset over the wasted effort, because even if the task is useless, you're still going to collect your pension. (This isn't often heard among reserve personnel, who are entitled to no pension; when a reservist's time is wasted, they generally blame regulars) (See also **If you can't take a joke, you shouldn't have joined!**)

> *What a waste of time this is!*
> *Relax, it's all pensionable time...*

JULIET

JABBERWOCK (RNAS; WWI) — "Jabberwock" was Royal Naval Air Service slang for the Sopwith "Baby", a First World War seaplane. The name clearly comes from the famous nonsense poem *Jabberwocky* by Lewis Carol, though it is unclear why the Sopwith attracted this nickname. [Ref: Partridge (8th)]

> *The trouble with flying a Jabberwock is that you can easily get your feet wet!*

JACK-KNIFE SPEC (Canadian military postwar to 1965) — "Jack-knife Spec" was slang for the "JCANAF Specification", or "Joint Canadian Army Navy Air Force Specification". [Ref: Sutherland]

JAG; Jag (CF; current) — A world of difference exists between a "JAG" and a "Jag".

> (1) **JAG** is the abbreviation for "Judge-Advocate General", the senior CF legal officer. Thus a military lawyer is inevitably called a JAG, as in: *Call the JAG and ask how low I can go before they'll charge me with Low Flying!*

> (2) **Jag** is current RAF and NATO shorthand for "Jaguar", an Anglo-French reconnaissance and fighter aircraft used both by the RAF and the French *Armee de l'Air*. It is an effective aircraft, though sometimes felt to be a bit underpowered, as in: *Do you know why the "Jag" has two engines? Because if one fails, the other will take the airplane all the way to the crash point!*

JAG/Jag

A world of difference exists
between a JAG and a Jag.

JAM FACTORY (RFC; WWI) — The first technical training school in the Royal Flying Corps, established in 1916 at Coley Park, Reading Park in England, was known as the "Jam Factory". This school, which turned out the thousands of aircraft mechanics needed to keep the RFC flying, was located in a factory originally built for the CWS Jam Company. [Ref: Sutherland]

Before they'll let you be a rigger or a fitter you'll have to spend a couple of months at the jam factory.

JAM, TO; JAMMING (military communications, since WW2) — "Jamming" is the practice of intentionally disrupting a radio or radar transmission by broadcasting a stronger electronic signal on the same frequency and amplitude. The stronger signal is received at the same time as the primary signal, and obscures it. Jamming is a critical weapon in electronic warfare, and is generally defeated by employing a transmitter capable of switching frequency. However, jammers exist now which can switch frequency along with the transmitter being attacked. This, in turn, has led to development of transmitters and receivers that can change frequency with each other, rapidly and at random. Unsurprisingly, this is being countered by more sophisticated jamming equipment.

Not only can we jam their signals, we can transmit enough wattage to burn their receivers out!

JAMMY (originally English, circa 1900; still current CF) — "Jammy" can mean "easy", "pleasurable", or "without worry". This adjective is simply a derivation of "jam". Jam is sweet, thus anything jammy is also sweet, as in a "jammy job", a "jammy trip", or even the nonspecific noun: "a jammy". This is Anglo-Canadian slang that appears to now be dated everywhere but in the CF. [Ref: Partridge (FS)]

It looks like I'm going to Las Vegas!
How do you get on so many jammy trips?

JANKERS (British Forces to WWII) — Jankers is yet another nickname for a military jail. (See also **Club Ed, Digger, D.B.'s**) [Ref: Harvey]

JERRY (British Commonwealth; WWI, WWII) — "Jerry" was an epithet for a German, common during both the First and Second World Wars.

Jerry, contrary to common belief, does not derive from the word "German". As slang for Germans, the word "Jerry" derives from the similarity in appearance between the unique German army helmet, and a chamberpot. During the First World War, the German Army

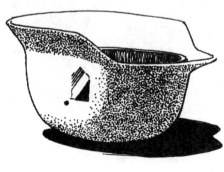

Jerry

abandoned the ceremonial Prussian spiked helmet and adopted its well-known and highly effective angled helmet. However, this new helmet reminded British soldiers of a chamberpot worn upside-down on the head and Jerry was contemporary British slang for a chamberpot! Thus, Germans - identified by their helmet - became Jerries, and anything German was described as being Jerry. (See also **Jerrycan**) [Ref: Partridge (8th)]

I hear that the Wing Commander shot down another Jerry.

JERRYCAN (originally British 8th Army, WWII; now universal) — A jerrycan is a reusable container for carrying liquids, which can be carried by one person. The basic design was developed during the Second World War for the German Army, and was used widely to carry fuel and water. British troops in North Africa preferred the Afrika Korp's fuel cans to the small, tin-and-solder British fuel cans, which leaked and were easily crushed. So when British Forces captured Afrika Korps vehicles or positions, they appropriated all the German fuel cans they could find. "Jerry" was the favoured slang term for things German, and these Afrika Korps fuel cans soon became known as "Jerry cans" as opposed to their own "British cans". The name stuck. Eventually, British forces copied the German design, manufacturing and issuing their own jerrycans. (See also **Jerry**) [Ref: Partridge (8th)]

I hate having to fuel the airplane straight from the jerrycan!

JERRY'S BACKYARD (1942-43; Coastal Command) — During the Second World War, "Jerry's Backyard" was the name given by Coastal Command aircrew to the Skaggerrak and Kattegat areas of the North Sea. As these areas were very near the German North Sea coastline, flying in this area would bring Coastal Command aircraft as close to Jerry (ie., the Germans) as if they were flying in his backyard. (See **Jerry**) [Ref: Partridge (FS)]

Where are we patrolling this time?
Jerry's Backyard again...

JESUS NUT; JESUS BOLT; JESUS WIRE; etc. (current) — This reference to the Son of God has little if any religious significance. The word "Jesus" is used as a prefix to describe any object that is either enormously large or enormously important. Folklore has it that when an observer confronts the object, the only possible reaction will be to utter the word: "JESUS!"

For example, the main nut and bolt holding the rotors of a helicopter to the drive shaft are the "Jesus Nut" and the "Jesus Bolt", because if either should fail, the crew and passengers will only have time to shout "JESUS!" before tumbling into a crash. Similarly, a very large hangar is occasionally termed a "Jesus Hangar" because, upon seeing the structure, the observer is dumbstruck, and can only mutter the word: "JESUS!". On an aircraft carrier, the last arrester wire is the "Jesus Wire". It is said that if a carrier-based aircraft lands, and its tail hook misses all the wires but the last, the pilot will be so relieved he can only sigh: "JESUS!".

Just make sure there's nothing wrong with the Jesus Nut!

JEZEBEL   See Girls

JIMMY (CF; current) — "Jimmy" is the occasional nickname for a member of the Communications and Electronics Engineering branch. The term seems to have its origin in army slang; the army signal corps cap badge depicted a running figure of Mercury who was called Jimmy by the troops. After unification in 1968, both army signallers and air force ground communicators found themselves in the new "Communications and Electronics Engineering Branch". Their new cap badge also depicted Jimmy, the running figure of Mercury. It seems that the army term stuck and has entered the airman's lexicon. [Ref: Partridge (8th)]

A new Jimmy is being posted into the Wing this week...

JINKING; JINK,TO (RAF, RCAF; WWII) — "To Jink" was Bomber Command jargon for the violent evasive action taken by a heavy bomber to avoid enemy fighters. "Jinking" was a standard, repetitive series of abrupt climbs and dives, coupled with violent turns. Formally termed "the corkscrew", it was taught to all Bomber Command pilots. It was a purely defensive tactic specifically designed to help the large, less-lively, heavy bomber to put the pursuing fighter off its aim, and give a clear shot to the bomber's rear gunner. Jinking was often enough to throw off an attacking night fighter. [Ref: Partridge (8th)]

There's a fighter behind us and below! Start Jinking!

JOB (RAF; since 1930's) — "Job" is slang for an aircraft type. Therefore a multi-engine aircraft was a "multi-engine job", a swept-wing aircraft was a "swept-wing job", etc. Airmen subsequently applied the word job to human typology as well, as in:

Twin Engine Job	a female (from twin-engine aircraft)
Blonde Job	a blonde woman
Brown Job	a soldier

(See also **Blue Job, Brown Job**) [Ref: Partridge (FS)]

JOCKEY, TO; JOCK; JET JOCK (American; current) — A "jockey" or "jock" is a pilot, specifically, a fighter pilot. Though common USAF slang, it is occasionally heard from Canadians. Therefore, "to manoeuvre" an aircraft is to jockey the aircraft.

The mess is full of American jet jocks.

JOE, TO (originally RAF 1930's; now universal Canadian military) — "To joe" someone is to give them a dirty job. Thus, a dirty job is a "joe job". The origin of this word is unclear, though it might be borrowed from the American "Joe Soap", a comic character of the 1930's who was rather simple and eager, and easily taken advantage of. (See also **Joe Erk; S.L.J.**) [Ref: Partridge (FS)]

We'd better joe somebody to clean up that garbage on the floor.

JOE ERK (RAF; WWII) — "Joe Erk" was the term for the quintessential Air Force "everyman", the AC2 or Aircraftman 2nd Class - the lowest rank in the air force. The term is probably a combination of "Joe Soap" (See **to Joe**) and "Erk", RAF slang for an Aircraftman (See **Acey-Deucey, AC Plonk, Erk**) [Ref: Partridge (8th)]

Joe Job

Joe Jobs are a fact of
military life.

I used to be in the air force. Mind you, I wasn't a Wing Commander or anything like that. I was just Joe Erk...

JOE JOB   See to **Joe**

JOHNNY TURK (British Empire Forces; WWI) — "Johnny Turk" was the First World War epithet for Turkish troops, both individually and collectively. Turkey and its Ottoman Empire were First World War allies of Germany and the Austro-Hungarian Empire. As such, "Johnny Turk" fought in Palestine and the Eastern Mediterranean, so Canadian land forces had few contacts with Turkish adversaries. However, Canadian aviators flew wherever the RFC and RNAS flew, and a number flew against the Turks.

I'd be careful about flying in that area. Johnny Turk is a good shot!

JOY; ANY JOY?, NO JOY! (RAF 1930's; still current CF usage) — "Joy" equates to "satisfaction", "luck", or "success". Thus, to make contact, or to enjoy a successful operation was to have joy. The converse was "no joy". Among electricians, it also appears to have been used to state whether a wire was "live", that is, whether it carried any electrical current. The term appears to have entered standard radio procedure because it conveys much information in a very short phrase. [Ref: Partridge (FS)]

Any joy in your patrol area?
Nope; No joy at all...

JOY-STICK (1915-25 RAF; now dated) — A "joy-stick" is an aircraft control column. According to Arch Whitehouse, an American who flew in the RFC, the word joy-stick was a corruption of the term "Joyce Stick". Presumably an Englishman named Joyce had been instrumental in standardizing aircraft flight controls. [Ref: Voss; Whitehouse]

To make the aircraft descend, push the joy-stick forward.

JR; JRC (CF; current) — "JR" or "JRC" are the initials for the "Junior Ranks Club", the base social centre and lounge for junior noncommissioned members of the CF.

Formal military social activities are generally organized by rank, and all CF members belong to the mess appropriate to their rank. The JR is part of the CF "three-mess system", and serves the "Junior Ranks", ie., those personnel below the rank of Sergeant. The JR, like the Officers' Mess, and the Sergeants' and Warrant Officers' Mess, promotes morale and cohesiveness, (to say nothing of enabling junior ranks to "blow off steam" away from the boss!)

The Mess or Club is the focal point for socializing with one's peers in rank. Rank and age generally correlate, so Junior Ranks Clubs tend to be dominated by young single men and women, whereas the Sergeants' and Warrant Officers' Mess has an older clientele. (See also **Menopause Manor**) The Officers' Mess on the other hand, suffers from the clash of ages. A nineteen-year old Officer Cadet and a fifty-year old Colonel share the same Mess but do not generally share the same taste in entertainment. This explains why on the occasional Saturday night, against all regulations, young Air Force officers sneak into the JR! The JR is more fun.

What time does the JR close on Saturdays?
I didn't know it closed at all...

JUGS (RCAF, CF; current) — "Jugs" are extra fuel tanks carried beneath an fighter aircraft's wing. The term dates back to the Second World War and may be American in origin. However, "Jugs" is also the nickname for a great American wartime fighter, the Republic P-47 Thunderbolt, also flown in the southeast Asia theatre by Commonwealth squadrons.

JUICE (RAF, RCAF; WWII) — During the Second World War and for a time thereafter, "juice" was slang for aircraft fuel. [Ref: Partridge (8th)]

The Spitfire was nearly out of juice...

JUICER (Canadian; WWII) — A "juicer" is an Englishman or Englishwoman. The term is probably derived from another epithet for Englishmen: "Lime-juicer", itself the root word for the most famous of all English epithets: "Limey". ("Limey" comes from the early Royal Navy practice of serving lime juice to its sailors on long sailing voyages to ward off scurvy.) (See also **Kipper, Brit(1)**)

The new Wing Commander is a typical juicer, all right!

JULIE   See **Girls**

JUMP SEAT (Universal Aviation usage) — A "Jump Seat" is a spare seat permanently installed on the flight deck of an aircraft, located to enable the occupant to observe activity without getting in the way of the crew. The seat is often used by instructors or check pilots, or by extra crewmembers. Aircraft designers borrowed the term from automotive slang, which in turn merely borrowed from earlier terminology. As early as 1846, a spare, movable seat in a horse-drawn carriage was a Jump Seat.

The Check Pilot normally sits in the jump seat, watching everything.

Kilo

KEROSENE CANSO (RCAF; 1950's to early 1960's) — "Kerosene Canso" was yet another rueful nickname for the Avro CF-100 "Canuck", a twin-engine, two-seat interceptor in RCAF and CF service from the early 1950's to the mid 1980's. Of all aircraft in Canadian military service, none has attracted such a collection of nicknames as the CF-100. The CF-100 was ungainly-looking, to put it mildly and though an effective interceptor, the CF-100 was not very manoeuvrable when compared with its contemporary, the F-86 Sabre. As a result it acquired many unkind nicknames that reflected this lack of agility. Kerosene Canso was one such nickname. This nickname alluded to another classic RCAF aircraft, the "Canso", a reliable but rather ungainly flying boat based on the Catalina flying boat. The word "Kerosene" reflects the fact that the CF-100 is powered by a jet engine which burns jet fuel, a form of kerosene. (See also Canuck (3), Clunk, Lead Sled) [Ref: Sutherland]

KICKER — The word "Kicker" can have two different meanings:

(1)   **Kicker**   See **Stick-Shaker**

(2)   **Kicker** (since WWII; military transport aviation) — A "kicker" was a transport aircraft crewman who "kicked" cargo out of the aircraft during an airdrop. During the Second World War, most military cargo aircraft were merely converted civil airliners, and were not configured to deliver cargo by parachute. Therefore it became necessary to have kickers, groundcrew "volunteers" who manhandled cargo bundles to the open door of an aircraft and kicked the cargo out into the slipstream, where it would descend to the ground. Most cargo was attached to a parachute, though certain more robust items (boots, for example) were occasionally free-dropped. A free-drop made things very exciting for those waiting on the ground (especially if the free-drop was slightly off-target).

Being a kicker was hazardous. At least one RCAF kicker fell out of his Dakota transport aircraft while manhandling cargo out the door during an air drop in the Burma campaign in the Second World War. Fortunately, his parachute "functioned as advertised", though he spent several days in the Burmese jungle before rejoining his squadron! He was lucky, parachutes weren't always worn.

Modern military transport aircraft are tailor-made to paradrop large, bulky equipment. Their cargo despatch systems incorporate rollers and palletized cargo bundles, so there is little need for a "kicker", except perhaps on very small aircraft. Today, these functions are performed by a loadmaster (See **Loadie**), though the loadmaster's job embraces many more reponsibilities.

KICK THE TIRES, LIGHT THE FIRES (AND BRIEF ON GUARD) (Aviation, Current) — To "kick the tires and light the fires" is to give an airplane a pre-flight inspection and start the engines, in preparation for take-off. The further exageration - "kick the tires, light the fires, and brief on guard"- describes a very rapid departure by several aircraft and their pilots. It suggests there isn't time to do the necessary pre-flight preparations, such as planning, briefing, and inspecting the aircraft before the takeoff. Instead of doing the customary pre-flight mechanical inspection, here one merely "kicks the tires". Starting the engines is "lighting the fires". "Brief on guard" suggests the pilots do not brief, or discuss, their flight before takeoff. Rather the crews discuss the flight on their aircraft radios on the emergency (often called the "guard") frequency - while already in flight, rather than on the ground, beforehand. (See **Guard**) [Ref: Partridge (8th)]

After we've checked the maintenance log, we'll go out to the airplane to kick the tires and light the fires!

KIPPER (general CF usage, since WWII) — "Kipper" is slang for an Englishman or can be descriptive of anything English, from the English custom of eating kippers for breakfast. [Ref: Partridge (8th)]

There's a Hercules due in at 0600.
One of ours?
No. Its a kipper...

KIPPER KITE (RAF; WWII) — "Kipper Kite" was Second World War slang for Coastal Command patrol aircraft that operated over the North Sea. It is in the waters of the North Sea that fishermen trawl for the fish known to Englishmen as the "kipper". Later the term was applied to Coastal Command aircraft generally. [Ref: Partridge (FS)]

KIT (general Commonwealth military usage) — Virtually any equipment issued by the military is "kit". Thus, a formal uniform for evening wear is usually termed a "Mess Kit", the attachments needed to turn an ordinary bomb into a precision munition is a "Laser Guided Bomb Kit", etc. [Ref: Partridge (FS)]

The CF-18 is an outstanding piece of kit!

KITCHEN PASS (CF; current) — A "Kitchen Pass" is spousal permission (perhaps grudgingly given) to attend a stag function at the mess. Kitchen Pass is an allusion to a military leave pass.

Doug! This is the first time you've been to the mess in a month. Did your wife give you a Kitchen Pass?!

KITE (RAF; 1914 to WWII) — Kite was a common nickname for aircraft in the general sense, like "plane", or "machine". It first arose as the formal name for the Bristol "Box Kite", an aircraft flown by the RFC from 1917-18. By the 1930's the term was becoming obsolescent. [Ref: Partridge (8th)]

There's a French kite orbiting overhead.

KITTENS, TO HAVE   See **Baby, to have a**

Kriegies

Allied prisoners-of-war, or Kriegies,
developed a whole new vocabulary.

KIWI; KIWI CLUB (CF, current) — In addition to applying to a New Zealander, the word "kiwi" can mean a non-flying air force officer, from the flightless bird native to New Zealand. On many bases, Kiwis have established their own social circle, termed the "Kiwi Club". Few laypersons realize that "Kiwis" outnumber aircrew in the Air Force, and that without them, aircraft could never leave the ground or perform their missions. At a typical Kiwi Club luncheon one might find the aerospace engineering officers, the air traffic controllers, the flight surgeons and nurses, administrators and logistics specialists. There would be military police and intelligence officers, and the construction and electronics engineers. Though they are all Air Force officers, none fly for a living. (See also **Penguin(2), Wingless Wonder**) [Ref: Partridge (FS); Partridge (8th)]

> *Are you a pilot?*
> *Yes*
> *In that case, you can't come in. This luncheon is for Kiwis only...*

KLICK (general military usage; probably American in origin) — A "klick" is a kilometer, as in: "the airport is only two klicks ahead..." [Ref: Elting]

KRIEGIE; KRIEGY (WWII) — "Kriegie" (or "Kriegy") was the nickname that Allied prisoners of war in German hands gave themselves, during the Second World War.

The term is short for *Kriegsgefangener*, German for "Prisoner of War". The Kriegies developed a whole body of slang unto themselves, a remarkable fact considering the difficulty experienced by POW's communicating between camps. Examples include:

- **big eats?**   How are you? (from the German *Wie geht's?*)

- **Big X**   The head of the Escape Committee;

- **circuit**   A well-worn track within in a POW camp, around which POW's walked to pass the time. Many POW's were aircrew, so it is unsurprising that this walk around the camp was reminiscent of flying "circuits and bumps" around the aerodrome in earlier, happier times;

- **Duty Pilot**   A POW who watched the main camp gate and made a record of the arrivals and departures of German staff. (Derived from the Duty Pilot on an air force aerodrome, whose duty it was to log all aircraft landings and takeoffs);

- **Ferret**   A guard who specialized in detecting POW escape routes, escape equipment, radios, etc. Ferrets were easily recognized by the fact that they always wore dark blue denim coveralls and usually travelled in pairs.

- **Fish Paste?**   What time is it? (from *Wie spät ist es?*);

- **Ghost**   A secret supernumary POW, ie., one who was surreptitiously present in the camp but not listed on official German records. Eric Williams records that at some camps early in the war,

POW's managed to confuse German records. There were sometimes more POW's in the camp than there were in the German record books! Of course, these POW's were kept in hiding during roll-call and, after a POW escaped a "ghost" took his place. However, not being on the roll call meant that a ghost received no rations and the other POW's had to share theirs!"

• **Goon**   A German guard (apparently coined from a bit of doggerel commonly learned during in operational flying training: *Beware of the Hun in the Sun and Beware of the Goon in the Moon!*);

• **Goon-Baiting** Making life difficult for the guards;

• **Kriegdom**   The world of the POW;

• **Little X**   An escape committee member responsible for recruiting and employing Stooges;

• **Nix Fish Tins** I don't understand (from *Nicht verstehen*);

• **Penguin**   A POW who unobtrusively disposed of the dirt that accumulated from the digging of an escape tunnel;

• **stimmt**   All OK (from *alles stimmt*);

• **Stooge**   A sentry POW who followed, or watched for "Ferrets" while other POW's conferred or worked to escape;

• **Tiger Box**   Guard Tower, with light, guns, telephone, etc;

• **X Organization** The Escape Committee.

[Ref: Partridge (8th); Williams]

KRO's; QRO's (ie., "kay-are-owes";"cue-are-owes") (Commonwealth military) — "K.R.O.'s" were King's Regulations and Orders, the legal rules and regulations that govern the internal workings of the armed forces. They are termed "King's" Regulations and Orders when the reigning monarch is male, and become "Queen's" Regulations and Orders when a female is on the throne.

L IMA

L-14 (RCAF, 1950's to late 1960's; still occasionally heard in 1990's) — The term "L-14" has lived for a long time in Canada's air force. The original L-14 of the immediate postwar RCAF was a form on which technicians recorded the line servicing actions taken on a given aircraft, on a given day. (The preface "L" indicated that it was part of a series of RCAF "Engineering" forms of the day). The L-14 was a key document in the daily life of an aircraft and of the people who maintained it and flew it. By 1957 or 1958 all RCAF maintenance forms for an individual aircraft had been integrated into a single set of documents bound in a loose-leaf binder. This format exists to this day though it will likely be replaced by a computer-based system. By the late 1950's the term L-14 referred to this binder. By the 1970's the L-14 designation had long since officially disappeared (to be replaced by the ponderous title: "Aircraft Maintenance Record Set"). Despite this, well into the 1980's and 1990's, many technicians who had not yet been born when the RCAF ceased to exist, referred to the daily aircraft log as the L-14! [Ref: Sutherland]

L-19   See **Bird Dog**

LAB (RCAF, CF; since 1960's) — "Lab" is the diminutive for the "Labrador" helicopter. The Labrador, built by Boeing Vertol and designated the CH-113 by the RCAF, is a twin-rotor helicopter capable of partial immersion in water. It was first acquired in the 1960's by the RCAF for Search and Rescue. The Canadian Army purchased a slightly different variant named the "Voyageur", which had auto-hover and which could sling cargo. When the CF purchased the "Chinook" helicopter for Army support, all Voyageurs were converted to Search and Rescue configuration and joined the "Lab" fleet.

A Lab took off half an hour ago to search for the missing aircraft.

LANC (RAF, RCAF; since WWII) — "Lanc" is the diminutive for the Avro "Lancaster", the preeminent British bomber of the Second World War. The Lanc entered Bomber Command service in late 1941 and was based on Avro's unsuccessful twin-engined Manchester bomber. The Lancaster, which ran on four Merlin engines, proved to be a classic. Its crews had great confidence in it, and it typically carried a 14,000-pound bombload (about two and a half tons more than the American B-17G Flying Fortress, which devoted much of its payload capacity for defensive armament). Later versions of the Lancaster could lift the massive 12,000 pound "Tall Boy" and the 22,000 pound "Grand Slam" bombs!

Ultimately fourteen RCAF bomber squadrons flew the Lanc in Bomber Command. Over seven thousand were built, and fittingly, most of the Lancasters flown by the RCAF's No. 6 Bomber Group, were built in Canada by Victory Aircraft Ltd., a Crown Corporation. A total of 422 were built in Canada. It is said that the Chief Inspector of Avro in Britain, after inspecting an early Canadian-built Lancaster, advised his senior inspectors to *go and look it over and see how an aircraft should be built*. After the war, the

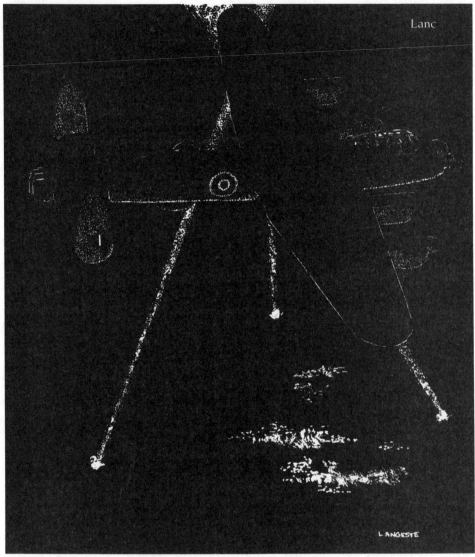

Searchlights cone a Lanc over the target.

RCAF modified its Lancasters for reconnaissance, aerial photo work, maritime patrol, search and rescue, and navigation training. The Lanc finally retired from RCAF service in the early 1960's. (See also **Clapper, Grand Slam, Tallboy**) [Refs: Partridge (FS); Molson and Taylor]

Last night a Lanc came in on only three engines...

LAND OF NO FUTURE (WWII; Bomber Command) — To Bomber Command aircrews, the land of no future was the Ruhr Valley, Germany's industrial heartland. Much of Germany's heavy industry is located in the cities of the Ruhr Valley. A primary target of

.

the bomber offensive, it was very heavily defended by German flak batteries and flying there severely diminished one's life expectancy. It was the land of no future. (See also **No future at all, Happy Valley**) [Partridge (8th)]

Well, gentlemen, tonight's trip takes us to the land of no future.

LAND OF THE ROUND DOORKNOBS (CF Europe; 1970's, 80's) — Canada was the "Land of the Round Doorknobs" to members of Canada's NATO contingent in Germany, during at least the last decade of the contingent's existence. The term is also current among American servicemembers in Germany, for whom it means the United States.

This unusual term alludes to the fact that doors in Germany typically do not have a doorknob. Indeed, doorknobs are virtually unknown in the German republic where nearly all doors open and close by means of a latch. (As many have observed, a latch has the advantage of allowing a person to open a door with one's elbow - even when one's hands are full). Consequently, Canada - being largely latch-free - is "the land of the round doorknobs". [Ref: Partridge (8th)]

LANSDOWNE EXHIBITION (RCAF; 1950'S, 1960'S) — The "Lansdowne Exhibition" was an annual "rite of spring" at RCAF Headquarters in Ottawa during the 1950's and 1960's. This was a two-week period during which all RCAF HQ personnel below the rank of Wing Commander reported every morning to Lansdowne Park, the home of the Central Canada Exhibition, for two hours of parade square drill. On the last day of the two-week period, a senior officer (See also **A.O.C.**) would come on parade and conduct a slow, ceremonious inspection of the assemblage. Many believed that the real purpose of the Lansdowne Exhibition was to ensure that everyone at air force headquarters still owned an RCAF uniform! (RCAF Headquarters was in downtown Ottawa. To prevent the downtown area from being inundated with military uniforms, air force headquarters staff only wore uniform one day a week!) [Ref: Sutherland]

You'd better start shining those shoes Terry! Its only two weeks until the Lansdown Exhibition!

LAPES, TO (pronounced "layps")(CF, current) — "To lapes" is a verb derived from the acronym LAPES, for "Low Altitude Parachute Extraction System". In LAPES, a pallet of cargo is sent out of the aircraft's tail ramp at extremely low altitude. This can only occur in aircraft having a cargo ramp at the tail, such as a Hercules. LAPES calls for the pilot to fly the aircraft to within 10 or 15 feet of the ground, when a parachute is deployed which drags the cargo out of the back of the aircraft. It then free-falls to the ground, sliding forward on its pallet. The procedure is only used for very well cushioned cargo and for very strong cargo, such as a bulldozer.

We'll lapes the bulldozer between the runways.

LAST CHANCE CHECK (military aviation; general) — A "Last Chance Check" is precisely that: a final inspection of a running fighter aircraft before it takes off. The Last Chance Check is performed by a specially qualified technician, while the aircraft engine is running, and just before the aircraft taxis onto the runway to take off. It is the last chance to discover a technical fault on the ground, before the aircraft flies.

Lapes

A Lapes run demanded split-second timing and a keen eye for distance.

LAST THREE (CF, current; originally British Army) — "Last Three" refers to the last three digits of one's service number. The Geneva Conventions require that all combatants have a personal serial number. Most, if not all, air force records identify members by this number. However, as a quick reference, it is often more useful to refer to the last three digits, rather than the entire service number (which may by anywhere from 7 to 9 numbers long). The theory behind reliance on only one's last three is that in any given small corner of the air force, no two people will have the same name, rank and last three. It is especially useful in units with lots of people with the same surname (as in *Are you Jones 245? Or Jones 682?*). (See also **Dogtag**) [Partridge (8th)]

> *What's your name, rank and last three!*
> *Tokuda! Corporal! 958!*

LATE ARRIVALS CLUB (Commonwealth Air Forces, WWII) — The "Late Arrivals Club" was a highly informal club whose membership is limited to Second World War allied aircrew who, having had to abandon their aircraft in enemy territory, made a belated return to their unit, ie. a "Late Arrival".

Late Arrivals Club

The Late Arrivals Club first appeared in the Western Desert, in June of 1941. Its precise origins are unknown; both RAF and South African Air Force units claim its founding. It is a highly informal "club" and those who qualified received a badge (consisting of a winged boot) and a Membership Certificate.

The text of the "Late Arrivals Club" certificate states:

> *Inasmuch as he, in _____(location)*
> *on _____19_____(date)*
> *When obliged to abandon his Aircraft, on*
> *the ground or in the air, as a result*
> *of unfriendly action by the enemy,*
> *Succeeded in returning to his Squadron,*
> *on foot or by other means, long after*
> *his Estimated Time of Arrival.*

IT IS NEVER TOO LATE TO COME BACK

The badge was intended to be worn by air force aircrew only on their flying clothing. (Though at least one photo exists of the "winged boot" badge worn on dress uniform by Canadian and Australian aircrew at Buckingham Palace, there to receive more formal decorations from King George VI). [Ref: Hampson]

LAUGHING, TO BE (CF; current) — This now-common term was coined by servicemen during the First World War. A person who is "laughing" has nothing to worry about. [Ref: Partridge (8th)]

> *Gerry couldn't meet his car payments until he won the squadron Grey Cup*
> > *pool!*
> *So, now he's laughing, eh?*

LAWN DART (CF current; originally USAF) — A "Lawn Dart" is a high performance fighter aircraft, though it was originally a nickname limited to the USAF F-16. (To the uninitiated, "Lawn Darts" was a commercially available child's game of the 1970's and 1980's, in which players lobbed steel darts with large plastic fins, for points, into marked areas on one's lawn. The "Lawn Darts" stuck into the lawn, just as normal-sized darts stick into cork. However, "Lawn Darts" was eventually removed from the shelves as a safety hazard; the large steel dart could stick into people, as easily as into grass!)

LAY EGGS, TO (RNAS, RFC; WWI) — During the First World War, when RNAS or RFC airmen laid mines at sea from their flying machines, they were often said to be "laying eggs". Presumably this was a reference to the shape of the mine. (See also **Gardening**) [Ref: Partridge (8th)]

LAY ON, TO (CF, general; originally RAF) — "To lay on" something is to arrange something, or to plan, or orchestrate it. (See also **Lay on Air, to; Tee-Up**) [Ref: Partridge (FS)]

> *We'll have to lay on a reception for the Commander when he visits the*
> > *squadron.*

LEAD SLED (RCAF; 1950's and 1960's) — "Lead Sled" was a derogatory nickname coined by RCAF "Sabre" crews for the CF- 100 "Canuck". This nickname soon spread throughout the RCAF.

It seems that no other RCAF aircraft has attracted the number of derogatory nicknames that the CF-100 has. During the 1950's, an RCAF Fighter Wing in France or Germany was usually comprised of two squadrons of F-86 Sabres, and one squadron of CF-100 Canucks. The F-86 Sabre was a magnificent day fighter. In contrast, the CF-100 Canuck was rather less manoeuvrable, having been designed from the outset as an all-weather interceptor. CF-100 pilots and navigators stalked intruders at night, at extremely high altitude, or in foul weather, relying on the radar and fire control system to bring them to close quarters. The CF-100 was robust for a fighter, but no one could ever claim it was graceful in appearance, let alone manoeuvrable!

Thus, to an aggressive young Sabre pilot of a 1950's Fighter Wing, the CF-100 was not a "real" fighter, and its crews worthy of mere pity or scorn for having to fly the graceless "Lead Sled". (See also **Canuck, Kerosene Canso**; For the CF-100 side of this story, see **Clunk**)

> *You mean Ray was actually bounced by a Lead Sled? That's it then! We'll have to post him off fighters!*

LEAF (CF; current) — "Leaf" refers to the Maple Leaf worn in the "vee" of the chevrons worn by a person holding the rank of Master Corporal or Sergeant in the CF. "Getting a leaf" refers to being promoted to the rank of Master Corporal, from Corporal. A Master Corporal wears chevrons identical to Corporal's chevrons except for this Maple Leaf. Less commonly, the word leaf can refer to a much higher rank - general officers in the CF are distinguished by the number of maple leaves embroidered on their epaulettes.

> *When did Willy put up a leaf?*

LEANS, THE (aviation; general) — "The leans" is a type of disorientation that may be experienced by a pilot flying under instrument conditions and without visual reference. Essentially the leans is a subjective, but powerful perception that the aircraft is turning or rolling, when in fact it is flying straight and level. In other words, all the senses tell the pilot to lean to one side, to compensate for an excessive roll that does not really exist. The leans results from a confusion of the senses that humans rely on to maintain equilibrium. Normally this loss of equilibrium occurs if references to the outside horizon are obscured, as can occur in instrument flight.

Healthy human beings maintain their equilibrium and balance using a combination of three senses: their sight, their "vestibular sense" (ie., the balancing senses of the inner ears), and their "muscle sense" (ie., the changes in pressure on the nerve endings in the muscles). Disorientation occurs when the signals sent to the brain by each of these senses conflict with each other. These senses have evolved to function well on the ground, the visual sense being the most powerful. In certain flight conditions the visible horizon may be obscured, which makes the visual sense much less effective. The pilot must then rely more on the other, less reliable senses. The muscle sense becomes much less reliable in flight due to the motion of the aircraft. Thus, the vestibular sense becomes much more influential over the pilots' orientation. When the pilots muscle sense and vestibular sense are telling the pilot that the aircraft is in a roll, while the pilot's instruments are saying the aircraft is flying straight and level, the pilot experiences the leans. The leans, like most forms of disorientation, is best counteracted by an awareness of its causes and by concentration on the aircraft's more reliable instruments. [Ref: Welch]

I started my instrument approach to landing when I felt a case of the leans coming on, so I cancelled the approach.

LEAN-TO (RCAF, CF; 1940's to present) — A "lean-to" is a structure built along the side of a hangar which houses offices and shops. In an architectural sense, the lean-to is an addition that does not bear the main loads of the hangar roof. [Ref: Sutherland]

You'll find the battery shop in the north lean-to of 6 Hangar

LEAVE VISITING CARDS, TO; LEAVE CALLING CARDS, TO (Bomber Command; WWII) — "Leaving visiting cards" was Bomber Command vernacular for bombing. The term alludes to the custom - in high society - of leaving a personal card ("visiting cards" or "calling cards") at the door of a home that one is visiting. [Ref: Partridge (FS)]

Last night we paid a visit to Essen and left some visiting cards.

LEFT, RIGHT, AND CENTRE (RCAF, RAF, WWII) — Originally, to say "left, right, and centre" was to say that everything went well. The phrase alludes to aerial bombing, where the Bomb Aimer ("Bombardier" in American air forces) tracks the fall of the bombs "left" of target heading, corrects to the "right" of the target, and finally "centres" the fall of the bombs directly onto the target, therefore: "Left, Right, and Centre". Its usage however, has expanded so that "left, right, and centre" can also be synonymous with "everywhere". [Ref: Partridge (FS), Partridge (8th)]

LEG (now general; originally RAF, circa 1925) — A "leg" is a stage between stops during a long-range trip.

LEGS   See **Long Legs**

LETCH, TO (general, WWII) — "To letch" is to aggressively and amorously seek out female companionship. It is derived from the word "lecher". [Ref: Partridge (8th)]

LET-DOWN (aviation, general) — An aircraft that "lets-down" is on a controlled, steady descent to a lower altitude. Often the term refers to a descent to a landing. (See also **Nylon Let-Down**)

We'll be commencing our let-down into Namao in about five minutes.

LET-DOWN CHART (RCAF, CF; 1950's to the present) — Strictly speaking, a "Let-Down Chart" (properly known as an "Approach Plate") is a navigation document that describes the instrument approach and landing procedures for a specific airport. All the Let-Down Charts for a given region of Canada are bound together in a small booklet - about the same dimensions as a small menu.

However, a Let-Down Chart can also be a menu in the officer's mess. Perhaps this usage was coined because a menu is about the same size as a Let-Down Chart, and must be carefully studied before committing oneself.

Let's see what's for dinner; Pass me the Let-Down Chart.

LEVY; LEVEE (CF; current) — A Levy is a formal reception held by a public figure such as the Governor-General, a Provincial Lieutenant-Governor, or a Mayor, at which members of the public and the military exchange greetings on a holiday or other occasion. Perhaps the most usual occasion for a Levy is the annual New Year's Day Levy given by the Governor-General and by each Provincial Lieutenant-Governor at their official residences. All serving Canadian Forces officers in the vicinity are expected to attend, wearing dress uniforms and medals, though in many capitals the custom is not restricted to officers.

Upon arrival at the official residence, attendees line up in order of seniority, and in turn exchange New Year's greetings with their host, the Governor-General or Lieutenant-Governor. Despite the apparent formality of the occasion, this is often followed by a round of visits to each mess in the area. It might be considered a formalized New Year's Day "pub-crawl".

LIB (Allied Air Forces; WWII) — The "Liberator", an American four-engine bomber built by Consolidated Aircraft, was often called the "Lib". The Lib is most commonly associated with the U.S. Army Air Force daylight bombing campaign over Germany. However, the Lib was also used by the RCAF, primarily in maritime patrol. The RCAF's 10 and 11 Squadrons, ranged over both the Atlantic and Pacific in search of submarines. As well, No. 168 Squadron flew the Lib in transatlantic transport. [Ref: Partridge (FS)]

Lib

RCAF Squadrons flew the
Lib primarily in anti-submarine ops.

LIGHT BLUE (CF; current) — The phrase "light blue" refers to things or people that belong to the air force, as opposed to "dark blue" which applies to things naval. The term, part of the colour-coding evident in Canadian military slang, is derived from the colour of service uniforms. Things or people belonging to the army may be referred to as "brown" or "green" (though "green" can also refer to things relating to the post-unification era, when everyone wore CF green uniforms). (However, see also **Blue Job; Brown Job; Purple**)

The new Chief Warrant Officer is light blue...

LIGHT COLONEL (CF; current) — An officer of the rank of Lieutenant Colonel is occasionally called a "Light" Colonel. The origins of this term are unclear but it may be supposed that it derives from the fact that the word "lieutenant" is abbreviated "Lt.", which is also an occasional abbreviation for the word light. The nickname is apt, as a Lieutenant Colonel's authority is slightly "lighter" than that of a full Colonel.

Did you hear that Harry got promoted?
So he's a Light Colonel now, eh?

LINE SHACK (RCAF; CF; general) — A "Line Shack" is a building located on the flight "line" or hangar "line" which houses the "Line Servicing" section, the technicians responsible for aircraft handling, servicing and marshalling. Sometimes the Line Shack was just that - a shack - in which the technicians would do their paperwork, hang around waiting for aircraft or aircrews, or drink coffee. On other air bases the Line Shack could be quite palatial, with locker rooms, showers, and a canteen. Just to confuse things, sometimes the Line Shack wasn't a separate building at all! Rather, it was simply a room in a hangar on the Hangar Line. Wherever it may be located, technicians everywhere will agree that a line shack isn't so much a place, as a state of mind. The ambience of an aircraft servicing section - created by its "aircraft status board" covering one wall, multiple telephones, technical logs and manuals, coffee pot in the corner, tables and chairs, and dozens of well-thumbed magazines - has probably not changed since the early days of military aviation. [Ref: Sutherland]

You'll find Sergeant Mills in the Line Shack.

LINE SHOOTING (general since WWII; originally RAF) — "Line-shooting" is boastful lying or exaggeration. [Refs: Partridge (FS); Jones]

LITTLE NORWAY (RCAF, Canadian general; circa 1941-45) — "Little Norway" was the nickname for the Royal Norwegian Air Force training bases established during the Second World War, in Toronto and in Ontario's Muskoka country. The Royal Norwegian Air Force-in-exile operated several aircrew training schools in Canada. These schools provided airmen for the Norwegian squadrons flying with the RAF in Britain during the Second World War. Thus the bright red, white and blue stripes that marked Norwegian military aircraft became a familiar sight in southern Ontario.

LIVING IN; LIVING OUT (CF; current since early 20th C.) — "Living in", or "living out", are descriptive of where a member of the air force is living. If they reside in military quarters on the base they are "living in". If living in civilian accommodations off the base they are "living out". Thus, persons quartered in military barracks are collectively termed, at least for administrative purposes, as "living-in members". (See also **On the Economy**)

> *Are you living in an apartment?*
> *No, I'm living in for now.*

LIZZY (RAF, RCAF; WWII) — "Lizzy" was the affectionate nickname for a classic aircraft of the 1930's and 1940's, the Westland "Lysander". The Lysander was designed in the 1930's to meet an RAF requirement for a rough-and-ready utility aircraft, to be used for Army Cooperation. It was high wing monoplane, with a short take off and landing (STOL) capability rare for aircraft of its time. The RCAF ordered 28 Lizzies for its Army Cooperation squadrons in 1938, and ultimately 225 flew in RCAF livery. Of the first RCAF squadrons sent overseas, the first and the third were air reserve units flying the Lysander; ultimately the Lysander did yeoman service in the European theatre, wherever STOL performance was needed, particularly in the dangerous role of transporting underground fighters to and from occupied France, under cover of dark. In Canada, the Lizzy saw much service in the British Commonwealth Air Training Plan, primarily in the Bombing and Gunnery Schools. [Ref: Molson and Taylor]

> *The first RCAF squadron sent to England in World War Two was a reserve*
> *unit flying Lizzy's.*

L.M.F. (British Commonwealth; WWI and WWII) — The initials "L.M.F." are shorthand for a highly controversial term used in both world wars: "Lack of Moral Fibre". "Lack of Moral Fibre" was the official designation given to an airman no longer capable of functioning in combat for behavioural reasons not diagnosed as medical in nature. Rightly or wrongly, L.M.F. status was often regarded as synonymous with cowardice.

As air historian John Terraine aptly put it, L.M.F was ascribed to aircrew who had *forfeited the confidence of their Commanding Officers in the face of danger in the air.* The isolated nature of air warfare, where the combatants fly alone or in a small crew, has meant that air forces rely to a far greater extent on individual self-discipline than on an externally imposed disciplinary hierarchy. What then, does the air force do with aircrew who are unable to master their fear and cannot cope with continued operational flying?

Squadron CO's had a great deal of discretion in deciding how to handle such airmen. Most would order the airman on leave, or to rest. However, asking to be relieved was often another matter; Mick Mannock, the leading RAF ace of the First World War and CO of 74 Squadron *...would rip the tunic wings off of any pilot requesting a desk job and order their replacement by a strip of yellow cloth.*

During the Second World War, most such cases were diagnosed as psychological conditions and were treated with rest, leave or psychiatric care. Still, a small number of cases (only about 0.3% of all Second World War Commonwealth aircrew) were deemed not to be a medical affliction. The category of "Lack of Moral Fibre" was created to deal with such cases, and such airmen were still treated very harshly. One wartime station commander stated: *I made certain that every case before me was punished by court-martial, and where applicable by an exemplary prison sentence, whatever the psychiatrists were saying.* Airmen deemed to be L.M.F. were treated by the air force system as being merely cowards by other name, and aircrew designated L.M.F. were usually stripped of rank, flying wings, and medals, and were assigned to the most menial of tasks. The designation L.M.F. no longer exists, but controversy lingers. Though there were undoubtedly some cases of outright cowardice, many such cases were in fact an adverse psychological reaction to the stress of combat. Even psychiatric cases were touched by the insinuation of cowardice. [Refs: Terraine, Winter]

LOADIE (CF; current) — "Loadie" is slang for "Loadmaster", the crew member of a transport aircraft who supervises the cargo, safeguards the aircraft from being overloaded, and ensures that the cargo is distributed safely, so as not to shift the aircraft's centre of gravity. The loadie's duties include handling passengers and cargo, and overseeing air drops of cargo.

Ask the Loadie whether we can take on another three passengers.

LOCK HIM UP, TO (military aviation; general) — The term "to lock him up" is a variation on the term "lock on". When a fighter pilot has a target "locked up" it means that the fighter's radar is tracking a target selected by the pilot, to the exclusion of all other targets. This enables a radar-guided missile to home in on it. The target, if it is to survive, must "break the lock" through aggressive evasive manoeuvres, electronic countermeasures, or by use of a decoy. (See also **Lock-on**)

The MiG never stood a chance; I had him locked up at three miles!

LOCK-ON (current; military aviation) — "Lock-on" has two meanings, a technical, tactical meaning, and a social meaning derived from the first.

Strictly speaking, "lock-on" is a technical term; a "lock-on" occurs when tracking radar distinguishes and isolates a selected target and follows its movement, to the exclusion of all else. (See **To Lock Him Up**) Not all radars can "lock-on". However, when a radar is capable of locking on to a target, it enables the aircraft, missile, or bomb to track to its target with great accuracy.

However, this technical and tactical term has been spread to the social arena. Someone whose attention focuses on one thing, to the exclusion of all else, has a "lock-on". Perhaps unsurprisingly, the term is most often associated with the sight of an attractive member of the opposite sex.

Did you see that hot brunette, two tables over?
Yeah, I've got a lock-on!

LOGGIE; LOG WOG (CF; current) — A "LOG Wog" or a "Loggie" is a member of the Logistics Branch, and more specifically, a Logistics Officer. The Canadian Forces Logistics Branch performs all duties related to Supply, Finance and Transportation. As such, the operational support of the CF is largely in the hands of LOG Wogs and Loggies. (See also **Air Mover, Bin Rat, Blanket-Stacker, Box-Kicker, Sock-Tucker**)

Those LOG Wogs run a really big operation!

LOH (inexplicably pronounced "loatch")(CF; current) — The letters LOH stand for "Light Observation Helicopter", but for some reason they are universally pronounced "loatch". A typical Canadian Tactical Helicopter Squadron comprises two operational flights, one of which is the LOH Flight (ie., "loatch flight"). The CF presently uses the Bell Kiowa helicopter for the LOH role, though it will soon be replaced by the Bell "Griffon".

Dave's a LOH driver in Edmonton!

LOITER, TO (Military Aviation, general; current) — An aircraft "loiters" when it is airborne but not yet engaged in operations and is waiting to be called upon to engage the enemy.

The CF-18's were loitering behind the battlefield, waiting to be called in to strike the enemy ground forces.

LONG LEGS; SHORT LEGS (aviation; general) — An aircraft which has "long legs" is capable of flying long distances without refuelling. Similarly, an aircraft with "short legs" has a relatively short range.

The Starfighter was a great airplane, but it had fairly short legs.

LONG WEIGHT (Military; general) — The similarity in sound between "long weight" and "long wait" has led to many an embarrassing moment for junior servicemembers over the years. Long weight falls into the category of: "useful but mythical apparatus". Typically, a senior airman will send a hapless apprentice on an errand: *to go and ask for a long weight.* The apprentice will proceed, asking the person in charge for a long weight. The person in charge will then invite the apprentice to take a seat. After awhile, the apprentice will be asked if he had waited long enough. (For other mythical but useful substances see **Flight Line; Hangar Line, Flight Lustre, Propwash, Radar Contacts, Relative Bearing Grease, Skyhook, Tartan Paint, Tacan Gate**)

Cameron, go to the tool crib and ask the Corporal there for a long weight...

LORRAINE (RCAF; Post-WWII) — The "Lorraine" was the biggest crane on an RCAF Station. It was a large, wheeled monster that could hoist 20 tons, and was made by the Lorraine Corporation. When an aircraft had to be lifted off the ground, you usually sent for the Lorraine. [Ref: Sutherland]

That Sabre's right undercarriage failed and it spun off the runway into the weeds. We'll need the Lorraine to get it back to the Wing Maintenance hangar.

LOST LEGION — "Lost Legion" is a term coined by Canadian aviation historians for all those Canadians who, during the Second World War, served in British, rather than Canadian, flying services. The "Lost Legion" includes Canadians serving in the Royal Air Force (rather than the RCAF), and members of the RCAF who served in RAF squadrons. These persons are "lost" because, whether by accident or design, British records do not list these personnel as "Canadian". Thus their contributions to the war effort have been ascribed to the RAF, rather than being attributed to Canada or the RCAF.

For many years Canadian citizens were "British Subjects", a legacy of membership in the British Empire and Commonwealth. With precious few career opportunities in the tiny prewar RCAF, Canadians who wished to become military aviators usually crossed the Atlantic to join the RAF. For example, the great Canadian naval ace of the First World War, Raymond Collishaw of Nanaimo, B.C., remained in the RAF after the First World War, rather than return to Canada. Ultimately he rose to become the senior Air Officer in North Africa during the Second World War, a level of command he could never have aspired to as an RCAF officer. Similarly, during the Second World War, RCAF personnel were posted about within the RAF at will. So a considerable portion of Canada's effort in the Second World War in the air has been ascribed to the Royal Air Force.

Unfortunately, it is very difficult to estimate the size of the Lost Legion due to RAF records policy. It has been strongly suggested that this policy reflected Imperial sensibilities, in which Colonies and Dominions were merely expected to provide replacements for larger "Imperial" armed forces, run by British leaders. Indeed, it has been further suggested that this sentiment lives on to this day in the Historical Branch of the Ministry of Defence. At least one researcher experienced difficulty obtaining cooperation in learning the size and extent of the Lost Legion from wartime RAF records.

Still, there is no doubt that the Lost Legion has an exemplary record of service, including:

-       50 "Aces" (out of the RAF total of over 900)
-       2 Victoria Cross Winners
-       2 George Cross Winners

Over 100 of the "Lost Legion" became Prisoners of War, and 870 were killed in action.

Besides Canadians who served in, or with, the RAF, many Canadian naval aviators served in the Royal Navy's Fleet Air Arm. Perhaps the most distinguished of these was Lieutenant Robert Hampton Grey, known as "Hammy" to his friends, a Naval Reservist who posthumously won the Victoria Cross by sinking a Japanese destroyer in a Royal Navy "Corsair" aircraft. [Ref: Allison]

LOWBOLD   See **Gremlin**

LOX, TO (aviation general) — "LOX" is the acronym for Liquid Oxygen, often used in military aircraft as a source of breathing oxygen for high altitude flight. "To LOX" an aircraft, is to replenish its supply of Liquid Oxygen. LOX is useful because it is highly compressed and a great deal of oxygen can be carried in a small volume. However, LOX is cold enough to destroy flesh, and when it contacts a petroleum product, instant combustion results. It is a very dangerous substance if mishandled, and it must be returned to its gaseous state before it is usable.

After the aircraft is refuelled, send the Safety Systems guy out to lox it.

MIKE

MACH (generally pronounced "mock") (aviation; general) — Mach is the term used to designate multiples of the speed of sound, ie., the velocity of a sound wave travelling through the atmosphere. Therefore, Mach 1 is the speed of sound, Mach 2 is twice the speed of sound, and so on. The precise speed of sound is not constant; it varies with air density and temperature, and therefore, with altitude. This usage Mach honours the German physicist who first calculated the speed of sound: Ernst Mach.

Use of the word Mach was largely confined to university labs and lecture halls until the 1940's, when aeronautical engineers encountered unforeseen obstacles while trying to build faster aircraft. They discovered that, as aircraft speeds approached Mach 1, the ordinary rules of flight dynamics changed and familiar aerodynamic principles became irrelevant. Many aircraft and pilots were lost in the attempt to exceed Mach 1, which became known as the "sound barrier". Finally, in October, 1947, Captain Chuck Yeager of the USAF exceeded Mach 1, flying a Bell X-1 rocket plane. Later research led to the discovery of the "area rule" principle, which allowed designers to build aircraft capable of easily making the transition from subsonic to supersonic flight. (See **Coke-Bottle Fuselage**)

> *These days, exceeding Mach 1 is no big deal.*
> *It is if you're flying an Aurora!*

MACHINE (RNAS, RFC; WWI) — In the First World War, and for several decades after, an aircraft was commonly called a "machine".

M.A.D.; MAD BOOM (military aviation; since 1950's) — "M.A.D." (generally pronounced "madd") stands for "Magnetic Anomaly Detection", one of several submarine detection systems carried on maritime patrol aircraft. MAD works on simple principles: a submarine contains much ferrous metal, and the presence of all this iron in the open sea, even if submerged, should easily deflect a sensitive magnet! Magnetic Anomaly Detection systems measure the earth's magnetic field. When the presence of iron in a submerged submarine disrupts the magnetic field, the MAD system senses it. An aircraft equipped with a MAD system is easily recognized by the a large, prominent appendage sticking straight back from the aircraft tail. This is the "MAD Boom" - sometimes called a "stinger" for its resemblance to a bee, or wasp stinger. (Some smaller anti-submarine aircraft however are equipped with a less prominent, retractable "stinger")

MAD systems are very accurate but have rather short range. When the presence of a submarine is suspected, the aircraft flies a tight, complex, clover leaf-shaped pattern within a very small area over the sea, localizing the submerged submarine with the MAD system. This is the "MAD run", and it calls for the pilot to throw the large sub-hunter around the sky like a fighter until the systems operators in the back of the aircraft locate the submarine. The MAD run is not popular among anti- submarine aircrews - at

Mae West

The inflatable life preserver owes
its nickname to Hollywood star
Mae West.

least not to those in the rear aircraft compartments. Lacking a view outside the aircraft, they must concentrate on monitoring their systems while enduring these gyrations. They say that being on a MAD run is like being inside a shoe box that someone has kicked down a flight of stairs... (See also **Honk Bag**) [Ref: Sutherland]

You can always tell whether an aircraft is a sub-hunter, by its MAD boom.

MAE WEST (Post-1939) — "Mae West" has been the nickname for an automatically inflatable life-preserver since the Second World War. The name honours Mae West, Hollywood actress and comedienne of the 1930's, whose voluptuous bosom and enticing demeanour made quite an impression on the male imagination. The nickname is apt when applied to a life preserver. The Mae West is worn like a vest, the front of which incorporates two large inflatable bladders. These two bladders, inflated with compressed CO2, keep the downed aviator afloat in the water.

The Mae West was certainly an improvement on earlier aircrew life preservers. Some earlier life preservers were made of kapok, and therefore too bulky for wear in an aircraft. Others were inflatable, but the wearer had to inflate it himself using lung-power, a difficult task for a wounded survivor or in a rough sea. The Mae West, quickly inflated from a small bottle of compressed gas, kept the wearer's nose and mouth above water even when the survivor was unconscious. [Refs: Partridge (FS); Greer; Harold]

MAGGIE, THE (general CF, but especially RCN; 1950's) — "The Maggie" was the affectionate nickname for HMCS Magnificent, the second aircraft carrier in RCN service. The Maggie was a British Majestic-class light fleet carrier of 19,000 tons displacement. Originally it was planned for British wartime service, but construction was halted at war's end. Construction was again commenced when Canada expressed interest in replacing its first aircraft carrier, HMCS Warrior (a "Colossus" class carrier, loaned to Canada by Britain in 1947). Like Warrior, HMCS Magnificent was "on loan" from Britain. Commissioned in 1951, the Maggie carried a variety of naval aircraft: Sea Fury fighters, Avenger ASW aircraft, and H04S helicopters. The Maggie was returned to Britain in 1955 and replaced by a Canadian-owned ship, HMCS Bonaventure. Like HMCS Magnificent, HMCS Bonaventure was also a Majestic-class carrier though it was extensively modified to Canadian requirements. (See **Bonnie, Turkey, Horse**)

MAHOGANY BOMBER (general, post WWII) — A "Mahogany Bomber" can be a desk-bound member of the air force, or it can mean the desk that member sits at. The term was coined because aircrew posted to a ground job, or who spend an inordinate amount of time at a desk doing paperwork, often call this "flying a desk". Therefore, they fly a Mahogany Bomber.

What do you do at Headquarters?
I fly a Mahogany Bomber...

MAJE (CF Air Element, current) — "Maje" is a subordinate's casual form of address to an officer of the rank of Major, formed simply by dropping the last syllable. Though common among air force officers and NCOs, it is perhaps ill-advised to address an Army Major as "maje", given the Army's more rigid view of military courtesy.

How's it going, Maje?

MAJOR — In the Air Force, the word "Major" has two possible meanings:

(1)   **'Major** (pre-1950's RCAF) — From the birth of the RCAF to the 1950's, the title of the senior noncommissioned officer on an RCAF squadron or station was "Sergeant-Major." Generally this was contracted to "'major". Thus, one might "get into trouble with the 'major", "report to the 'major", and "be assigned to extra duties by the 'major". This all occured in an air force that had no such rank as Major. (Sergeant-Major is an appointment, not a rank, and the rank of Major belonged to the army, not the RCAF. Others have suggested this was all part of a larger RCAF plot to confuse the army!)

This may all come as a shock to RCAF veterans of a younger generation, for whom Sergeant-Major is purely an army title. Still, the founders of the RCAF felt that the senior Warrant Officer ought to be accorded this traditional title, which remained in use for over three decades - abbreviated as 'Major. In the early 1950's the rules changed and the senior noncommissioned officer became the Station, or Squadron Warrant Officer - the "SWO". (See **SWO**) [Refs: Harvey; Sutherland]

Ask the 'major to report to Wing Commander Campbell.

(2)   **Major** (RCAF, CF; current) — "Major" is a technician's shorthand for a "major unserviceability", that is, a technical malfunction serious enough to prevent the aircraft from flying until the major is rectified. A major is to be distinguished from a "minor", a malfunction not serious enough to prevent safe flight. (See **Pink Sheets; Snag**)

How's the repair of that major coming along?

MAKE A NAME FOR ONESELF, TO (CF current) — "Making a name for oneself" means attracting the attention of ones' peers or superiors - in a thoroughly negative sense, generally after repeated professional or social failings.

I hear Andre is beginning to make a name for himself!
I'm afraid so...

MAKE-AND-MEND DAY (RAF, RCAF; WWII; originally naval) — "Make and Mend" is naval slang that slipped over into air force usage during the Second World War. "Make and Mend" is a "stand down", a period set aside - or bestowed by fortune - and devoted to rest, performing minor repairs and doing housekeeping chores. [Ref: Harvey]

That rain's not going to let us fly today. Apparently we've got a make and mend day on our hands.

MANNING (RCAF; WWII) — "Manning" was RCAF shorthand for "Manning Depot", the recruit's first taste of the air force. Each of the RCAF recruit training schools was called a Manning Depot. At Manning, RCAF recruits were introduced to drill, weapons, air force law, dress and discipline, physical training, pay and career policies, and of course, they met the dreaded "discip", the disciplinary NCO's who ran the training. The four Second World War Manning Depots were located at Brandon, Edmonton, Toronto and Lachine. After the Second World War, the sole RCAF Manning Depot was located at St. Jean, Quebec. After unification of the armed forces in 1968, all CF anglophone recruit training was centralized at CFB Cornwallis in Nova Scotia, formerly the home of the RCN's recruit school. Recruit training for francophone recruits remained at St. Jean. (See **Discip, Muscle Bosun, Squarebashing, Spitshine**) [Ref: Collins]

I was never happier than when I finished Manning...

MAPLE FLAG (CF/NATO; current) — Maple Flag is a large and highly realistic air fighting exercise held several times annually at CFB Cold Lake, 300 miles northeast of Edmonton, near the Saskatchewan border. The title "Maple Flag" borrows from "Red Flag", a USAF air combat exercise conducted at Nellis Air Force Base, just outside Las Vegas, Nevada. Exercises such as Maple Flag, Red Flag, and the US Navy "Top Gun" provide the most realistic air combat training possible, short of firing live weapons. Computer and electronics technology makes it possible to accurately simulate an air battle occurring over a range several thousand miles square.

Exercises such as these resulted from lessons learned in the Viet Nam war. There, the USN and USAF found that the greatest risk of being shot down was early in an aviator's tour of combat duty, before the pilot had acquired the skills and knowledge needed to survive. Top Gun and Red Flag were developed to teach American pilots air combat skills before meeting the enemy. They proved so successful that Canada and other NATO air forces copied the program and have added unique twists of their own.

In some respects, Maple Flag is superior to other exercises because the air fighting range is large, isolated, and closely resembles the terrain of the former Soviet Union. Canadian squadrons train at Maple Flag, and are often joined by squadrons from all American service branches and from NATO air forces. Just as aircrew compete in the sky, squadron groundcrews strive to keep aircraft serviceable and maintain a high flying rate. Recently, the air defence artillery has joined the list of participants, much to the chagrin of some fighter pilots who have learned about SAM's and "triple A" the hard way! As well, transport squadrons often participate, to give transport crews training in tactical airlift in a high threat environment, and to give fighter crews training in escort and interception.

Maple Flag is characterized by fierce competition between squadrons, both in mock air war and in the nightly contests around the "Crud Table"! Crud is a unique and demanding indoor sport which had its origins in the messes of Canadian fighter squadrons. Thanks to Maple Flag, it is now becoming popular in United States flying units, RAF squadrons, and among NATO air forces. (See **Crud (3), SAM; Triple A**)

MARGUERITE   See **Dispersal**

MARK I EYEBALL (general military usage) — To use the "Mark I Eyeball" is to actually look at something, as opposed to using some other mechanical, electrical or optical aid to examine it. Sometimes it is the "Mark I, Mod 1 Eyeball". Successive designs and variants of aircraft, weapons and equipment are often designated by their "Mark" number or by their Modification (or "Mod") number.

MASTER OF CEREMONIES (WWII RAF, RCAF) — The "Master of Ceremonies" is the

"Master Bomber" on a night bombing attack during the Second World War.

In the Second World War, Bomber Command aircraft flew to their targets at night, independent of one another, albeit along the same route. In any given raid, hundreds, even thousands, of bombers flew along a common corridor, called the "stream", to a common target. As the number of aircraft increased, the need for traffic control immediately over the target became critical.

The solution was to appoint a Master Bomber, who flew his aircraft over the target throughout the raid, and who guided the bomb-aimers* towards their targets. The Master Bomber was exposed to flak and night fighters for hours, and typically flew a Lancaster bomber (See **Lanc**), though later, smaller Mosquito aircraft were employed (See **Mossie**). This was a very dangerous job and only the most experienced Bomber Command aircrew had the skill required.

> *   In the Commonwealth air forces, he was a "Bomb-Aimer", not a "Bombardier". "Bombardier" was a US air force term, and was also a rank in the Royal Canadian Artillery, equal to an air force corporal.

[Ref: Partridge (FS)]

MATERNITY JACKET (RFC; WWI) — The "Maternity Jacket" was the distinctive dress tunic adopted during the First World War by the Royal Flying Corps (...*available from Dunhill tailors for 5-and-a-half Guineas!*). This dress jacket distinguished RFC members from members of other British Army corps and regiments. The Maternity Jacket was characterized by a high closed "military" collar and by a jacket front that draped right across the body. The front of the jacket was closed with hidden buttons on the wearer's extreme right. The effect was that the front of the tunic became an unbroken expanse of fabric, without either buttons or pockets - rather like a lady's maternity dress of the day. [Ref: Winter]

MAYDAY (universal Aviation; since WWI) — "Mayday" is the universal radio codeword indicating that an aircraft is in distress. It is a corruption of a French term thought to indicate that a person needs help: *m'aidez*. Purists suggest that the Mayday code must have been coined by an English speaker, as the proper French is *aidez-moi!* Grammar hardly matters though, as the usefulness of a radio codeword lies in its universal acceptance, and clarity of its sound and meaning. (See also **Guard**)

If you hear a Mayday, stop talking and listen!

MEATBALL (RCN; 1950's to 1969) — In the early days of naval aviation, a pilot was guided down to a landing by a Landing Signals Officer, (Deck Landing Control Officer, or DLCO on British carriers) who signalled to the pilot with lights, or with bright paddles in each hand (See **Bats**). In modern aircraft carrier landings, the LSO has been replaced by a mechanical/optical aid that shines a light into a specially focussed mirror. This mirror reflects the light beam up and along the correct flight path to landing. The pilot aligns the aircraft to descend along this beam, and adjusts his course and rate of descent to remain "on the beam". The pilot was assisted by a marker placed in front of the mirror. The marker was fixed such that, when the aircraft descended correctly along the beam, the marker interrupted the light beam and blocked it from the approaching the beam, the marker interrupted the light beam and blocked it from the approaching pilot's view. This marker is the "Meatball". Thus the pilot, adjusting his rate of descent and heading, could perform a correct carrier landing by keeping the Meatball in the centre of the mirror. However, the short deck, and the roll and pitch of the ship always makes for a challenging landing.

> *Finally I broke free of the cloud layer; then all I had to do was fly the Meatball down onto the deck.*

MEATHEAD (RCAF, now CF generally; since at least WWII) — A "Meathead" was an Air Force Policeman. The nickname lives on today in the Canadian Forces, where it refers to the Military Police (though it is rarely - if ever - used to their faces). Therefore, Military Police headquarters on a CF base is occasionally the "Meathead Shack." (See also **A.F.P, A.P., Gestapo, S.P.**)[Ref: Harvey; Partridge (8th)]

Meathead

> *This padlock has been broken; call the Meatheads!*

MEATWAGON (origins obscure, but probably WWI) — The "meatwagon" was the ambulance that attended at aircraft crashes and remove the injured - or the remains. (See also **Hungry Liz**) [Ref: Partridge (8th)]

> *How come the meatwagon is waiting on the tarmac?*

MECH   See **Tech**

MED A (CF; current) — "Med A" is both abbreviation and slang for that ubiquitous servicemember, the "medical assistant". The Med A is a non-commissioned aide who assists military nurses and doctors in all aspects of their medical duties. There is no real civilian equivalent to the Med A, whose duties range from simple orderly and nurses aide duties in a clinic, to emergency para-medical duties in isolated locations or on the battlefield. (The U.S. Army equivalent is nicknamed a "medic", and in the U.S. Navy and Marines the title is "corpsman", for "Medical Corpsman".)

MENOPAUSE MANOR (CF; current) — "Menopause Manor" is the humorous, if slightly disparaging, title for the "Sergeants and Warrant Officers Mess", the social forum and watering-hole for the senior noncommissioned officers. The "Senior Noncommissioned Officers" are the Sergeants, Flight Sergeants (in the RAF and RCAF), and Warrant Officers of all grades. Menopause Manor reflects the fact that the Sergeants and Warrant Officers taken as a group, are generally older than everyone else on the base. (See also **J.R.**)

Where's Warrant Officer Griffiths?
I believe you'll find him having a lemonade in Menopause Manor...

MENOPAUSE ROW; MENOPAUSE CIRCLE (RCAF, CF) — Menopause Row and Menopause Circle are both rather disparaging references to the street in an air base's "married quarters area" where senior officers live. Like the comparable term "Menopause Manor", these terms suggest that the senior officers on a base, taken as a group, are generally older. [Ref: Sutherland]

Squadron Leader Gibbons lives on Menopause Row.

MESS KIT — "Mess Kit" is the universal, though incorrect, name for formal military "evening wear". The proper name is Mess Dress. (Properly, a mess kit is a set of metal tins, and a knife, fork and spoon, carried in the field.) Each service branch has its own style of Mess Dress. Usually it comprises a short jacket and trousers (or long skirt for ladies), white shirt or blouse, a black bow tie, and cummerbund. Rank badges, and miniature medals and flying badges are worn. (See also **Kit**)

Mess Kit

MET; MET MAN (aviation; general) — "Met" is the universal shorthand for meteorology. Therefore, the "Met Man" is the meteorologist who gives everyone the weather report at the "Met Briefing". (See also **Cloudy Joe**) [Refs: Partridge (FS); Partridge (8th)]

METAL-BASHER (RAF, RCAF, WWII to the present) — "Metal-Basher" is the nickname for a Metals Technician, the ground crew technician responsible for fabricating metal components for aircraft repairs. Immediately before the Second World War, RAF (and RCAF) slang referred to almost all specialist groundcrew as some type of "basher" (e.g., Clock-Basher for an instrument technician). Metal-Basher seems to be the last surviving usage in Canadian air force slang. (See **Basher, Clock Basher**)

MFWIC (pronounced "miff-wick") (CF Current) — "MFWIC" is the acronym for "Mother-Fucker Who's In Charge", ie. the person running things - the boss, or the Commanding Officer. The term is doubtless American in origin, but has achieved a certain Canadian following.

Who's the MFWIC in this Section?!

MICKEY MOUSE (Originally American; since WWII) — Something that is "Mickey Mouse" is simple, crude, or has been hastily improvised without thought.

Of course, this term derives from the famous Walt Disney cartoon character. Originally, if something was "Mickey Mouse", it was comical and childlike, rather like the character himself. However, in Air Force operations, anything comical and childlike is also usually dangerous. Therefore, this term gradually took on a highly disparaging aspect when used in a military context.

MiG (since WWII) — MiG is the universal acronym for Soviet aircraft built by the superlative Mikoyan- Gurevitch design bureau. The term is formed from the first letters of each of their names: "Mi" and "G".

MIKE-MIKE — "Mike-Mike" is slang for "millimetre", from its abbreviation: "mm." which, if pronounced according to the NATO phonetic alphabet, becomes mike-mike. Mike-mike is generally used to refer to aircraft cannons, the calibre of which is expressed in millimetres. [Ref: Elting]

> *What's this aircraft armed with?*
> *A pair of 40 mike-mikes*

MILK RUN (military aviation; since WWII) — A "milk run" is a routine scheduled flight, typically uneventful. The term probably alludes to an old horse-drawn milk cart, routinely making morning milk deliveries throughout the neighbourhood. The term is relative, though. A milk run to a bomber squadron may not seem like a milk run to other types of unit! Second World War bomber crews considered certain operations to be a milk run, not because they were uneventful, but because they were merely less risky than other operations. [Ref: Partridge (FS)]

MILSPEC (ie., "mill-speck")(NATO, CF; general) — "MilSpec" is the acronym for "Military Specification", a set of very specific standards of engineering quality applied to the design and manufacture of various armed forces equipment. Armed forces have an inherent need for predictably high quality in all materiel, from nuts and bolts, to bootsoles. The MilSpec system was developed in the United States to ensure this high quality. These standards generally exceed those of the commercial marketplace. However, defence procurement programs are lately being criticized for requiring expensive MilSpec standards, even in equipment where there is no need. For example, is there any need for a specially designed MilSpec garbage can when a garbage can from a hardware store will suffice?

> *Are these diodes MilSpec?*

MINIATURES (military; general usage) — "Miniatures" are small-sized versions of one's medals, orders and decorations. They are worn exclusively on the Mess Dress uniform. (See **Mess Kit**)

MINI-WARRANT (CF; current) — A "Mini-Warrant" is a person who holds the rank of Warrant Officer. In the CF rank structure, there are three levels of Warrant Officer. From highest to lowest they are: Chief Warrant Officer, Master Warrant Officer, and the Warrant Officer. The lowest level is sometimes called the Mini-Warrant, to distinguish it from the two higher levels of Warrant Officer. A Warrant Officer ranks immediately above a Sergeant and is equivalent to the old RCAF rank of Flight Sergeant. (See also **Crowns**)

Did you hear that Sergeant Forbes got promoted?
So, she's a Mini-Warrant now, eh?

MINOR   See **Major(2)**

M.I.R. (ie., "emm-eye-are")(universal; Commonwealth military forces) — M.I.R. is the "Medical Inspection Room", the outpatient clinic in a military hospital. Customarily, "Sick Parade" was held first thing in the morning, and was a scene that could (and often did) attract a most amazing collection of military ill and injured, together with the occasional malingerer or hypochondriac.

I think I've got the flu; I'm going to M.I.R.

MISSILE FARM (RCAF, CF; current) — The "Missile Farm" was the missile storage area at an air defence base, and was a common term during the service of the CF-101 Voodoo. (See also **Coffin, One-o-One; One-o- wonder**)

M.O. (Military; general usage) — In military circles, "Medical Officer" (inevitably abbreviated as "M.O.") always refers to the doctor.

MOD (Aviation, general; since 1920's) — "Mod" is shorthand for "modification". Aircraft are the product of precise design engineering, but inevitably, improvements or alterations to the existing aircraft design become necessary. These alterations are termed modifications but are inevitably referred to by aircraft maintainers as mods. (Ref: Partridge (8th)]

Twin Otter 804 is grounded for a Mod

MOG (ie., "mogg")(RCAF Europe; late 1950's and early 1960's) — "Mog" was the Canadian airman's shorthand for "Unimog", a German aircraft towing tractor built by Mercedes-Benz. The Mog was in RCAF overseas use in the late 1950's and early 1960's, during the latter days of the Sabre and early days of the Starfighter. RCAF ground crews tended to prefer it to the "Mules" used at RCAF Stations in Canada. (See **Mule**) [Ref: Sutherland]

Wing Maintenance has finished the special inspection. Take a Mog down
there and bring that aircraft back here.

MONKEY CHAIN   See **Monkey Harness**

MONKEY HARNESS (RCAF, CF; current) —A "monkey harness" is a restraint harness worn by a crewman who must move around the aircraft cabin in flight, near an open aircraft door. Essentially a monkey harness is a parachute harness (of course, minus the parachute and bag), tethered to the aircraft fuselage by strong nylon webbing. The monkey harness prevents crewmembers from falling out of the open door should they lose their footing. This makes it possible for the crewman to safely assist in paradrops or cargo drops.

The term may be a development on "monkey chain". During the latter part of the First World War, gunners and observers in RAF aircraft were tethered to their seat by a monkey chain. This was a steel chain attached to the crewman's waist belt, which allowed the crewman to move and turn around in the open cockpit, while remaining secure. Both terms appear to allude to the harness worn by an organ-grinder's monkey. However, it has been suggested in American circles that monkey harness alludes to the fact that the wearer, like a monkey, has a long "tail" attached to the aircraft.

MOOSE CALL (RCAF, CF; early 1960's to late 1980's) — The "moose call" was a distinctive howling noise unique to the engine of the Lockheed Starfighter. This sound was best described as an abrupt and sometimes unnerving change of pitch, caused by movement of the variable exhaust nozzle on the Starfighter's J-79 engine. The sound of the moose call was compared by some to the call of a bull moose in rut! The sound was not produced by other fighters, and thus will forever be fondly associated with RCAF and CF Starfighter operations. (See **One-O-Four, Widowmaker**)

> *You can always tell the sound of a CF-104!*
> *How?*
> *By the Moose Call, of course!*

MOOSE MILK (CF; universal) — In the 1920's, Moose Milk was one of several types of home-brewed cocktail common to the Yukon Territories. A common type of Moose Milk was condensed milk stiffly laced with rum. Today, the term is common throughout the Canadian Forces for eggnog, also stiffly laced with rum, and topped by a sprinkling of cinnamon. Moose Milk, like eggnog, is a beverage usually served during the festive season. Moose Milk is inevitably served at inter-mess functions, such as when officers and sergeants are invited to each other's messes, or at the annual Lieutenant-Governor's Levee. Moose milk is a deceptive beverage, and ought to be consumed with respect. [Ref: Partridge (8th)]

> *Nobody makes Moose Milk like Sergeant Tanchuk makes Moose Milk!*

MORNING PRAYERS (CF; current) — "Morning Prayers" is the term often given to a daily morning staff conference. The term dates back to the Second World War and is certainly current in the CF for morning meetings conducted by the unit senior aircraft engineering officer. Morning Prayers is attended by all of the aircraft engineering officers and senior technical NCO's on that squadron. [Ref: Partridge (8th)]

> *Does the Deputy Aircraft Maintenance Officer have to attend morning*
> *   prayers?*
> *At this Wing, everyone attends Morning Prayers!*

MOSSIE (pronounced "mozzy") (Commonwealth air forces; WWII) — "Mossie" was the nickname for one of the most remarkable combat aircraft of the Second World War: the Mosquito. The Mosquito, a private venture, was designed as a small, fast, twin-engine bomber, with a crew of only two: a pilot, and an observer who navigated and dropped bombs. From this, the Mossie developed into a fighter, a fighter-bomber, night intruder, and photo-reconnaissance aircraft. It was a truly versatile aircraft. It was fast and maneouvrable, yet could also carry a bombload equal to that of an American B-17 Flying Fortress (albeit for a shorter distance). Its service ceiling was so high that no

Luftwaffe aircraft could touch it until the first of the German jet fighters entered service.

The most striking feature of the Mossie was its construction; to reduce wartime metal use, the airframe was constructed almost entirely of plywood! As well, Mosquito production was dispersed throughout Britain and elsewhere. Sub-contractors included groups which were as small as seven people! One of every seven Mossies was produced in Toronto. Use of wood enabled fast construction and repair, and by applying sheets of balsa in layers, and by aligning the wood grain properly, strength was maintained. A shell fragment that might sever a strong metal member would scarcely weaken a thick, continuous wood shell or a stout wooden spar.

Repair of the Mossie was sometimes unusual because of its wooden construction. In 1942-43, a Mosquito squadron quickly deployed from England to Malta and had to conduct operations before its stock of spares and its technicians had arrived; ...*woodwork repairs were carried out with cigar box wood, old tea chests and bits of (wooden aircraft) bomb doors. Aid was also obtained from the local coffin-maker, whose woodworking was of the highest order. His presence spread a slight gloom over the pilots, one of whom was heard to remark "to watch that blighter working on my aeroplane makes me expect to find it fitted with brass handles when I next go to fly."* Wood made the Mossie very light, and gave the aircraft a poor image on enemy radar; it has been described as the first "stealth" fighter. This use of wood also led to its other nickname, coined primarily for the wartime public: "The Wooden Wonder". [Ref: Sharp and Bowyer]

The Mossie needed a carpenter as often as a mechanic!

MOTH (RAF, RCAF; still current though rare) — "Moth" could be shorthand for any of the De Havilland "Moth" series of biplanes (ie., Gipsy Moth, Cirrus Moth, Fox Moth, etc), though the term primarily referred to that classic wartime trainer, the "Tiger Moth". The Tiger Moth, often called the "Tiger" by its pilots, was a slow, forgiving and reliable biplane used by both the RAF and RCAF for initial pilot training. Its gentle nature made it ideal for initial flying training. (De Havilland Aircraft named this series of aircraft after various species of Moth in honour of their pioneering designer Geoffrey De Havilland, an ardent Lepidopterist!) (See also **Tiger; Tigerschmitt**)

The Moth was the first airplane I ever flew!

MOTHBALLS, IN (aviation, military; general) — An aircraft that has been placed "in mothballs" has been placed in long-term storage. The term alludes to the old practice of putting "mothballs" alongside cotton or wool clothing destined for long-term storage. (Mothballs were a substance noxious to insects, which thereby dissuaded them from dining on your clothes.)

Aircraft placed in long term storage are drained of all fluids, high pressure gases are bled off, and usable parts are removed. Finally, the entire aircraft is painted with a rubber-based paint, to inhibit corrosion or the introduction of foreign substances. When taken "out of mothballs", an aircraft undergoes a thorough overhaul before reentering service. (See also **Cocoon, to**)

M-SLASH (ie., "emm-slash") (CF; current since 1968) — "M-Slash" is occasional Canadian Forces slang for the rank of Master Corporal, and derives from an early abbreviation: "M/Cpl". "M-Slash" refers to the letter "M", followed by the "slash" symbol: "/" .

Did you hear? Doreen got her M-Slash!

MUD-MOVING (CF; current) — "Mud-moving" is slang for close air support or battlefield air interdiction. These involve the direct use of attack aircraft to support the army in the land battle. These involve direct attack of enemy ground forces, using bombs, air-to-ground rockets, antitank missiles, napalm, and of course, guns. The effect of any of these is usually to throw large amounts of soil and debris into the air, therefore the term mud- moving. (See also **Air-to-Mud**)

Though the CF-5 is good at mud-moving, the A-10 is superb!

MULE (RCAF, CF; universal) — A Mule is an aircraft towing tractor. The origins of the nickname are obvious considering the usual role of a (four-legged) mule.

Not only does a mule have to be able to tow this Aurora, its brakes have to be able to stop it once it builds up momentum!

MURPHY'S LAW; TO MURPHY — Murphy's Law is a planning principle ignored at one's peril. Originally there was one so-called Murphy's Law, but research has revealed a set of three:

Murphy's First Law:	*If anything can go wrong, it will go wrong.*
Murphy's Second Law:	*If everything is proceeding on time, within budget, and without any failures, you have overlooked something.*
Murphy's Third Law:	*If there is a possibility of two or more things going wrong, the first to go wrong will be that which has the worst consequences.*

(Note however, that the same principles which find expression in Murphy's Law have been known in Britain for over a century, as "Sod's Law". Also, students of this phenonomenon ought to be aware of the so-called 4th Law of Physics which states that the cussedness of the universe tends to a maximum.)

According to the Concise Oxford Dictionary of Proverbs, there actually was a man named Murphy after whom these laws were named! The Oxford states that the three Murphy's Laws above were coined in 1949 by George Nicholls, an engineer with Northrop Aviation, and were based on comments made by his friend, Captain E. Murphy, of the Dayton Aircraft Research Establishment. The laws appear to be valid, and are now part of Twentieth Century folklore. (Readers should also be aware of "O'Toole's Axiom", which states: "Murphy was an optimist.")

In contemporary CF jargon, the above axioms have also been turned into a verb: "to Murphy". An errant technician "murphies" a component when he or she succeeds in installing an aircraft component in a manner completely contrary to the way it was designed to be installed. In other words, the technician has proved Murphy's First Law:

If anything can go wrong, it will go wrong. [Ref: Oxford - Proverbs]

MUSCLE BOSUN; MUSCLE MECHANIC; MUSCLE MERCHANT (CF; current) — A "Muscle Bosun", or a "Muscle Mechanic" is a physical training instructor, a serviceman or servicewoman trained in fitness training and in coaching sports. Servicemembers usually first encounter them during recruit training, where they begin the difficult and unpopular task of getting into top physical condition. The term Muscle Bosun probably came from the navy, where a "Bosun" (a contraction of "boatswain") is the sailor who actually handles the ship (as opposed to operating its engines or weapons, etc.) Thus, the seaman instructor who ran physical training became known as a Muscle Bosun. The term likely spread to the rest of the CF after Unification in 1968. Muscle Mechanic would appear to be more air force oriented, given that the air force has so many mechanics of all types. [Ref: Partridge (8th)]

Muscle Bosun

We need a soccer ball; can we get one from the Muscle Bosuns?

MYSTERY MEAT (Canadian military; universal) — "Mystery meat" is meat, served in military food, the origin of which is uncertain or which is generally unappetizing. Most often the term refers to canned or processed meat. [Ref: Sutherland]

> *What's for lunch today?*
> *Mystery meat sandwiches, as usual.*

OVEMBER

NAAFI (pronounced "naffy") (British Forces, and Commonwealth during WWII) — The "NAAFI" was the Navy, Army, Air Force Institute, the organization that runs British military canteens and sells creature comforts to servicemen at low cost. Canadians in wartime England relied on the NAAFI along with their British comrades. However, in those days it could offer only very basic service, due to wartime austerity. Still the volunteers who staffed the canteens made up for it with much good cheer.

The NAAFI was associated with rest and relaxation and by implication, the avoidance of responsibility. So, during the Second World War the name of this fine organization became part of other slang terms describing idle servicemen, who were described as "NAAFI cowboys" with "no aim, ambition, or fucking initiative." [Ref: Partridge (8th)]

I'm going to the NAAFI for a cup of tea. Coming?

NATIVES WERE HOSTILE, THE (RAF, RCAF; WWII) — "The natives were hostile" was a euphemism (probably borrowed from Hollywood or turn of the century travel and adventure books) meaning that fierce enemy resistance had been encountered during an attack or a raid. [Ref: Partridge (FS)]

How was the trip?
The natives were hostile!

NATO STANDARD (NATO forces, current) — "NATO Standard" is coffee with cream and sugar. In the NATO alliance nearly every aspect of military organization, from inventory accounting to tactics, was standardized among the sixteen member nations. This term alludes to this standardization.

How do you want your coffee?
NATO Standard, please...

NAUSE (pronounced "nozz") (CF current; probably naval in origin) — "Nause" is perhaps best translated as "lots of stuff", especially trivial stuff. The origins of the word are unknown, but most probably it comes from the word nausea. Therefore, nause is stuff that is apt to cause nausea because of its large volume and triviality.

There's a lot of nause to learn on this course...

NAV (universal military aviation) — "Nav" is shorthand for Navigator, or occasionally, for Navigation. (See also **A.I., Alligator**) [Ref: Partridge (FS)]

Who's the Nav on this trip?

NAVIGATORS' UNION (RAF, RCAF; WWII) — The late Eric Partridge defined "the

Navigators Union" as "a select, most unofficial body which met in pubs anywhere near a Bomber Station." At most wartime Bomber Command stations an unofficial, but very exclusive fraternity of navigators seemed to develop spontaneously, the existence of which probably reflects a phenomenon of aircrew social psychology.

Navigators
Union

The "glamour boys" of the air force are the pilots. Pilots were (and are) notorious for wallowing in this prestige whether or not, as individuals, it was merited and other airmen are quickly made aware of this exclusivity. However in Bomber Command squadrons, navigators had a pivotal role and everyone knew it. Bomber Command crews fought at night, and with few navigation aids and fewer electronic aids, it was the navigator's skill that found the target. Consequently, there was a kind of freemasonry among Bomber Command navigators.

Mindful of the unfair image they had as "second string" airmen, Bomber Command navigators made it their duty to remind the pilots that they are not the font of all flying wisdom, nor the source of all skill. Navigators knew that pilots owed them, if not blind faith, then at least, the courtesy of not second-guessing their decisions! Navigators learned early not to "think out loud" over the intercom, as this merely invited unnecessary worry among the rest of the crew. This was especially so in Pathfinder Force whose aircraft each carried two Navigators. One pathfinder navigator put it well: *It was a fairly general rule...that the navigation team did not defer too much to the Captain.* It seems this sentiment lives on in maritime patrol squadrons where, though the pilot may fly the aircraft, navigators are the tacticians and the releasers of weapons.

So perhaps it was inevitable that these spontaneous wartime gatherings of navigators, whether social or operational, became known as the "Navigators Union". [Refs: Bowyer, Partridge (8th)]

> *You look hung over, Rick!*
> *I am... The Navigators Union met at the village pub last night...*

N.C.M.   See **Airman**

NECK OIL (RCAF; WWII) — "Neck Oil" is beer, presumably because it lubricates the throat, as in: *Pass me a pint of Neck Oil!* [Ref: Partridge (8th)]

NEGATIVE; NEGATORY (universal) — "Negative" is the word that airmen often use instead of "no", and is borrowed from radio voice procedure. Occasionally to alleviate boredom, people say "negatory" or "negat" or some other variation. (See also **Affirmative**)

> *I'll have a hamburger, negative onions.*

NERVOUS AIR — "Nervous Air" is rhymed slang for "service air". Service Air is the military administrative term for travel using military transport aircraft (as opposed to "commercial air", or travel by airline). The word "nervous" reflects the fact that passenger comfort is not as high a priority on military missions. Military air transport squadrons are not an airline, so passengers must put up with the air force approach to operations, which are rough-and-ready when compared to an airline. (See also **Service Air, White Knuckle Airlines, The Boeing, Yuke, Pri-5, Blue Bark**)

> *How will you get from Comox to Halifax?*
> *I'm taking Nervous Air.*

NEWZIE (RCAF; WWII) — The term "Newzie" was an occasional nickname for New Zealanders. [Ref: Alcorn, Souster]

NICKEL OPERATIONS　　　　　See **Bumf**

NIGHT LANDINGS (RCAF; CF; since 1950's) — "Night Landings" is a mess game, occasionally played in RCAF officer's messes. As such, there is no particular reason for its existence except merriment.

The principles of Night Landings are very basic. A "Runway" is prepared by clearing away a long section of the Mess Floor. This game simulates a landing at night, therefore "Landing Lights" are required! These are prepared by lining candles down both sides of "runway". (The candles are generally liberated from mess candelabra). The runway is then liberally soaked with beer, the candles are lit, and the room lights are extinguished, all to simulate a wet runway at night. A bar tray is placed at the near end of the runway. Then the person runs towards the runway (simulating an aircraft on final approach to landing) and leaps headlong onto the tray, hydroplaning on the beer-soaked runway/floor, to the runway's end. If the person does so successfully, without knocking down any candles, he wins. If not, he buys a round, or contributes towards a round for the mess. To appreciate the true subtleties of Night Landings, participants should be thoroughly inebriated. Otherwise, it seems quite pointless. A similar game is played in the USN and USMC, called "Carrier Landings", which differs in that a long table is used instead of the floor. (Compare with **Dead Ants, Crud(3)**)

> *They're setting up for Night Landings! Go get me a beer!*

NINAK; NINACK (RAF; WWI) — "Ninak" was the nickname coined for the De Havilland 9A, designated the DH9A. The DH9A, a modification of the earlier DH9, was a two-seat biplane bomber that saw service during the latter days of the First World War and into the early 1920's.

The name Ninack arose because of its designation: 9A. During the First World War, the word ack represented the letter "A" in the British Army phonetic alphabet. Thus the DH9A became the DH9 Ack, then the 9 ack, and finally the ninack.

> *The Ninak was an improvement over the DH9.*

NIT-NOY (CF; current) — "Nit-Noy" is both noun and adjective for things best described as petty, time- consuming details. [Ref: Elting]

> *I'll eventually go flying today, if I can just get past all this nit-noy stuff!*

NO-BALL (RAF, RCAF; WWII) — "No-Ball" was the Second World War codeword for any of the 96 launching sites for the much-feared V-1 Flying Bomb, developed by the Germans late in the Second World War. (See **Diver**) The V-1, one of Germany's secret "vengeance weapons", was a crude cruise missile launched at England from sites on the European coast. Each V-1 carried about one ton of high explosive for 120 to 140 miles. The V- 1 was launched by a small rocket that accelerated the missile up a long, concrete inclined plane (often termed a "ski-jump", for its appearance from the air). Once airborne the V-1's own pulse jet started, and the missile proceeded towards England at speeds up to 400 miles per hour. These "No-Ball" sites were a high priority target for Bomber Command and the American 8th Air Force.

The origins of the codename "No-Ball" are unknown, though one wonders if it comes from a jingle often heard in wartime Britain (sung to the tune of 'Colonel Bogey'):

> *"Hitler has only got one ball,*
> *Goering has two - but very small,*
> *Himmler has something similar,*
> *But poor old Goebbels has no balls at all!"*

[Refs: Jones, Rawling]

NO FUTURE (IN IT) AT ALL (British Commonwealth Forces since WWII; now rare) — Any extremely risky or hazardous activity is said to have "no future in it". This phrase draws from everyday civilian slang, in which a job or a career opportunity might "have a good future", or alternately, might have "no future in it." (See also **Land of No Future**) [Ref: Partridge (8th)]

> *I'm volunteering for the Bomb Disposal Team.*
> *Not me! There's no future in that at all!*

NO-LONE ZONE (US; Canadian Forces, 1960's to 1980's) — The "No-Lone Zone" is a security area within which a nuclear weapon (or a nuclear armed aircraft) may be placed. The term describes the precaution to be observed in this area, ie., that no one is to enter the area without an escort. The penalty for so doing could be lethal, as these aircraft are extremely well-guarded. This term entered the Canadian lexicon in the early 1960's when U.S. tactical nuclear weapons armed Canadian aircraft. These weapons were deployed both in Europe, with the NATO forces, and in North America for air defence. Canadian involvement in nuclear weapons ended in the early 1980's when the CF-18 entered service, replacing the nuclear-capable CF-101 Voodoo in NORAD duties.

> *...and whatever you do, don't enter the No-Lone Zone without an escort!*

NO NAMES - NO PACK DRILL (British and Commonwealth military; since early 1900's) — "No Names - No Pack Drill" is a warning to fellow conspirators, upon having committing a breach of military discipline, to "shut up" and admit to nothing. After all, the military authorities cannot impose punishment if they do not know who to punish! This aphorism dates from the early part of this century (and perhaps even earlier) and originated in the British Army. "Pack Drill" was a common punishment for petty breaches of discipline in the 19th Century British Army; a person detailed to do Pack Drill did ordinary marching and arms drill for hours at a time, but while wearing a field back pack, often weighted with bricks or rocks. From the British Army, this aphorism spread throughout the military forces of the Commonwealth, including Canada's air force. [Ref: Partridge (8th)]

> *Grant! They're trying to find out who deflated the tires on the military police car!*
> *Remember, Bob, we're in this together! No names - No Pack Drill!*

NORTH LUFF (RCAF; 1950's) — "North Luff" was the short nickname for RAF Station North Luffenham, in England. "North Luff" was the main RCAF staging and logistics base when Canadian NATO forces in Europe grew during the early 1950's. Materiel and aircraft destined for Canadian fighter bases in Europe all passed through RAF North Luffenham.

> *Today, another four Sabres arrived from North Luff.*

NOSE ART (general military aviation usage) — From the earliest days of military aviation, both air and ground crews derived their collective unit identity and self-image from the type of aircraft they operated. To enhance this, the pilots or crews of individual aircraft often placed unique illustrations or slogans on aircraft, to identify it as their "own". These illustrations were known as "Nose Art".

Perhaps the best examples of Canadian Nose Art existed during the Second World War, on the Lancaster and Halifax aircraft of Bomber Command. Individual crews painted colourful slogans, illustrations of scantily-clad ladies, nicknames, or popular cartoon characters on the nose of their aircraft. Both the aircrews and groundcrews derived much of their unit social and operational identity from it. Sometimes a unit would adopt a "theme", and all aircraft in that unit would bear Nose Art in keeping with that theme. For example, the Mosquito aircraft of 418 "City of Edmonton" Squadron, a night intruder squadron, each bore a cartoon character from the popular *Li'l Abner* comic strip. The creator of *Li'l Abner*, the late Al Capp, had given his permission to the squadron to do so.

> *Though Nose Art was quite common on American and Canadian aircraft, it was rare on British aircraft.*

NOT A SAUSAGE (British Commonwealth forces to WWII) — "Not a sausage!" is an expression meaning "no luck", "nothing", or "nothing seen". It has its origins in British street slang, where a person who had not a sausage, was "broke", or hadn't any money. [Ref: Partridge (FS)]

> *Did you spot any bandits?*
> *Nope. Not a sausage...*

NOTHING ON THE CLOCK (RAF, RCAF, CF; now obsolescent) — Depending on the context, this term means either that an aircraft is flying at almost zero altitude, or alternately, is so slow, it has virtually no airspeed. The "clock" is early aviation slang for either, or both, the altimeter and airspeed indicator. [Ref: Partridge (8th)]

> *There I was: barely flying - at an altitude of a hundred feet - with nothing on the clock except the manufacturer's name!*

NUKE; TO NUKE (Originally American, now nearly universal) — "Nuke" is a shorthand term for a nuclear weapon. Similarly, "to nuke" is to use a nuclear weapon (though the term has found a new meaning: the heating of food in a microwave oven).

After the cancellation of the Avro Arrow in 1959 (See **Black Friday**), a decision was made to equip the Canadian Forces with several new weapons systems: the CF-101 Voodoo, a long-range interceptor, the CF-104 Starfighter, a fast low-level strike aircraft, the Bomarc Surface-to-Air Missile, and for the army, the Honest John Surface-to-Surface missile. All of these had one thing in common: they were designed to deliver tactical nuclear warheads. However the Progressive Conservative government of John Diefenbaker, which had first acquired these weapons, balked at establishing a Canadian nuclear capability or putting Canadian Forces into the United States nuclear arsenal. This led to phenomenal political debate and the downfall of the Diefenbaker government. Lester Pearson's Liberals assumed power in Ottawa and shortly afterwards Canadian units were armed with tactical nuclear weapons, though under American control and direction. (Canada was not the only nation whose military would be armed with United States nuclear weapons; several other NATO air forces were also so armed.) Canadian Forces were nuclear-capable for less than two decades. The Bomarc surface-to-air missile squadrons stood down in 1972 and the Europe-based CF-104 Squadrons relinquished their tactical strike role in the same year. The Canadian Forces retained their nuclear capability a bit longer, until the CF-18 Hornet replaced the CF-101 Voodoo in air defence squadron service.

The extraordinary precautions needed in handling and protecting Nukes introduced a whole host of new terms to the Canadian military vocabulary. Some unclassified ones include:

G.R.A.:	General Restricted Area, an area of the air base that was cordoned off and secured from the domestic and administrative parts of the base. No one got past the wire or the armed guards without a "G.R.A. Pass". The term lived on into the conventional weapons era.
F.O.A.:	Follow-On Area, an area within the G.R.A. that could be further secured for "uploading" or "downloading" of nukes onto additional aircraft.
L.A.D.D.:	Low Altitude Drogue Delivery, the method by which a CF-104 dropped a Nuke. For a Starfighter pilot to drop his nuke and survive, he had to fly at his target very fast and very low. The pilot released the bomb (which was attached to a parachute) as he pulled the aircraft up into a loop. The parachute slowed the bomb's descent down while the pilot rolled level, descended to very low altitude and escaped as fast as his aircraft and the enemy would allow. Thankfully, as history showed, this whole exercise proved to be hypothetical.
S.A.S.:	Special Ammunition Storage, the place where nukes were stored.

(See also **Ground Zero; Poopy Suit(1); Shape; White Bullet**) [Ref: Sutherland]

There aren't any more nukes in Canada...

NUMBER 1; NUMBER 2...NUMBER 99 (originally Korean War, American) — "Number 1" was Korean street English for "very good" or, "the best", as opposed to "Number 99", which meant "the worst". Part of American military slang, the term may have entered Canadian vocabulary via the Canadian Brigade of the Commonwealth Division that fought in Korea. Post-Korean War contact with the American military would have promoted its use. [Ref: Partridge (8th)]

How did your vacation go?
Number 1!

NYLON LET-DOWN (Post-War; general military usage) — A "Nylon Let-Down" is a parachute descent. In the normal turn of events, an aircraft's approach to landing is termed a "Let-Down". However, given that parachutes are made of nylon, a pilot who has had to bale out of an aircraft has made a Nylon Let-Down.

When Bill's engine failed, he had to make a Nylon Let-Down.

Nylon
Let-Down

SCAR

OATMEAL SAVAGES — "Oatmeal Savages" are Scots or people of Scottish descent. Presumably the term derives from this national staple food of Scotland (celebrated by Scots and mothers for its restorative powers) and from the approach taken by Highland Regiments to soldiering.

Cameron ain't a bad navigator - for an Oatmeal Savage, that is!

OBOE (RAF Bomber Command; WWII) — "Oboe" was an early electronic navigation aid that helped Bomber Command navigators guide their aircraft to their targets at night.

The name Oboe was apparently coined by a technician named Bates, who frequently flew on operations to test the Oboe system. Early versions of Oboe called for the pilot to listen over his headphones for an audible tone that indicated whether the pilot was left or right of the desired course. Bates, a keen musician, thought this electronic tone sounded like an Oboe. The nickname stuck and Oboe became the official codeword.

Oboe relied on two ground-based radars in England, an aircraft-mounted receiver, and basic geometry. Well before takeoff, the distance from each radar site to the target was calculated. Oboe equipment on the bomber sensed each of the two radar signals emanating from England and automatically calculated the range from the aircraft to each radar transmitter. On nearing the target, the navigator of the Oboe-equipped Bomber would use this information to direct the pilot; when the two distances provided by Oboe equalled the (previously calculated) distance to the target, the aircraft was over the target city. (See also **Gee, on the Beam**) [Ref: Bowyer]

OFFICER DEVELOPMENT (CF; current) — "Officer Development" was that part of an RCAF officer's initial training devoted to learning about the military profession, as opposed to learning purely technical or occupational topics. However, "Officer Development" is also a euphemism for mutual, informal discussion of information of topical or social interest then circulating among the officer corps. To properly be "Officer Development", such discussion requires an informal setting - such as the Officer's Mess. This usage mocks those more formal professional development activities. (See also **Sports Afternoon**)

O-GROUP (CF; current) — "O-Group" is shorthand for "Orders Group". This is standard NATO terminology for a briefing where a Commanding Officer issues orders to subordinate officers and NCO's and is very common army usage. In more general air force usage however, it has come to mean a "briefing".

O CHRIST-THIRTY; O DARK-THIRTY (military general; originally RAF) — "O-Christ Thirty" and "O-Dark Thirty" each mean the same thing: very, very early in the morning - before sunrise.

Each is a play on the military "twenty-four hour" clock phraseology where for example, the time 0530 Hours is spoken as: "oh-five-thirty". A person who is forced to arise at such an early hour might easily mutter, on being woken, "Oh Christ...". Therefore, "Oh-Christ-Thirty" is that very early time of day that invites such a rude comment. "Oh Dark-Thirty" is a variation that of course, alludes to the predawn darkness. (See also **Crow Fart**) [Refs: Elting; Partridge (8th)]

> *What time do we have to get up?*
> *Oh-Christ Thirty!*

OLD NEWTON (GOT HIM) (RAF, RCAF; pre-WWII) — "Old Newton" is gravity, which can pull an airplane from the sky. The usage honours of course, Sir Isaac Newton. [Ref: Partridge (8th)]

> *Don't let your airspeed drop too much or else Old Newton will get you!*

OLD SWEAT (military general) — An "old sweat" is an experienced or veteran serviceman, a person with lots of "T.I.". (See also **T.I.**) [Ref: Partridge (FS)]

O.L.Q.'s (CF; current) — "O.L.Q.'s" are "Officer-Like Qualities", those amorphous attributes such as leadership, skill, integrity and courage that are easy to describe but difficult to find. Whether on duty or off-duty, junior officers and officer cadets are constantly evaluated for demonstrations of O.L.Q.'s.

OLYMPIC BAND, THE (CF; current) — The Air Command Band was occasionally known by military musicians as The Olympic Band - because it is bigger, faster, louder.

ONE-EYED STEAKS (RCAF; WWII) — "One-eyed steaks" is a Canadian airman's term for kippers, the small fish that Britons love to eat for breakfast. The term one-eyed steaks derives from the fact that a kipper lies on a plate on its side, with one eye visible. Canadian airmen and airwomen in wartime Britain lived and served on RAF stations and enjoyed British - not Canadian - military cuisine. This diet invariably included kippers.

> *What's for breakfast?*
> *What else? One-eyed steaks...*

ONE IN THE HANGAR, ONE (TWO, etc) ON THE RAMP (unknown origin) — "One in the hangar, one on the ramp" means that the speaker (usually male) has one child and that his lady is expecting another. The phrase suggests the placement of aircraft on an airfield and perhaps unsurprisingly, this phrase is almost never heard from women.

> *How many children do you have?*
> *One in the hangar, one on the ramp...*

ONE-O-FOUR (ie., '104) (NATO; general usage) — Military aircraft types, especially in North America, are generally assigned a design number as well as a name. Not surprisingly, such aircraft are as often known by this number as by their name. The "one-o-four", or '104, was the Lockheed F-104 Starfighter, flown by the RCAF and the CF until the late 1980's.

Though formally named the "Starfighter", Canadians almost always called it "the 104". However, the aircraft also attracted a much less savoury nickname in the media - the "Widowmaker" - because of a very high German air force accident rate (See also **Widowmaker**)

The '104 was a classic aircraft, one of the so-called "Century Series" of American fighters of the 1950's. The Starfighter was designed during the Korean War by the Lockheed "Skunkworks" design team led by famous designer Kelly Johnson. After discussions with American pilots during the Korean War, Johnson concluded that there was a need for an aircraft with outstanding climb and altitude capabilities. The result was the '104, which first flew in 1953.

The '104 originally served as a short-range point interceptor, that is, its job was to defend a specific target from air attack. However, it was redesigned and the F-104G variant served as a low-level strike and interdiction aircraft. This variant was marketed heavily around the world by Lockheed, and many nations allied to the U.S. purchased it, including Canada. The Canadian Starfighter was designated the CF-104 and 238 were built for the RCAF under licence by Canadair in Montreal. The '104 was intended to replace the F-86 Sabres then in service at Canada's European-based fighter wings. The '104 differed from the Sabre, however. Whereas the Sabre was an interceptor, RCAF Starfighter wings in France and Germany became strike and reconnaissance specialists, and rearmed with tactical nuclear weapons (though under American control). RCAF aircraft would carry tactical nuclear weapons - fast and low - into Warsaw Pact states in case of an east-west nuclear war. When Canada relinquished the tactical nuclear role in the 1970's, Starfighter aircraft were converted to a conventional air-to-ground attack role - a role that this light, fast, thin-winged aircraft was never intended to perform. The '104 was gradually phased out as the new McDonnell-Douglas CF-18 "Hornet" replaced it. [Refs: Molson and Taylor; Reed]

The 104 could accelerate faster than any surface-to-air-missile the Soviets had.

ONE-O-ONE; ONE-O-WONDER (ie., '101) (RCAF, CF, USAF; general usage) — Just as with the "one-o-four" (see **One-O-Four**), "one-o-one" was the shorthand nickname for the McDonnell F-101 Voodoo, a twin engined, two-crew jet interceptor. The McDonnell F-101, originally designed as a single-seat, long-range escort fighter, was another of the so-called "Century series" supersonic fighters that entered American service in the 1950's. Voodoos were to accompany American B-47 and B-52 bombers as they penetrated enemy airspace in war. Designed to carry fuel and weapons over long ranges, this large escort fighter was a brute of an airplane. The basic design was later developed into a single-seat photo-reconnaissance fighter and a two-seat all-weather interceptor.

The RCAF procured the two-seat interceptor variant after the cancellation of the Avro Arrow program in 1959. (See **Black Friday**) It remained operational in NORAD air defence duties until the early 1980's when the McDonnell Douglas CF-18 Hornet replaced the Voodoo.

The bragging nickname "One-O-Wonder" was occasionally heard from its crews, a term that was taken from the flying suit badge worn by its pilots. (The Voodoo's air intercept Navigators, Engineering Officers, and Technicians wore occupational badges with similar, bragging slogans: "Scope Wizard", "Witch Doctor", and "Medicine Man", respectively.)

The one-o-one had no guns at all, only missiles...

ONE-STAR; TWO-STAR; THREE-STAR; FOUR-STAR — Many servicemembers in the NATO armed forces have taken up the American habit of referring to general officers (and their naval and air force equivalents) not by their rank, but by the number of stars they wear as rank insignia. Even though Canadian, British, Norwegian, and other NATO general officers do not all wear stars, this American slang makes useful short-hand. It is easier to say that an Italian air force "three-star" outranks a Greek "two-star" than to say that a *Generale di Division Aerea* is higher than an *Ypopterarchos*!

Wilkins will become a two-star, effective next November.

ON THE CARPET (Military, General) — To be "on the carpet" is to be in trouble with one's superior officer. The implication is that one is summoned to stand before the Commanding Officer's desk - standing on the carpet - to account for one's actions. [Ref: Harvey]

After that low flying stunt, Harv got called up on the carpet...

ON THE ECONOMY (CF Current) — To a servicemember posted to Europe on NATO duties, living "on the economy" meant living in a European town or village as would a local resident, rather than living in quarters on the base. In other words, someone "on the economy" lived in the civilian community of their host nation. As such, the costs of their rent and utilities were subject to the vagaries of the civilian economy. [Ref: Elting]

How did you learn to speak German so well?
After living on the economy for four years, I couldn't help but learn it!

ON THE STEP (aviation general) — An aircraft that is "on the step" has attained stable level flight and is gaining airspeed after a steep, abrupt climb that imposes a lower than usual airspeed.

This term is often associated with floatplanes or seaplanes. To take off, a waterborne aircraft must overcome the severe friction of contact with the water. This is often done by pulling back on the control column earlier and much more steeply than in a normal runway takeoff, to lift as much of the aircraft as possible out of the water. However, this abrupt nose up attitude cannot be maintained, lest the aircraft stall. So, once the aircraft is in stable flight, ie., once it is on the step, the pilot then relaxes the back-pressure on the control column and levels off to build up airspeed for a more protracted climb - even though part of the float or hull is still trailing in the water.

ON TOP (aviation; general) — "On top" refers to flying above the clouds. However, in anti-submarine warfare, to be "on top" can mean that an anti-submarine aircraft has located a submerged submarine and is orbiting immediately overhead. That is, the aircraft is on top of its target.

On the surface the weather was nothing but fog and rain, but on top it was
as clear as could be.

ON TRACK, ON TIME (CF; current) — "On track, on time" is a phrase borrowed from air navigation which means that "everything is going according to plan". An aircraft is "on track, on time" when it is flying exactly over its planned route ("on track") at the speed planned by its crew ("on time"). "On track, on time" is the exact opposite of the phrase: "Same way, same day". The phrase "on track, on time" is sometimes applied in non-navigational situations, also. (See also **Same way, Same day**)

> *How's your project coming along?*
> *We're on track, on time!*

OPEN ONE'S ACCOUNT, TO (RAF, RCAF; WWII) — A Second World War fighter pilot "opened his account" by shooting down his first enemy aircraft. The term alludes to a bank account; one always hoped to increase one's tally of victories, just as one hoped to increase one's bank balance.

> *Young Andy opened his account yesterday, over Calais...*

OPIE-DOPIE (CF; current) — "Opie-Dopie" is the nickname for the Officer's Professional Development Program, and derives from the program's abbreviation: "O.P.D.P". Opie Dopies are a series of examinations on six military topics, all deemed critical knowledge for a member of the profession of arms. Officers are expected to study their Opie-Dopies on their own initiative.

> *How come Darlene can't come to the Mess tonight?*
> *She's studying for her Opie-Dopies...*

O PIP (RFC; WWI) — "O Pip" was First World War slang for "Offensive Patrol", an operation where allied fighter aircraft crossed the front lines and aggressively sought out enemy aircraft. The term is derived from the First World War phonetic alphabet, where the word "pip" denotes the letter "P". There was then no phonetic codeword for the letter "O", so the Offensive Patrol became known as the O Pip. (For other examples see also **Ack Emma, Ack W, Emma Toc, Pip Emma**) [Ref: Voss]

> *"Charlie is on his second O Pip of the day..."*

OPS; OP (since at least WWII) — "Ops" and "Op", respectively, are the universal shorthand terms for the plural and singular of the word "Operation". In military doctrine, "operations" describes the primary activity of one's unit or element, whatever that activity may be. In the air force, the word "ops" generally implies flying - though it isn't always so. For example, flying on ops should be distinguished from flying training. As well, ops need not always occur in the air; thus, "maintenance ops" describes the actual repair and servicing of aircraft as opposed to staff engineering duties. Similarly, "supply ops" describes the actual delivery of materiel to users in the field, as opposed to headquarters management. From the word Ops comes the acronym: "OpEval", for Operational Evaluation.

Since the Second World War, the word "op" described a single operation or mission, as in "there's an op scheduled for tomorrow night". Today the singular, op, seems limited to formal usage in the title of an Operation, such as OP BOREAL or OP BOXTOP.

> *Art is the new Ops Officer.*

O.R.'s   See **Airman**

ORBIT (since WWII; now general) — To "orbit" is to "circle" over a designated point on the ground, a term that appears to have started as RAF Fighter Command slang during the Second World War. [Ref: Partridge (8th)]

OSCAR; OSCAR TRUCK (CF; current) — "OSCAR" is the acronym and radio codeword for the "On-Scene Control And Response" truck.

The OSCAR Truck is a vehicle used by an airbase operations staff as a mobile command and control vehicle, during an emergency or an aircraft crash away from base. OSCAR trucks contain a host of communications equipment needed to coordinate and direct the activity at the accident scene. The OSCAR truck is kept in readiness near the Base Operations centre.

OUT OF ALTITUDE, AIRSPEED, AND IDEAS (aviation; general) — This phrase describes that critical situation just before an aircraft crashes. When an aircraft has sufficient altitude and airspeed, there is usually time for the pilot to attempt to recover the aircraft from an emergency, or eject. However, when the pilot is out of altitude, airspeed, and ideas, there is nothing left to do but crash.

Fred bailed out, just as he ran out of altitude, airspeed, and ideas!

OVERHEAD BREAK (general usage, 1950's to present) — An "overhead break" is a manoeuvre used by a formation of military aircraft returning to base at high-speed. The overhead break enables the formation to slow and separate the aircraft, and to allow independent landings.

An Overhead Break can be quite dramatic in appearance. An aircraft returning to land flies down the runway at an altitude of about 1000 feet. The pilot then executes a steep 180 degree turn, to fly "downwind". It goes downwind until it is positioned to commence another 180-degree turn, and roll out onto the final approach to a landing. When several aircraft return together, they join up in "echelon formation" and fly over the runway, each aircraft executing an overhead break in succession. (See also **Battle Break**)

OVERSHOOT (aviation; general) — "Overshoot", both noun and verb, refers to an aircraft aborting its landing approach, and its ensuing climb. Occasionally, however, the term "overshoot" describes the result when a pilot has indeed landed the aircraft, but was unable to slow the aircraft down before rolling off the end of the runway. When the air traffic controllers direct an aircraft to overshoot, it is mandatory for the pilot to do so. In naval aviation at sea, this command is termed a "Bolter" or a "Wave-off". (See **Bolter, Wave-Off**)

Jim began the overshoot when he spotted the deer on the runway ahead.

OX-BOX (RAF, RCAF; WWII) — "Ox-Box" was an occasional nickname for the Airspeed "Oxford", a light twin-engine monoplane used by the RAF as a trainer and as a station "hack". (See **Hack(1)**) The term is rhymed slang and reflects the fact that the Oxford, when compared with other service aircraft of the day, was fairly basic and box-like. [Ref: Peden]

The new Air Vice Marshal arrived this afternoon in an Ox-Box.

P APA

PACK IT IN, TO (military; since at least WWII) — The phrase "to pack it in" has two meanings pertinent to military aviation:

> *(1)* First, to **pack it in** can mean to stop, as in: *The sun's setting and it's too dark to search any longer. Let's pack it in and go home.* This phrase, now common usage, apparently had its origins in Second World War service slang.

> (2) Also, to **pack it in** is to crash an aircraft, as in: *Rudy packed it in just west of Fort Churchill.* Sometimes the phrase "to pile it in" is used instead.

[Ref: Partridge (8th)]

PACKAGE; PACK (military aviation: current) — A "package", or "pack", is a discrete group of aircraft assigned to perform a particular task. (The term would appear to be derived from current operational terminology, where "route package" is an area targeted for air attack.) Naturally, if there are six aircraft in the group, it is a "six-pack", a further allusion to a small case of beer. [Ref: Elting]

> *A package of F-18's is en route.*

PADRE (military; general) — "Padre" is Portuguese for "father", and is the traditional moniker for a military chaplain. Though one might expect the word "Padre" to apply strictly to Roman Catholic Chaplains, this is not so. It seems that all military chaplains, whatever the denomination (or even gender, for females ordained in Protestant denominations), are referred to by servicemembers as "the Padre".

The role of the Padre in the military hierarchy is unique. The following description by an RCAF Padre of the Second World War fairly sums it up:

> *If a Padre was on to his job he was the confidant and advisor to a whole hash of problems incurred by airmen overseas. "See the Padre" was advice handed out liberally. "Try it on the Padre for size, and then go on from there." The Padre could with discretion circumvent the chain of command and take a problem directly to the C.O. or the M.O. or the Adjutant. Even service problems, working conditions, food, or promotion came to him. An RAF commissioning board asked one of our NCO's what wine should be served with pheasant. "The Padre should know!"*

[Ref: Carlson; Partridge (8th)]

PANCAKE, TO (aviation; general) — "To pancake" an aircraft is to crash it so that it lands flat on its belly, with minimal forward motion, rather like a pancake flopping down onto a plate. Such a landing must occur at a very low airspeed, indeed, just above the stall speed, but if carried out effectively it minimizes damage. With the high approach speeds of modern aircraft, the decision to pancake the aircraft is always a last resort.

Though they'd run out of fuel, the pilot still managed to pancake the airplane on the beach.

PANIC BOWLER   See **Battle Bowler**

PARTY (Commonwealth forces; WWII) — A "party" is a combat operation. [Ref: Partridge (FS)]

You'd better get some sleep, there is quite a party laid on for tonight.

PASS-OUT, TO (Commonwealth military; general) — Contrary to what it may appear to mean, "to Pass-Out", in the forces of the Commonwealth, has long meant "to graduate from training". Thus, when one "passes out", one "passes" the course, and attends a "Passing-Out Parade." (However, this is not to say that one cannot "pass out" in the physiological sense, at one's Passing-Out Parade.)

What time is the Passing-Out Parade?

PATCH (military, general; predominantly American) — A "patch" is a cloth unit badge or crest, as worn on a flying suit or jacket.

PATHFINDER (RAF, RCAF; WWII) — The term "Pathfinder" had two meanings, an operational meaning, and a social, colloquial meaning derived from the operational meaning.

(1)   A **Pathfinder** was an aircraft (or a crewmember of such an aircraft) whose special task it was to mark out targets for bombing.

Second World War Bomber Command aircraft bombed at night, with few navigation references. Thus there was great risk of missing the target altogether, a risk that was magnified by the various decoys and deceptions used by the Germans. To ensure bombing accuracy, RAF Bomber Command formed the "Pathfinder Force". "Pathfinders" were special bomber squadrons and crews that led the way, found the target, and marked it with flares for the rest of the Bomber Force.

Pathfinding was very dangerous and Pathfinder aircrews were combat-experienced volunteers of uncommon ability, especially the Navigators. Pathfinder aircraft were priority targets for Luftwaffe night fighters, because by defeating the Pathfinders, they could disrupt the entire raid. Typically, Pathfinder squadrons flew Lancasters, though later in the war, Mosquito light bombers were also used. The RCAF had one Pathfinder Squadron, 405 Squadron. Its motto is apt: *Ducimus*, Latin for "We Lead".

(2)   The Pathfinder's reputation for seeking out and finding the target led to another, more colloquial meaning of the word **Pathfinder**. In day-to-day air

force slang, during the Second World War, a Pathfinder was an airman who was particularly successful in meeting women.

[Ref: Partridge (8th)]

PAUL BUNYAN (RCAF, CF; current) — A "Paul Bunyan" is a large, aluminum, air-portable storage box. The Paul Bunyan was used to easily ship articles too small to be secured on their own to the floor of a transport aircraft or vehicle. The term seems to derive from the fact that the box, like the legendary lumberjack Paul Bunyan, is rather large.

PAX (CF; current) — In Air Transport units, "pax" is written shorthand for "passenger". However, it did not take very long for "pax" to become verbal shorthand as well.

> *What's our load today?*
> *We've got 1800 pounds of general cargo and 23 pax.*

P.B.I. (WWI, general) — "P.B.I.", a common abbreviation in the British and Commonwealth forces during the First World War, meant "Poor Bloody Infantry". These letters were a sober acknowledgment that it was the infantryman in the trenches who experienced the worst that the war had to offer, and whose lot was least enviable. It was never a term of denigration. [Ref: Partridge (8th); Voss]

> *As we flew over the front, we could see thousands of the P.B.I. below in their trenches!*

P.B.O. (RFC,WWI) — The common abbreviation P.B.I. (for "poor bloody infantry") led to its being adapted by the airmen of the Royal Flying Corps, where "P.B.O." meant "poor bloody observer". This abbreviation was, like P.B.I., a recognition that the lot of the Observer was an unenviable one. The Observer maintained a constant watch over the terrain below, plotted the fall of artillery, spotted enemy concentrations, defended the aircraft with his Lewis Gun, and signalled headquarters, risking enemy fire all the while, and was totally at the mercy of the pilot. It is wise to recall that the RFC was very loathe to issue their aircrews with parachutes during the First World War. However, the initials P.B.O. were never quite as implicitly sombre as P.B.I., perhaps a reflection of the fact that it was still the infantry whose lot was the worst. [Ref: Partridge (8th);Voss]

P.C. (ie., "pee-see") (RCAF; to early 1960's) — In the post-war RCAF, "P.C." was the abbreviation for "Permanent Commission". Up to the 1960's, the regular RCAF enrolled officers as either "Short-Service Officers" who served for only a few years and then returned to civilian life or the Auxiliary, or as "Permanent Officers" who served on a career basis until retirement. For those who joined on a short-service basis and enjoyed RCAF life, the Holy Grail was to obtain a P.C.

PEDRO   See **Horse**

PENGUIN — A penguin is of course, a bird that cannot fly. As such, its name has been borrowed and applied to two other flightless entities:

>   (1)   (RFC, WWI) During the First World War, the nickname **penguin**

described an aircraft whose wings had been removed and was used to train flight cadets to run up and handle aircraft engines. [Refs: Partridge (8th);Winter]

(2)   (RAF, RCAF; since WWII) A **penguin** is a non-flying air force officer. (See also **Kiwi;Kiwi Club, Mahogony Bomber, Wingless Wonder**) [Ref: Partridge (FS)]

(But see also **Kriegie**)

PER ARDUA ASBESTOS (WWII) — "Per Ardua Asbestos" is a mock Latin phrase that alludes to the slang term: "fireproof", and to the motto of the air force: *Per ardua ad astra.*

The official air force motto is *Per Ardua Ad Astra* (officially translated as "Through adversity to the stars"). As such it is a phrase that every airman and airwoman becomes familiar with very early in their service.

Asbestos is a non-flammable mineral of fibrous composition, often used as a flame insulator. Thus, it is often associated with articles that are fireproof. However, in air force slang, the word "fireproof" also describes a person who can rely on rank, seniority or appointment to escape difficulty.

So it is perhaps unsurprising that someone should note the assonance between "asbestos" and "ad astra" and alter the air force motto, to allude to another's "fireproof" status. (for other mock Latin see: **Argi, Albatri, Excrementum vincit cerebellum, Illegitimus non carborundum**) [Ref: Partridge-Catchphrases]

> *Did you notice that Billy hasn't been in trouble even once since we started training!?*
> *Well, I guess it's like they say, Per ardua asbestos!*

PERCH (RCAF, CF; current since the 1950's) — In fighter tactics, to be "on the perch" is to be flying above one's opponent, in a position where the opponent can be "bounced", or attacked from above. The word "perch" suggests a bird on a branch, sitting in wait for prey below. To fly at an altitude higher than one's opponent in air-to-air combat gives an overall advantage. The aircraft's potential energy is quickly converted into kinetic, manoeuvring energy, simply by diving. This was discovered early in the history of air combat; the maxim of British First World War ace Mick Mannock was: *Always above, seldom on the same level, never underneath.* (See also **Bounce**)

> *There I was, on the perch, with a section of USAF Sabres about 8000 feet below..."*

PERIM; PERIMETER — The perimeter is the common term for the outward boundary of an aerodrome. Therefore a "Perimeter Road" is a road around the airport. Occasionally it is shortened to "perim". [Ref: Partridge (8th)]

PERMS (CF, to early 1950's) — Up to the 1950's, Canada's regular military component was termed the "Permanent Force", as distinguished from the part-time, reserve component that was the "Non-Permanent Force". Consequently, regular members were collectively known as the "Perms" among reservists or militiamen. By the 1950's the names had changed; the Permanent Force became the "Regular Force" and Perms became "Regs". (See also **P.F.**)

PETER HEATER (aviation; general) — "Peter Heater" is rhymed slang for a device called a "Pitot Heater". ("Pitot" is pronounced "peet-owe")

Aircraft are equipped with a "pitot-static system" which measures airspeed and altitude. One very critical component is the "pitot tube", a small hollow tube attached to the outside the airframe, pointed forward into the airstream. Outside air flows into this tube, and its pressure is compared with static air pressure. The differences in pressure are used to measure the aircraft's "airspeed". However, in cold, damp weather there is a risk of the pitot tube becoming iced over, blocking the airflow into the pitot tube and making it impossible to measure how fast the aircraft is flying. To prevent this, aircraft designers build a powerful electrical heating element into the pitot tube to melt any ice. This is commonly called the "Peter Heater", though its proper name is pitot heater.

Don't touch the Peter Heater while I test it. You'll burn your fingers!

PETRIFIED FOREST (RAF Bomber Command; WWII) — The "Petrified Forest" was Bomber Command Headquarters during the Second World War. All RAF and Commonwealth heavy bomber units were controlled by Bomber Command Headquarters.

At first, Bomber Command HQ was not known for enlightened thinking, and it is said that weather over the target rather than strategic goals or tactical concerns was the most critical element in target planning. However, after Air Chief Marshal Harris took over Bomber Command, systematic operational planning began, which included the creation of Pathfinder units, and operational and scientific research. (See also **Bullshit Towers, Chateau, Castle Dismal, Disneyland-on-the-Rideau, Fort Fumble, Fraggle Rock, Glass Menagerie; Glass Palace**) [Ref: Bowyer (Pathfinders)]

Tomorrow's Operations Order has arrived from the Petrified Forest.

PETROL BOOZER   See **Gremlin**

P.F. (RCAF, to 1950's) — The initials "P.F." were common shorthand for "Permanent Force", the peacetime standing air force (as opposed to the reserve), as in: *I'm transferring from the P.F. to the Auxiliary.* Today, instead of P.F., one would speak of the "Regs" or "Regforce", for Regular Force. (See also **Perms**)

P.F.M.; P.F.M. BOX (aviation, general; current) — The initials "P.F.M." mean "pure fucking magic". This phrase is often used to explain to the uninformed how aircraft electronics and computer equipment works. This phrase suggests that such equipment is so complicated that it is unnecessary to learn how and why it works, unless you are a technician repairing it or a designer modifying it. (In the same sense that one need not learn how an ignition system works to drive a car!)

Therefore, when someone asks "how does it work?" it is often easier to answer "P.F.M.", rather than go through a long, complicated, and ultimately incomprehensible explanation. Consequently, a piece of highly complex electronic or computer equipment is sometimes called a "P.F.M. Box".

> *How does the Inertial Navigation System really work?*
> *...through P.F.M., laddie, P.F.M.*

PICKLE, TO (Military aviation; since WWII) — Since the Second World War, to drop a bomb was to "pickle the bomb". Not surprisingly, a "pickle switch" is the switch or button pressed by the pilot or bombardier to release a bomb. The origins of this term seem to derive from the Second World War, when the U.S. Army Air Corps equipped its heavy bombers with the Norden Bombsight, advertised by its makers as being accurate enough to place a bomb "into a pickle barrel from 20,000 feet."

> *Okay, I'll approach down the valley at low level and about 350 knots. I'll pull*
> *up and roll over the top of the hill, spot the target, and roll level again. Then*
> *I'll pickle the bombs and get the hell out of there.*

PICKLIES (CF postwar; current) — "Picklies" is a common nickname for the Princess Patricia's Canadian Light Infantry (PPCLI), and is a feeble attempt at actually pronouncing the initials "PPCLI"!

> *We'll be flying a company of picklies to Gagetown.*

PIECE OF CAKE (originally RAF from 1938, now universal) — Anything easy, or a golden opportunity, is a "Piece of Cake". The phrase implies that the problem is as easy to dispose of as a piece of cake. This term, which has now entered everyday English usage, originated among RAF fighter pilots just before the outbreak of the Second World War. [Ref: Partridge (FS); Partridge - Catchphrases]

> *How was your flight?*
> *...a piece of cake!*

PIECE OF PISS (Canadian, since WWII) — The phrase "a Piece of Piss" is an earthier, and slightly contemptuous equivalent of "Piece of Cake" (see **Piece of Cake**). [Ref: Partridge (8th)]

PIGEON (Army, Navy; general usage) — "Pigeon" is naval and army slang for a member of the air force, and was the soldier's and sailor's preferred term for airmen and airwomen into the 1960's. (See also **Brylcreem Boys, Crabfat, Shithawk, Zoomie**) [Ref: Partridge (8th)]

PILE IT IN; PILE IT UP — To "pile in" an aircraft is to crash it. (See also **Prang, to Pack It In(2)**) [Ref: Partridge (8th)]

> *Brian piled it in, just across from the Fire Hall.*
> *That was obliging of him...*

PINEAPPLE   See **Cornflake**

PINECONE   See **Cornflake**

PINK DINK (RCAF; 1960's) — The "Red Knight", the official RCAF solo aerobatic display pilot of the 1950's and 1960's, was occasionally known as the "Pink Dink". This nickname was coined at Toronto's CNE Airshow in the early 1960's by U.S. Navy pilots of the "Blue Angels" formation team, after a convivial evening and early morning spent in the company of the Red Knight. The Red Knight flew a bright red T-33 aircraft (later, a Tutor) and it may be safely speculated that the aircraft's red colour (perhaps faded?) was the origin of the nickname. [Ref: Milberry]

Pink Dink

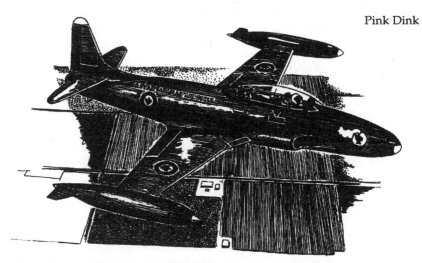

To airshow crowds, he was the Red Knight. To most in the Air Force, he was the Pink Dink.

PINK SHEETS (RCAF, CF; current) — The "pink sheet" is the technician's nickname for the CF Form 349, the document upon which is recorded any major aircraft mechanical or electronic failure. These forms are printed on pink paper, to easily distinguish them from other aircraft forms. (See also **Blue Sheets, Major(2), Snag**)

PINKS — The word "pinks" can have two meanings:

(1)   **Pinks**   See **School Solution**

(2)   The word **Pinks** (RCAF; 1950's, 1960's) (like "Blues" or "Khakis") was a noun that referred to a specific type of air force uniform, by its colour. Of course the RCAF never issued a uniform that was actually pink. However, the "Summer Number 6" khaki uniform of the 1950's and 1960's, had an unfortunate propensity for changing colour. When exposed to excessive heat the original khaki of the tunic and trousers transformed itself (permanently) into a pale pink or dusty rose colour. Consequently they were occasionally called "pinks". These uniforms were tailored from an early synthetic fabric whose chemical propensity for changing colour was apparently lost on those

213

who selected it. Airmen were advised to use extreme caution when pressing their "Summer Number 6" trousers and tunics (also notorious for not holding a press very well). (See also **Blues, Tee-Dubs**)

It looks like Don has exchanged his summer khakis for a set of summer pinks...

PIPELINER (RCAF, CF; current) — In the modern Canadian air force, a "pipeliner" is an aviator, usually a pilot, on their first posting after graduation from training. The term is derived from the "Training Pipeline", the mythical machine which produces trained personnel, ie., one feeds trainees into the pipeline and qualified aircrew emerge from the other end. Thus, a pilot who has recently emerged from the training pipeline, is a "pipeliner".

However, the term "pipeliner" occasionally refers to a pilot who entered the pilot ranks without prior military or aviation experience. Thus a pilot who first graduated from a military college, or one who was trained other than through the standard pilot training system, is not a "Pipeliner." Both of the above usages are current.

Most of the pilots on this squadron are pipeliners.

PIP EMMA (WWI, general) — "Pip" and "Emma" were the First World War phonetic codeword for the letters "P" and "M". Joined together as "pip emma" they most commonly meant "post meridiem". Time after noon is described as "P.M.", or post meridiem, as in "2:00 PM". During the First World War, before the 24 hour clock standard became universal, it was common to describe a time after noon as time pip emma, as in *Two o'clock pip emma*. Similarly, times before noon were described as "ack emma" for "A.M." or "ante meridiem". (See also **Ack Emma**) [Ref: Voss]

At ten pip emma, to the minute, the barrage started.

PIPPER (military aviation; general) — A "pipper" is the central aiming reticule on a fighter aircraft's gunsight.

Once I had the pipper lined up on the enemy tanks, I began firing...

PISSING CONTEST (CF; current) — A "Pissing Contest" is a petty dispute. The term alludes to the type of contest occasionally held by very small boys to prove who can urinate farther. (See also **Bunfight**)

I hear that the Operations Officer and the Air Traffic Controllers are in another Pissing Contest!

PISS POOR (originally CF; now general) — Piss Poor, originally military slang but now civilian vernacular also, means "very bad". [Ref: Partridge (8th)]

PISSPOT (RCAF; WWII) — "Pisspot" was the denigrating nickname for the RCAF men's winter cap, a very unpopular article of clothing among Second World War airmen. The characteristic airman's cap in the Second World War was the "wedge" hat. Though smart-looking, the wedge was never very practical in a sub-zero Canadian winter.

Pisspot

Sensibly the RCAF issued Canada-based airmen with a round wool cap, with a visor and ear-flaps that could be laced together at the top, out of the way. It was much warmer than the wedge, but simply lacked its panache, so airmen risked their ears. [Ref: Collins]

*Jeez, I hate wearing
that pisspot...*

PIT; TO PIT (CF; since at least 1920's) — A "pit" is a bed, presumably because, like a pit, it is a place where one enters darkness. Therefore, the verb "to pit" means to go to bed and sleep, and to be "pitted out" is to be asleep. (See also **Flame Out, Rack**) [Ref: Partridge (8th)]

*Where's Paul?
I think he went back to
barracks, to pit.*

PITCH-UP (aviation; general) — In aerodynamics, to "pitch-up" is to raise the nose of an aircraft, as in a climb. From this fact comes an additional, informal meaning "to depart", as in: *Its getting late - I think I'll pitch up and go home...*

PLANE — A plane is a flat, level surface mathematically defined in space by three points. On the other hand, an *airplane* is a machine that flies due to lift generated by air flowing over an airfoil embodied in a wing, or mainplane. Aviation professionals seem to avoid the word "plane" when formally referring to aircraft, just as sailors do not refer to their ship as a "boat" and as infantrymen do not refer to their rifle as a "gun". The famous RAF Group Captain and fighter ace Douglas Bader described his early lesson in this aspect of airmanlike vocabulary:

He (Bader's flying instructor) heard Douglas refer one day to a 'plane'. Straightaway he took him to an Avro parked beside the hangar. Touching the lower wing of the biplane, he said in his precise and pedantic way: This - this - is a plane. That - that', pointing to the whole aircraft 'is an aeroplane.' He would allow 'aeroplane' or 'aircraft' but nothing else. The other bastardized abbreviations - kite, plane and no doubt, the Americanism, ship - were absolutely forbidden.

Of course, this has not stopped military aviators from coining their own nicknames for specific aircraft types, nor has it prevented common use of nicknames among themselves. As well, aircraft technicians have invented thousands of slang and shorthand terms for various aircraft components. Still, it seems that the word "aircraft" is preferred in formal or public usage. [Ref: Lucas]

PLAY SILLY BUGGER, TO (originally British Forces; still current) — To "play silly bugger" is to go on military exercises, or to engage in time-wasting, though official, activity in the name of military need.

Pack your kit; we're all going to play silly bugger for six weeks...

PLUMBER (originally RAF since at least WWII, now obsolescent, but see Gun Plumber) — In the RAF, "plumber" was originally the cognomen for an Armourer, a technician who maintains aircraft weapons and armaments. (It may be related to another Armourer nickname, "Gun Plumber", still occasionally heard in the CF of the 1990's). In the Second World War, Plumber came to refer to any aircraft mechanic, and indeed, among aircrews, the "Squadron Plumber" was the Squadron Engineering Officer. (See also **Engines, Gun Plumber**) [Ref: Partridge (8th)]

The plumbers are looking at the guns now.

PMQ BRAT — A "PMQ Brat" is the child of a serviceman or servicewoman who lives in "PMQ's", the "Permanent Married Quarters". PMQ's are military housing located next to a military base, where many servicemembers posted to that base live and raise families. There is a unique subculture associated with life in PMQ's. Though not "military" in the strictest sense of the word, this subculture is inextricably bound up with the CF and its peculiarities. Children of course, do not appreciate military order and structure and often rebel against rules. Therefore, the term PMQ Brats.

POLE-HOG (RCAF, CF; current) — A "pole-hog" is a pilot (in a two-pilot aircraft) who rarely yields control of the aircraft to the other pilot, and who "hogs" (ie., covets) the "pole" (ie., the aircraft's control column). To be a pole-hog is a social sin in the pilot fraternity, where it is accepted that everyone wants to fly and that the opportunity to do so ought to be shared equitably.

I hate flying with Hughes! He's such a pole-hog!

POND, THE — The "pond" is the Atlantic Ocean, as in: *Crossing the pond in a North Star aircraft is a long, loud, and uncomfortable flight.* [Ref: Partridge (8th)]

PONGO — "Pongo" is a sailor's and airman's mildly derogatory nickname for a soldier. The word pongo originates in "Pongid Ape", apparently an early term for the Orangutan. One description of the Pongid Ape given to the author (probably incorrect, but nonetheless delicious) said that this ape was *noted for its habit of digging holes in the earth and filling them up again, for no apparent reason.*

The use of the word Pongo to describe soldiers developed in the Royal Navy in the 1890's, where it originally applied to Royal Marines. Major warships always carried a complement of marines on board, and it is no secret that the inherent differences in temperament and attitude between the "marines" and the "mariners" led to a longstanding rivalry. One imagines a section of marines drilling smartly on the quarterdeck of a Dreadnought, being observed by a group of casual and languid sailors making disparaging allusions to "trained monkeys"! Hence, the reference to Pongid

Pongo

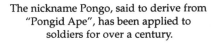

The nickname Pongo, said to derive from "Pongid Ape", has been applied to soldiers for over a century.

Ape, and to Pongo. Eventually, the term Pongo came to apply to soldiers generally, rather than marines in particular. Its use spread throughout the British Empire and Commonwealth forces, where it entered Canadian air force usage. The term is becoming obsolete in Canadian usage. The American term "grunt" seems to be overtaking it. [Ref: Partridge (8th)]

I see that this will be a casual affair - by the fact that the pongos are here...

POOPY SUIT — "Poopy Suit" is a term applied to any of several bulky overall-like garments worn in military service, such as:

(1)   Immersion suits: An Immersion Suit is a rubberized one-piece garment worn over flying clothing intended to keep a wearer dry, should one's flight be cut short by a crash landing into cold water. The first variants were designed for the pilots of Second World War "Hurricat" fighters whose every landing was a "ditching" into the sea. (See also **Hurricat**) These early suits were made of horse leather, which could "breathe" but which sealed tight when immersed in water. They were very successful and were also called "Goon Suits" by airmen. Modern Poopy Suits are made of rubber, which is less bulky than leather and provides a better "seal" against the water. They are, however, renowned for being very, very hot. [Ref: Greer, Harold]

(2)   Nuclear-Biological-Chemical Warfare Suit (NBCW Suit): An NBCW Suit is a sealed garment worn over the entire body, including head, feet and hands, which protects the wearer from exposure to low-yield radioactive fallout, and chemical and biological weapons. Though such a suit will not protect the wearer from strong direct radiation, the wearer is generally safe from the effects of fallout, for a while. The suit is also lined with a filtering material which protects the wearer from contact with chemical weapons or germs. Not unlike a snowmobile suit in appearance, an NBCW Suit is hot and

bulky and when fully "closed up", the wearer breathes through a respirator. Though such clothing is the best personal protection now available from the effects of "special weapons", an NBCW Suit also drastically reduces the ability to perform normal duties. Still, Canadian Forces personnel in Germany and in the Gulf War were trained and ready to fly, service and defend combat aircraft wearing an NBCW Suit.

POPULAR (RAF; WWII) — "Popular" was the Second World War RAF codename for a free-ranging, low-level offensive patrol by one or several photo-reconnaissance aircraft. In such an operation, the pilots had enormous personal discretion in the selection of targets, within a given area. A Popular was to photo-reconnaissance pilots, what a "Rhubarb" was to fighter pilots. (See also **Rodeo;Rhubarb**)

Get ready! You and Walt are scheduled for a Popular this afternoon.

PORPOISE, TO (aviation; general) — When an aircraft "porpoises", it pitches slightly forward and back about its lateral axis. Its flight path undulates slightly, suggesting a porpoise swimming rapidly and arcing up, out of the water, and splashing back into the water, over and over...

If you look carefully at a Spitfire as it climbs away after takeoff, you'll notice
it porpoising slightly, several times.
That's because the pilot pumps the undercarriage up by hand.

POT — Depending on the context, a "pot" could be slang for either of:

(1)   A cylinder on a piston engine, presumably because like a kitchen pot, a cylinder is hollow and circular; and

(2)   A potentiometer, an electrical device for limiting or measuring Electromotive Force.

POWER ON, TO (CF Europe; 1960's to 1980's) — "To power on" is to get started, to get underway, or to begin. Thus, "powering on" alluded to a time, as in *we're powering on at 1136 hours*. The term was used by the air and ground crews of CF-104 Starfighter squadrons, who probably picked it up from the USAF. There, power on occurred when groundcrew technicians applied auxiliary ground power to an individual aircraft. This enabled the pilot to align the Inertial Navigation/Attack system with the autopilot and start the engine for takeoff.

PRANG; TO PRANG (originally RAF WWII; now aviation general) — To "prang" an aircraft is to crash it. It is said that the word is a "verbal sound effect", representing the noise of metal vibrating after impact. Hence, the noun prang, meaning a crash. (The coining of this term was most unfortunate for one element of the American air reserve forces, the Puerto Rico Air National Guard, or PRANG.) It entered civilian slang briefly, where it simply meant "to break something". Prang was very common during and after the Second World War, though its use is now fading. [Ref: Partridge (FS)]

Be careful to keep your airspeed up! You don't want to prang it!

PREGNANT DUCK (RAF, RCAF; WWII) — "Pregnant Duck" was the occasional nickname for the Lockheed Hudson, a twin- engined patrol bomber of the Second World War. The nickname probably derives from the aircraft's somewhat portly appearance on the ground.

The Hudson was designed at the outset of the Second World War on very short notice by Lockheed Aircraft to meet a British requirement for a fast patrol bomber. It was derived from the Lockheed Lodestar airliner of the late 1930's. The British Purchasing Mission approved of Lockheed's proposal, and the Pregnant Duck entered both RAF and RCAF service very shortly after. The Hudson was primarily employed as a coastal patrol and anti-submarine aircraft, though it was not very long before faster aircraft began to surpass it in performance. The Hudson was the direct antecedent of Lockheed's uprated Ventura patrol bomber. (See also **Flying Pig**) [Ref: Partridge (FS)]

Another dozen Pregnant Ducks will be leaving for Britain tomorrow.

PREGNANT FROG (RCAF; WWII) — "Pregnant Frog" was the unkind nickname given by Canadian airmen to the Grumman Goblin, a biplane fighter that equipped RCAF fighter units in Eastern Canada early in the Second World War.

The Grumman Goblin would have been an effective fighter early in the 1930's, but it was sadly outdated by 1939. Still, it was used for Eastern Canadian air defence in the first years of the Second World War because no other aircraft were available. It was not a handsome aircraft, a fact which was the probable origin of its nickname.

PRESSING BLANKETS — "Pressing Blankets" is occasional air force vernacular for "sleeping".

PRESS-ON-ITIS   See **Get-there-itis**

PRI-5 (CF; current) — Pri-5 is shorthand for "Priority 5". Synonymous with flying on a "stand-by" or "space available" basis, Pri-5 is the lowest travel priority that is possible for a military passenger to be allocated. It is accepted that there are usually fewer available seats on military transport aircraft than there are people who need to travel. However, when a spare seat is available, it is accepted that it would be preferable for a servicemember travelling on leave to have the spare seat, rather than letting it go to waste. To bring order to this volume of demand, a system of priorities has been established; Pri-5 is the lowest priority, and is designated for those travelling on leave. Pri-5 passengers are only boarded after all higher priority passengers are assured a seat, so travelling Pri-5 carried a certain amount of risk. You generally got a seat, but you might wait several days to get it! This fact led to another aphorism of military air transport: *Got Time To Spare? Fly Service Air!*

I'm trying to get a Pri-5 flight over to Germany.
Good luck, you'll need it!

PROP(S) — Of course in aviation, "prop" is merely shorthand for an aircraft propeller. Thus, one "feathers the props", or "changes a prop".

However, on RAF and RCAF uniforms, a "prop" was the badge of rank for a Leading

Aircraftman or Leading Aircraftwoman (LAC, LAW). On each upper sleeve, an LAC or LAW wore a cloth rank badge depicting a silver two-bladed propeller, or prop. Therefore, to be promoted to LAC or LAW was to "put up your props", and to toast the promotion was to "wet your props". [Ref: Partridge (FS)]

PROPWASH (aviation, general) — Strictly speaking, "propwash" is the blast of turbulent air driven towards the rear of an aircraft engine by the propeller.

However, propwash has another, more unusual meaning. "Propwash", in this sense, is a useful but mythical substance that has for decades been the source of much embarrassment for apprentice technicians. The unaware apprentice is typically sent on a simple errand: "to go get a can of propwash" - an apparently plausible item (used to clean aircraft propellers, no doubt!), but which simply does not exist. A hapless rookie in the hands of others who play along with the joke can be sent hither and yon for hours before anyone lets him in on the joke. (*Propwash? Sorry, we're fresh out, but ask over at 442 Squadron. They might have some!*) Hardly anyone falls for it anymore, but every now and then... (For other mythical but useful substances see **Flight Line, Hangar Line; Flight Lustre; Long Weight; Radar Contacts; Relative Bearing Grease; Skyhook; Tartan Paint; Tacan Gate**)

Propwash

Where's McGillivray?
He went to 5 Hangar to look for a gallon of propwash!

PRUNERY; PRUNISM — "Prunery" and "Prunism" both refer to flying which is likely to cause a crash. Both words are derived from one of the least auspicious characters in RAF folklore: Pilot Officer Percy Prune.

Pilot Officer Percy Prune was a very popular Second World War cartoon character, an RAF pilot best described as earnest, cerebrally uncomplicated, and thoroughly unsafe. Pilot Officer Prune lived in the pages of the RAF's safety-oriented training memorandum, "Tee Emm", where fellow aircrew learned by his exploits, what *not* to do while flying! Prune was created by two RAF officers, Anthony Armstrong Willis (who recorded Prune's exploits) and Bill Hooper (who illustrated them). Prune became extraordinarily popular and soon the words "prunery" and "prunism" entered the air force vocabulary.

The words "prunery" and "prunism" described behaviour that was worthy of Percy Prune. For example, Tee Emm told of the aircraft and crew that landed at an unknown RAF station in the middle of the night, during the war. The pilot nonchalantly left the aircraft and walked around the station until he found the mess, where he carefully noted the name of the station from the bulletin board. He then returned to his aircraft and the crew flew home. This is prunery at its finest!

Pilot Officer Prune was an Englishman, but his crew was drawn from all over the Commonwealth and included Flying Officer Freddy Fixe, an RCAF navigator! Although there was no hope of Prune ever being promoted past Pilot Officer (for youngsters, this is equivalent to Second Lieutenant), he did become a "Companion of the Most Highly Derogatory Order of the Irremoveable Finger". (For the full implications of this, see **Fingertrouble**) Captured German records apparently showed that Prune had been awarded the Iron Cross *in absentia*, for having destroyed so many RAF aircraft. Prune is now apparently retired and lives happily in England. [Ref: Gunderson]

> *I heard that Dave oversped the propeller again!*
> *Yeah, he's always involved in some Prunery...*

PUCKER; PUCKER FACTOR — The "Pucker Factor" is a mythical scale by which one measures the stressfulness of a situation faced (usually) in flight. Therefore, a "pucker" situation is a stressful, or difficult one.

The "Pucker Factor" is an allusion to the fact that, while under stress, one's muscles tense up. More specifically, Pucker Factor refers to the tendency, in a dangerous situation, for the muscles of the anal sphincter to close so tight that a certain "puckering" effect seems to occur. Whatever the physiological realities may be, aviators gauge stress by the Pucker Factor.

> *I'm lucky to be alive! The starboard engine failed while flying through the*
> *mountains, and my Pucker Factor suddenly tripled!*

PUKE (CF current; originally USN) — "Puke" is a mildly disparaging term for a person of a particular type or category. (For the uninformed, "puke" is common slang for vomit.) The term "puke" is usually used by aircrew to describe other aircrew, and is prefaced by a descriptive category, as in "Fighter Puke", "Transport Puke", etc. In this sense it is an equivalent of the RAF slang words "type" and "basher", or the USAF slang word "weenie". (See also **Type, Basher, Weenie**)

> *He's a typical fighter puke...*

LANGESTE

Pucker Factor

The Pucker Factor is a useful (though
mythical) gauge of stress.

PUKKA (originally British Indian Forces; later more general use) — *Pukka* is a Hindi word that has entered the lexicon of British and British Commonwealth military slang and translates as "good", "proper", or "reliable". It was first picked up by British troops in India, from where it entered Empire and Canadian military usage. The most common air force usage is with the word "gen" (which means "information"), therefore the term "pukka gen", for "reliable information". Pukka is becoming very rare in Canadian usage. (See **Gen**) [Ref: Partridge (8th)]

The new Commanding Officer is a pukka sort of fellow, I hear.

PULVERIZER (Bomber Command; WWII) — "Pulverizer" was the ironic nickname for the Short "Stirling", one of the first of the RAF's four-engine heavy bombers of the Second World War. Though the Stirling looked very impressive, its performance never lived up to expectations, largely because prewar RAF specifications imposed ridiculous, and sometimes contradictory constraints on the Pulverizer's designers.

The Stirling was expected to carry a heavy bombload over thousands of miles at high speeds. This role requires an aircraft with a wide wingspan, to generate the needed lift. Yet, the RAF also demanded that the Stirling's wingspan not exceed 100 feet, so that the aircraft could fit inside prewar RAF hangars! To create enough lift from such a narrow wingspan, designers had to increase the camber (ie., relative thickness) of the wing. This in turn increased drag, and reduced the Stirling's maximum speed and ceiling! Reliable though it was, the Pulverizer was a bundle of compromises, and was soon surpassed by other, better-designed bombers such as the Lancaster and Halifax. [Ref: Partridge (FS)]

So you fly Pulverizers?

PULL THE CHOCKS; PULL THE PINS (aviation general) — When an airman or airwoman "pulls the chocks" or "pulls the pins", it means they are leaving. Both phrases seem to be borrowed from aircraft handling terminology and are metaphors for departure.

The term "to pull the chocks" derives from the fact that aircraft are normally parked with chocks beneath the wheels that prevent an aircraft from rolling forward or aft. Pulling the chocks is a metaphor for departure, because the last thing to be done before the aircraft can depart is to remove the chocks from beneath the wheels.

"To pull the pins" is also "to depart", though the origins of this term may not be in aviation. To an aviator, the word "pins" would seem to refer to "safety pins". Safety pins are steel rods inserted into mechanical locks in various parts of an aircraft. These pins prevent undercarriages from being retracted on the ground, flight control surfaces from being moved around by the wind, and weapons from being inadvertently armed. They are removed, or pulled immediately before flight - and are therefore the metaphor for "departure".

However, as far back as the 1930's, to "pull the pins" has also been Canadian railway slang for "departure"! In the railways of the 1930's, railway cars were uncoupled from each other by pulling, or removing, steel pins linking each car to the next. Thus, at the end of a trip, railway crew members would "pull the pins" and uncouple the cars from the engine before leaving the train in the siding. It is uncertain whether the phrase to pull the pins, as spoken by aviators, was unconsciously borrowed from the railways, or whether it emerged independently. [Ref: Partridge (8th)]

Well, its time to go home, so I think I'll pull the pins (pull the chocks) and leave.

PULPIT (RFC, RAF; WWI) — "Pulpit" was the nickname for a First World War fighter, the "BE9". The nickname arose because of the unique configuration of the BE9. Its designers placed the engine and propeller in the rear of the fuselage, the gunner in an open cockpit in the nose, and the pilot between. The aircraft was a "taildragger", so as the aircraft sat on the ground, the nose (with the gunner's position) sat quite high, rather like a minister's pulpit in a church. [Ref: Partridge (8th)]

PUNCH OUT, TO (military aviation; since 1950's) — "To punch out" is to eject from an aircraft equipped with an ejection seat. Presumably the term is borrowed from civilian slang where to punch out means "to leave". The term originally stems from industry, where one "punches in" on a time clock when arriving at work, and "punches out" on leaving.

When a jet fighter's engine fails at low altitude, there is nothing you can do except punch out - fast!

PUP — The word "Pup" has had two meanings relevant to military aviation. During the First World War, "Pup" invariably referred to the Sopwith Pup, a very effective biplane fighter introduced in the last year of the war. However, during the Second World War, a "Pup" was a student pilot, the allusion being to a puppy, of course. [Ref: Partridge (FS)]

PURPLE (CF; current) — Up to the late 1980's all members of the Canadian Forces wore a dark forest-green uniform, regardless of service affiliation. Though the army was generally happy with the green uniform, sailors and airmen were not and in 1988 changes were finally announced. Soon airmen and airwomen were back in light blue uniforms, sailors were in dark blue, and soldiers stayed in the CF green (although the army, navy and air force did not return as separate legal entities). Along with this change came new slang. The colour of the uniform became synonymous with the service that wore that colour. Thus a member of the air force was a "light-blue type", and a sailor was "dark-blue". Military trades were similarly identified; for example, "Airframe Technician" and "Pilot" were considered "light blue" occupations, "Infantrymen" and "Field Engineers" were "green" trades, and "Boatswains" and "Divers" were "dark blue" trades.

This colourful nomenclature broke down however, when applied to those trades that were common to all three environments of the CF, such as administration, logistics, medical, military police, etc. In National Defence Headquarters slang these occupations became known as "purple" trades - purple being a colour not associated with either the army, navy or the air force. (See also **Blues**)

Administrative Clerks are one of those purple trades.

PUSSER SPITFIRE (Fleet Air Arm; WWII) — "Pusser Spitfire" is sarcastic slang for the Royal Navy's Swordfish torpedo-bomber, also known as the "Stringbag". The word "pusser" (itself a corruption of the word Purser) is navy slang that means official or navy issue. The term implies that the Swordfish, a slow, open cockpit biplane, is a "navy-issue Spitfire!" Both the Swordfish and the Spitfire were developed in the 1930's as war threatened Europe, the Swordfish for the Navy, the Spitfire for the RAF. It is beyond question that, in terms of funding, the navy's Fleet Air Arm was a poor cousin to the RAF. So the nickname Pusser Spitfire is a sarcastic allusion to the preference enjoyed by the Royal Air Force over the Fleet Air Arm, in aircraft development. (See also **Stringbag**) [Ref: Partridge (8th)]

> *Oh, the Fleet Air Arm flew Spitfires all right - Pusser Spitfires, with two sets of wings!*

PUZZLE-PALACE (CF current; possibly American in origin) — "Puzzle Palace" is a generic term for a higher military headquarters, presumably because activities of headquarters (in the eyes of many line unit personnel) are often puzzling, at best. (See also **Bullshit Towers, Castle Dismal, Disneyland-on-the-Rideau, Fort Fumble, Fraggle Rock, Glass Menagerie; Glass Palace, Petrified Forest**)

PYROTECHNIC   See **Rocket**

 UEBEC

Q, THE (CF, current) — The "Q" is shorthand for the "QRA" or "Quick Reaction Area". The "Q" is an area at fighter bases in which fighter interceptor aircraft and their crews wait around the clock for the signal to launch. The Q comprises a hangar, aircraft servicing facility, and quarters, all self-contained and adjacent to the runways. These aircraft are "cocked and loaded"; that is, the aircraft are armed and their crews are ready for immediate takeoff to intercept any unidentified or hostile aircraft. Hostile intruders are destroyed. (See also **Cocked and Loaded**)

Two interceptors and their crews are in "the Q", ready for immediate launch.

QRO's; QR and O's (ie., "cue-are-owes") (CF; since 1953) — Hardly slang, but universal enough to be a permanent part of the air force lexicon, "QRO's" are Queen's Regulations and Orders. QRO's are the rules that govern the armed forces and all who serve in it. When a King wears the Crown, the term is "King's Regulations and Orders", or KRO's. Prior to integration of the three services they were termed QR(Air) - Queen's Regulations for the Air Force - to distinguish them from navy and army regulations. (See also **KRO's**)

What do you think I am, a library? Look it up in QRO's!

Q'S, THE (CF, current) — The "Q's" is shorthand for "PMQ's", the universally used abbreviation for "Permanent Married Quarters". PMQ's are the houses built for married service personnel on, or near, a military base. (See also **PMQ Brat**)

My husband and I are living in the Q's again.

QUACK, THE (RCAF, RAF; WWII) — The "quack" is the Medical Officer - a military doctor - as in: *If you've got a cold, you'd better go see the Quack.* The term is clearly borrowed from civilian slang. [Ref: Partridge (FS)]

QUEEN BEE (RCAF/RAF, WWII) — The senior female officer at an RAF or RCAF Station was often termed the "Queen Bee" (though rarely to her face). The Queen Bee had a special responsibility to look out for the welfare of all female personnel on that station, a task not deemed suitable for male officers. [Refs: Harvey; Partridge (FS)]

Squadron Leader Houston is the Queen Bee at this Station.

QUEEN'S CORPORAL   See **Hellyer's Corporal**

QUEEN MARY (RCAF; WWII to late 1960's) — "Queen Mary" was the airman's nickname for a large flatbed trailer used to haul away wrecked or salvaged aircraft. The nickname, referring to its size, suggested the trailer was big enough to haul the ocean liner, the Queen Mary! The term lived in RCAF usage until the late 1960's. [Refs: Partridge (8th); Sutherland]

Jeez - we'll need a Queen Mary to get this tail section back to the base!

QUICK PUSSY (RCAF Europe: early 1960's to early 1980's) — "Quick Pussy" was the somewhat lewd nickname for "Fast Cat", a NATO codename for a secure communications system. Fast Cat linked NATO's "Supreme Headquarters Operations Centre" to the air bases armed with nuclear weapons. [Ref: Sutherland]

Wing Commander, there's a call for you on Quick Pussy...

QUIRK, THE (RFC,WWI) — The "Quirk" was the nickname given to the Be2c, a First World War two-seat observation aircraft remarkable for its slow speed. However, the word quirk also described an officer undergoing RFC training. This usage may have been borrowed from "erk", an airman. [Ref: Partridge (8th)]

Quirk

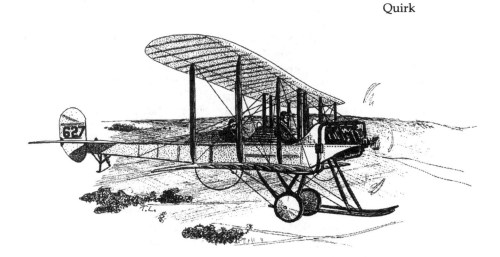

I used to fly the Quirk, then I was posted back to England.

Romeo

RACK; TO RACK (CF, current) — A "rack" is a bed. Therefore, "to rack" is to sleep, as in: *I'm going back to the barracks to rack for a while.*

RADAR CONTACTS — To most aviators, a "radar contact" is the indication that radar has detected an object, such as an aircraft or ship. However, the term radar contact is occasionally used in another, entirely different context: as part of a practical joke played on apprentice avionics technicians, where the radar "contact" is deliberately confused with other types of electrical "contacts".

Avionics (a contraction of "aviation" and "electronics") is a highly complex and demanding subject, one in which possessing only a "little bit of knowledge" is dangerous. This is certainly true for the apprentice technician struggling to keep track of all the new things to be learned - including all sorts of hardware, like various types of electrical "contacts". So, it is perhaps not surprising that when a more senior technician - with a straight face - tells an apprentice to go get a "box of radar contacts", the apprentice will generally scurry away to locate them! Later, when the unfortunate technician realizes he or she has been "had", there is usually much embarrassment. In this sense, a "radar contact" falls into the category of the useful, but mythical. (For other mythical but useful substances see **Flight Line, Hangar Line; Flight Lustre; Long Weight; Propwash; Relative Bearing Grease; Skyhook; Tartan Paint; Tacan Gate**)

Kerry, go up to the avionics lab and ask for a box of radar contacts...

RAF (pronounced "raff") — The Royal Air Force is often called the "raff" (as is the RAAF, or Royal Australian Air Force, in Australia). However, within the Royal Air Force the term is usually regarded as being in bad form. The early history, customs and traditions of the RAF are very relevant to the study of Canadian military aviation. For most of the first half of the twentieth century Canada's domestic military activity was minimal and overseas involvement was conducted as part of the British Empire and Commonwealth. Consequently the RCAF tended to borrow RAF procedures and Canadian airmen received much RAF advice and training.

However, it would not be fair to say that Canadians merely "copied " the RAF and its traditions; given the enormous number of Canadians who served in the RAF it is more accurate to say that Canadians had a great deal to do with establishing the RAF. Indeed, British historian Denis Winter has written: *By the end of the (first world) war Canadian pilots had the lion's share of killings: Bishop 72, Collishaw 60, Barker 59, Maclaren 54, McEvoy 46, Claxton 39, McCall 37, Quigley 34, Carter 31, McKeever 30 - without such scores the RAF list would have been thin gruel...* A nation with only 10 percent of the British Empire's population had produced one-third of the imperial air force. This strong link with the RAF persisted until after the Second World War when the exigencies of continental defence forged equally strong links with the United States Air Force. Still, the RAF influence is strong and a Canadian airman visiting a raff station today would recognize much in his surroundings. [Refs: Partridge (8th); Winter]

RAISE, TO (commonwealth military; general) — "To raise" a document is to issue it, or to complete it. Thus one can raise one's Travel Orders, or raise a cheque, etc. [Ref: Partridge (8th)]

Get the orderly room staff to raise a travel claim for you.

RAMROD   See **Circus**

RANGER (RAF, RCAF; WWII) — "Ranger" was Second World War code for a freelance offensive air operation carried out by groups of RAF fighters. These groups ranged in size from a single squadron to several wings. These operations were carried out extensively before the Normandy invasion of 1944. The goal of this program of Ranger operations was to engage enemy fighter forces and wear them down through attrition. Typically, a Ranger operation would target Luftwaffe fighter bases and their areas of operations. This was one of several types of offensive fighter operation introduced by Air Chief Marshal Sholto Douglas, chief of Fighter Command after the Battle of Britain. The Germans had just invaded Russia and there were loud cries for the western allies to relieve pressure on the Russians by opening a second front. The western allies were unable to open up a second front immediately, though other offensive actions were commenced. Offensive fighter sweeps such as Ranger operations began, but they proved to be less than successful. The Luftwaffe realized the aim of the operations and simply did not respond with the alacrity that the RAF expected. It was not until RAF bombers became involved that the Luftwaffe responded, though even these operations did not achieve the aim of wearing out the Luftwaffe. (See also **Circus, Rodeo; Rhubarb**) [Ref: Rawlings; Terraine]

RCEME (pronounced "ree-mee") (CF; since WWII) — Despite the awkward spelling, "RCEME", the initials for the Royal Canadian Electrical and Mechanical Engineers, are pronounced "ree-mee". The RCEME was that corps of the Canadian Army that maintained the army's equipment and weaponry, including its aircraft and helicopters. (Though during the Second World War and immediately after, the aircraft technicians for Canadian Army aviation units came from the RCAF.) After unification, RCEME aircraft maintainers, like their counterparts in the Navy, were absorbed into the air force-dominated Canadian Forces aircraft maintenance structure.

The acronym is pronounced "ree-mee" (ie., without the "C" sounding at all) because it is borrowed from the British Army, whose analogous Corps is the REME. [Ref: Partridge (8th)]

REALLY NOT A SAILOR (Royal Navy; WWI) — During the First World War, "Really Not a Sailor" was the spurious meaning for the initials "RNAS", which actually meant "Royal Naval Air Service". "Really Not A Sailor" fairly summed up the saltwater sailors' opinion of the upstart Royal Naval Air Service.

The RNAS was established in 1912 by the Royal Navy which, like almost all military services of the day, had no real appreciation of the potential of air power. In part this resulted because the RNAS flew largely on the western front alongside the army's RFC. It was not as involved with the fleet and naval officers had less to do with its air arm than did the army. Thus, more tradition-bound naval officers looked down on the upstart RNAS, which enjoyed much more recognition than was felt deserved. They were "of the navy", but not seamen. (The naval airman's common retort was *seamanship is merely airmanship at 10 knots, and in two dimensions, rather than three...*) [Ref: Partridge (8th)]

> *I see Sub-Lieutenant Watt is transferring to the RNAS...*
> *What you mean is that he's 'really not a sailor', eh?*

RECCE (pronounced "recky") (Commonwealth military) — "Recce" is the universal abbreviation and shorthand slang substitute, for "reconnaissance". Therefore, one "goes on a recce", or "flies a recce trip", "receives a recce report", etc. [Ref: Partridge (FS)]

> *Who's leading the recce flight?*

RECSPEC (RCAF; 1950's, 60's) — "RecSpec" was the RCAF abbreviation and acronym for "Recreation Specialist". A RecSpec was an airman trained to conduct physical education and training, and to run the recreation facilities on any given RCAF Station. (It is not to be confused with a "Rescue Spec".) With Unification in 1968, terminology changed and these personnel became known as "Peri's" (pronounced "perry") for Physical Education and Recreation Instructor. (See **Rescue Spec, Muscle Bosun**)

RED BARON (WWI) — "Red Baron" was (and remains) the nickname for German ace Rittmeister Baron von Richthofen, the leading fighter ace of the First World War, with 80 victories. Richthofen was indeed a baron, born of Prussian aristocracy. Like many First World War pilots, he began service as a cavalry officer (his rank, *Rittmeister* is the cavalry rank equal to Captain); he soon transferred to the Imperial German Flying Service where he quickly earned a reputation as a deadly shot. However, records show he was a cautious attacker; two-seat reconnaissance aircraft accounted for 60% of Richthofen's victories. By all accounts he revelled in each kill; for each victory he ordered a small silver cup engraved with the date of the victory and the type of aircraft destroyed.

He became known as the "red" baron because of his practice of painting his aircraft a vivid bright red. However, it is quite possible that this idea was in fact borrowed from Jean Navarre, a French ace who flew a bright red Nieuport biplane, and who flew against Richthofen for a time. Richthofen was killed on April 21st, 1918 in air combat with two Canadians. Richthofen had rolled in to attack a Sopwith Camel flown by Canadian Lieutenant "Wop" May, when a fellow Canadian, Captain Roy Brown dived after the Baron. Wop May survived to become a great Canadian bush pilot and Roy Brown was credited with having shot down the famous "Red Baron". Roy Brown's combat report on this fateful day follows:

> *SOPWITH BR NUMBER 7270. 21 APRIL 1918. TIME 10.45 AM LOCALITY 62DQ2. DUTY OP. AT 1035 I OBSERVED TWO ALBATROSSES BURST INTO FLAMES AND CRASH. DIVED ON LARGE FORMATION OF 15-20 ALBATROSSES AND D-5 SCOUTS AND FOKKER TRIPLANES. TWO GOT ON MY TAIL AND I CAME OUT. WENT BACK AGAIN AND DIVED ON A PURE RED TRIPLANE WHICH WAS FIRING ON LIEUTENANT MAY. I GOT A LONG BURST INTO HIM AND HE WENT DOWN VERTICAL AND WAS*

*OBSERVED TO CRASH BY LT. MELLISH AND LT. MAY. I FIRED ON
TWO MORE BUT DID NOT GET THEM.*

Some controversy remains about whether Richthofen was killed by Captain Roy Brown or by ground fire from Australian ground troops; however, the army doctors who first examined Richthofen's body agreed that the angle of entry of his fatal wounds meant that another aircraft was almost certainly responsible. (See also **Flying Circus**) [Refs: Longstreet, Winter]

RED FLAG (USAF; current) — Red Flag is a large and highly realistic air fighting exercise conducted at Nellis Air Force Base, near Las Vegas, Nevada. From time to time Canadian fighter squadrons deploy to Nevada to participate. (See **Maple Flag**)

RED OUT   See to **Black Out**

REGS — "Regs" is a term with two meanings pertinent to military aviation:

(1)   **Regs** is simply abbreviated shorthand for "Regulations", as in *go check out the regs!*

(2)   **Regs** is also shorthand for "Regulars", as in "Regular Force", as opposed to the Reserve Force. Servicemembers who serve on a full-time, career basis are members of the Regular Force (ie., "the Regs", and are generally called regs by Reservists. (See **Perms, P.F.**)

RELATIVE BEARING GREASE — "Relative Bearing Grease" is useful but mythical substance that has occasionally become the source of much embarrassment to very junior aviators. A "bearing" is a mechanical device used in aircraft and much other equipment to reduce friction between components; bearings come in many configurations: roller bearings, ball bearings, etc. To further reduce friction, these bearings are lubricated with grease. In contrast, in navigation a "bearing" is a direction relative to a reference point, and is expressed in degrees of the compass. Aviators learning navigation learn how to take a "relative bearing". Junior airmen are expected to keep this, and all sorts of other information clear in their minds. However, it is not always possible for novices to keep all this straight, and occasionally someone will be sent off to get a can of "grease" to lubricate a "relative bearing". (For other mythical but useful substances see **Flight Line, Hangar Line; Flight Lustre; Long Weight; Propwash; Radar Contacts; Skyhook; Tartan Paint; Tacan Gate**)

*Mister Cooper, ask the maintenance sergeant for a small can of relative
bearing grease.*

REP (military; general) — "Rep" is short for Reprimand, a formal rebuke noted on one's records resulting from a breach of regulations. [Ref: Partridge (FS)]

The court-martial found him guilty and gave him a severe rep.

RESCUE SPEC; R.S. (RCAF, CF 1950's to 1980's) — "Rescue Spec" and "R.S." are both shorthand terms for "Rescue Specialist". The Rescue Spec was a highly trained NCO who parachuted from a Search and Rescue aircraft down to a crash site, helped the survivors, and helped extricate them. The term Rescue Spec yielded to "Search and Rescue Technician" or "SARTECH" in the early 1980's, as the rescue specialty became a full-fledged occupation. Up to then, Rescue Specialists were seconded to the job from other occupations, and in theory at least, could return to their former jobs.

RE-TREAD (military, general; since WWII) — A "Re-tread" is an airman who is already fully trained in one skill, and who, for personal or organizational reasons, becomes a "journeyman" in a different air force occupation. Thus a fully trained navigator who reclassifies to become a pilot is said to be a "retread". The term sometimes alludes to a retired servicemember who is recalled for war service. The obvious allusion is to a worn rubber tire that can be "retreaded" to give it a longer useful life. [Ref: Partridge (8th)]

> *Isn't Stobbs a bit older than the other pilot trainees?*
> *Not when you consider that he's a retread observer.*

RHIP (military, general) — The initials "RHIP" mean "Rank Has Its Privileges." Throughout the armed forces of the world, higher rank generally does bring privileges. However, officers and NCOs in the best military organizations believe more strongly that "rank has its responsibilities".

> *Why does the Station Commander's office have such a nice carpet?*
> *RHIP*

RHUBARB   See **Rodeo**

RIGGER (RAF, RAF; since 1920's) — Today, a "rigger" is an airframe technician, that is, a technician who specializes in repair and maintenance of aircraft structures, flight controls, fuel systems, undercarriage, hydraulics, pressurization, etc. The term dates back to the First World War when a rigger's primary job was the "rigging" of flight control cables, and adjusting them to the correct tension. Plans exist for the rigger trade to amalgamate with the "fitters", the aero-engine technicians. (See also **Fitter, Super-Rigger**)

> *Call a Rigger. We've got a problem with the undercarriage.*

RIGGER MORTIS (RCAF; 1940's, 1950's) — A "Rigger Mortis" is a useless airman. The term is a play on "rigor mortis", the bodily stiffness that accompanies death, and the word "rigger", an airframe technician. (See **Rigger**) [Ref: Partridge (FS)]

> *What's Dennis like?*
> *He's a real Rigger Mortis...*

RIGGER'S NIGHTMARE   See **Harry Tate**

RING-KNOCKER (CF, current; originally U.S. Army) — "Ring-Knocker" is a disparaging American army term for a graduate of West Point, the United States Military Academy. Consequently, it has been adopted by some Canadian servicemembers to refer to graduates of the Royal Military College of Canada. Apparently the term has its origins in the custom of the "Class Ring" - now common at high schools, colleges and universities - a custom which began at West Point early in the

Twentieth Century. West Point graduates enjoy a certain privileged status in the U.S. Army social pecking order. Reportedly, when a West Point graduate wishes to emphasize their superiority to non-West Point graduates, they do so by audibly knocking their graduation ring against a table. Whether the practice was common or not, the term ring-knocker has come to imply smug reliance on ostensibly superior status, derived from being a military college graduate.

The new Base Commander is a Ring-Knocker.

RINGS (RAF; RCN; RCAF; CF; still current) — "Ring" is the nickname for the rank braid worn about the lower sleeve by naval and air force officers, and by CF officers. Consequently, one speaks of "two-ringers" (naval Lieutenants, air force Flight Lieutenants, and CF captains), "two and a half ringers", "three-ringers", etc. Often one hears the words "hoop" or "stripe" instead of ring. (See also **Count the Hooks!, Scraper, Two-Striper**) [Ref: Partridge (8th)]

ROB, TO (CF, current) — In aircraft maintenance, "to rob" is to obtain a needed component immediately by removing it from a serviceable aircraft, rather than to wait for the component to be obtained through the military supply system. The practice of "robbing" components is always a last resort, because not only does it render a serviceable unit unserviceable, it imposes extra work on technicians who must now repair two units rather than just one.

ROCK APE (RAF, since WWII) — "Rock Ape" is the nickname for a member of the Royal Air Force Regiment, a corps of the RAF that defends air bases on the ground and provides anti-aircraft defence. In addition to aircrew losses, during the Second World War the RAF lost 14,000 ground staff as airfields were overrun by enemy troops in France, Greece, Crete, Burma, and North Africa. Winston Churchill authorized the creation of the RAF Regiment. He reasoned that the air force was full of fit, intelligent and courageous men and ought to be responsible for its own ground defence, rather than relying on soldiers detached from the Army to protect airmen. The army agreed and the result was the RAF Regiment. (The USAF followed suit with its own extensive ground security forces.) Though trained as infantry and air defence artillerymen, it would be unwise to call someone in the RAF Regiment a "soldier". As far as a Rock Ape is concerned, a "soldier" is in the army, and a Rock Ape is definitely a member of the air force. They use RAF rank titles and are formed into "flights" and "squadrons" (as opposed to the "platoons" and "companies" of the Army). The RAF Regiment customarily works and fights in close proximity to flying operations, though when necessary units have been detached to fight in army formations.

RCAF units flew from RAF airfields during the Second World War, so Canadian airmen also relied on the protection of the Rock Apes. The nickname Rock Apes refers to the Barbary Apes that inhabit the Rock of Gibraltar, a strategic spot where the RAF Regiment served with distinction. The Canadian Forces has no equivalent and the army would likely be called on to withdraw troops from the line to protect air force units. This was certainly the case during the Gulf War. (See also **Servicing Commandos**) [Ref: Partridge (FS)]

This airfield is too bloody close to the front lines. I'd feel more secure if there were some more Rock Apes here.

ROCKET (RAF, RCAF; WWII and postwar) — A "rocket" is a written reprimand, or a blast of verbal abuse from a superior. This term led to the wry synonym, pyrotechnic, as in: *we can expect some pyrotechnics from the boss!* [Refs: Harvey; Partridge (8th)]

> *Here, read this! Wing Headquarters just sent down this rocket!*

ROCKS, THE (aviation, general; Canada) — The "rocks" are mountains, especially the Rockies.

> *Where did the aircraft go down?*
> *In the Rocks, northwest of Jasper...*

RODEO; RHUBARB (RAF, RCAF; WWII) — "Rodeo" and "Rhubarb" were Second World War RAF code for two similar types of offensive fighter sweeps. These sweeps, instigated by Air Chief Marshal Sholto Douglas, successor to Hugh Dowding as chief of Fighter Command, were an attempt to increase pressure on the Germans in the west and to relieve the pressure on the Russian front. Rodeo operations were fighter sweeps aimed at drawing Luftwaffe fighters up to fight. These sweeps ranged in size from squadron strength, to one or two wings of 36 aircraft apiece. Rhubarbs were smaller scale fighter and fighter-bomber attacks on targets of opportunity. As historian John Terraine put it: *...the Germans appeared to be largely unimpressed.* The lack of success of these operations led to the creation of the "Circus" sweeps. (See **Circus, Ranger**) [Ref: Milberry and Halliday; Rawlings; Terraine]

ROGER; ROGER WILCO (Universal since 1940's) — Today, the word "roger" is a radio codeword that officially means *I have received all of your last transmission*. However, the term is also a synonym for "yes", "OK", or "acknowledged!", and has been:

> - shortened (ie. "rodge!"),
> - put to rhyme ("Roger Dodger!", in turn shortened to "Roger D") and,
> - intentionally mispronounced: ("roe-gurr", or, as in French: "ro-jhay"!)

Furthermore all these are merely a corruption of the original meaning of Roger, which has its roots in 1940's radio procedure. Before the Second World War the word Roger was the American radio codeword for the letter "R"; indeed Roger may have been used in Morse telegraphy on American railways since the 1800's. (Up to 1943 the equivalent British Commonwealth codeword was Robert). The arrival of American forces in Britain during the Second World War had made it necessary to standardize the Allied phonetic alphabet, so in 1943 the Allies accepted Roger as phonetic code for the letter "R".

How then did the meaning of the word Roger change from being a phonetic codeword to a synonym for "yes"? Roger's meaning changed when telegraph operators began to acknowledge receipt of a telegraph message by telegraphing back the word "RECEIVED" to the originator of the message. Rather than sending all the codewords for the word "RECEIVED", operators shortened the message to Roger, code for "R", the first letter in "received". Soon Roger itself came to mean "I have received all of your last transmission." .

In radio voice communications, Roger was often followed by another codeword: "Wilco", a contraction of "will comply". Therefore, someone who transmitted: "Roger,

Wilco!" was acknowledging that he had received his orders and would comply with them. Soon, Wilco was dropped and most merely transmitted the word Roger. As a result, Roger became synonymous with "OK", to such an extent that it became useless as phonetic alphabet code and was replaced by the word "Romeo". [Ref: Partridge (FS); Gentle and Reithmaier]

> *Are you going to the dance tonight?*
> *That's a big ROGER!*

ROMAN CANDLE (aviation, parachuting; general) — When a parachute "Roman Candles", it fails to deploy and streams, unopened, above the doomed parachutist. The term derives from a type of firework, the Roman Candle, which emits a bright white flame when ignited. The useless fluttering white parachute is said to resemble the white flame of the firework. [Ref: Partridge (FS)]

> *I saw him bail out all right, but then his parachute Roman Candle'd...*

ROOSTERTAIL — A "roostertail" is a plume of water or earth thrown up by the exhaust and turbulence of an aircraft flying extremely low. Its appearance is similar to the tail of a rooster.

ROPEY (RAF, RCAF; WWII) — Anything that is peculiar, inferior or awkward could have been described as "ropey" by a serviceman of the Second World War, or of the postwar years. [Refs: Harvey; Partridge (FS)]

> *You sure listen to some ropey music, Tom!*

ROTORHEAD (CF; current) — A "Rotorhead" is a person who flies, or works on, helicopters. In fact a rotorhead is the hub of a helicopter's rotor, and contains a very complex array of mechanical links and controls, critical in controlling a helicopter. From there, it was not hard to make the leap to calling a person associated with helicopters a Rotorhead, in the tradition of other, similar nicknames, such as "hothead".

> *What kind of aircraft do you fly?*
> *I'm a rotorhead!*

ROUNDEL (RAF, RCAF, CF; current) — Any circular heraldic badge may be termed a "Roundel". In military aviation, a roundel is the circular badge applied to the fuselages and wings of military aircraft to identify nationality and service. Such badges trace their origins to the opening shots of the First World War. Military aircraft carried no national markings for the opening weeks of the First World War. However, the risk that ground troops would mistake them as hostile quickly made it necessary to adopt national identifiers. The result was a new branch of heraldry.

The Imperial German Air Service was the first to identify their aircraft, using their famous black Teutonic cross. The first roundel in aviation was that of France. The French Air Service's roundel had a blue disc at the centre, around which was a white ring, itself all surrounded by a red ring. The French roundel - still used today - was apparently based on the cockade worn in the cap by revolutionaries during the French Revolution.

Until the end of the Second World War, Canadian military aircraft bore British markings and Canada's postwar roundel evolved from that used by the British. However, the now-famous RAF roundel was *not* Britain's first choice for military aircraft markings. Instead, the first British military aircraft bore a painted Union Jack on the wings and fuselage. Unfortunately, in poor light conditions, the Union Jack (with its dark-red crosses outlined in white) was often mistaken for the "Iron Cross" of the German Air Services, by Allied troops! After RFC aircraft were repeatedly shot at by friendly troops, the British air services adopted it's now-famous roundel merely by reversing the order of the three colours in the French roundel! Indeed, by agreement all the First World War allies (France, Britain, Italy, Belgium, the United States and Russia) adopted a circular roundel format for their respective national aircraft markings. All these nations use their original roundels today, except the United States and Russia which both changed to their respective "star" insignias after the 1918 armistice.

Both the Canadian Air Force in 1920 and in 1924 the Royal Canadian Air Force, used Royal Air Force markings, a policy that continued until 1946. This policy resulted

Roundel

because Canadians felt that if they were ever again to fight, they would be fighting alongside the British. Indeed this proved to be the case in 1939 when the Second World War broke out and the RCAF overseas was integrated into the RAF. However, in 1942, burgeoning Canadian nationalism led the RCAF to create a new, Canadian roundel by replacing the central red disc in the RAF roundel with a red maple leaf. This new RCAF roundel first appeared during the Second World War on the RCAF Ensign, the air force flag; Canadian aircraft did not bear the new roundel until after the end of the Second World War.

After the Second World War, a purely Canadian system of aircraft markings was developed for all three services that included the distinctively Canadian roundel. Despite this new system however, the roundel on RCAF and Army aircraft differed from that on Navy aircraft. The Navy roundel bore a leaf from a "Silver Maple" at its centre, while the air force and army roundel bore a "Sugar Maple". All Canadian roundels were changed to a common pattern in 1965, when Canada adopted its now famous red-and-white national flag. The maple leaf on the roundel was matched to the maple leaf on the new flag. This roundel is now borne on Canadian military aircraft, though for tactical purposes, the badge is often applied in grey or black tones, rather than in the traditional red, white, and blue.

In the Commonwealth air forces, the roundel is often seen as the "trademark" of the service. Roundels are sometimes applied both officially and unofficially to vehicles, air force marine craft, and buildings. Indeed, the tanks and armoured personnel carriers of the RAF Regiment often bear a small RAF roundel. Likewise, the name of the RCAF Magazine before unification was "Roundel"; this proud name was revived in 1993 as the magazine of Canadian Forces Air Command. (See also **Fin Flash**) [Refs: Phelan; Petipas]

ROVER (RAF, RCAF; WWII) — "Rover" was the Second World War RAF codename for offensive fighter operations where small sections of fighters would conduct armed reconnaissance against targets of opportunity, just behind enemy lines. These operations were pioneered in North Africa and continued in Europe after the Normandy invasion of 1944. (See also **Ranger, Rodeo; Rhubarb**) [Ref: Rawlings]

R.P. (RCAF; WWII) — "R.P." was the shorthand abbreviation for "Restricted Privileges", a minor non-judicial punishment for airmen who strayed from the RCAF's standards of discipline. (See also **C.B.**) [Ref: Milberry and Halliday]

I was late for parade, so the Flight Sergeant gave me 7 days R.P....

R.T.U. (ie., "are-tee-yew") (Commonwealth military; general) — "RTU" is the abbreviation for "Return To Unit", a designation given to military personnel who are required to return to their parent organization, after having been attached to another. As such, it has become synonymous with failing a training course, and has become a verb, as in: "to RTU" someone, or "to be RTU'd".

How did you do on your final exam?
Not good enough, I guess. I'm being RTU'd.

RUBBER ON THE RAMP, PUTTING (CF; current) — "Rubber on the Ramp" is a recent phrase that can be taken to mean "aircraft ready to fly". The word "rubber" refers to the rubber tires that support an aircraft as it sits on the ground, and "ramp" is the paved area around a hangar, where aircraft operate on the ground. The phrase has been adopted by members of the aircraft maintenance and engineering community who believe that putting rubber on the ramp is a fair summation of their job. In the final analysis, the efforts of aircraft engineers and technicians aim at providing airworthy and battleworthy aircraft, ready for operations. In otherwords, they put a serviceable aircraft, resting on its rubber tires, on the ramp.

In the final analysis, the job of a technician is to put rubber on the ramp.

RUMBLE — The word "rumble' has two distinct meanings:

(1)   **Rumble**   See **T-Bird**

(2)   (RCAF, CF; since WWII) In an air force flying squadron or flying training unit, **to rumble** someone is to accuse them of a minor professional or social faux pas. Later the custom developed of convening a Kangaroo Court of one's peers, called a Rumble Court, for a good- natured accounting. This court was usually convened annually, or after completion of a course or deployment and was mostly an excuse for a party. A person who is rumbled is expected to respond to the accusation with a lively and entertaining explanation for their actions. Tradition called for nearly everyone to be rumbled for some offence, real or imagined, and generally speaking, no one who was rumbled was ever acquitted. Modest fines are usually assessed, the proceeds of which go into a party fund. It is a custom that seems to have been relatively common in the RCAF of the 1940's and 1950's, but which is now rare. [Ref: Harvey]

> *Can you believe it? I was rumbled just because I'd drifted off*
> *course!*
> *They decided to rumble you for drifting off course and not noticing*
> *for fifteen minutes!*

RUMPETY (RFC; WWI) — For unknown reasons, the Maurice Farman Shorthorn aircraft earned the nickname "Rumpety" among airmen of the RFC. The Shorthorn was used for a time as a trainer in the early years of the First World War. [Ref: Voss]

RUN CHICKEN, RUN (CF; current) — The words "Run Chicken, Run" are possibly the worst insult that a member of the air force - or anyone else for that matter - could ever give to a member of the Royal Canadian Regiment. It is at once, an allusion to the initials of the regimental title, RCR, and to chickens, a fowl that has gained an unfortunate association with the regiment.

It is important to realize that the word "chicken" does not, as one might imagine, insinuate cowardice. The battle honours of the RCR are testament to their valour in combat. Rather this insult, which began in the army, alludes to a story, perhaps apocryphal, which alleges that a member of the regiment was found, *in flagrante delicto*, with a chicken. On hearing this story, members of the RCR sometimes counter with information that the individual was a cook, not an infantryman and therefore not a member of Canada's senior infantry regiment; alternately, they may just counterattack with whatever blunt object is within reach. Whether the story is true or not, members of the RCR have had to put up with it for decades.

RV (military; universal) — "RV" is the abbreviation, and shorthand, for "rendezvous". Though more common in the army, the term has become part of Canadian air force slang. [Ref: Partridge (FS)]

> *"What's the location of the RV?"*

SIERRA

SALLY ANN (general usage) — "Sally Ann" is the universal nickname for the Salvation Army. Nearly every overseas Canadian base or station had a canteen run by the Sally Ann where servicemembers could buy snacks or goods at inexpensive prices. When troubled by life's problems, members of the Sally Ann were there to lend an ear. The Salvation Army has justly earned a good reputation for taking care of servicemembers away from home, both in a spiritual sense and in a material sense. [Ref: Partridge (8th)]

I'm going to the Sally Ann for coffee and a doughnut. Coming?

SAM, or S.A.M. (ie., "samm") (general; current) — "SAM" is the acronym for "Surface-to-Air Missile", as in: *watch out for the SAM sites south of the target!*

SAME WAY, SAME DAY (CF; current) — "Same way, same day" describes a formation of aircraft which is decidedly loose. Ideally, aircraft in formation fly at precisely the same speed, and there is no variance in the positions of the aircraft relative to one another. This is not the case when a formation is described as "same way, same day". That is, there is so much variance in the speeds of the various aircraft, and in spacing between aircraft in the formation that the best that can be said is that the aircraft are flying in the same direction, on the same day! The phrase "same way, same day" is occasionally used in non-flying discussions to mean "casual" or "imprecise".

How did the formation look to you?
Uh, let's just say it was 'same way, same day'

SARTECH —   See **Rescue Spec; R.S.**

SAUSAGE — The nickname "sausage" was applied to both the barrage balloon, and the windsock. Both are oblong and tubular in shape, therefore the allusion to a sausage.

(1)   A Barrage Balloon was a large limp balloon inflated with helium and tethered aloft over targets vulnerable to air attack. They were especially prevalent in Britain and northwest Europe during the Second World War. The idea was to make it difficult for attacking aircraft to get low enough or close enough to the target without colliding with the balloon or its guide wires.

(2)   A Windsock is a tube of fabric, held open at one end by a metal ring, and mounted on a pole. Windsocks are placed around an airport to give a visual indication of the wind direction and provide a rough and ready guide to wind velocity.

SCARLET SLUGS (WWII) — During the Second World War, "scarlet slugs" were tracer rounds fired from an anti- aircraft gun. When a "tracer" round is fired from a gun, a small amount of chemical burns and the resulting flame illustrates the path of the round.

This helps the gunner to adjust his aim. The tracer round burns bright red, hence the nickname scarlet slugs. Tracer rounds are mingled with ordinary rounds. (See also **Flaming Onions, Tracer**) [Ref: Partridge (FS)]

SCHOOL SOLUTION, THE (CF current; Originally British) — The "School Solution" is the "official" or "approved" solution to a hypothetical military problem - whether that solution makes sense or not. This term derives from Staff College training, where senior officers study staff skills, tactics, and strategy. These subjects are often best understood through exercises and simulations, where candidates play roles that require them to prove their abilities to the Directing Staff (also known as "DS"). The solution developed by the students is compared with the "school solution", ie., the ideal solution as defined by the Directing Staff. Thus, the school solution (sometimes the "DS Solution") is a plan that is perfect, ties up all loose ends, solves everything, and is generally unimpaired by any intrusions of reality.

Other terms are used, such as "the greens" or "the pinks", for the colour of paper on which the approved solution is printed. (Staff College seems to use pink and the air force staff course uses green.) (See also **D.S.; Coprolite**)

Okay, if you're so smart, what's the School Solution?

SCOPE DOPE (RCAF, CF; since 1950's) — "Scope Dope" is rhymed slang for any airman or airwoman whose job requires the continuous monitoring of a radar screen (ie., a "scope"). Thus, Air Traffic Controllers, Fighter Controllers, Air Weapons Controllers, Airborne Electronics Operators and Air Navigators, have all been referred to by their fellows as Scope Dopes.

Scope Dope

The nickname "Scope Dope" was
applied to anyone whose job
demanded they monitor a radar scope.

SCORE, THE (since WWII) — "The score" is "the situation", or "the truth", as in: *What's the score?* [Ref: Partridge (8th)]

SCOTCH MIST (RAF, RCAF; WWII) — "Scotch Mist" was drizzle, as in: *Look at that Scotch Mist; we're not flying today!* [Refs: Harvey; Partridge (8th)]

SCRAMBLE, TO (general military aviation; since WWII) — An aircraft is "scrambled" when it and its crew are launched on operations with little or no notice. When operations demand it, military aircraft and their crews can be kept at immediate readiness to launch. Thus, fighter aircraft can be scrambled to engage intruding enemy aircraft, maritime patrol aircraft can be scrambled to take up a submarine contact, and rescue aircraft can be scrambled to search for survivors in distress. The process of launching such aircraft is termed a scramble. [Ref: Partridge (FS)]

SCRAMBLED EGGS (military general) — "Scrambled Eggs" is the nickname for the gold wire braid adorning the visor of a senior officer's dress cap. This braid is called "scrambled eggs" for the fact that it appears as a jumble of yellow-gold on a black visor. (See also **Brass Hat**) [Ref: Partridge (FS)]

SCRAPER (RAF, RCAF; now dated) — A "scraper" was the narrow, "half-width" loop of rank braid located between the two loops of wider rank braid on a Squadron Leader's (or CF major's) rank badges. RAF and RCAF officers normally wore their rank braid around the lower sleeves of their tunics. Officers of the rank of Squadron Leader wore two normal-width rings of braid, between which was a ring of half-width braid. The narrow middle stripe is often termed a scraper; thus, being promoted to Squadron Leader was to "get your scraper". The usage was also applied - though less commonly - to the CF major's rank braid.

The word scraper refers to the piston rings in a reciprocating engine. Circular metal rings are wrapped about each piston to ensure a seal between it and the cylinder wall. This serves to maintain compression and to prevent engine oil from entering the zone of combustion. The most prominent of these are the "compression ring" and the "oil retaining ring", between which is found another, smaller ring called the "scraper ring". Just as the scraper ring sits between the two other piston rings in an engine, on a Squadron Leaders' rank braid the scraper sits between the two other cloth rings of rank braid. Therefore, the middle braid was the scraper, and to be promoted to Squadron Leader (or major) was to "receive your scraper". [Ref: Partridge (8th)]

> *Did you hear that Flight Lieutenant Kelly got his 'scraper'?*
> *He's a Squadron Leader now, eh?!*

SCREAMERS, THE (RAF, RCAF; WWII) — The "screamers" was an intense dislike of operational flying, often to the extent that it becomes a disabling phobia. The term seems to be derived from another phrase, "the screaming shits", likewise a fear of combat flying. Fear is a reality of flying, especially combat flying, and is hardly uncommon. Post-1945 American research showed that most fighter pilots were unable to function effectively at some time or other, due to fear. Indeed, over 40% of all "kills" were credited to less than 1 percent of fighter pilots. Usually, the screamers developed after prolonged exposure to the stress of combat. During the Second World War, Allied air forces limited the length of combat flying tours, due to the onset of stress-related illness. Such illness interfered with the ability to fly and fight effectively. (See also **L.M.F.**) [Ref: Partridge (8th)]

I think Ken is developing a case of the screamers...

SCREWED, BLUED AND TATTOOED (Military, general; becoming rare) — The term "screwed, blued and tattooed" means "an abundance of misfortune". It is an elaboration of the verb "to be screwed", meaning "to meet one's demise". Originally, however the phrase described the activities experienced by many servicemen during a spot of leave. The word "screwed" and "tattooed" are perhaps self-explanatory, but the word "blued" requires some elaboration. The word "blued" refers to the blue ointment applied to the genitalia by a doctor treating a person afflicted by pubic lice, or "crabs". (For another example of this usage, see **Crabfat**) [Refs: Harvey; Partridge (8th)]

Now that you guys have been screwed, blued and tattooed, maybe you'll be ready for some operational flying again!

SCROUNGE, TO (universal military; since 1914) — "To scrounge" is to acquire needed military property without any authority apart from one's innate guile, stealth and imagination. "Scrounging" differs from outright theft only in that in a "theft" one acquires the article for one's own benefit, whereas an article that is "scrounged" is generally obtained for service use - although not for its intended use. Wing Commander 'Dizzy' Allen, Commanding Officer of a wartime Spitfire squadron wrote: *To be an effective squadron commander, it is essential that one is a better 'scrounger' than one's NCO's.* The practice is not lawful, but it is nonetheless common. One can also "scrounge" intangibles, such as "scrounging a ride" or "scrounging help". [Refs: Allen; Partridge (FS)]

Now, just where did that Spitfire come from, Doug?!
I scrounged it, sir!

SCRUB, TO (aviation general; origins unclear though dating back to circa 1910) — "To scrub" something is to cancel it. [Ref: Partridge (8th)]

SCRUFF, THE (North Africa; WWII) — The "Scruff" was the "Desert Air Force", that is, the RAF squadrons and support elements that fought alongside the 8th Army in the North African desert during the Second World War. The nickname is both a gentle insult and a play on the word "raff" (ie., "RAF") for "Royal Air Force". Only one RCAF unit, 417 Squadron (flying Spitfires) flew as part of the Scruff, though many Canadians served in RAF desert units. (See **Lost Legion**) Of the Scruff, Journalist Peter Sanders (Sunday Times Magazine; Sept 10th, 1967) wrote: *Men of the Desert Army used to think that men of the Desert Air Force were even dirtier and scruffier than themselves. A debatable point.* [Ref: Partridge (8th)]

SEA PIG   See **Sea Thing**

SEA THING (RCN, CF; current) — "Sea Thing" is rhymed slang for "Sea King", the large anti-submarine helicopter built by Sikorsky, and flown from Canadian warships since 1963. The Sea King is twin-engined and amphibious (though in practice it is less amphibious than advertised), and can operate at sea on instruments. It was intended for use on aircraft carriers or Canada's frigate-sized Helicopter Destroyers. It carries dipping sonar, which enables it to track a submerged contact, and allows the ship's combat control team to triangulate sonar readings. The Sea King became the primary weapons system on Canadian warships. It can investigate potential submarine contacts much more quickly than a warship, and can sink the submarine with its homing torpedoes or depth bombs.

It is said that the nickname Sea Thing was coined by Tracker pilots of 880 Squadron on the carrier HMCS Bonaventure, though the origins of the subsequent variation, "Sea Pig" are uncertain. (See also **DDH**) [Ref: Snowie]

They say that landing a Sea Thing on a destroyer in heavy seas is the most stressful flying there is.

SECOND DICKEY (RAF, RCAF; WWII and prior) — The Second Dickey is the co-pilot. The origins of this term are uncertain, though it is known that "dickey" was an old term for the back seat in a carriage. Perhaps there is a link here in that the second pilot, particularly in older RAF aircraft such as the Lancaster and the Wellington, sits in an temporary folding seat. Such early RAF aircraft, although equipped with dual controls, did not have a permanent co-pilot's seat. These aircraft were flown most of the time by the pilot; the co-pilot (often doubling as navigator) only had a collapsible, folding seat. However, it has also been suggested that the term Second Dickey was simply appropriated from merchant mariners, for whom it has always meant the Second Mate. [Ref: Partridge (8th)]

I flew as Second Dickey for about 300 hours before they let me upgrade to Captain.

SERGEANT-MAJOR   See **Major(1)**

SERVICE AIR (CF, current) — Travel on military aircraft is universally known as "Service Air". This is an administrative term and is used in contrast to "Commercial Air" (for military duty travel, though on an airline). There is often a stark contrast between "Commercial Air" with its beverages, fixed schedules, and movies, and Service Air, with its variable schedules, spartan amenities, and subordination to operational needs. This contrast has resulted in a rhyming variation on Service Air: "Nervous Air". Because certain of these flights follow fixed schedules, they are sometimes known as "Scheduled Flights", or "Sked Flights". (See also **White Knuckle Airlines**)

SERVICE BRAT   See **PMQ Brat**

SERVICING COMMANDO (RAF; WWII) — Servicing Commandos were aircraft technicians who advanced with the Army during the Second World War, in the latter part of the Second World War in Europe. These teams of aircraft maintainers serviced Allied tactical aircraft immediately behind the front-lines, and often under fire. During the advance up the "boot" of Italy, and in France after the Normandy invasion, a drill had been worked out, where field squadrons of the RAF Regiment (See **Rock Ape**) advanced with the army to seize and secure enemy airfields for immediate use by Allied aircraft. Within hours, army field engineers would repair the runways while a party of air force "servicing commandos" prepared to receive the Spitfires that would arrive in several hours. On their arrival, the servicing commandos would keep the Spits flying until that squadron's own maintenance personnel caught up. Sometimes, the whole process took a matter of hours, and Spitfires began flying combat sorties from the newly captured airfield within a day, often before the RAF Regiment had even finished "mopping up" enemy resistance. [Refs: Clostermann; Terraine]

You Servicing Commando guys must enjoy being shot at!

S.F.A. (ie., "ess-eff-eh") — The initials "S.F.A." are a euphemism meaning "nothing", and has been coined to avoid having to use the full phrase "Sweet Fuck All". (See also **Sweet Fanny Adams**) [Ref: Partridge (8th)]

What did Gord say at the briefing?
S.F.A.!

S.F.O. (RCAF; 1930's) — "S.F.O." is the acronym for "Senior Flying Officer". In the RAF and the RCAF, Flying Officer was a rank equal to an army or CF Lieutenant or a naval Sub-Lieutenant. On RCAF Stations of the 1930's, the "SFO" was appointed from among all the other Flying Officers as sort of a "first among equals". The SFO was responsible for keeping all the other junior officers in the Mess in line. The SFO had a reserved parking spot at the Mess and wore a special badge, but it was a thankless job and often the SFO was as much a ringleader in hi-jinks as a moderating influence. [Refs: Hampson; Sutherland]

Where's the S.F.O.? The Station Commander wants to see him!

SHAGBAT (RAF, RCAF; WWII) — "Shagbat" was the nickname for a classic aircraft of the 1930's and 1940's, the Supermarine "Walrus". The Walrus was a single-engine seaplane flown by the Royal Navy and RAF from 1935 to 1945, and is renowned for its record in Air-Sea Rescue. The Walrus was designed by R.J. Mitchell, better known for having created the legendary Spitfire. However, the Walrus could not have looked less like the streamlined "Spit". Ungainly in appearance, this seaplane with two wings had one pusher propeller mounted above the flying boat hull, and had a small angular hull and cabin. However, it was still a classic, because like the Spitfire, the Walrus excelled at the tasks that it was designed for, and was an "honest airplane" without bad handling characteristics. Shagbats were amphibious, and could be launched from catapults mounted on Royal Navy battleships.

According to lexicographer Eric Partridge, the nickname Shagbat relates back to the Sopwith "Bat Boat", which, during the First World War, performed much the same role as the Walrus did in the Second World War. However, the Bat Boat nickname was altered slightly for the Walrus. Partridge suggests that because Walrus whiskers are "shaggy", some unknown aviator began to call it the "Shaggy Bat", and then the "Shagbat". That name stuck. (See also **Bat Boat**) [Ref: Partridge (8th)]

That poor air gunner was in the water for about twelve hours before the
Shagbat crew spotted him and picked him up.

SHAKE AND BAKE (fighter aviation; general) — "Shake and Bake" is a napalm canister, or as it is often called, a "fire bomb". Napalm is jellied gasoline contained in a bomb-shaped canister made of thin aluminum, dropped from an aircraft onto ground targets. The term appears to be American in origin, and may have been coined because the optimum trajectory for a napalm canister is to tumble (ie., "shake") on leaving the aircraft, so that it bursts open at the seams on impact, spreading the burning jellied gasoline on the ground. Napalm is one of the uglier air-to-ground weapons, though its usefulness against "hardened targets" such as concrete bunkers, is limited.

SHAKER   See **Stick-Shaker**

SHAKY DO (RAF, RCAF; WWII) — A "shaky do" is a combat operation fraught with uncertainty, risk, or danger. (A "do" is an affair, or an occasion) [Ref: Partridge (8th)]

> *Tonight's trip looks like a shaky do.*

SHAKY JAKE (RCAF; WWII) — The "Shaky Jake" was the Jacobs radial engine, used to power Canadian-built variants of the "Anson", a twin-engined monoplane used primarily for training and liaison. The Jacobs engine earned a reputation for rough running, therefore the nickname Shaky Jake. (See **Annie**)

SHAPE (RCAF, CF; 1960's and 70's) — "Shape" was the nickname given to the concrete replica of a 2000 lb. tactical nuclear weapon that was used - instead of the real thing - for training, when Canadian Starfighter squadrons in Europe were employed in the nuclear strike role. The nickname is apt, as this concrete replica was simply a thing that was "shaped" like the real bomb. The shape was used to train the load crews in arming the aircraft, and in training the pilots in the special high-speed low-altitude delivery needed to drop a "nuke" and survive. [Ref: Sutherland]

SHARP END, THE (CF; current since at least WWII) — The "sharp end" is the operational end of the military, as opposed to its headquarters and support elements. The term alludes to the point of a sword or knife blade - which is directed at the enemy - as opposed to its hilt, which is not. [Ref: Partridge (8th)]

> *Some of those people at Group Headquarters just don't understand life at the sharp end.*

SHIP — A "ship" is an aircraft. The word seems to have had its origins in the United States services during the First World War but is not as common among Canadian and Commonwealth personnel, where its usage was often more jocular. (See **Plane**) [Refs: Collins; Partridge (8th)]

SHIT-HAWK (Army, Navy; to 1960's) — "Shit-hawk" is a derogatory nickname for airmen, common among Canadian soldiers and sailors until perhaps the late 1960's. Its origins are uncertain, though the word shit-hawk is also a nickname for the seagull. The term is also used in Britain to describe members of the RAF, though with a slight variation: "Shite-Hawk." (Indeed for a time members of the RAF Regiment were also known as "Shite-Hawk Soldiers".)

SHIT HOT (CF, current; probably American origin) — Something that is "shit hot", is superb, or excellent. (See also **Sierra Hotel**)

SHIT (PISS) AND CORRUPTION (RAF, RCAF; WWII) — Poor weather, marked by rain, cloud and wind, was often termed "shit, piss and corruption". [Ref: Partridge (8th)]

> *What's the forecast for tomorrow?*
> *...shit, piss and corruption!*

"SHIT ROLLS DOWNHILL" (military general) — "Shit rolls downhill" is an aphorism that illustrates a universal military truism: that displeasure at a high rank level is soon felt at lower levels. Thus, if the Squadron Commander is unhappy with things, the Flight Commander will be made unhappy before too long. The Flight Commander in turn makes the Warrant Officer unhappy, who wastes no time in conveying his own unhappy message to the troops. This in turn has led to the euphemism for receiving a reprimand from higher rank: *to be shit upon from great height.*

SHIT, SHAVE, SHINE, AND SHOWER (CF, current; origins uncertain) — Today "shit, shave, shine and shower", or the "Four S's", refers to an airman's typical morning routine in barracks. However, during the Second World War it was as likely to refer to the preparations necessary before going out for an evening's entertainment. [Ref: Collins; Partridge (8th)]

SHOOTING A LINE   See **Line Shooting**

SHOOT THE SHIT (Canadian, general) — To "shoot the shit" is to pass the time in amiable, if unproductive conversation.

SHORT ARM INSPECTION (military, general; WWI to 1950's) — "Short-arm inspection" was the rueful nickname for a service practice that was common during the Second World War and shortly after. A short-arm inspection was a compulsory, mass visual inspection of airmen's genitalia for symptoms of venereal disease. It was a rather dehumanizing process. Airmen lined up, opened their uniform trousers and, one by one, passed by a seated Medical Officer who performed a quick visual examination.

The following description from the memoirs of wartime airman Robert Collins, captures something of the moment:

> *But the most shocking and humiliating moment by far was short-arm inspection. "Short-arm" was the armed forces official euphemism for penis. You lined up with your fellows by the score, unbuttoned your fly (no zippers in those days) if you were so lucky as to be wearing pants at the time, and held your private parts at the ready.*
>
> *As you rounded in front of the medical officer and his grinning orderly you whipped out and presented your penis. "SQUEEZE!" urged the orderly, to us reluctant and bewildered ones. With a weary glance the MO checked for chancre, discharge, rash, or other evidence of foul disease.*
>
> *At the first short-arm, I couldn't believe it was happening. We were on the indoor parade square, surrounded by tiers of seats from its previous incarnation as an arena. As I shuffled in line, face flaming, I glanced up in the stands. A couple of WDs (RCAF Women's Division) high up in the cheap*

Short Arm Inspection

A Short Arm Inspection was no place
for surprises.

seats, were looking down with amused smiles. Given our mass embarrassment, they wouldn't have seen much even at arm's length, but it was the final indignity.

The short-arm inspection was an exercise in military efficiency, but was totally lacking in privacy. The practice faded out of the RCAF in the 1950's. [Refs: Collins; Sutherland; Partridge (8th)]

Ron, remember that short-arm inspection this morning? Well, there's bad news.

SHORT LEGS   See **Long Legs**

SHORTY   See **Gremlin**

SHOT DOWN IN FLAMES (RAF, RCAF; WWII) — One can be "shot down in flames" in either of two ways. Originally the phrase described an aircraft that fell prey to hostile fire. The term was adapted to other, analogous defeats, such as to be bested in an argument, or when a lady dashed the amorous hopes of an admirer. [Ref: Partridge (8th)]

What's the matter with Russ?
I think Alice shot him down in flames.

SHOULDER FLASH   See **Canada Flash**

SHOW (originally RAF, now general) — A "show" is an operation, a mission, a happening, an event, or a performance. Thus, an important mission is a "big show". Respectable performance is a "good show", and the opposite is a "poor show". (See also **Good Show, Party**) [Ref: Partridge (8th)]

You'd better get ready; there's a big show on tonight.

SHOWER (RAF, RCAF; WWII) — In Second World War British military slang, a "shower" is an absolute disaster or a fiasco. Likewise, shower can be used to describe a motley-looking collection of servicemen. The term is shorthand for "a shower of shit". [Refs: Harvey; Partridge 7th]

Put your caps on and do up your tunics, you horrible shower!!

SIDCOT (RNAS, RFC, RAF, RCAF; 1917 to 1945) — The first flying suit ever developed for British and Commonwealth aircrew was called the "Sidcot". Named for Sidney Cotton, the man who conceived it, the Sidcot flying coverall was intimately familiar to Commonwealth aircrew who wore it in all but hot or temperate climates, from 1917 to the end of the Second World War. The Sidcot replaced the leather flying clothing worn by RNAS and RFC aviators during the First World War. In an unheated, open-cockpit biplane, leather will not keep an aviator warm - even if worn over a woolen uniform. Hypothermia and frostbite become real hazards.

Sidney Cotton, an Australian flying in the RNAS, developed his idea for a new flying suit after a fortunate accident. While stationed on the Western Front in 1917, Cotton fell into the habit of helping the mechanics service his aircraft. One day while doing so, his squadron was alerted without notice to go aloft on patrol. Cotton had no time to change into his leather overcoat and leggings, so, he flew wearing his greasy mechanic's coveralls over his uniform. On return, Cotton noted that, though he remained relatively comfortable, his fellow squadron pilots - all wearing leather jackets and leggings - were cold and shivering.

Cotton realized that it was his cotton mechanic's coveralls that had kept him warm, so he wrote to Robinson and Cleaver, his tailors in London, and asked them to fabricate several sets of tailor-made coveralls made of burberry fabric, with a thin fur lining and silk inside. He christened this the "Sidcot Flying Overall", after the first syllables of his first and last name. When his fellow pilots saw the Sidcot, they enthusiastically ordered their own from the same tailors (who were soon inundated with orders from aviators on the Western Front. The tailors took the wise precaution of patenting the Sidcot suit).

Unsuccessful attempts were made to convince the RFC and the RNAS to issue Sidcots to all pilots and observers. Ultimately however, the Sidcot flying suit was adopted by the RAF, and by the RCAF, and was the most common flying suit in the Commonwealth air forces until the end of the Second World War. The basic pattern of the Sidcot changed little over the thirty years of its service. Interestingly, Baron Manfred von Richthofen, the "Red Baron", was wearing mechanics coveralls over his uniform - his own form of "Sidcot" flying suit - when he was shot down and killed!

Sidcot

Invented by accident, the Sidcot flying suit
remained in use until the end of the Second
World War.

Sidney Cotton continued in aviation, and in the Second World War, as a private consultant, was responsible for many improvements in RAF photo-reconnaissance. He died after the Second World War, flying arms into Hyderabad. [Refs: Greer and Harold; Jones]

Where's my Sidcot?

SIERRA HOTEL (NATO; general air force usage) — "Sierra Hotel" is a euphemism for "Shit Hot"; something that is "Shit Hot", is superb, or excellent. "Sierra" and "Hotel" are the NATO phonetic codewords for the letters "S" and "H" which, by no coincidence, are the first letters of each of the words "Shit" and "Hot". However, it would be indelicate to use this pithy expression in polite company or over the radio, so to convey the meaning while remaining prudent, aviators often use the phonetic code Sierra Hotel instead. (See **Shit Hot**)

How did you do in the gunnery competition?
Sierra Hotel!

SIGNATURE (military aviation general; since 1930's) — "Signature" is a term for a characteristic signal or trace that suggests the presence of a target to a detection system. For example, an aircraft easily detected on radar is said to leave a clear "signature". In contrast a Stealth Fighter - which is not easily detected on radar - will leave virtually no "signature" at all. Likewise, an aircraft that emits a lot of heat from its engine exhausts leaves a clear "infrared signature", whereas a cold aircraft on the ground leaves no such signature. The term appears to date from the 1930's, when the RAF was experimenting with sound-based aircraft detection systems, and the term "sound signature" was coined. [Ref: Quill]

An aircraft as big as a Hercules has a very clear radar signature.

SILENT HOURS — On a CF Base, "silent hours" are the hours outside the normal administrative working hours. Of course, these hours will vary from base to base, but typically silent hours will be from 1630 hours to 0800 daily and all weekend. The litmus test for whether silent hours have commenced is whether you can receive a meaningful answer to your pay inquiry.

SIM, THE — The "sim" is merely shorthand for "simulator". (See also **Box**)

SISKIN NOSE (RAF, RCAF; 1930's) — A "Siskin Nose" was a pilot's nose that was broken in a singularly unique way: by its impact against the instrument panel of the Siskin aircraft.

The Siskin was a biplane fighter of the 1920's and 30's which equipped several RAF squadrons, and which also became the RCAF's first fighter aircraft. In the RAF it gained the reputation for being tricky to land; it was prone to pitching forward on its propeller if mishandled even slightly. Enough pilots cracked their noses on Siskin instrument panels to establish, at least in air force folklore, a new category of injury: the Siskin Nose. [Ref: Greer; Harold]

Is that a Siskin Nose, or were you actually born looking that way?

SISTER ANNA (RAF; WWII) — "Sister Anna" was the affectionate nickname for RAF nursing sisters, a term commemorated in the following bit of doggerel, common in wartime Britain.

> *Sister Anna will carry the banner,*
> *I carried it last week!*
> *-but she's in the family way!*
> *...she's in everybody's way!*

SIT COURSE (RCAF, CF; since 1950's) — The term "SIT Course" has nothing to do with reclining in a chair. Rather, members of the RCAF once received instruction in how to teach at an establishment called the "School of Instructional Technique", commonly known as "SIT". Consequently, the basic classroom instructor's course became known as the SIT Course. The nickname persists, though SIT has long since changed its name to the CF Training Development Centre.

How long does the SIT Course last?

SITREP — Sitrep is an acronym for "Situation Report", as in: *Colonel, when can I get a sitrep?* The term dates back to at least the Second World War and remains current NATO parlance in the 1990's. [Ref: Partridge (FS)]

SITUATIONAL AWARENESS (aviation; current) — Situational awareness is a faculty that is critical to a military aviator. This is the ability to appreciate, simultaneously, the orientation of one's aircraft, its mechanical state, the disposition of the enemy, and the ability of friendly aircraft to help, and to use all this information to fly safely and accomplish the mission.

SIX — In Canadian military aviation, the word "six" has two common associations:

(1)   First, it could mean the "Six o'clock" position according to the "Clock Code", used to describe the location of another aircraft relative to one's own. The term "six" means the location immediately behind oneself, though it can have a more symbolic meaning, referring to an area of personal vulnerability. In combat, having an enemy aircraft at your "six" is to be at your enemy's mercy. Peacetime allied fighter pilots engage in mock combat, the goal of which is to place oneself at your opponent's "six". It is the height of professional embarrassment for a self-respecting fighter pilot to allow this, so the battle begins! (see also **Clock Code, Check Six!(1)**)

(2)   The word **Six**, during the 1950's and early 1960's, also referred to the Canadair "Sabre" Mark 6. The Canadair Mark 6 Sabre was the penultimate version of the F86 Sabre, first designed by North American Aviation. With its Canadian Orenda engine, the Six was more powerful than its American counterpart, which led to a new catchphrase in the NATO air forces of the 1950's *Check Six for the Mark Six!*

SIX PACK   See **Package, Pack**

SKED FLIGHT   See **Service Air**

SKEW L   See **Squadron Bleeder**

SKI JUMP   See **No-Ball**

SKIPPER (RAF, RCAF; since WWI) — During the Second World War, the captain of an aircraft was commonly called "skipper", or "skip", words that are clearly borrowed from seagoing slang. [Ref: Partridge (8th)]

> *When do we take off, Skipper?*

SKYHOOK — The word "skyhook" has had two connotations in military aviation:

> (1) **Skyhook** could refer to the De Havilland DH6 aircraft. During the First World War, De Havilland produced the DH6 to meet an RFC requirement for a basic trainer. It was not built in great numbers, probably because it possessed "reprehensible" features that resulted in it earning several unflattering nicknames, such as "Skyhook" and the "Clutching Hand." It was evaluated for use in Canada as a trainer, as an adjunct to the Curtiss JN-4 "Canuck", though only one was built in Canada. [Ref: Molson and Taylor; Partridge (8th)]

> (2) A **Skyhook** is also a useful, though mythical piece of equipment that enables an airplane to hover over one spot. This word would seem to pre-date helicopters and VTOL aircraft, such as the Harrier. (For other mythical but useful substances see **Flight Line, Hangar Line; Flight Lustre; Long Weight; Propwash; Radar Contacts; Relative Bearing Grease; Tartan Paint; Tacan Gate**)[Ref: Partridge (8th)]

SLED See **Lead Sled**

SLIP, TO (Aviation, general) — In aerodynamics, a "slip" or a "sideslip" is a manoeuvre used to lose altitude by forcing the aircraft to yaw sideways slightly, while still tracking forward.

S.L.J. (CF; current) — "S.L.J." means "shitty little job", a term needing little elaboration.

> *MacIntosh!! Report to the Base Warrant Officer!! He's got an S.L.J. picked out just for you!*

SLJO (CF; current) — SLJO means "S.L.J. Officer", an officer whose duties seem to consist largely of "SLJ's". SLJO is not an official title; it is usually applied informally to officers whose bad luck or limited abilities have resulted in a series of rotten or petty jobs. (See also **S.L.J.; Snackbar 2**)

SMART BOMB (Military aviation; general, since 1960's) — "Smart Bomb" is vernacular for a "precision-guided munition" (also known by the abbreviation: "PGM"). A Smart Bomb is a bomb or missile equipped with a guidance system that directs it to its target. The rationale behind the Smart Bomb is to dramatically increase the probability of a hit, thereby making it possible for aircraft to carry fewer and smaller bombs.

Before the advent of "smart" bombs, the probability of hitting a ground target from the air was very low. It was routine for bombers to drop many, many more bombs than necessary to destroy a target, simply because it was accepted that the majority would miss. This was due to the notoriously poor accuracy of gravity bombs (often known as "iron bombs"), even when released by a trained bomb-aimer with a good bombsight. The inherently poor accuracy of iron bombs meant that many bombs had to be dropped to ensure a few would hit the target. The United States pioneered the use of smart bombs during the Viet Nam war, but it was during the Gulf War of 1991 that their capability really made an impact on the public.

Let me guess! You give the smart bombs to the dumb pilots?

SMOKEY (RCAF) — "Smokey" was an RCAF nickname for a fire-fighter. Additionally though, Smokey was the radio call-sign for the Canadian Forces transport aircraft permanently stationed at Colorado Springs, Colorado, the headquarters for NORAD. [Ref: Sutherland]

SMOKING HOLE IN THE GROUND (RUNWAY, TARMAC, ETC), A — "Smoking hole in the runway" is a common euphemism for, or an allusion to, an aircraft crash.

SNACKBAR 2 (RCAF Europe; 1960's) — "Snackbar 2" was a term for meaningless secondary duties assigned to RCAF officers serving on Starfighter squadrons in Europe in the 1960's. (See also **SLJO**) [Ref: Sutherland]

Bob, why are you spending so much time in the Publications Room?
Haven't you heard? I'm the new Snackbar 2...

SNAFU (WWII; originally American) — "SNAFU" is an acronym, coined in the American military during the Second World War, for the phrase: "Situation Normal, All Fucked Up". The implication is one of a confused, disorganized situation. It has since become a verb (as in: *Apparently Frank snafu'd things pretty badly!*), and a noun (as in: *We've run into a Snafu...*). (See also **Balls-Up, FUBAR, TCCFU**)[Refs: Harvey; Partridge (8th)]

SNAG (RCAF, CF; since at least WWII) — A "snag" is an aircraft unserviceability, that is, a mechanical or electrical fault that prevents an aircraft or its equipment from being safely used. More particularly, it is a persistent unserviceability that defies a tech's best efforts at diagnosis or repair. The term has achieved official recognition and Maintenance Squadrons usually have a "Snag Recovery Section". (See also **Blue Sheet, Major(2), Pink Sheets**) [Ref: Harvey]

When will that snag on 804 be fixed?

SNAKEPIT (CF, current) — In a Canadian Forces mess, there are usually two bars, a formal lounge area and a smaller, less formal bar generally called the "snakepit". Mess regulations demand that persons in the lounge area wear more formal uniform. The snakepit is the casual bar, or the "back bar", where dress regulations are more relaxed and the amenities more basic. Having a snakepit allows members the luxury of enjoying a drink without having to "dress up" for the occasion.

SNARGASHER (RCAF; WWII) — In the Second World War RCAF, a training aircraft was a "Snargasher". It has been suggested that this unusual word is merely a corruption of "tarmac-smasher". [Ref: Partridge (8th)]

SNOOZE AND BOOZE (CF current) — "Snooze and Booze" is rhymed slang that describes any training course or seminar that is decidedly less than taxing. (See also **Gentleman's Course**)

> *Is the final exam difficult?*
> *No, it's a Snooze and Booze Course...*

SNOWBALL (RCAF, CF; since 1960's) — "Snowball" is the widely used codename for a rapid recall to duty during a military alert to prepare for hostilities. The codename Snowball arose because a recall of personnel starts with one phone call to the Commanding Officer, who then calls the senior officers; these senior officers in turn call all of their senior subordinates, who in turn call their deputies, etc. Thus, this one phone call to the Commanding Officer snowballs into hundreds of calls. Of course, cynics suggested that the real reason for this codename was that, if we ever went to war we wouldn't stand a "snowball's chance in hell!!"

However, the term also described a party that moved from one house to another, picking up new partygoers with each stop. Thus the number of people frolicking would snowball. This usage was common among airmen and airwomen stationed in Europe on NATO duties and was no doubt adapted from the official meaning, above. (See also **Egg-in-the-hole**)

> *Why do they always start the Snowball alert at some ungodly hour in the morning?*

SNOWTURKEYS (CF; current) — "Snowturkeys" is an unkind epithet occasionally applied by other members of the Forces to members of the Canadian Forces Flying Demonstration Team, the "Snowbirds". The term is not a professional criticism. Rather, it usually results from envy over the hordes of females who seek the acquaintance of individual Snowbirds. (It is said that members of the RAF flying team, the "Red Arrows", are occasionally called the "Dead Sparrows", for similar reasons.) These terms don't seem to bother either the Snowbirds or the Red Arrows very much, however...

SOCKED IN (aviation, general) — An airport that is "socked in" is closed due to low cloud or fog that prevents safe landings.

> *We can't land at Shearwater because it's socked in, so we'll have to divert to Greenwood.*

SOCK-TUCKER (RCAF, 1950's-60's) — "Sock-Tucker" was a mildly disparaging nickname for a supply clerk, probably because to those on the outside, the job seems not to be very demanding. (See also **Box-kicker, Blanket-Stacker, Bin Rat**)

S.O.L. (pronounced "ess-oh-ell")(current) — "S.O.L." is the abbreviation for "Shit Out of Luck", as in: *When the fuel ran out, they were S.O.L.!*

SOLO (aviation general) — "Solo" is a term implying that an aircraft is being flown by one pilot, rather than two. The word is most often used in flying training, to indicate that a student pilot is flying without the supervision of an instructor. The "first solo", the first time a student pilot takes off without an instructor, is a pivotal point in a student's development and is generally celebrated with much merriment - after a successful landing, that is.

We've got three cadets doing their first solos tomorrow.

SOP (RFC; WWI) — Any aircraft built by Sopwith Aeroplanes, founded by Tommy Sopwith, could be termed a "Sop", though the term was most commonly used to refer to the Sopwith "Pup".

SORTIE (military aviation, general) — A "sortie" is one mission, flown by one aircraft. Thus if two different aircraft each fly three missions, a total of six sorties has been flown. Occasionally the word is used as a verb, to describe the process of flying the mission, as in: *The Aurora sortied out of Greenwood at 0200 hours.* This term appears to have been derived from the French verb "sortir". (See also **Chalk**)

Last week the Wing flew 147 sorties.

SOULS ON BOARD — "Souls on board" is a common euphemism used during radio communications to indicate the total number of persons - both crew and passengers - presently on board an aircraft.

CanForce 312, how many souls on board?
Tower, this is CanForce 312. We have twelve souls on board.

SOUND OF FREEDOM (probably American originally; 1950's) — The "sound of freedom" was an ironic nickname for uncomfortably loud noise produced by a military jet aircraft. The origins of this term are unclear but air force folklore suggests that the "sound of freedom" was a catchphrase used as part of a public relations campaign. It seems to have been invented by Public Affairs officers in answer to complaints about jet noise around military air bases. The implication is that we all have to make sacrifices in the name of freedom. Air force personnel however, generally used the words in a more jocular or ironic sense as a synonym for sheer noise.

Plug your ears Major! We're about to hear the sound of freedom.

SOUP — "Soup" or "Pea Soup" is fog or other bad weather, as in: *unless this soup lifts, we'll never take off.*

S.P. (RCAF; 1940's, 1950's) — "S.P." is an abbreviation for "Service Police", the name by which the RCAF's "Air Force Police" went during the Second World War. (See also **A.P.'s, A.F.P.'s, Gestapo, Meatheads**)[Ref: Collins]

Quiet! The S.P.'s are downstairs!

SPACE CADET (CF, current) — "Space Cadet" is the less-than-kind alternative to "Flight Cadet" or "Officer Cadet". Officer Cadets are not yet officers. They are trainees who, if successful, may some day become officers. The term may have its origins in science fiction television programs of the 1950's, many of which featured a young, earnest and naive member of the "space rangers", or some such organization, a space cadet. In civilian slang, the term Space Cadet has come to mean a mindless person, a person who is "spaced out". Thus the behaviour of an Officer Cadet is often expected to be earnest, naive, and sometimes little more than mindless. In the RCAF of the early 1950's, the term was often shortened to "spacey". [Ref: Sutherland]

SPAD (Allied Air Services; WWI) — The Spad was a superlative French fighter aircraft of the First World War. The name "Spad" was actually the abbreviation of the first letters of the name of the company that built it: *Societe pour Aviation et ses Derives.*

A new Spad squadron is flying into this sector tomorrow.

SPAM MEDAL — The "Spam Medal" was the Canadian Volunteer Service Medal, given to all Canadian servicemen during the Second World War who volunteered for service (as opposed to being conscripted; see **Zombies**). This meant that most Canadian servicemembers during the Second World War were entitled to this medal, thus making it "nearly as common as spam". (Spam was a type of processed meat food, developed in the Second World War. For another commentary on Spam, see **Dead Air-Gunner**). [Ref: Collins]

SPANDULE   See **Gremlin**

SPANJER   See **Gremlin**

SPARKS   See **Spider**

SPARROW FART (military; WWII) — "Sparrow fart" is a pithy term that means "very, very early in the morning". Presumably the term arose because things are so still at this time of day that you can hear a sparrow pass gas! (See also **Crow Fart, O-Christ-Thirty;O-Dark-Thirty, Wakey-Wakey**) [Ref: Partridge (FS)]

Am I ever tired! I had to get up at sparrow fart this morning!

SPATS (aviation general, since 1930's) — "Spats" are wheel fairings, that is, streamlined covers fitted over the wheels of a fixed undercarriage aircraft to reduce drag. The term is borrowed from men's clothing, where spats are short gaiters worn over the ankle and the uppers of one's shoes or boots. [Ref: Partridge (8th)]

Spider

SPIDER (RAF, RCAF; WWII, still current RAF) — "Spider" was the nickname for the badge worn by an RAF or RCAF Wireless Operator. The badge depicted three crossed lighting bolts, with a hand grasping them all at the centre, a composition that resembled a spider when seen from afar. It was worn on the upper right sleeve of one's tunic. Sometimes the badge-wearer was also known as "Sparks". (See also **WOP/AG**) [Ref: Partridge (8th)]

When you're finished the course, you're entitled to wear the spider badge.

SPIFFY (RCAF; post-WWII) — "Spiffy" was RCAF airman's slang for a small, springy, wire brace which was inserted, behind and out of sight, into the points of the collar on one's dress shirt. In the days before permanent press fabrics, there was always the risk that one's shirt collar would go awry unless it was heavily starched. Even on a heavily starched collar however, there was still a remote chance that the points of the collar might be deflected upwards, revealing the black RCAF tie beneath and around one's neck. This was especially true when the airman was engaged in vigorous activity, like rifle drill in a ceremonial guard. An airman certainly did not want to risk having one's collar lift while "presenting arms" for the Queen! The wrath of Her Majesty would pale in comparison to the wrath of the SWO, so it was worthwhile to obtain a spiffy.

Your shirt collar looks terrible! Did you lose your spiffy?

SPIKE-BOZZLE (RNAS; WWI) — The fantastic verb "spike-bozzle" was invented by members of the Royal Naval Air Service, for whom it was synonymous with "to destroy, completely" as in *the hangar was totally spike-bozzled by fire.* [Ref: Partridge (8th)]

SPINNING INCINERATOR (RFC; WWI) — "Spinning Incinerator" was the unkind epithet given to the De Havilland 2, or DH2. The DH2 was an early fighter characterized by its pusher propeller, and by the fact that the gunner sat ahead of the pilot, facing forward with a clear arc of fire. Presumably the term "spinning incinerator" arose because of the fact that the DH2, like most First World War aircraft, was prone to catching fire, and could not easily be recovered from a spin.

SPIT (Allied Air Forces; WWII) — "Spit" is the shortened nickname for one of the classic aircraft of all time, the Supermarine Spitfire. The Spitfire's success resulted from matching a superb airframe, designed by Reginald Mitchell, and the powerful Merlin engine built by Rolls-Royce. The name "Spitfire" was proposed by Sir Robert McLean, the Chairman of the Board of Vickers, and had originally been given to an earlier, unsuccessful fighter prototype. Ironically, Mitchell, its designer, did not favour the name Spitfire. He is said to have remarked that "Spitfire" was ...*just the sort of bloody silly name they would give it!*

The Spitfire became the standard fighter of the RAF, the RCAF, and other Commonwealth air forces. It was navalised, to become the "Seafire", and served in both Royal Navy and Royal Canadian Navy units. Millions of words have been written about the Spit, but perhaps this testimony by RAF ace "Sailor" Malan encapsulates the feelings about the Spit:

> *"The Spitfire had style and was obviously a killer. Moreover, she was a perfect lady. She had no vices. She was beautifully positive. You could dive till your eyes were popping out of your head, but the wings would still be there - till your inside melted, and she would still answer to a touch."*

Spit

Ironically, R.J. Mitchell, the Spitfire's designer, did not care for the name Spit.

Thirteen RCAF squadrons flew the Spitfire during the Second World War, and Seafires flew from Canadian aircraft carriers until the early 1950's. [Refs: Quill; Turner/Bowyer]

After I finished training, I went straight onto Spits.

SPITSHINE (military; general) — A "spitshine" is an extremely glossy shine on one's service boots or shoes, which is obligatory in basic training and desirable thereafter. The military demands cleanliness and a smart turnout, including shiny shoes. This encourages servicemembers to look and feel good, and is a way of teaching recruits to pay attention to detail. Indeed, shining one's service dress shoes becomes something of a fetish for some. The term "spitshine" is something of a misnomer, as saliva is not the optimum solvent for a good polish. The experts use water, hence the less common term: "watershine". Occasionally one hears the term "glass shine" as well, as befits a shine that reflects light like polished glass.

Bloggins! Do you call that a spitshine?! Its not a spitshine until I can shave using your boots as a mirror!!

SPLASH (military aviation, general; since WWII) — "Splash" is a military radio codeword that means "to shoot down another aircraft" or "to have shot down an aircraft."

Splash one bandit!

SPLIT-ARSE (British Army; WWI) — "Split-arse", a term common in British cavalry regiments in the early 1900's, described a rider who was addicted to stunting and taking dares. Ex-cavalry officers introduced this term into the RFC during the First World War, where it survived, denoting a pilot with a similar taste for stunting and taking dares. This usage of the term died out some time ago, though it survived in "Split-Arse Turn".

259

Split-Arse turn may also have been the genesis of the term "Split-S". (See also **Split Arse Turn; Split-S**) [Refs: Partridge (8th); Voss]

Donald is quite a split-arse pilot!

SPLIT-ARSE CAP; SPLIT-ASS CAP (British Commonwealth; since WWI) — A "Split-Arse Cap" is a wedge cap, a term coined because a wedge cap is "split" longitudinally, rather like certain parts of the anatomy. (See **Wedge Cap**) [Refs: Partridge (8th); Voss]

SPLIT ARSE TURN; SPLIT ASS TURN (RFC, RNAS; WWI) — During the First World War, a "split-arse turn" was a flat turn, where the aircraft was turned but without any appreciable angle of bank. This remarkable feat was only possible in certain aircraft, such as the Sopwith Camel, which were equipped with very powerful rotary engines. In a rotary engine, the propeller and the pistons are permanently fixed together, and rotate together about a fixed crankshaft fixed to the fuselage. The result was that tremendous torque was established which, at the right power settings, could exactly offset the aircraft's roll in a turn. The term "split-arse" alludes to "stunting", so presumably this manoeuvre was not common. (See **Split-Arse**) [Ref: Partridge (8th); Voss]

SPLIT-S — A "Split-S" is an aerobatic manoeuvre where an aircraft flying level changes direction and altitude by rolling inverted and pulling hard down into a vertical dive, recovering by pulling out to the horizontal position but at a lower altitude. At the end of the Split-S, the aircraft is flying in the opposite direction from its original heading. In British service the Split-S is more often called a "Half-Roll". One wonders if the practice of calling this manoeuvre a "Split-S was somehow borrowed from that similar First World War term: "Split-Arse". (See **Split-Arse**) [Ref: Spick]

SPOOK (military, general, probably American in origin; from 1950's) — A "Spook" is a person who works in military intelligence. Therefore, an operation that relates to intelligence activity is described as "spooky". For a time, the training academy for the Canadian Security Intelligence Service (CSIS) was located at CFB Borden; to Borden personnel the academy was universally called "the Spook School". (See also **Spy**) [Ref: Partridge (8th)]

SPORTS AFTERNOON (CF; current) — In the name of physical fitness and general military efficiency, peacetime air force units are encouraged, from time to time, to devote part of a day to organized sports. However, occasionally, this is interpreted very loosely, and sports activities are less organized than might otherwise be. Indeed, "afternoon off" might be the more accurate description. (See also **Officer Development**)

How come everyone is leaving? It's only noon!
It's sports afternoon!

SPROG (CF, current; dates back to circa 1910) — "Sprog" is air force slang for a recruit or a novice. The term was originally used in reference to a newly graduated pilot, but its use has spread such that one can also speak of "sprog navigators" or "sprog technicians", as well. The origins of the word are unclear, though it has been explained as a mere variation of "sprout". It has also been described as an acronym for "Student Pilot Right Off Graduation". Others suggest that it originated in the Royal Navy early in the twentieth century, and is a contraction formed from the words "sprocket" and "cog". [Refs: Harvey; Partridge (8th)]

A dozen sprog pilots are due to arrive next week.

SPY (RAF, RCAF; WWII) — During the Second World War, the Intelligence Officer of an air force squadron, station or wing, was often termed the "Spy". (See also **Gen Merchant; Spook**)

Ask the Spy if those target photographs are ready yet.

SQUADRON BLEEDER, SQUALID BLEEDER (RAF, RCAF; to 1968) — "Squalid Bleeder" and "Squadron Bleeder" are less-than-complimentary substitutes for "Squadron Leader", the air force rank immediately senior to Flight Lieutenant. The term "Skew L" was also heard (though never written); this was an attempt to pronounce one of several abbreviations for Squadron Leader: "Sq/L". (See also **Scraper, Two-Striper;Two-and-a-Half Striper**) [Ref: Partridge (8th)]

Did you hear that Terry got promoted?
So he's a Squalid Bleeder now, eh?

SQUAREBASHING (military, general; originally British, but now rare) — "Squarebashing" is foot drill, or, "bashing about on a parade square." [Refs: Harvey; Partridge (8th)]

What do you do in Recruit School?
A hell of a lot of squarebashing!

SQUAWK (aviation; general) — To "squawk" is to transmit a radio signal that specifically identifies one's own aircraft from all others on a radar screen. This is normally done in response to an Air Traffic Controller's request

CanForce 311, Squawk 1203

SQUEAKER, TO SQUEAK (aviation; general) — A "squeaker" or, to "squeak it down", refers to a very, very smooth landing. In a squeaker the only indication that one has returned to Earth is the faint squeak of the tires on the runway. Occasionally one hears the term "greaser" (or the phrase "to grease it on the runway") instead. The suggestion is that the landing was so smooth it was as though the runway had been greased!

Nice landing, Lucy! You really squeaked it down!

STAB (aviation; general) — "Stab" is shorthand for "stabilizer". An aircraft has two sets of stabilizers, the vertical stabilizer, on which the rudder is mounted, and the horizontal stabilizer, where the elevators are located. Thus one speaks of a "horizontal stab" or a vertical stab".

STACKED; STACK, THE (aviation; general) — In instrument flying, aircraft waiting to land are required to orbit over the airport. Each aircraft orbits at a different altitude, to minimize the likelihood of a collision while aircraft fly on instruments. This array of aircraft orbiting over the airport at thousand-foot increments is "the stack". To require aircraft to orbit this way, is to stack the aircraft. [Ref: Partridge (8th)]

We've got aircraft stacked up to ten thousand feet today!

STALL (aviation; general) — A "stall" is an abrupt loss of lift that results when the "angle of attack" of an aircraft's wing becomes excessive. The angle of attack is the angle formed between the relative wind and the chord of the wing. A smooth airflow above and below the wing is needed to produce lift, and this airflow remains smooth when the angle of attack is relatively small. The pilot increases the angle of attack by pulling back on the control column, but if this angle becomes excessive, the smooth airflow is disrupted and lift ceases.

Many people are under the erroneous impression that a stall is caused by flying too slowly; in fact, a stall can occur at any airspeed, weight, attitude, or G-loading. All it takes is a dangerously high angle of attack.

Do not stall, lest the Earth arise to smite thee.

STAND TO; STAND DOWN; STAND UP (CF, current) — The terms "stand to", "stand up" and "stand down" do not refer to changes in seating, rather they refer to levels of military readiness.

"Stand to" is an old army term and is but a shortened version of the phrase: "stand to your arms". Thus, to stand to is to be ready for action, or to receive orders. One might say *tell the guard to stand to*, or one may schedule a "stand to inspection". Similarly, the term "stand down" is a shortened version of "stand down your arms", and implies a relaxation of readiness, though it can also imply disbandment, as in: *We're standing down 421 Squadron.*

The origin of the terms "stand to" and "stand down" (as relating to weapons) seems to have been lost in the air force, which may explain the emergence of another usage: "to stand up", as the opposite of "stand down". In the late 1980's one started to hear airmen and airwomen speaking of "standing up" a unit, instead of "activating" or "creating" it. [Ref: Partridge (FS)]

> *There's an operation on tonight. Signal 433 and 434 Squadrons to stand-to*
> *at 1330 Hours*
> *Tell "A" Flight they can stand down now...*
> *After the DEW Line radar stations stand down, we'll stand up the new*
> *North Warning System.*

STATIONMASTER (RAF; WWII) — In the RAF, the "Stationmaster" was the Station Commanding Officer, clearly, a humorous allusion to the fellow in charge of a railway station. In the RAF and the RCAF (to 1968), air force establishments were termed "stations", not "bases", and the Commanding Officer was the "Station Commanding Officer". In 1968, with the Unification of the Canadian Forces, major military establishments became "Canadian Forces Bases", while only minor establishments were known as "Canadian Forces Stations". (See also **Base Conductor, Bravo Charlie**) [Ref: Partridge (8th)]

Where's the C.O.? The Stationmaster is on the telephone.

STEADY UP (military; general) — "Steady Up" is a parade-square order that admonishes personnel in the ranks to cease moving, and to be alert for commands. From time to time, the phrase is heard off-parade, in other circumstances, to convey the same message: to "stop fooling around!"

STEAM OTTER (CF; current to mid 1980's) — The "Steam Otter" is the nickname that distinguishes the single piston-engined DHC-3 Otter, from its later derivative, the twin turbo-prop De Havilland "Twin Otter".

The Otter is an outstanding short-take-off-and-landing bush aircraft that combined simplicity with ruggedness. The Otter was itself derived from the outstanding DHC-2 "Beaver". The RCAF operated 69 Otters, several of which were stationed with the United Nations Emergency Force in the Middle East. (Indeed, the last aircraft to take off from the RCN aircraft carrier HMCS Magnificent was an RCAF Otter. It was being transported to the Middle East, when Magnificent was still in commission, but after it had ceased service as an operational carrier and was used as a transport. On arrival in the Middle East it was decided to simply fly the Otter aircraft off the deck.) The Otter remained in service through to the early 1980's, serving its last years as the standard mount of Air Reserve squadrons.

The name Steam Otter alludes to the fact that the single-engined "Otter" was a lot slower and relied on 1940's technology, in contrast to its younger cousin, the "Twin Otter". (See **Twotter**) [Ref: Molson and Taylor]

STEP ON THE BALL, TO (aviation, general) — "Step on the ball" is an admonition, from one pilot to another while flying, to take care to execute a coordinated turn. It refers to a small ball in the "Turn and Bank Indicator", an instrument that tells the pilot whether the aircraft is in a turn, and if so, whether the turn is a "coordinated turn". In a sense, the ball is like a bubble in a spirit level. If a pilot's turn is uncoordinated, the ball will be deflected to either side of the instrument. To correct this and execute a coordinated turn, pilots are taught to step on that rudder pedal that is on the same side that the ball has deflected in the instrument. Thus if the pilot executes a turn and notices the ball being deflected to the left, the pilot corrects this by applying left rudder. That is, one "steps on the ball", by applying left rudder, because the ball is deflected to the left. The same is true for an uncoordinated turn where the ball has been deflected to the right.

STICK (aviation; general) — The "stick" is an aircraft's control column. (See also **Joy Stick**)

STICK HANDLE, TO (CF; current) — To "stick-handle" something (especially a problem) is to cope with it, or to deal with it, on an ongoing basis until complete. The word stick-handle is, of course, borrowed from hockey, where it means to skilfully manoeuvre the puck past the opposition.

STICK-SHAKER (aviation; general) — The "Stick-Shaker" is an automatic safety device installed in many high speed aircraft which reduces the likelihood of stalling the aircraft. (See **Stall**) A stall is an abrupt loss of lift occurring when the angle of attack of the wings is too high. The Stick shaker senses when the angle of attack is excessive, and warns the pilot by vibrating the control column. Often, this system is simply called a "shaker".

If the pilot persists in keeping on the unsafe angle of attack, the Stick-Shaker engages a hydraulic actuator that literally forces the control column forward, reducing the angle of attack. The system which forces the control column forward is termed a "kicker" because it literally "kicks" the control forward automatically.

The pilot pulled back until the aircraft's nose was so high that he felt the stick-shaker.

STITCH AND BITCH (CF; current) — "Stitch and Bitch" is the less-than-kind nickname for the Officer's Wives Club at an air base. The social tone set at an Officer's Wives Club varies, though until quite recently, some bases seem to perpetuate the medieval notion that the prestige of a female spouse is directly proportional to the rank of the officer husband. Mind you, this attitude didn't always prevail. There is the story of the confrontation between a senior officer's wife, and a new service bride: *Hello, my husband is Air Commodore Smithers; and your husband is?   ...Twenty two!*

Ian, how come the upper Mess Bar is closed tomorrow?
The Stitch and Bitch is having a meeting...

STOOF (RCN, to 1970's; originally USN) — "Stoof" was the nickname for the Grumman Tracker aircraft, flown by the RCN and the Canadian Forces until 1990. The nickname is derived from the USN designation for the Tracker: "S2F" (ie., "S two F"). In the RCN, it became the "CS2F" but was occasionally termed the "stoof" as in the USN.

STOOGE AROUND, TO (WWII, still current) — "Stooging around" is loitering, hanging around idle or unproductive, or waiting to go into action. In Second World War fighter operations it meant patrolling in a non-combat situation. In Prisoner of War parlance, a "stooge" was a POW sentry warning other POW's of guards, thus, stooging around was feigned loitering while keeping watch. (See also **Kriegie; Loiter, to**) [Ref: Partridge (8th)]

We stooged around over our lines for a few minutes before crossing into enemy territory.

STOP THE PROP, TO (CF current) — When a photographer "stops the props", it means that the photographer has taken a picture of a running aircraft using such a fast shutter speed that the propellers appear motionless in the photo.

STOVEPIPING; TO STOVEPIPE (CF; current, originally American) — "Stovepiping", or "to stovepipe", refers to a military bureaucracy where decisions are made in an atmosphere of tunnel-vision, and where decision-making tends to occur outside the chain of command or without adequate participation from critical elements of the chain of command. A typical example of stovepiping might be a headquarters where the senior staff pilots habitually make operational plans in isolation from senior engineering or logistics staff, whose input is critical to the success of flying operations. The result is a poor flow of information and the rise of parochialism. [Ref: Flanagan]

We've got to stop the stovepiping in this headquarters, and increase the information flow!

STRAFE (universal; since WWI) — Today, "to strafe" is to attack a ground target from the air, with machine guns or cannon. However, in the First World War, it had a more general meaning as a fierce assault or a bombardment in land warfare. Later, the term strafe was also used to describe a punishment or a verbal reprimand, or alternately an efficiency campaign or a disciplinary crackdown. [Ref: Partridge (8th); Voss]

STRAINER   See **Stranny**

STRANNY (RCAF; WWII) — "Stranny" was the nickname for the "Stranraer", a large twin-engined biplane flying boat used by the RCAF for coastal patrol on both the east and the west coast during the Second World War. Occasionally it was known by its crews as the "Strainer". It was designed by Supermarine, the famous British flying boat manufacturers. Mindful of the threat of war, the RCAF ordered the Stranny in 1936. The Stranny was built in Canada for the RCAF under licence by Canadian Vickers. It was a good seaplane; it had a crew of five: a pilot, navigator, radio operator, and two gunners. Its bombload was approximately 1200 lbs. However, its relatively short range led to it being supplanted by other aircraft, such as the Canso, by 1944. (See **Cat(3)**) [Refs: Emmott; Molson & Taylor]

STREAM (Bomber Command; WWII) — The Stream was the path taken by the night bombers of RAF Bomber Command as they flew to bomb targets in Germany and occupied Europe. RAF bombers (including the Canadians in the RCAF's No. 6 Bomber Group) flew at night, individually, and could not fly in formation due to the lack of visibility at night.

These bombers, ranging in number from hundreds, to over a thousand, all took the same path to the target. Therefore it was important that navigation was accurate and that a sharp lookout was kept, not just for Luftwaffe night fighters, but to avoid colliding with other allied bombers! (See also **Gee(2); H2S; Master of Ceremonies; Oboe; Pathfinder(1)**)

We entered the stream about twenty minutes after takeoff.

STREAMER (RCAF, CF; current since WWII) — A "Streamer" is a peacetime air force officer who has been identified as having potential for high command, and who is selected for early promotion. A "Streamer" often attracts a certain amount of scepticism from the rank and file, who tend to place a great deal of faith in experience, over unrealized potential.

The new Station Commander looks awfully young!
Yeah, he's a Streamer, all right!

STRINGBAG (RN, RAF; WWII) — "Stringbag" was the affectionate nickname for the Fairey "Swordfish" torpedo-bomber, the mainstay of the Fleet Air Arm for the early years of the Second World War. The nickname "Stringbag" resulted from the fact that it could, and did, carry all kinds of equipment. Charles Lamb, a Royal Navy Swordfish pilot explained:

No housewife on a shopping spree could cram a wider variety of articles into her stringbag. The name stuck and from that moment the pilots always called it the Stringbag when talking about it amongst themselves.

Stringbag

The Fairey Swordfish became known as the Stringbag and, less commonly, as the "Pusser Spitfire".

The Swordfish was the answer to a British requirement for an aircraft that, except for fighter combat, could perform all the functions required of carrier-based aircraft. This was indeed a tall order but, amazingly, the three-place biplane Swordfish fitted the bill and was used as a bomber, torpedo-bomber, scout, and liaison aircraft. Equipped with floats, the Swordfish was the standard catapult aircraft on Royal Navy battleships and battlecruisers. On wheels, it flew from the Royal Navy's seven large aircraft carriers and was used in limited quantities by the RAF.

The Swordfish won glory in the Fleet Air Arm's attack on the Italian Fleet anchored at Taranto. There the Italians lost one destroyer, one cruiser, and three battleships in a surprise strike by four squadrons of Stringbags. (Interestingly, the attack on Taranto caught the attention of the Japanese Navy, which used it as the model for their subsequent attack on Pearl Harbour!)

The Stringbag was familiar to Canadians serving in the Royal Navy's Fleet Air Arm; as well, the Royal Navy operated the Stringbag in support of its No. 1 Naval Gunnery School at Yarmouth, Nova Scotia. Following the end of the Second World War, the Royal Canadian Navy obtained a number of Stringbags and sent them to Naval Reserve Divisions across the country, to assist them in training reserve naval aircraft technicians.(See also **Hally;Hallybag, Pusser Spitfire**) [Refs: Lamb (p. 56); Partridge (FS)]

SUCK - SQUEEZE - BANG - BLOW (CF, current) — "Suck, Squeeze, Bang, Blow" is a memory aid often used by airmen (though less frequently by airwomen) who have trouble remembering the "Otto Cycle" that is, the four strokes of an internal combustion engine:

Intake	Suck
Compression	Squeeze
Power	Bang
Exhaust	Blow

SUCTION RAID (RAF; WWII) — A "Suction Raid" is an aerial attack on enemy ground forces just ahead of one's own lines, designed to "create a vacuum and suck the brown jobs (ie., soldiers) forward." [Ref: Partridge (8th)]

SUPER RIGGER (RCAF; early 1950's) — In the RCAF and the CF, "rigger" is slang for an airframe technician, a technician trained in maintenance and repair of flight controls, fuel systems, undercarriages, cabin pressurization and aircraft structures. In the RCAF of the early 1950's, a "Super- Rigger" was an airframe technician who received advanced training at Trenton in the "Non-Destructive Testing" (NDT) specialty. Non-destructive testing techniques are an engineering tool used to detect cracks and imperfections in metal that are too small for the naked eye to see. These techniques include, among others, use of X- rays, fluorescent dyes, and electromagnets. Today NDT specialists are chosen from all technician specialties, but during the infancy of non-destructive testing only Airframe Technicians were selected. Consequently they became known as "Super-Riggers". (See also **Rigger**) [Ref: Sutherland]

SUSTOPS (RCN, to 1969) — Sustops is an acronym formed from the words "sustained operations", a condition requiring a Canadian aircraft carrier to conduct flying operations, day and night, indefinitely. Sustops was a period of very intense activity for the air complement of an aircraft carrier. Sustops on the light fleet carriers that served the Royal Canadian Navy, demanded that, at any given time the ship have four aircraft and two helicopters airborne, on patrol. [Ref: Snowie]

Get some sleep while you can; At 2400 we go on Sustops!

SWAG (current, aviation engineering general) — "SWAG" is an acronym for "Scientific Wild-Assed Guess", a phenomenon that is more common than might be imagined. It would seem to be a further development of the acronym "WAG", for "Wild Assed Guess".

Are you sure of the answer?
Nope...
Then give me a SWAG.

S.W.A.K., S.W.A.L.K. (military general) — The initials SWAK and SWALK mean "sealed with a kiss", and "sealed with a loving kiss", respectively. SWAK and SWALK are occasionally to be found printed on the flaps of servicemen's letters to, and from sweethearts. [Ref: Partridge (FS)]

SWAN (CF, general; originally British) — A "swan" is a trip which, though it professes to be in the line of duty, is as much a pleasure trip as a military obligation. (See also **Jammy**) [Ref: Partridge (8th)]

So, you're off on another swan, eh, Mike?

SWEEP (military aviation: since WWII) — A "sweep" is a tactical operation where a group of aircraft, seeking out the enemy, try to maximize the area covered by arraying themselves laterally, or in echelon. (See **Circus, Ranger, Rodeo; Rhubarb**)

SWEET FANNY ADAMS (WWII; originally British) — "Sweet Fanny Adams" is a euphemism for the letters S.F.A., meaning "Sweet Fuck All", in turn a euphemism that implies "absolutely nothing". [Ref: Partridge (FS)]

> *What have you been doing to pass the time?*
> *...Sweet Fanny Adams!*

SWINDLE SHEET (CF; current, since early 20th Century) — A "Swindle Sheet" is a Travel Claim, the document that authorizes a servicemember to travel and to reclaim money for expenses incurred by the servicemember during the trip. For petty, routine expenses, an automatic allowance is made and a receipt need not be produced. The servicemember will be compensated whether or not they have incurred the expense; hence, "swindle sheet". Abuse however, gets you into trouble, as some have discovered to their detriment. [Ref: Partridge (8th)]

SWITCHOLOGY (CF; current) — "Switchology" is the study and understanding of the layout of the instruments and switches in an aircraft cockpit. Before a pilot can learn to fly an aircraft competently, it is necessary to understand its "switchology". (See also **Fingertrouble**)

> *You'll be more comfortable flying this aircraft once you master the*
> *switchology.*

SWO (RAF, RCAF, CF; current since the 1950's) — The "SWO" is the "Station Warrant Officer", or "Squadron Warrant Officer", the senior noncommissioned officer in an air force unit. The SWO's duties are to monitor and promote unit discipline and to look out for the interests of the unit's noncommissioned airmen and airwomen. Up to the 1940's, the senior noncommissioned officer in an RCAF unit was known by the same title as his Army equivalent: "Sergeant-Major", though during the Second World War, this title was changed to Squadron Warrant Officer, or "SWO". The term is pronounced rather like Elmer Fudd saying "slow". (See also **'Major**)

> *After a brief period of chaos,*
> *the SWO restored order..*

SWO

SWORD (RCAF; 1950's to early 1960's) — "Sword" was the insider's name for the Canadair-built variant of the North American F-86 Sabre, perhaps the superlative air combat fighter of the 1950's. RCAF Sabre squadrons were a force to be reckoned with in the European skies, as an American Sabre pilot relates:

> *The Canadian fighter jocks in Europe loved to dogfight us in their own lighter, more manoeuvrable Mark V Sabres. They were merciless and there wasn't much we could do about it.*

In designing the Sabre for the USAF, the North American Aviation corporation relied heavily on captured German wartime research. The result was a highly successful fighter that maintained air superiority in the skies over Korea. The design was so successful that Sabres were supplied to many other nations, and as well, were built under licence in Australia and Canada. The Canadian variants were built by Canadair, which improved the original North American design. Six Sabre variants were built in Canada. (See also **Six(2)**) [Refs: Molson and Taylor; Yeager and Janos]

> *I flew the Sword right up to the end of its service.*

Sword

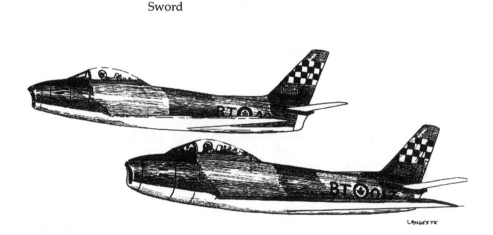

LANGESTE

To its pilots and groundcrews, the Canadair
Sabre was the Sword.

ANGO

T'S AND P'S (general aviation; current) — "T's and P's" is rhyming shorthand for "temperatures and pressures". Among the engine instruments in an aircraft cockpit are the gauges displaying engine temperatures, and fuel and oil pressure. Pilots and Flight engineers closely monitor these instruments because an engine problem usually first reveals itself through abnormal T's and P's.

Before we take off, we'll run the engine up and check the T's and P's.

TACAN GATE — A "Tacan Gate" is yet another useful but mythical device that, if described out of context, can be highly misleading to novices. It is therefore fruit for practical jokes.

Tacan is the acronym for "Tactical Air Navigation", a radio navigation system that provides both bearing and distance information to a pilot or navigator. Tacan relies on ground-based UHF transmitters and aircraft-mounted receivers and instruments. Aviation authorities have placed Tacan ground transmitters across the country, often enclosed within a fence to keep out intruders. The term "Tacan Gate" would suggest a gate in this surrounding fence, and it has been known for novice air traffic controllers to be sent to *look for the key to the Tacan gate*. Though this sounds plausible, in fact a Tacan gate is a 1950's term for what is now called a "precision approach point". This is the point in the air where an aircraft landing on instruments begins its approach to land. Thus the term Tacan gate (and the key to its lock) falls into the category of useful but mythical devices. (For other mythical but useful substances see: **Flight Line; Hangar Line; Flight Lustre; Long Weight; Propwash; Radar Contacts; Relative Bearing Grease; Skyhook; Tartan Paint**)

Go pick up George. He's waiting at the Tacan gate.

TACCO (CF, current; originally USN) — "TACCO" is the acronym for "Tactical Coordinator". On anti-submarine aircraft, the Tactical Coordinator is a senior air navigator who plans the stratagems and manoeuvres to detect, track, and - in wartime - sink, a submerged submarine. This is a highly involved operation. The Tacco analyses information gained from sonar, radar, magnetic anomaly detectors, and a variety of other sensor systems. With this information, the Tacco develops the tactics appropriate to engage the submarine. In days past it was the pilot who did this job; however, the task is simply too complex to be performed by someone already engaged in flying the aircraft. Thus, the pilot is the Aircraft Commander, whereas the Tacco is usually the mission commander.

In anti-submarine warfare, the pilot flies the aircraft, but the Tacco fights the battle.

TAC JENNY (CF, current) — "Tac Jenny" is technician's shorthand for "Tachometer

Generator". This is an electrical generator that runs off the aircraft engine drive shaft; as engine RPM increases, the generator creates a proportionately higher current. The cockpit tachometer is essentially an ammeter that measures the current, and displays the result in terms of engine "revolutions per minute" all thanks to the Tac Jenny.

I think the Tac Jenny is unserviceable.

TAIL-END CHARLIE (WWII; RCAF, RAF) — "Tail-End Charlie" is Second World War slang for the rear gunner in aircraft equipped with a tail turret. (Contrast with **Arse-End Charlie**) (See also **Dustbin; They Hosed Them Out**) [Refs: Harvey; Partridge (8th)]

What do you do on this airplane?
I'm the Tail-End Charlie - I fly around backwards for a living!

Tail-end Charlie

TAIL NUMBER (CF, current) — A specific aircraft is occasionally referred to as a "tail number". Each Canadian military aircraft has an identity number, specific to that aircraft. The number is usually painted on the aircraft's vertical stabilizer, so the identity number is usually called a "Tail Number". Therefore, one might refer to specific aircraft by its tail number. On occasion, the words "tail number" are used as a synonym for "aircraft".

Many systems of designating Tail Numbers have been used over the years, though the current CF system uses six digits. The first three digits represent the aircraft "type", and the second three digits represent the individual aircraft's specific identity number. Thus, an aircraft with the tail number 130338 is a CC130 Hercules, number 338.

The operations officer has assigned two tail numbers to that tasking.

TAJ MAHAL (RCAF, CF; to 1990's) — "Taj Mahal" is slang for the spherical domes covering the heavy radar antennae at any of the NORAD air defence radar stations. The term derives from their similarity to the famous Taj Mahal temple in India.

Only a few of us actually work at the Taj Mahal. The rest of the people at this radar station do the support jobs.

TAKE THE AIR, TO (RAF, RCAF; WWII) — "To take the air" is to go flying, a phrase adapted by aviators from its original meaning, to go for a walk in the fresh air. [Ref: Partridge (8th)]

TALLBOY (RAF; WWII) — The "Tallboy" was a massive conventional aerial bomb designed to destroy targets that were well-armoured or which were susceptible to damage from a shock wave transmitted through the earth. The Tallboy was heavy, weighing 12,000 pounds. It was so heavy that only a specially modified Lancaster bomber with uprated engines, a reduced crew, and with as much equipment removed as possible, could only carry one of the six-ton Tallboys! These specially modified Lancasters became known as "Clappers" by their crews, for the high speeds they could attain once they had released their heavy load. Such aircraft were flown only by two Bomber Command squadrons: Number 9 Squadron and 617 "Dambuster" Squadron, both of which had many Canadians on strength. Indeed for a time, 617 "Dambuster" squadron was commanded by Johnny Fauquier, an RCAF Wing Commander who voluntarily accepted a demotion to this rank to take on the job!

The Tallboy was designed by Barnes Wallace, the engineer who designed the Wellington Bomber (See **Wimpey**) and who was the scientific expert behind the "Dams Raid". The Tallboy was 21 feet long and was cast in special chrome molybdenum steel; it contained 5000 pounds of Torpex D1 explosive and a delayed fuse was usually employed, allowing the bomb to penetrate the earth before exploding. It was first tested in February, 1943.

The Tallboy was occasionally called the "earthquake bomb". It was dropped from extremely high altitudes and had a delayed reaction fuse. Its weight caused it to penetrate up to fifty feet into the earth before exploding, when the resulting explosion transmitted a massive shock wave through the earth. Thus, one Tallboy could dislodge all the railway tracks in a railway yard, or topple all the buildings in a city block. It was a series of hits from Tallboys that sank the German Battleship Tirpitz as it lay in a Norwegian fjord. The success of the Tallboy led to a further development, an even larger, 22,000-pound bomb called the "Grand Slam". (See also **Clapper; Grand Slam**) [Ref: Cooper; Partridge (FS)]

TALLY-HO (RAF, WWII; now universal) — "Tally Ho" is the radio codeword that means "I have sighted enemy aircraft and I am attacking." The term was coined during the Second World War by RAF fighter pilots and is clearly drawn from the English fox hunt. Use of the term spread, and in the absence of any competing code, it attained official recognition. It is now universal among the English-speaking air forces. Occasionally, the term is transformed into a noun, synonymous with the word "target", as in *I have a Tally Ho at two o'clock!* [Ref: Partridge (8th)]

Tally Ho! Tally Ho! Bandits, bearing 165; 9 miles and closing!

TANK-BUSTING (RAF, RCAF; WWII) — "Tank-busting" was Second World War air force slang for using tactical fighter aircraft to destroy German armour in France and Northwest Europe. At the beginning of the Second World War, tanks were regarded as perhaps the most important element in the land battle. The success of the blitzkrieg and the excellence of German armour made it critically important for the Allies to learn to defeat tanks. One very successful antitank weapon was the air-to-ground rocket that became standard equipment for the RAF and RCAF squadrons of the 2nd Tactical Air Force. These rockets became devastating antitank weapons, and perhaps more than any other factor, produced the phenomenon of tank-busting. After D-Day in June 1944, squadrons of Allied fighter bombers ranged ahead of the advancing armies, searching out enemy tanks. Tank-busting fighter-bombers, such as the Typhoon and Tempest (and their American counterparts, the P-47 Thunderbolt and the P-51 Mustang) steadily reduced the effectiveness of German armour on the western front. (See also **Cab Rank; Can-Opener; Winkling Out**) [Ref: Partridge (8th)]

Uncrate the rockets! B Flight is going tank-busting tomorrow morning!

TANK TRACKS (CF; current) — To an airman or an airwoman who wears a beret, "tank tracks" are that regular series of folds at the top of the beret that are so tough to get rid of. To wear a beret in proper "Monty-fashion", there should be no tank-tracks. The term is doubtless army slang and arose because these wrinkles are reminiscent of the regular grooves left in the earth by a tank's treads.

Though often worn by Canadian airmen and airwomen, some traditionalists still view the beret as an "army" cap. Since the Second World War, soldiers of the Canadian Army-including aviators - had worn the beret in a colour appropriate to their corps or regiment. (The first berets worn in the commonwealth military were the black berets of the armoured corps.) By the end of the Second World War the RAF had exchanged its wedge caps for air force-blue berets, and by the late 1940's, the Royal Canadian Navy had adopted a navy-coloured beret as the working headgear for naval airmen. However the RCAF never followed suit. Later, airmen and airwomen in the unified Canadian Forces were issued a CF-green beret as working headgear, and air force Search and Rescue Technicians established their proud tradition of wearing a scarlet beret. Though the traditional blue "wedge cap" returned in 1988 as the dress cap for Canadian Forces airmen and airwomen, slate-blue air force berets are also now issued to all air force personnel as a working cap. So, airmen and airwomen will continue to search for ways to rid themselves of tank tracks.

TANNOY (RAF, RCAF; WWII) — Tannoy was a corporation that manufactured public address systems and speakers in England during the 1930's and 40's. Consequently, one referred to public address systems generally as a "Tannoy".

The CO is making an announcement on the Tannoy at 1200 hours.

TARFU (pronounced "tar-foo") (military general; WWII) — TARFU was a very popular Second World War acronym for "things are really fucked up!" (See also **SNAFU, FUBAR, TCCFU**) [Ref: Partridge (8th)]

> *What's the situation up there?*
> *TARFU, as usual!*

TARGET FOR TONIGHT (RAF, RCAF; WWII) — In airman's slang of the Second World War, one's "Target for Tonight" was one's lady friend. Originally, *Target for Tonight* was the title of a wartime dramatic movie about the crew of a Wellington bomber on a night raid over Germany. The movie was well received and the title *Target for Tonight* became popularly associated with the night bomber campaign. However, airmen were quick to adapt the term to refer to another, more feminine sort of target for tonight. [Ref: Partridge (8th); Sargent]

> *Where are you going after dinner?*
> *I'll be seeking out my Target for Tonight. Her name is Debbie!*

TARGET-RICH ENVIRONMENT (CF current; originally American) — Being in a "target-rich environment" is a droll way of saying that you are seriously outnumbered by the enemy. Everywhere you turn, you face a target! The term appears to have been a mocking echo of the bureaucratic military doublespeak associated with the Viet Nam war.

> *How many hostile aircraft were there?*
> *Let's just say that it was a Target-Rich environment!*

TARMAC (aviation, general) — "Tarmac" is a common British term for asphalt pavement, but in Canada it has become synonymous with the ramp area of an air base hangar line. The word tarmac is an agglomeration of "tar macadam", the original British term for pavement (from the use of tar as an additive to "macadam", that is, gravel where the stones are of uniform size. It was named for its inventor, a man named Macadam). In Britain, tarmac can refer to any type of pavement but this usage seems to be more rare among Canadians (who speak of "pavement" or "asphalt"). In Canada, tarmac seems limited to aviation circles, where it refers to the ramp area. (See also **Ramp, Flight Line; Hangar Line**) [Ref: Partridge (8th)]

> *Park the aircraft on the tarmac, just opposite the maintenance hangar...*

TARTAN PAINT — "Tartan Paint" is another of those ostensibly useful, but mythical substances that are the occasional source of embarrassment to novice airmen. Since the Second World War, the Royal Canadian Air Force has had its own distinctive highland tartan - indeed it is the only air force to have its own tartan. As such, "RCAF tartan" has had a high profile on Canadian air bases, and is of course, worn by air force pipe bands. Where does it come from? Well, it is apparently possible to successfully convince - at least some - air force recruits that there is such a thing as tartan paint. Of course, when they really think about it, the absurdity of it all becomes apparent. (For other mythical but useful substances see **Flight Line, Hangar Line; Flight Lustre; Long Weight; Propwash; Radar Contacts; Relative Bearing Grease; Skyhook; Tacan Gate**)

> *Haskell, go to supply and get a can of air force tartan paint.*

TASKING; TASK, TO (CF, current) — A "tasking" is an official order to carry out a mission or an operation. Therefore a squadron may be "tasked", the unit may receive a "tasking message", and when performing the mission, the aircraft is "on task". Terminology has changed over the years. During the Second World War, Canadian and commonwealth aircrews would have gone on an "op", short for operation. Americans would have gone on a "mission". (See **Ops**)

Headquarters just called. We've got another airlift tasking.

TAXI-DRIVER (RFC, RNAS; WWI) — "Taxi driver" is First World War slang for a staff pilot (as opposed to a combat pilot). The job of a staff pilot was liaison, which generally involved flying on short hops, like a taxi carrying a fare. [Ref: Partridge (8th)]

T-BIRD; T-BAG (CF, current; originally USAF) — "T-Bird" is the universal moniker for the Lockheed T-33 "Shooting Star", a very successful jet trainer built in Canada under licence as the "Silver Star". The nickname T-Bird was probably coined from the "T" (a designation for training aircraft) in "T-33" and the fact that T-Bird was also the nickname for the Ford Thunderbird" automobile, introduced during the mid-1950's. By the 1980's the aircraft was occasionally described as the "T-Bag".

The T-Bird is a two-seat, single engine trainer developed in the 1950's from the Lockheed F-80, the first successful American jet-propelled fighter aircraft. The Canadian T-Bird differs from its American counterpart in that it was powered by the Rolls-Royce Nene 10 engine, which gave it slightly more power. In the early stages of engine start, the T-33 engine emitted a low pitched, low-frequency rumbling noise often termed the "T-Bird Rumble". This was caused by unstable combustion during the early stages of engine start.

The T-Bird is a classic aircraft by any standard. It was the RCAF's standard advanced pilot trainer from the 1953 to the 1970's, when it was removed from the pilot training curriculum. The RCAF solo aerobatic demonstration pilot, the "Red Knight", flew a bright red T-33. (See also **Pink Dink**) The T-33 equipped several RCAF reserve squadrons as a gunnery trainer, and was used by the Royal Canadian Navy for fleet air defence training. Nearly 40 years after its introduction, the T-33 remains in CF service in the 1990's for fleet air defence training and as an electronic countermeasures aircraft. It is not scheduled for retirement until the 21st Century. [Ref: Molson and Taylor]

Our T-Birds had a bit more power than the American T-Birds.

TCCFU (RAF Coastal Command; WWII) — Coastal Command of the RAF was responsible for conducting oceanic air patrols, and for joint operations with the navy during the Second World War. Coastal Command squadrons, including many RCAF squadrons, flew anti-submarine, anti-shipping and convoy escort patrols. TCCFU was the abbreviation for "Typical Coastal Command Foul Up", a designation wryly applied to the situation when operations didn't go on as planned by Coastal Command headquarters. (See also **FUBAR, SNAFU**) [Ref: Partridge (FS)]

T.D. (CF; current) — "T.D." is the CF abbreviation for "Temporary Duty", that is, where a servicemember is sent away from home base for a short period to perform duties. T.D. is synonymous with travel, therefore one "goes on T.D.", "plans a T.D. trip", and receives a financial "T.D. Allowance". (The U.S. equivalent is "T.D.Y.")

I'm going on T.D. for a few weeks!
Don't forget to bring your golf clubs!

TECH; MECH (CF, current since approximately 1950) — "Mech" and "Tech" are the short forms of "Mechanic" and "Technician", respectively. In the early days of the air force, people who repaired and maintained aircraft and equipment were almost always referred to as "mechanics" (See **Ack Emma**). However, since the Second World War the skills and knowledge demanded of aircraft maintainers has grown to the extent that the aircraft mechanic became known as a technician.

Flying operations simply could not occur without technicians and a very high proportion of any air force are technicians. In the latter days of the service of the CF-104 Starfighter, over forty man-hours of maintenance were needed for every single flying hour! Every "mech" or "tech" is a specialist in a difficult discipline; indeed, even in a lifetime, no single individual can master all the skills and knowledge of aircraft maintenance engineering. Though the aircrew may fly the aircraft, it does not follow that they are capable of keeping it flyable. So, aircrew must take it as an article of faith that each technician has done their job well. Air forces (and naval and army air services) quickly discovered that the people who became aircraft mechanics or technicians were a different breed. Though techs gave all credit to the aircrews who flew the aircraft, they also knew that their own skills were unique and irreplaceable.

In the 1930's Colonel T.E. Lawrence (better known as "Lawrence of Arabia") served incognito in the RAF for nine years as "Leading Aircraftman Shaw" and observed that air force junior ranks were very different from the men he knew and commanded while an army officer. Airmen regarded themselves as the equal of their officers in competence and: *...the officers were treated by the men off parade as rather humorous things to have to show respect to.* RAF historian John Terraine further described groundcrew:

> *"These were men with skills, and implicit in that was a generally higher level of education than one would normally expect to find in the mass of sailors and soldiers. Such men tend to have enquiring - or at any rate, questioning - minds; they do not take readily to discipline; they are impatient of "bull"; they grouse; they answer back."*

One cannot understand - let alone lead or command - the "techs" without understanding this. In latter days however, the words technician or tech have also been applied to a variety of military occupations that are decidedly non-technical. For example, today, people in the supply branch are "Supply Techs", NCO's who direct an air battle from their radar screens are "Air Defence Techs". Even infantrymen now jokingly refer to themselves as "Death Techs"! (See also **Armourer, Basher, Clock-Basher, Fitter, Gun Plumber, Rigger, WEM**) [Ref: James, p. 108; Terraine]

TEE-DUBS (RCAF; since at least WWII) — "Tee-Dubs" is the shortened form for "T.W." (ie., "tee double-U), the abbreviation for "Tropical Wear", or perhaps "Tropical Worsteds". The term "tee-dubs" was applied to any khaki air force uniform, from the cotton shirt and shorts worn in the desert or jungle during World War II, to the RCAF's synthetic khaki dress trousers and tunic of the 1950's and 1960's (renowned for turning pink under a too-hot iron). Unification in 1968 brought dark-green uniforms for all seasons in the CF and ended khaki tee-dubs in the CF. (Though when the "Distinctive

Tee-Dubs

Welcome to
COLD
LAKE

Environmental Uniforms" appeared in the late 1980's, the army returned to a Khaki summer uniform; the air element adopted a new "air force blue" for all seasons) (See also **Blues; Pinks(2)**)

If you're being posted to North Africa, then you'd better get some Tee- Dubs..

TEE-UP, TO (commonwealth military; universal; originally British Army) — To "tee-up" something is to arrange it, or to assure that it will happen. Tee-Up entered air force slang from the British Army, though it would appear to have earlier origins in golf. The air force equivalent was "to lay on", as in *to lay on a staff car*. (See also **to Lay On**) [Ref: Partridge (8th)]

Russ, tee-up a staff car for the Colonel's visit.

TEN-FOOT TWO (CF; current) — "Ten-Foot Two" is the nickname for 10 Field Technical Training Unit, the school responsible for training personnel to maintain fighter aircraft at CFB Cold Lake. The nickname Ten Foot Two is derived from the school's initials: 10 FTTU", which can be twisted into "10 ft. tu", and then into "10 foot-two"! Similarly, 3 Field Technical Training Unit is "3 foot two", 6 Field Technical Training Unit is "6 foot two", etc.

TEN-TON TESSIE   See **Tallboy**

TGIF (RCAF, CF; current) — "TGIF", meaning "Thank God Its Friday", is a weekly "happy hour" at the mess, held late on Friday afternoons to allow attendees to blow off the week's accumulated steam. There are normally three "messes" on a military base: the Junior Ranks' Mess (for those below the rank of Sergeant), the Sergeants' and Warrant Officers' Mess, and the Officers' Mess. Each is a centre of social activity for its members and at the end of the week, each Mess holds a TGIF. TGIF is characterized by cut-rate drinks, a buffet meal for all members and guests, and heightened Military Police traffic patrols. (See also **Weepers**)

Its pizza night at TGIF this Friday!

THEIRS (universal military) — "Theirs" refers to one of the enemy, as in "its one of theirs". (See also **Bandit; Bogey**)

"THERE ARE OLD PILOTS AND THERE ARE BOLD PILOTS, BUT THERE ARE NO OLD BOLD PILOTS" — This aphorism (which dates back to at least the Second World War, and probably earlier) has become something of a cliche; still, its message remains valid. It warns pilots that, if they wish to live to a ripe old age, they should avoid being "bold". That is, they should avoid taking unnecessary risks. [Ref: Peden]

"THERE WE WERE, UPSIDE DOWN IN CLOUD, FUCK ALL ON THE CLOCK AND STILL CLIMBING!!!" (WWII) — This stock phrase was used as a way to curb a "line-shooter", a person prone to stretching the truth while telling "war stories", especially about aerial exploits. [Ref: Partridge-Catchphrases]

> *Anyway lads, as I was saying, we had just crossed the enemy coast when...*
> *(...and from across the room): Yessir, there we were, upside down in cloud,*
> *fuck all on the clock and still climbing!!!*

"THEY CAN MAKE YOU DO ANYTHING IN THE AIR FORCE EXCEPT HAVE A BABY" (WWII) — This catchphrase, apparently coined during the Second World War, is a wry commentary on the broad reach of military authority. [Ref: Partridge-Catchphrases]

"THEY HOSED THEM OUT" (Bomber Command WWII) — This graphic catchphrase refers to all those who flew as a rear gunner. The allusion is to the tragic death rate and the fact that the rear gunner fought his war in very confined spaces. (See also **Dustbin; Tail-End Charlie**) [Ref: Partridge-Catchphrases]

THIRD, TO GET ONE'S (Commonwealth military) — "Third" refers to one's third chevron. Only a sergeant wears three chevrons, so "to get one's third" means to be promoted to sergeant. [Ref: Partridge (8th)]

> *Keep up the good work and someday you'll get your third.*

THIRTY-SIX; FORTY-EIGHT; SEVENTY-TWO; NINETY-SIX (Military; general) — When a servicemember talks of a "36", they refer to period of leave which is thirty-six hours long. Similarly, a "48" is forty-eight hours of leave, two days. "72" is three days of leave, and "96" is four days. [Ref: Collins]

> *I've got a "36" due to me next month...*

THOUSAND-MILER (CF; current — A "thousand-miler" is a reusable envelope used for internal administrative correspondence. Unlike most envelopes, which are used but once, a thousand miler is said to travel a thousand miles before being thrown out.

> *Just send the memo to the adjutant in a thousand-miler.*

THREE-POINTER   See **Wheeler**

THUNDERBUMPER (aviation, general) — "Thunderbumper" is slang for a cumulonimbus cloud, more often known as a "thunder-head". The cumulonimbus cloud can bring fierce thunder and lightning, and is associated with heavy rain. Old folk tales spoke of thunder and lightning being caused by thunderclouds "bumping" into one another, therefore the name Thunderbumper.

> *A line of thunderbumpers will move through the area tonight, so we'll probably get rain.*

T.I. (CF; current) — "T.I." is an occasional abbreviation for "time in", that is, a long time spent in air force service. [Ref: Carlson]

> *Wait till you get some T.I. before you complain...*

TICKETY-BOO (RAF, RCAF, CF; current) — "Tickety-boo" is an adjective that denotes that things are in proper order, or satisfactory. The word seems to have had its origins in the RAF of the 1920's, and may be derived from a Hindustani term. Once everyday British usage, it is less common in Canadian civilian language. However, it remains fairly common in Canadian air force usage. [Ref: Partridge (8th)]

> *Is your project finished?*
> *Yes, and everything is tickety-boo!*

TIFFIE; TIFFY (RAF, RCAF; WWII) — "Tiffie" is the affectionate nickname for the Typhoon, an excellent British fighter- bomber of the Second World War. The Tiffie was designed as a general-purpose fighter by the Sydney Camm design team at Hawker Aviation and was a follow-on to Hawker's earlier success, the Hurricane. However, disappointing performance at medium to high altitudes caused the team to rethink the future of the "Tiffie", and it was reborn as a ground attack aircraft. It could carry a heavy weight of rockets and bombs, and at low altitudes was very manoeuvrable. Many RAF squadrons and four RCAF squadrons flew the Tiffie in the 2nd Tactical Air Force. Tiffies earned an enviable reputation as ground support aircraft after the D-Day landings. (See also **Cab Rank, Tank-Busting, Winkling; Winkle Out**) [Refs: Harvey; Partridge (FS)]

> *At low altitudes, nothing could match a Tiffie!*

TIGER; TIGERSCHMITT (RAF, RCAF; WWII) — "Tiger" and "Tigerschmitt" were both affectionate nicknames for the De Havilland "Tiger Moth", the major primary trainer of the 1930's and 1940's. Tigerschmitt is an obvious allusion to German Messerschmitt aircraft.

The Tiger Moth was developed from the earlier Cirrus Moth. (This series of aircraft was named in honour of Geoffrey De Havilland's hobby of Lepidoptery). In 1937, work began on modifying the basic Tiger Moth for Canadian winter conditions; a clear canopy was added and the undercarriage was beefed up to take skis. The Tiger Moth was flown extensively throughout the British Empire; just over 1500 Tigers were built in Canada, where they were used in the British Commonwealth Air Training Plan for both Elementary Pilot Training and for Wireless Operator Training. (See also **Moth**) [Ref: Molson and Taylor]

> *A student gets about 25 flying hours on the Tiger before they send him to advanced training on the Harvard.*

TIGER TEAM (CF; current) — "Tiger Team" is a current military buzzword for a committee whose members are drawn from many disciplines and whose task is to solve a particular organizational problem as quickly as is possible. Tiger Teams are intended to provide a rapid solution to a problem by taking the problem-solving process out of the routine, bureaucratic chain of command.

TIN OTTER   see **Twotter**

TINKERTOY (CF; mid 1960's) — The CF-5 fighter was first acquired by the CF in 1968, and for a time, became known as the "TinkerToy", after the popular children's construction toys. It earned this nickname because of its simpler construction and features when compared to its contemporaries, the CF-104 Starfighter and the CF-101 Voodoo. Occasionally, the aircraft was called the "SST", or "Supersonic TinkerToy" (also a play on the initials "SST" which ordinarily means Supersonic Transport).

By 1965 the RCAF had to replace its Canada-based Sabre aircraft, and several aircraft types were under consideration. The air force favoured other aircraft, the F4 Phantom,

TinkerToy

the A-6 Intruder or the A-7 Corsair. Ultimately the government selected the CF-5, the Canadair-built variant of the F-5 "Freedom Fighter", a light tactical fighter developed by Northrop aviation from its T-38 Talon, the standard USAF advanced jet trainer. The United States military was never seriously interested in acquiring the F-5 for front-line service, and Northrop marketed the aircraft heavily under American foreign military assistance programs. The Canadian government selected the CF-5 in no small measure because it could be built in Canada under licence. Ultimately two tactical fighter squadrons flew the CF-5, and one fighter training squadron. When the CF-18 Hornet entered Canadian service, the CF-5 was relegated to the advanced fighter pilot-training role.

The CF-5 differed from the stock F-5 Freedom Fighter in that it employed more powerful engines, improved navigational and communication equipment, and had a basic photo-reconnaissance capability. Later, in-flight refuelling capability was added. Canadair produced 105 similar aircraft for the Royal Netherlands Air Force, designated the NF-5. [Ref: Molson and Taylor]

TOOLS (RCAF, RAF; WWII) — To airmen and airwomen during the Second World War, "tools" were cutlery. (See also **Eating Irons**) [Ref: Collins]

You'll find the tools over at the end of the steam table, next to the plates.

TOOL CRIB (RCAF, CF; current since at least 1930's) — The "Tool Crib" is a central point in a maintenance hangar from which tools and certain types of aircraft supplies can be drawn by aircraft maintainers.

TOOT   See **Tute**

TORBEAU   See **Beau**

TORQUE IT TIGHT, THEN BACK IT HALF A TURN (CF; current) — "Torque it tight, then turn it back half a turn" is a phrase used occasionally by technicians. The term advises a technician to tighten a bolt without worrying about whether the bolt must be tightened to any specific torque.

TOTAL LOSS (general; since WWII) — "Total Loss" is descriptive of anyone, or anything, which is worthless. The term may have entered aviation usage from the fact that, from an accounting perspective, a wrecked aircraft is a "total loss". It doesn't take much of a leap of the imagination to apply the same term to a person whose usefulness is zero. (See also **Write-Off**) [Ref: Partridge (8th)]

What's your new Commanding Officer like?
He's a total loss...

TOUCH DOWN, TO (aviation general) — To "touch down" is to land an aircraft, as in: *See if you can touch down on the first half of the runway this time, okay?* [Ref: Partridge (8th)]

TOWER (aviation; general — "Tower" always refers to the control tower, where air traffic control activities are centred. Thus, the radio frequency on which visual air traffic control communications occur is "Tower Frequency".

Ottawa Tower, Canforce 335 is ready for takeoff.

TRACER (military, general; since WWI) — Tracer is a type of ammunition that burns brightly after it leaves the cannon or machine gun. This allows the pilot or gunner to note the direction that the rounds are travelling and adjust the aim. (See also **Flaming Onions, Scarlet Slugs**)

I like to have one tracer round for every 10 explosive rounds.

TRAINING BEER (CF; current) — "Training Beer" is low alcohol beer, the implication being that, just as a training aircraft is less hazardous to fly, Training Beer is less hazardous to drink. (Sometimes called "Near Beer")

When you're finished drinking that training beer, have a real drink.

TRAIN TRACKS (CF; general) — To have "train tracks" is to improperly iron one's uniform trousers, so as to press "double-creases" into them. That is, instead of having trousers with a single knife-edged crease, one has a series of parallel creases that create the impression of parallel railway tracks.

Bloggins! Look at the creases in your trousers! You've got train tracks!!

TRAP (RCN; to 1969) — "Trap" is naval aviation slang for an aircraft carrier landing. An aircraft landing on a carrier deck only stops if the tailhook engages the arrestor cable, "trapping" the aircraft - as though in a snare.

There's going to be a party in the wardroom tonight! Lieutenant-Commander Rodney made his 200th trap this morning!

Trap

TRASH HAULER (CF; current) — "Trash Hauler" is a mildly derogatory nickname for air transport personnel, especially aircrew. The term suggests that airlift, the mere carriage of freight and personnel, is something less than a "military" vocation, as opposed to directly inflicting mayhem upon the enemy! Nowhere is this view more apparent than in the fighter pilot's fraternity. However, airlift crews know better and the term "Trash Hauler" often attracts a certain pride, also. The term is possibly American in origin.

It's lonely being the only Trash Hauler in a fighter wing!

TRICYCLE; TRIKE (aviation; general) — "Tricycle" or "trike" refers to aircraft with tricycle undercarriage (as opposed to "conventional" or "tail-dragger" undercarriage, or any of the other types of aircraft landing gear types). In a trike, the aircraft's centre of gravity is between the nose wheel and its two main wheels, rather like a child's tricycle. (See **Wheelbarrow**)

TRIPE (WWI) — "Tripe" is short for the word "triplane", an aircraft with three mainplanes, or wings. The idea behind the tripe was to create an aircraft with reduced wingspan and chord, but to make up for the lost wing area by adding a third wing. Only two tripes earned their spurs in combat: the Sopwith Triplane (See **Tripe Hound**) and the Fokker DR-1 made famous by Richthofen. (See also **Red Baron; Flying Circus**) Indeed the Fokker triplane was inspired by the earlier Sopwith Triplane. [Ref: Voss]

TRIPE HOUND (RNAS; WWI) — "Tripe Hound" was the unkind nickname for the Sopwith Triplane (see **Tripe**), a fighter introduced into the Royal Naval Air Service (RNAS) in the First World War to counter the threat of Germany's new Albatros fighters. The nickname Tripe Hound suggests that the aircraft was a "Tripe" (a triplane) that behaved like a hound, ie. a "bitch". The Sopwith Triplane was a highly manoeuvrable aircraft with a good climb rate, but it occasionally attracted the unkind nickname Tripe Hound.

The Sopwith Triplane was occasionally criticized for being under-powered and under-armed. Still, despite the poor reputation suggested by the nickname Tripe Hound, the all- Canadian "Black Flight" of RNAS No. 10 Squadron, scored 87 victories between May and July of 1917 while flying the Triplane. The Black Flight was led by Flight Lieutenant Raymond Collishaw of Nanaimo, B.C.

The origin of the unkind nickname "Tripe Hound" is perhaps to be found in how the Triplane was manufactured. Though a Sopwith design, many Triplanes were built by subcontractors that had reduced the gauge of the airframe cables, weakening the airframe. Also, due to shortages of the Bentley rotary engine intended for the Triplane the lower-powered French Clerget engine was fitted; this reduction in power forced the removal of one of the Triplanes' two guns, reducing its firepower. As if this weren't enough, Clerget engines built by British subcontractors were less reliable than the original French powerplant. Canadian ace Raymond Collishaw reckoned that the ideal was a Sopwith-built Triplane powered by an original French Clerget engine. Otherwise, the airplane was a Tripe Hound. (See **Black Flight**) [Ref: Hadington; Partridge (8th); Phelan]

TRIPLE-A (military aviation, standard since 1960's) — "Triple A" is verbal shorthand for "A.A.A.", the abbreviation for Anti-Aircraft Artillery. Anti-aircraft artillery is comprised of guns and cannon, together with their tracking systems. As such, triple A is distinguished from "SAMs", or "Surface to Air Missiles. (See **Flaming Onions; SAM**)

There was a lot of 'Triple A' over the target.

TRIPLE-FOUR (RCAF, CF; since WWII) — "Triple-four" has been the moniker for 444 Squadron since its inception in 1947. Originally formed as an air observation post unit, triple four reformed as a fighter squadron in 1953, flying the Sabre and Starfighter. It was stood down in 1967, only to be reactivated several years later as a tactical helicopter squadron.

Malcolm was bounced by a triple-four bird this morning.

TRUCKER (CF; current) — The nickname "Trucker" refers to CF logistics officers who specialize in transport (as opposed to the other two logistics specialties, finance and supply). This subclassification includes "Air Movements", the control of air cargo and passengers. Consequently, Air Movements Officers are occasionally called truckers. The term would appear to have originated in the army, where it applies to the members of the transport company in a Service Battalion. (See also **Air Mover**)

"TRUE VIRGINS MAKE DULL COMPANY" — "True virgins make dull company" is a mnemonic device used in teaching basic air navigation. This odd phrase helps student pilots and navigators to remember how to convert from "True" heading to "Compass" heading.

"True Heading" is the direction in degrees that an aircraft flies relative to the geographic north pole, ie., true north on the map. However, navigation is complicated because compasses do not point to true north, they point to magnetic north, located in Canada's arctic archipelago and not at the top of the world. Therefore in planning a cross-country flight, a pilot or navigator must mathematically convert the desired heading according to the map, to the heading as it must be read from the aircraft compass in flight. This is "Compass Heading".

Converting from True Heading to Compass Heading requires the aviator to make two arithmetic calculations. First, the difference in degrees between the direction to the geographic and magnetic north poles must be mathematically accounted for. This difference is called "variation": compass heading adjusted for variation is known as "Magnetic Heading".

However, computing an aircraft's magnetic heading isn't enough. An aircraft compass can be offset by the magnetic field induced by the aircraft's own electrical system; the amount that the compass is thrown off is called "Deviation" and it too must be accounted for. So, the second computation that the aviator must make is to convert from "magnetic heading" to "compass heading". All these variables and computations are remembered through the mnemonic device: "True virgins make dull company". This is illustrated below:

True	TRUE HEADING
	(plus/minus)
Virgins	VARIATION
	(gives you)
Make	MAGNETIC HEADING
	(plus/minus)
Dull	DEVIATION
	(gives you)
Company	COMPASS HEADING

The reverse conversion is remembered by the mnemonic device: "Can Dead Men Vote Twice?"

TUCK IT IN, TO (aviation; general) — "To tuck it in" is to narrow the distance between aircraft flying in formation, as in: *Tuck it in tight!*

TURKEY (RCN, originally USN) — "Turkey" was the affectionate nickname given to the Grumman Avenger by naval airmen of the United States Navy during the Second World War. The nickname "Turkey" came to the RCN when it purchased the Avenger for anti-submarine duties following the Second World War.

The origins of the nickname Turkey are uncertain, though it may be a reference to its ungainly appearance when compared to other USN aircraft of the era. The Avenger was designed as a torpedo-bomber and earned an exemplary reputation during the Second World War. However, the RCN acquired the "Turkey" after the Second World War and used it primarily as an anti-submarine patrol aircraft. Its large carrying capacity and robust structure made it easily adaptable to this task. A later variant, nicknamed the "Guppy" by Canadian naval airmen, mounted a large, bulbous fairing containing a surveillance radar. The Guppy was used for airborne early warning with the east coast Canadian fleet. The Turkey was gradually phased out of service and replaced by the Grumman Tracker, when HMCS Magnificent was replaced by HMCS Bonaventure in 1956. (See also **Stoof, Bonnie, Maggie**) [Ref: Petipas]

The Turkey squadron has deployed to sea.

TUTE; TOOT (RCAF, CF; current) — "Tute" (or "Toot") is shorthand for "Tutor", a two-seat single engine jet trainer designed and built by Canadair. The Tutor resulted from a privately funded design program in 1958, intended to market a light jet aircraft that could be used as both a trainer and as a counterinsurgency fighter. In 1961, Canada ordered 190 Tutor advanced trainers, and in 1967 Malaysia purchased 20 as light ground attack and training aircraft. In Malaysian service it was known as the "Tebuan".

The Tutor has side-by-side seating for the instructor and student pilot (to make for more easy visual communications between student and instructor). The Tute, powered by a General Electric J-85 gas turbine engine, replaced the venerable Harvard as the RCAF's advanced training aircraft in 1961. The Tutor is in service with No. 2 Canadian Forces Flying Training School at Moose Jaw, and in Winnipeg at the Central Flying School and the Instrument Check Pilot School. The Canadian public however, will most likely associate the Tutor with the "Snowbirds", the Canadian Forces Aerial Demonstration Team. The Snowbirds however, are not the only flying team to have flown the Tute. During the 1967 Centennial, several years before the inception of the Snowbirds, the "Golden Centennaires" flew nine gold and black Tutors in airshows across the country to celebrate Canada's 100th birthday. [Ref: Molson and Taylor]

After you finish your initial pilot training course, you'll go on to advanced flying training on the Tute.

TWEAK, TO — "To tweak" is to make a minor adjustment. Thus one can tweak radio frequencies, tweak a trim setting, etc.

"TWELVE YEARS OF UNDETECTED CRIME" (CF since 1950's) — "Twelve years of undetected crime" is the cynic's criteria by which a person is awarded the Canadian Forces Decoration. The Canadian Forces Decoration is a medal awarded for good conduct over a long period, specifically, twelve years. It is commonly called the "C.D.", for the letters that the recipient is entitled to place behind his or her name. The medal is only awarded to those whose service record is unblemished, though it is acknowledged that one must actually be "caught in the act" to blemish one's service record! Those whose crimes go undetected will still receive their "CD"!

> *What did you get that medal for?*
> *...twelve years of undetected crime!*

TWIN-ENGINE JOB (WWII) — Though an aircraft with two engines is often called a "Twin-Engine Job", the term has also been known to refer to a female, because both twin engine aircraft and the female form have a certain bifurcated symmetry. (Aircraft are often referred to as a "job", hence "twin-engine job") (See **Job**)

TWITCH (RAF; 1930's) — To have "the twitch" is to be visibly nervous about military flying. This term has now entered standard English. (See also **All of a doodah; Screamers**) [Ref: Partridge (8th)]

TWO-STRIPER; TWO AND A HALF; THREE-STRIPER (CF, current) — A "two-striper" can be a Corporal, from the number of chevrons worn on the sleeves. Alternately, among officers it can be a Navy Lieutenant, an RCAF Flight Lieutenant, or a Canadian Forces Captain, each of whom wear two loops of braid as a rank insignia. (See also **Flight Looie**)

A "two-and-a-half" is a Navy Lieutenant-Commander, an RCAF Squadron Leader or a Canadian Forces Major. These officers wear rank badges consisting of two loops of rank braid, between which is another smaller, half-wide loop of braid. (But see also **Scraper, Squadron Bleeder; Squalid Bleeder**)

Likewise, a "three-striper" can be a Sergeant or alternately, a naval Commander, an RCAF Wing Commander, or a Canadian Forces Lieutenant-Colonel. (See also **Hoops; Light Colonel; Rings; Wingco**)

> *Who's the new Three-Striper?*

TWOTTER (CF; current) — "Twotter" is the unofficial contraction and nickname for the "Twin Otter", a light twin-engined bush aircraft flown by the Canadian Forces since the late 1960's. The Twin Otter is flown from Yellowknife (and until recently, from Edmonton) for both light transport and search and rescue duties.

The Twin Otter was developed from the earlier single piston-engined Otter (which became known as the "single Otter" or the "Steam Otter", to distinguish it from the turbine-powered Twin Otter). Only after small, light gas turbine engines such as the United Aircraft PT-6 became available was the development of a twin-engined STOL (short takeoff and landing) aircraft with performance comparable to the single-engined Otter possible. Occasionally the Twin Otter is called the "Tin Otter", a term that is at once a play on the name, and an allusion to the basic construction of this rugged bushplane. [Ref: Molson and Taylor]

> *The Twotter doesn't need much runway to land.*

T.X. (pronounced "tea-ex"); **TO BE T.X.'d** (CF; current) — "T.X." is written shorthand for the term "time-expired". Aircraft equipment has a limited life; it can only be used for a fixed number of flying hours, or a given number of calendar days. After this time expires, technicians must replace or overhaul the component. A component that has been in use for that specified period is said to be "time-expired" or "T.X.'d". Occasionally this term is applied to servicemembers who have completed a fixed period of military service and are due for release from the military, as in: *Ray is T.X.'d next November.*

> *Check the hours on that propeller. It's probably T.X.'d!*

TYPE (RAF, RCAF, CF; since 1920's) — Different makes or categories of aircraft are known as aircraft "types". Consequently, persons can also be known as a "type", as in "good type", "fighter type", "supply type", etc. The word is particularly RAF in origin and is analogous to the U.S. Navy's favourite, "puke", or the USAF's "weenie". (See also **Basher; Puke; Weenie**) [Ref: Partridge (8th)]

> *What about the new Commanding Officer?*
> *I think he started as a bomber type...*

UNIFORM

UMBRELLA (British; since 1914, now obsolete) — "Umbrella" was once slang for a parachute, as in: *when the engine conked out, I got out and opened my umbrella.* From this, one gets another early nickname for a parachute, "brolly", also a nickname for an umbrella. [Ref: Partridge (FS)]

UNACCOMPANIED (CF; current) — A servicemember who is "unaccompanied" is posted somewhere without his or her spouse, family, and effects. Usually servicemembers are posted from base to base and bring their family with them. However, an unaccompanied posting is sometimes arranged where moving the family would prove to be a burden.

I'm here unaccompanied, so I'm living in barracks.

UNDERCART (British, since WWI, still occasionally heard) — "Undercart" is shorthand for "undercarriage" or landing gear, as in: *don't forget to lower the undercart this time!* [Ref: Partridge (8th)]

UNDERSHOOT (general aviation) — To "undershoot" is to touch the ground (or risk touching the ground) short of one's intended landing spot. It is the opposite of "to overshoot". [Ref: Partridge (8th)]

If you undershoot at Comox you'll wind up in the sea!

UNLOAD — To "unload" is a term with two common meanings in military aviation:

(1)   To **unload** is to drop bombs, a usage that dates from the Royal Flying Corps of the first World War, as in: *We had to unload our bombs sooner than we expected.* [Ref: Partridge (8th)]

(2)   To **unload** while manoeuvring an aircraft, is to decrease the "G's"(or "gees") acting on an aircraft and its occupants by pushing forward on the aircraft control column. One might say: *I levelled out of the turn, unloaded the stick, and felt my weight go back to normal again.* When a pilot pulls back hard on the control column, whether to turn very tightly, or to pull out of a dive, the aircraft and its occupants experience the sensation of weighing much more than they normally do. The force which causes this sensation, centrifugal force, is measured in multiples of the force of gravity. It therefore is called "Gee", "G Force", or "G Load", with the G referring to gravity. Thus aviators speak of the G Load acting on an aircraft. Consequently, to increase the G's is to load on the G's, and to decrease the G loading is to "unload".

UPLOAD, TO; DOWNLOAD, TO (NATO air forces, current) — Armourers "upload" an aircraft when they arm the aircraft with rockets or bombs. Consequently, to "download" an aircraft is to remove those same rockets or bombs (other than by dropping them on the bad guys). This peculiar term entered Canadian usage via the USAF, when the CF-104 Starfighter entered Canadian service. One would think that the words "load" and "unload" would suffice!

It will take the armourers at least an hour to upload all these aircraft.

UPSTAIRS (general aviation usage since 1918) — "Upstairs" is vernacular for any altitude higher than one's own, as in: *We're only at 5000 feet altitude; let's get upstairs.* [Ref: Partridge (FS)]

UP THE YING-YANG (CF; current) — To use the phrase "up the ying-yang" is to allude to plenty, or great numbers, in the same way that one might say "up to the armpits" (as in "we're up to the armpits in spare wheels!") or "we're swimming" (as in "we're swimming in spare wheels!"). The phrase seems vulgar in a vague sort of way, an allusion to the sexual. Although there is no way of being certain, it is certainly possible that this usage of the term originated with Allied servicemen posted to the Orient where they would have been exposed to Asian culture and religion.

"Ying" and "Yang" are concepts central to the Confucian faith. Ying and Yang are two different but complementary components of the cosmos, components that moderate each other and foster each other's growth. "Ying" (sometimes "Yin") represents, among other things, the female, whereas "Yang" represents the male; the union of the two makes the universe complete. "Ying" and "Yang" are often represented graphically as two dynamic halves of a circle; an example of this depiction is found at the centre of the flag of South Korea and on the insignia of the South Korean air force. It may be that the phrase "up the Ying-Yang" originated among Allied servicmen stationed in Korea.

Given its gender-oriented symbolism, it is perhaps unsurprising that western servicemen would refer to the "ying-yang" as though it were part of the body! So whenever someone speaks of having something "up the ying-yang", they mean that they have plenty of it! [Ref: Benet]

Have you got any spare wheels?
We've got lots! We've got spare wheels up the ying-yang!

UPWARD CHARLIE (RAF, RCAF; to 1950's) — An "Upward Charlie" is a vertical roll. The term Upward Charlie seems to have its origins in pre-1939 RAF "Rules for Air Fighting", a series of rigid, standardized fighter tactics developed during peacetime. These rules were founded on the mistaken belief that by the 1930's, aircraft flew too fast for a freewheeling "dogfight" to be possible. One such standard attack called for the fighter, on spotting the bomber, to dive below the bomber to gain speed and then pull up into a vertical climb towards the bomber. (Throughout this, the bomber was expected to obligingly maintain position and not take evasive action). While climbing up towards the enemy bomber, the fighter would roll to allow a firing pass while inverted, after which the fighter pilot would pull back on the controls and descend. This roll was the upward charlie. The RAF's "standard attacks" did not last after 1940. The fluidity of air fighting rendered them useless, indeed dangerous. Though the "Standard Attacks" did not last, the nickname for the upward roll did, and even in the late 1950's, student pilots still referred to the upward charlie. [Refs: Brickhill; Fletcher and MacPhail]

The new Squadron Leader promptly took off in his Hurricane and did three
Upward Charlies right over the aerodrome!

U/S (pronounced "yew-ess"; CF) — "u/s" is the standard military abbreviation for "unserviceable" (or "broken", as civilians would say). This abbreviation is common in English-speaking air forces, with the notable exception of the American military, ie. the "U.S." military. The US Air Force for example, presumably does not want to be known as the "u/s air force". (Ref: Patridge (8th)]

This damned altimeter is u/s again!

USAF (pronounced "yew-saff") — The United States Air Force is known by the initials USAF. Often these letters are pronounced "yew-saff", from the succesful attempt to turn the abbreviation "USAF" into an acronym.

We're expecting a "yew-saff" Hercules in tonight.

ICTOR

VAMP (RAF, RCAF; 1940's, 50's) — "Vamp" was the short form of "Vampire", the name of a pioneer jet fighter built in Britain in the late 1940's by De Havilland. The Vamp was easily recognized by its twin-boom configuration, a design based on captured Second World War German research. It was nimble and a gentle aircraft to fly, but by later jet fighter standards the Vampire was very basic indeed. It was small, it had no ejection seat, and parts of the fuselage were made of balsa (like the earlier De Havilland Mosquito).

The RCAF took delivery of its first Vamps in 1949 and they remained in service with both regular and reserve RCAF squadrons until the mid-1950's.

Did you know that the Vamp had no ejection seat?

Vamp

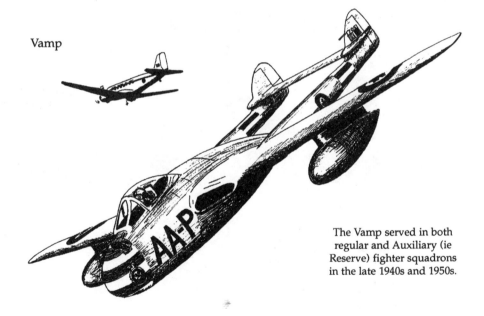

The Vamp served in both regular and Auxiliary (ie Reserve) fighter squadrons in the late 1940s and 1950s.

VANDOOS (Canadian Army, CF; WWI to present) — In the Canadian Forces, "Vandoo" is the nickname for soldiers of the Royal 22e Regiment, Canada's premier French-speaking army regiment. Vandoo is but an English corruption of the French word for "22", *vingt-deux*. Often beyond the capability of your basic "anglo", *vingt-deux* was simply altered by English tongues to "van-doo". Hence, soldiers of the *Royal vingt-deuxieme regiment* are Vandoos.

You can tell a Vandoo, although you can't tell him much...

VIC (RAF, RCAF; 1920's to present) — "Vic" is the common term for a "vee-shaped" formation of aircraft. The lead aircraft flies at the apex of the "V", and is followed by two other aircraft flying on either side and slightly behind. The term "vic" is actually an old phonetic alphabet code for the letter "V". This phonetic codeword became the the name for this formation simply because of the formation's "V-shape".

Prior to the Second World War, the three aircraft "vic" was the favoured fighter formation in the RAF; indeed until well into 1940, RAF fighter squadrons were based on four "vics" of three aircraft each. This proved disastrous for many young RAF fighter pilots, however. As a tactical formation, the "vic" was inferior to the "finger-four" formation used by the Luftwaffe. The German four-aircraft formation could split into two equal halves, with two pairs of fighters complementing each other in combat. The three-aircraft "vic" could not be so divided and it was more difficult for three RAF aircraft to fight in a coordinated manner against the more fluid German pair. The RAF, largely at the instigation of aces Douglas Bader and Robert Stanford-Tuck, soon adopted the "finger-four". (See also **Finger-Four**) [Ref: Partridge (8th); Spick]

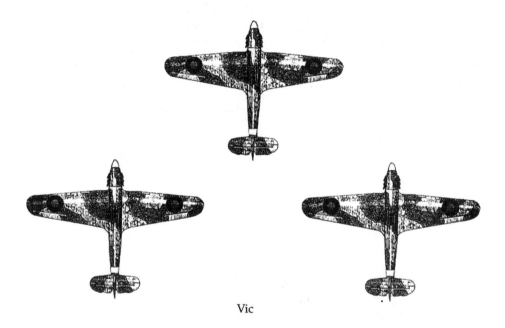

Vic

...three Hurricanes arced overhead in a vic...

VIS; VIZ (universal aviation) — "Vis" is the short form for "visibility", the meteorologists' term for the distance that a person with average vision can see in current weather conditions. For example, visibility in thick fog is zero, whereas in extremely clear skies visibility can be measured in miles. In the Antarctic, where smog and fog are virtually unknown, visibility has been reported to be as much as 80 miles!

What's the vis at Winnipeg?

VOLLEYBALL U (CF; current) — "Volleyball U" was a nickname for the Canadian Forces Staff School. This school trained officers of Captain rank for senior officer responsibilities. The course is an intensive, three month program of leadership, management and administration training, broken by occasional periods of physical activity - usually volleyball. Therefore, the school is "Volleyball University" or "Volleyball U".

It looks like I'm in for a couple of months at Volleyball U

VOLUNTEER (military, universal) — In conventional military wisdom a "volunteer" is someone who didn't understand the question. Alternately, it can be a euphemism for someone who was not fast enough to escape. (See also **They can make you do anything in the air force except have a baby!**)

I need three volunteers! You, you, and you!

VPI; VP INTERNATIONAL (NATO Air Forces; current) — "VPI" or "VP International" is an international fraternity of aviators from the NATO air forces who have completed at least 1000 flying hours in "VP", or "maritime patrol" aircraft. The "VP" designator was an invention of the US Navy, which uses such alphabetic designators to identify its patrol squadrons; the system has spread to the other NATO air forces. The letter "V" indicates that the unit is a fixed-wing squadron, and the letter "P" means "Patrol". Thus, the international fraternity of fixed-wing patrol aviators is known as "VPI".

The local chapter of the VPI is having a luncheon next week.

WHISKEY

WAAF ("Waff") (RAF;WWII) — "WAAF" is the acronym for the Women's Auxiliary Air Force, the women's branch of the RAF during the Second World War. This acronym described both the service as a whole, and its individual members. Therefore, a woman joined the WAAF and in so doing, became a WAAF.

Although WAAF became a common term among Canadians overseas, the Women's Auxiliary Air Force was a British, not Canadian, organization. RCAF airwomen served in the Canadian Women's Auxiliary Air Force (CWAAF), which was renamed the "RCAF Women's Division" in 1942. Canadian airwomen were usually called "W.D.'s" (the abbreviation for "Women's Division") but occasionally, if inaccurately, they were also called WAAF's. Though many Canadian men served in the RAF, it is unclear how many Canadian women travelled to Britain to become WAAFs; most would have joined the "W.D." in Canada. (See **Queen Bee, W.D., Wid**) [Ref: Partridge (8th)]

WAFFERY (RAF; WWII) — "Waffery" was Second World War slang for the WAAF's barracks, that is, women's quarters at RAF Stations in England. (See **WAAF**) The word Waffery may have been adapted from "Wrennery", the slang term for female quarters on a naval base. ("Wren" is the official name for female naval personnel and is adapted from the initials W.R.N.S., for Women's Royal Naval Service.) Waffery and Wrennery both played on the word Nunnery. Perhaps the allusion to a nunnery resulted because military authorities regard female quarters as sacrosanct and inviolate. Males, regardless of rank, must not darken the doorstep of female quarters except on the most pressing of official duties, and even then, only if escorted by a female NCO or Officer. This cloistering suggests a nunnery. [Ref: Partridge (8th)]

> *Don't get caught inside the Waffery again, Bill!*

WAG — "WAG" is an abbreviation with two possible meanings in the air force:

> (1)   A **WAG** was a Wireless Air Gunner, a Second World War aircrew category more properly called a Wireless Operator/Air Gunner (See also **WOP/AG**) This was a radio operator cross-trained as an air gunner. (See also **Spider**) [Refs: Harvey; Partridge (8th)]

> (2)   A **WAG** is also a "Wild-Assed Guess". (There is as well the improved version: SWAG, for "Scientific Wild-Assed Guess". (See also **SWAG**)

WAKEY-WAKEY (RCAF, RAF, RN, RCN; from 1920's) — Wakey-Wakey is reveille, the beginning of the military day in barracks. An RAF term which has spread into Canadian usage, "Wakey-Wakey!" is the traditional early morning cry of the Duty NCO. The Duty NCO had the job of rising early and entering a barracks full of sleeping airmen at 0530 or so, to shout: "WAKEY, WAKEY!! DROP YOUR COCK, GRAB YOUR SOCKS! ITS DAYLIGHT IN THE SWAMP!" - or some such similarly ironic refrain. This cry was repeated without tenderness until all the room's occupants were awake and cheerfully ready to face the day. (See also **O-Christ-Thirty; O-Dark-thirty, Crow Fart, Sparrow Fart**) [Refs: Collins; Partridge (8th)]

What time is Wakey-Wakey around here?

WARM FUZZY FEELING (CF; current) — "Warm fuzzy feeling" is a mildly sarcastic term for a feeling of contentment. In military circles it is also synonymous with "subjectivity", as opposed to "objectivity". In otherwords, a person who gets a "warm fuzzy feeling" about something, has made an evaluation without objective standards. They have given their approval on only subjective emotional or temperamental factors.

Sergeant Jones has no particular criteria when he qualifies a technician; he just waits until he gets a warm fuzzy feeling about the guy.

WARTHOG (NATO general, originally USAF) — "Warthog" is the unofficial but universal nickname for the Fairchild A-10 "Thunderbolt II", a USAF close air support aircraft with phenomenal firepower and manoeuvrability. The nickname results from the fact that this aircraft, like its namesake, could never be accused of being eye-pleasing.

The Warthog was the air force's attempt to prove that they could design a tank as well as the army could!

WASH OUT, TO (general; originally American) — During the First World War, a patrol that was cancelled due to rain or bad weather was said to be "washed out". Later the usage of this term expanded to imply any type of cancellation, failure or disappointment. Consequently, today, to "wash out" is to fail to be selected for a coveted training course, or to not succeed in passing such a course. Therefore, a person who fails is often termed "a washout", and the term is most often associated with persons who fail aircrew training. Though occasionally heard in Canada, this usage is primarily American; Canadians were more apt to use the phrase "to be C.T.'d", for "Ceased Training". (See **C.T., Scrub**) [Ref: Partridge (8th)]

WASH-UP (CF; current) — A wash-up is a debriefing, a group discussion and review after the end of some activity. Just as "washing up" is the last thing that one does after completing chores, a debriefing is the last thing one does after completing a military operation. (See also **Debrief(2)**) [Ref: Partridge (8th)]

What time's the wash-up?

WASTE OF RATIONS, A (CF; current) — "A waste of rations" is an insulting description of a person so thoroughly useless that it probably isn't worth feeding them, as it only encourages them to remain and foul things up more.

What's the new Sergeant like?
...a waste of rations...

WAVELENGTH, TO BE ON THE SAME (originally RAF; now general) — When two or more people are in a state of concordance, or agreement, they are "on the same wavelength". In older radio terminology, the word "wavelength" was used instead of the now more common term "frequency". For radios to be useful in communication, they must be on the same "frequency", or "wavelength". Similarly, two people whose ideas are in accord are "on the same wavelength".

WAVE-OFF (RCN and naval aviation; general) — On an aircraft carrier landing, a "wave-off" is an order from the Landing Signals Officer (LSO) (See **Bats**) instructing the pilot to abort the landing approach, pull up, and fly around again. Up to the 1950's, navy pilots adjusted their landing approach to the deck of a carrier by observing visible arm signals given by the LSO, who stood at the edge of the flight deck, observing the approach in a position where he could be easily seen. If the LSO felt the approach was unsafe, he signalled the pilot to abort the landing by waving both arms over his head. This signal was termed a "wave-off". Although the LSO's arm signals eventually gave way to an electro-optical system with lights and mirrors, a command from the deck to abort the landing is still "a wave-off". (See **Bolter**)

His airspeed was down to 87 knots before he got the wave-off!

WAX, TO (originally Cockney; now general military) — In mock aerial combat, "to wax" one's opponent is to "have him dead to rights" - the aerial equivalent of a checkmate, in chess. The term is Cockney in origin, and by 1906 had become common slang in the British services for a decisive demonstration of superiority. Presumably, the term migrated to the RCAF via the RAF. The term is also heard occasionally from American military aviators. [Ref: Partridge (8th)]

W.D. (RCAF 1941-1968) — "W.D." was the abbreviation for the "Women's Division" of the RCAF. As such, it also became the universal nickname for female members of the RCAF.

Though women had served in the RAF during the First World War, opportunities for Canadian women to join the air force did not surface until the Second World War. The first women in the RCAF were a small number of flight nurses who joined in 1940, but it wasn't felt necessary to establish a distinct RCAF "women's branch" due to their small numbers. The war, however, led to a greater need for personnel and in 1941, the RCAF established the "Canadian Women's Auxiliary Air Force" (CWAAF), renamed the RCAF Women's Division in 1942. The common abbreviation was "RCAF (WD)", so Canadian airwomen became known as "W.D.'s".

The task of the RCAF (WD) was to recruit and train females for non-operational air force jobs, thereby releasing males for operational duty. The motto of the Women's Division was: *That Men May Fly*. This approach to employing females may appear antiquated in the light of changes in society since 1945. Still, it was a radical step that might have taken years to happen had the war not forced it. We often forget that the decision to employ women in the armed forces was not universally popular among Canadians of the 1940's, male or female and among traditionalists, female servicemembers were sometimes suspected of being mere "camp followers," though nothing was further from the truth. Women were assigned to a variety of RCAF technical, logistics, and support jobs and performed them well.

The first peacetime members of the WD were enrolled in 1951, and the scope of women's air force duties gradually expanded. However, women were still not employed in the

In the beginning, airwomen served to free males for operational duties.
Now women serve in all Air Force jobs.

full range of air force duties. With Unification in 1968, the RCAF, together with its Women's Division, disappeared as a legal entity. For the new Canadian Armed Forces, it was decided that there was no need to create a special "female branch". Personnel policies, for the most part, treated females as they did males - although women were still not entitled to serve in all occupations. However, by 1982, Canada had its own Charter of Rights and Freedoms that forbade governmental discrimination based on gender. This in turn prompted reevaluation of female employment in the military. Today all recruits, male and female, are assigned to military occupations on the basis of physical, behavioural, and educational requirements, and not gender. (The only exception is submarine duty, which remains an exclusive male bastion due to the abject lack of privacy in a submarine.) (See also **WAAF, Waffery, Wid**)

How do you like that? My sister is gonna be a W.D.!

WEATHER DAY; WEATHER PLAN (CF; current) — The term "weather day" is really just shorthand for a "bad weather day", a day in which no flying can occur due to poor weather. Thus it follows that a "weather plan" is a standby schedule or program held in readiness should a weather day occur, so that the day is not entirely wasted. The term is occasionally used in non-flying situations, but it is definitely aircrew usage.

If this rain doesn't stop, we'll have to plan a weather day.

WEDGE CAP, WEDGIE — Whenever an airman or airwoman refers to a "wedge cap" or a "wedgie" they are referring to a piece of headgear once known as the "Field Service Cap". The wedge has become the characteristic dress cap of Canadian airmen, and now airwomen. It takes its name from its appearance; the cap is long and narrow, but closed at the top seam, giving it a wedge-like appearance when worn.

The wedge was first introduced in the 1880's into the British Army to satisfy a requirement for a light, practical field cap and to replace more ornate headgear in common use. The wedge cap was patterned after an Austro-Hungarian Army cap that incorporated a fold-down cloth flap and visor, secured by a pair of buttons, which was folded down over the forehead and ears in cold weather for warmth. The British and Canadian wedge cap also incorporated a fold-down flap and visor; these features remain today, though they are now purely ornamental. The wedge cap was standard issue for most of the regiments and corps of the British Army, including the Royal Flying Corps. However, it was probably not known as the "wedge cap" until later in the 20th Century.

The wedge was favoured by airmen in the Royal Flying Corps because when removed, it folded neatly flat, and could be easily carried in a pocket, or inside flying coveralls. Not surprisingly, when the RFC amalgamated with the RNAS to become the Royal Air Force, the RAF adopted the wedge cap. The RCAF and most Commonwealth air forces adopted the wedge cap as well, but it never entered naval use. Both the British Army and the RAF ceased issuing the wedge in favour of the beret late in the Second World War (though occasionally one sees wedge caps in British use). Similarly, the Royal Australian Air Force has altered the

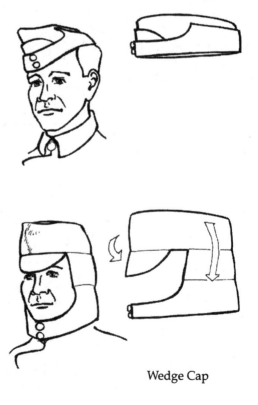

Wedge Cap

pattern and cut of its own wedge cap, and it no longer resembles the original RFC cap.

The RCAF stopped issuing the wedge in the late 1950's, and began issuing its airmen with a rakish, officer-style "flat hat", instead. Afterwards, airmen who wished to wear the wedge had to buy one, though wedges remained part of the uniform of the Royal Canadian Air Cadets until Unification. Shortly after, the air cadets switched to CF green uniforms and a soft, American-style wedge cap.

Ironically Unification in 1968, which had brought the end of the RCAF as a legal entity, revived the wear of the traditional wedge among airmen. The creation of the "Canadian Armed Forces" in 1968 brought forest-green uniforms to all soldiers, sailors and airmen. The CF "working" cap was to have been a green beret. However, airmen and airwomen, conscious of a distinct loss of air force identity, voiced a preference for a wedge cap (albeit made of "CF green" fabric). The powers-that-be authorized the green wedge for wear as an "optional item" (that is, you could wear it, but you had to buy it yourself). As well, for the first time, women wore the wedge; up to then, the old RCAF wedge cap had been exclusively male headgear. Airwomen had worn a variety of other caps, all specifically designed for females.

In 1988, the CF returned to distinctive environmental uniforms reflecting one's service identity; uniforms and wedge caps in "air force-blue" reappeared (as did an air force blue beret at a later date). It also returned to the Air Cadets. Very few other nations issue the wedge to their services (though it lives on in certain British units), so it seems the blue wedge will remain the distinctive dress headgear for Canadian airmen and airwomen. (See also **Pisspot**)

WEEKEND WARRIOR (universal military) — "Weekend Warrior" is a denigrating term for a reservist, a member of the armed forces who serves on other than a full-time, career basis. Generally speaking, the reservist serves on either a part-time basis (on top of civilian commitments), or if on a full-time basis, for a short, temporary period. The primary advantage of maintaining reserve forces is economic; though they cannot respond as readily as full-time regulars, they are far less expensive. Reservists often bring costly civilian skills to the air force and indirectly foster public awareness of military matters, simply by their very presence in the civilian community.

Canada's first air force reserve units were formed in the early 1930's, part of the RCAF's expansion in the face of the impending world war. Indeed the first RCAF squadron to go overseas to war in 1939 was a mobilized reserve squadron. (The second, a regular squadron, was only sent after it had absorbed the personnel from a co-located reserve squadron and the third was also a reserve squadron.) After the Second World War the RCAF planned a large reserve and a small regular force, but the advent of the Cold War put an end to this notion. Still, the RCAF Auxiliary of the 1950's was a respectable force which peaked at ten fighter squadrons and two light bomber squadrons, plus support units. Its strength was about 5500. As well, the RCN had a Naval Air Reserve of five squadrons, and naval air reservists occasionally deployed for carrier qualification to HMCS Magnificent.

In 1960, defence cutbacks saw the reserve slashed. From its peak strength of twelve squadrons, the RCAF Auxiliary was reduced to six. Its 5000 personnel were cut by 90%, and the Naval Air Reserve was disbanded outright. The rationale for this cut was the belief that Canada's next war would be nuclear, and that therefore there would be no time for reserve mobilization. (Ironically, Canada cut its reserves just as the United States began to beef up its own neglected air reserves reasoning that conventional conflicts, not nuclear, would be more likely. Time proved the American strategy correct.) Only in the mid 1970's was renewed Canadian attention paid to the air reserve, and the first steps were taken towards integrating the reserve with the regular air force. Today the CF has adopted the Total Force policy that integrates air reservists into all air force operations, though the biggest obstacle in implementing Total Force has been an antiquated system of regulations and policies governing reservists. Today air reservists fly and maintain the full range of CF aircraft, including the CC-130 Hercules, the Challenger and the Griffon helicopter. Air Reservists serve in virtually all air force occupations. (See also **Guard(2)**)

Those weekend warriors will fly Herks over my dead body!
Anything you say, General...

WEENIE (CF current; originally American) — A "weenie" is the mildly derogatory term for a person belonging to some particular group. It is usually combined with an adjectival prefix, as in "fighter weenies" or "armament weenies", etc. A "wing weenie" is a person from headquarters. In its usage, "weenie" is akin to the words: "type", or "basher", or "job", or "puke." The term may have its origins in the USAF. (See **Basher, Job, Puke, Type**) [Ref: Partridge (8th)]

How can you associate with those training command weenies? They have
absolutely no sense of humour!

WEEPERS (RCN and CF Maritime Command) — "Weepers" is to the navy and its air arm, what "TGIF" is to the air force and army. "Weepers" is a Friday night "beer call" at the Wardroom (the officer's mess in Her Majesty's Canadian Ships and at naval shore establishments). All off-watch mess members are encouraged to attend. The term weepers refers to its celebrated purpose: it is a time when everyone can "weep in their beer" over that week's disasters and unwind for the weekend ahead. Typically, drinks are sold at cut-rate prices, a light meal is served, there is good company, and the mess closes late. In some naval units, including the aircraft carrier HMCS Bonaventure, the term "POITS" was preferred to "weepers". (POITS is the acronym for *Piss On It, Tomorrow's Saturday!*) (See **TGIF**)

Are you going to Weepers at the dockyard? Its steak night tonight!

WEM (pronounced "wemm") (RAF circa 1935) — "WEM" was the longstanding RAF and RCAF abbreviation and acronym for "Wireless & Electrical Mechanic". [Ref: Partridge (8th)]

This antenna is damaged; you'd better tell the WEM.

WET — In the air force, the word "wet" has several possible meanings.

(1)   **Wet** (in aviation) In aviation, the word "wet" often alludes to the presence of aircraft fuel. An airlift of fuel is a "wet airlift" whereas an airlift of other cargo is a "dry airlift". Similarly, an aircraft with empty fuel tanks might weigh 8000 pounds; this is the "Dry Weight". If the aircraft is filled with fuel to

capacity (say, for argument's sake, fuel weighing 2000 pounds), the same aircraft will weigh 10,000 pounds "wet".

(2)   **Wet** (in the mess) (universal; British Commonwealth forces) "Wet" is also an allusion to alcoholic beverages, as in *I'm going to the Mess for a Wet. Coming along?*

Thus a military canteen which serves alcohol is a "Wet Canteen". The word "wet" appears in many other terms and phrases. "To have a wet" is to have a drink. To "wet your prop" is to drink a toast to your promotion to Leading Aircraftman (whose rank badge was a single-bladed propeller, or "prop"); likewise toasting one's promotion to Corporal or Sergeant was to "wet your stripes", etc. [Ref: Partridge (8th)]

WETP (pronounced "wet pee") (RCAF; WWII) — "WETP" was the acronym for "War Emergency Training Program". This was an air force-sponsored academic upgrading program that prepared prospective RCAF recruits for later air force technical training. During the depression that preceded the Second World War, many young men were unable to obtain an adequate education, a vital prerequisite to success in aviation. However, the short but intense "wet pee" system filled the gap. WETP candidates were sworn into the RCAF but often wore civilian clothes while training; their status was indicated by an official badge worn on the lapel. [Ref: Collins; Conrad; Hampson]

After I finish WETP, I'm putting in for Aircrew training.

WHALEBACK (RAF; WWII) — "Whaleback" was the nickname for a class of fast crash rescue boats in Royal Air Force service. The nickname was coined due to the "hump-backed" appearance of the boat when compared to other small war vessels. Both the RAF and RCAF maintained an extensive fleet of marine craft, ranging from fast crash-rescue boats (resembling Motor Torpedo Boats) to slow tenders for seaplane maintenance or refuelling.

I was lucky! I baled out and was in the water for only six hours before the Whaleback found me.

What-A-Pity

WHAT-A-PITY (RCAF; 1930's) — "What-a-pity" was the rueful nickname for the "Wapiti", a light biplane bomber built in the late 1920's by Westland. The Wapiti had been developed from the DH 9A (See also **Ninack**), a two-place biplane bomber of the First World War. However, the Second World War was looming by the time the RCAF acquired its Wapitis in 1936. The RAF had long since retired the Wapiti as a combat aircraft, except for a few serving on the fringes of the empire. Other nations were developing modern attack aircraft; the Americans were developing the B-17 Flying Fortress, the RAF was introducing the Wellington into squadron service, and the Luftwaffe was preparing to counter them with the Messerschmitt 109. Meanwhile, RCAF aircrew trained in bombing in an RAF surplus, two-place, biplane bomber. The nickname What-a-pity fairly described the attitude of Canadian airmen towards the Wapiti. [Ref: Milberry]

WHAT'S THE DRILL?; WHAT'S THE FORM?; WHAT'S THE SCORE? (RAF, RCAF, CF: since 1930's) — When an airman wanted to know what was happening, or what the normal procedure was, the questions "What' the drill?", or "What's the form?" or "What's the score?" were asked. [Ref: Partridge (8th)]

WHEELBARROW, TO (aviation; general) — To "wheelbarrow" a tricycle-gear airplane is to land it in a decidedly non-recommended manner. Tricycle gear airplanes have two main wheels and a nose wheel. To "wheelbarrow" such an aircraft is to land it, but to inadvertently set the nosewheel down onto the runway first, rather like a man pushing a wheelbarrow! As a landing technique, it is not recommended. Placing all the aircraft's weight on the nosewheel renders the aircraft difficult to control on the runway and places undue strain on the nose landing gear. Ideally, in landing a tricycle gear airplane one sets the airplane onto the earth so that the mainwheels touch first, after which the nose wheel touches the runway. (See also **Squeaker, Tricycle**)

WHEELER (aviation general) — A "wheeler" is a type of landing unique to "tail-dragger" aircraft, that is, aircraft with conventional undercarriage. Ideally, taildragger aircraft land such that all three wheels, the two mainwheels and the tailwheel, touch the runway simultaneously. This is the so-called "three-point" landing. However, a "three-pointer" is not always possible, especially in heavy or gusting winds, so in such conditions the "wheeler" is preferred. The aircraft is flown down to the runway at slightly higher than usual speed. However, rather than cutting engine power just above the runway, the aircraft is literally "flown onto" the runway with power on and is set down on the two main wheels. Only then does the pilot completely reduce the power so that the airplane slows, the tail settles and the tailwheel touches down.

WHEELS IN THE WELL (aviation general) — "Wheels in the well" is that time in an aircraft's flight when the wheels are retracted, and the journey proper begins. Specifically, it is just after takeoff when the aircraft's undercarriage (ie., the "wheels") are retracted into their wells inside the wings or fuselage.

We'll have wheels in the well at 0545!

WHEN KRO'S WERE CARVED IN STONE; WHEN PONTIUS WAS A PILOT (AND NERO WAS HIS NAVIGATOR) (RAF, some RCAF; since 1920's) — To say *when KRO's were carved in stone* or *when Pontius was a pilot* is to really say: *a very, very long time ago.*

KRO's were "King's Regulations and Orders" the system of rules that governed the air force. (They are "KRO's" when a King is on the throne; they have been Queen's Regulations and Orders since Elizabeth II was crowned. Its been several millennia since they were issued in stone tablets.) "When Pontius was a pilot..." is a punning reference to the Pontius Pilate of Biblical notoriety. [Ref: Partridge (8th)]

How long have you been in the air force, Flight?
I joined when KRO's were carved in stone...
...huh?
I joined a long time ago, lad, when Pontius was a pilot...

WHEN THE BALLOON GOES UP (Military, general; since at least WWI) — The time that fighting starts is often referred to as "when the balloon goes up". This interesting phrase seems to come from the trench warfare of 1914-1918. First World War battles generally began with a massive artillery barrage, sometimes lasting days and weeks. Both sides in this war used gas-filled balloons as artillery observation posts. These balloons were tethered to the ground behind one's own lines and were raised several thousands of feet, with a trained artillery observer in the basket; the observer watched the fall of the shells through field glasses and reported this to the gunners, far behind the lines, through a telephone cable. Consequently, the ascent of an observation balloon was often the first visual indication that an offensive was to begin. The barrage and the battle begins "when the balloon goes up." Even though observation balloons fell out of use after the First World War, this term has remained current military usage for the balance of the 20th century. No doubt the use of barrage balloons during the Second World War fostered use of the phrase. [Ref: Partridge (8th)]

Let's get the squadron ready, in case the balloon goes up this month...

WHIP UP A SMART ONE, TO (RAF, RCAF; CF) — To "whip up a smart one" is to execute a proper, crisp air force salute, as in: *Here comes the Station Commander! Be sure to whip up a smart one for him!* [Ref: Partridge (8th)]

WHIRLY BIRD (aviation; general) — "Whirly Bird" is post-Second World War rhyming slang for a helicopter, from the fact that its blades whirl overhead.

WHISPERING DEATH   see **Beau**

WHITE BULLET (RCAF, CF; early 1960's to 1980's) — "White Bullet" was the occasional nickname for the MD-1 "Genie" rocket intended for use on Canadian CF-101 Voodoo interceptors. This air-to-air rocket was armed with a small nuclear weapon capable of destroying inbound bombers striking at North American cities, packing their own nuclear weapons. The Genie rockets and their warheads belonged to the United States but were assigned to Canadian CF-101 Voodoo interceptor squadrons allocated to the air defence of North America. When CF air squadrons re-equipped with the CF-18 Hornet, the "White Bullet" ceased operational life in Canada and Canadian nuclear capability in air defence ended. The nickname comes from the colour of the rocket. (See also **Nuke, One-O-One; One-O-Wonder**) [Ref: Sutherland]

See that compound with all the guards and the fence around it? That's where they store the white bullets.

WHITE HOUSE, THE (RCAF, CF; since at least the 1950's) — The world knows the "White House" as the official residence of the President of the United States. However, in the RCAF and the Canadian Forces the "White House" was also the nickname for the home of the Canadian Forces Photo Unit, at Rockliffe, in Ottawa. Closed in 1995, the building was the central facility for military photography in Canada, and took its name from the structure's colour.

WHITE KNUCKLE AIRLINES (RCAF, CF; current since at least the 1960's) — "White Knuckle Airlines" is one of several nicknames given to Canada's military air transport units. The term suggests that, in terms of passenger comfort, flying as a passenger of Air Transport Command (later, Air Transport Group) doesn't compare with flying as a passenger on commercial airlines. The nickname suggests that military passengers must become used to gripping their seat so tightly from apprehension, that their knuckles turn white! (See also **Pri-5; Grey Funnel Airlines; Service Air; Nervous Air**)

WHITE OUT (aviation; general) — "White Out" is a dangerous atmospheric condition that can occur in winter. In a white out, severe blowing snow, snow on the ground, and overcast conditions combine to obscure the horizon and obliterate visual references to the earth. Pilots flying in a white out describe it as like "flying inside a ping-pong ball". White Out is a very dangerous condition, where landings or takeoffs are undertaken only in the last extreme.

WHITE TICKET   See **Green Ticket**

WID (RCAF; WWII) — A "Wid" is a member of the RCAF Women's Division. The term derives from the attempt to actually pronounce the letters "W.D." (for Women's Division), the more common nickname for Canadian airwomen. (See **W.D.**) [Ref: Partridge (8th)]

WIDGET   See **Gremlin**

WIDOW-MAKER (popular; since the 1960's) — "Widow-Maker" was a dark nickname coined by the press for the Lockheed F-104 Starfighter, flown in Canada under the designation CF-104. The nickname appears to have been coined after the West German Luftwaffe lost several hundred of their own F-104G Starfighters within a very short period during the 1960's! No public consensus has been reached about why the Luftwaffe lost this extraordinary number of aircraft within such a short period. However, it has been suggested that a combination of factors, including operational doctrine, low pilot experience levels, and the inherent dangers of low-level strike missions, all played their part. In any event, the press was quick to condemn the Starfighter as a killer of pilots and a maker of widows.

The epithet "Widow Maker" was generally regarded by Canadian airmen as unfair to the aircraft and the term was not part of their vocabulary. The Starfighter was a demanding aircraft to fly but it was also regarded as an "honest" aircraft, that is, its characteristics were known and predictable. If the pilot flew the aircraft within its performance envelope, it performed like a thoroughbred.

WIMPEY (RAF, RCAF; WWII) — "Wimpey" was the affectionate nickname for the Vickers "Wellington", a twin-engined RAF medium bomber designed by the superb design engineer Barnes Wallace. The nickname "Wimpey" is taken from the popular "Popeye" cartoons by Max Fleischman. "Wimpey" is Popeye's rotund and hamburger-addicted friend, whose full name is "J. Wellington Wimpey".

The Wimpey went into production in late 1937 and became the mainstay of Bomber Command for the first two years of the Second World War. The striking characteristic of the Wellington was its unique "geodetic" construction; rather than using conventional bulkheads, spars, longerons and stringers, the fuselage and wings were formed in a metal "basket weave" type of construction. This enabled the Wimpey to absorb a tremendous amount of damage and still fly. It could carry a three-ton bombload at about 180 mph. However, its relatively small capacity caused larger, faster bombers such as the Lancaster and the Halifax to supersede the Wellington in Bomber Command. However, the Wimpey remained in service in Coastal Command and as an operational trainer, and the RAF kept it in service until the early 1950's. Twelve RCAF bomber squadrons were equipped with the "Wimpey" at one time or other. [Ref: Partridge (8th)]

The Wimpey could take a lot of punishment because of its "basket-weave" construction.

WINGCO (RAF, RCAF; since 1920's) — The "Wingco" is the unofficial acronym for an RAF or RCAF officer of the rank of Wing Commander, equivalent to a Lieutenant Colonel or a navy Commander. [Ref: Partridge (8th)]

Harry, tell Ron that the Wingco wants to see him!

WINGLESS WONDER (RAF, RCAF; 1940's 1950's) — A "wingless wonder" is a non-aircrew air force officer. (See also **Kiwi; Kiwi Club, Penguin(2)**) [Ref: Partridge (8th)]

WINGMAN (military aviation; since WWII) — The basic element in fighter combat is a pair of aircraft, which manoeuvre and fly in cooperation with one another. The pair are named the "Lead" and the "Wingman". The Lead is responsible for hunting the enemy and is usually the more experienced or proficient combat pilot. The Wingman helps the Lead in the hunt, but more importantly, the Wingman keeps a lookout behind, leaving the Lead free to stalk the enemy.

WINGS (Universal; Military Aviation) — The badges worn to indicate the wearer's aircrew specialty have been known as "wings" since their inception, because they invariably incorporate a set of stylized bird's wings in the design.

The design of Canadian aircrew "wings" has changed over the years, but the British influence is obvious. Canadian airmen of the First World War served in British flying organizations, and as such, wore wings of either the Royal Flying Corps (RFC) or the Royal Naval Air Service (RNAS). The woven silk pilot's and observers wings of the Royal Flying Corps tended to serve as a model for all those aircrew wings yet to come. The short-lived Canadian Air Force (1920 to 1924), which issued unique metal aircrew wings, was an exception to the Canadian tendency to adapt British badges. But in 1924 the CAF became the RCAF, and adopted wholesale RAF-pattern uniforms and wings. Later, the RCN and Canadian Army adapted British Fleet Air Arm, and British Army flying badges, respectively.

 Canadian Army Pilot's
Wings

RCN Pilot's Wings

 Canadian Forces
Pilot's Wings

RFC Pilot's Wings

 CAF Pilot's Wings
ca 1921

RCAF Pilot's Wings

RCN
Observer's
Wings

CAF Observer's Wing
ca 1921

RFC/RAF/RCAF
Observer's Wing
(a.k.a. The Flying
Arsehole)

Flight
Surgeon

RCAF Flight
Engineer's Wing
ca 1943

RCAF Airman's
Flying Badge, the
precursor to many
other types of
'Flight Crew' Wings

Loadmaster
(1974 to 1995)

Navigator's Wing

The RFC pilot's badge, which served as the model for nearly all pilot's wings to follow, was embroidered in silver-white silk and depicted two wings in the "downstroke". Between each wing was a wreath, containing the initials "RFC", beneath a crown. (The wings were said to depict those of a Swift, a bird known for its speed.) This badge was worn over the left breast pocket, and above any medal ribbons. The RAF, born in 1918 out of a marriage of the RFC and the RNAS, copied the RFC wing, only substituting the letters "RAF" for "RFC". In Canada, the letters "RCAF" were inserted between the wings.

First World War naval pilots originally wore a small brass "eagle" (similar to that still seen on the air force badge) on the lower left sleeve of their tunic, over the rank lace. However after the First World War new naval pilot's wings were introduced. They were similar in appearance to RAF and RCAF wings, though woven in gold wire and bearing a naval anchor in the centre. (As well, naval wings were said to be modelled on those of the Albatross, rather than the Swift.) Unlike RFC, RAF, and RCAF wings (and unlike United States Navy wings), Royal Navy and RCN pilot's wings were not worn over the uniform's breast pockets; rather they were worn on the lower left sleeve of the tunic, above the rank braid.

The British Army created aviation units during the Second World War, and the Canadian Army followed suit. Army pilot wings differed yet again from the air force and navy wings. Army pilot's wings were embroidered in light blue silk, and were upswept at a slightly different angle. They bore a crown and lion at the centre and were worn by Canadian Army pilots until Unification in 1968.

Up to 1941, the only non-pilot aircrew were the Observers - aircrew jacks-of-all trades who performed the duties of gunner, navigator, wireless telegraph operator, and intelligence analyst! (Before the Second World War, "air gunner" was not a permanent aircrew trade. They were usually drawn on a casual basis from ground crew volunteers.) The original RFC Observer's wing was used by RAF and RCAF observers until 1941. The RFC Observer wore a badge that depicted a woven letter "O" supported by a single, upswept wing. The use of the "O" led to its highly unflattering nickname: the "Flying Arsehole". Ultimately, it became impractical to train one person for all the tasks performed by the Observer. So, in early 1942, "specialist" aircrew categories were created, each entitled to wear a specialist flying wing patterned on that of the Observer. Thus, the Navigator's single wing bore the letter "N"; a Bomb-Aimer's wing, a "B", and a Gunner's wing bore the initials "AG", or "WAG" (for "air gunner" or "wireless air gunner", respectively).

Following the Second World War the RCAF retired the "single wing" for specialist aircrew, patterned on the original RFC Observer's wing. All aircrew - pilots and non-pilots alike - would now wear a broad wing like a pilot. The wings of non-pilots would be distinguished from pilot's wings by a distinctive insignia in the centre. While pilot's wings bore the letters "RCAF", Navigator's wings bore a globe, Flight Engineer's wings showed a three-bladed propeller, etc.

After the Second World War, the RCN maintained the system of having three aircrew types, Pilots, Observers and Observers Mates. Observer's wings depicted the letter "O" between two smaller wings in the upstroke (as distinct from the pilot's wings that depicted two large wings in the downstroke). The Observers Mates wings were the same as the Observers except it had an anchor inside the "O". Like Army wings, naval wings were worn until Unification in 1968.

In the 1960's, a new category of RCAF aviator evolved which continues in the CF of today: Flight Crew. Flight Crew were ground personnel called upon to perform their duties while flying (as opposed to Aircrew, whose job could only be done while airborne). Flight Crew included technicians who flew as "Technical Crewmen" (See **Flight Magician**), soldiers who flew as "Tactical Helicopter Observers", or Stewards who flew as "Flight Stewards". Flight Crew wear a flying badge with two upswept wings, somewhat smaller than aircrew wings, reminiscent of navy observer's Wings.

Today, all Canadian Forces wings are made of gold embroidered thread. The RCAF system has prevailed in that aircrew badges depict two broad wings in the "downstroke", while flight crew badges have two smaller wings in the "upstroke". The wearer's specialty is identified by the insignia between the wings.

WINKLING; WINKLE OUT, TO (RAF, RCAF; WWII) — "Winkling out" was Second World War slang for the use of Allied fighter-bombers to destroy small enemy strongpoints that slowed the Allied armies advancing through France and the Low Countries, after D-Day. The term suggests the difficulty of finding and hitting a well-camouflaged and well dug-in target. A "winkle" is a type of clam and originally, "winkling" referred to finding and digging out clams, hidden beneath the sand of a beach. (See also **Cab Rank**) [Ref: Partridge (8th)]

The battalion advance would have lost its momentum if the Typhoons hadn't winkled out that bunker.

WIRELESS (British) — "Wireless" is what most Britons called a radio until well into the 1950's (ie., a "wireless telephone" or "W/T"). The term is now obsolete, and never really entered Canadian usage but, because the RCAF adopted many RAF terms and policies, Canadian airmen and airwomen of the Second World War became "Wireless Operators" rather than "Radio Operators". The term "wireless" yielded to "radio-telephone" (more commonly abbreviated to "R/T"), and ultimately to "Radio". [Ref: Harvey]

WIRING DIAGRAM (CF; current) — A "wiring diagram" is an organization chart, a chart that illustrates in graphic form, the various positions in an organization, with their reporting relationships. In large organizations - like the air force - these become sufficiently complex as to resemble complicated electronic wiring diagrams. (See also **Empire**)

Now, where will the new Major be on this wiring diagram?

WIZARD (RAF, 1930's and 40's) — "Wizard" was an RAF phrase that meant "exceptional", "wonderful", or "splendid". Along with "prang", "wizard" is the perhaps the penultimate RAF slang word of the Second World War. It appears to have been used as far back to the 1929-30 Schneider Cup races, where the Supermarine S.6, the antecedent of the famous Spitfire, was first introduced to the public. [Ref: Partridge (8th)]

My first trip in a Spitfire was wizard!

WONG-WONG (RFC, RNAS, RAF; WWI) — The German "Gotha" bomber, an early strategic bomber of the First World War, was occasionally known by the Allies as the "Wong-Wong". The Gotha was a twin-engine, multi-crew biplane bomber used by the Imperial German Air Service. It saw service in the Western Front, and was used (along with the early zeppelins) to bomb England at night.

The origin of the nickname Wong-Wong is unknown, though perhaps it derives from the sound its unsynchronized engines and propeller made. An irritating, rhythmic vibrating sound resonates through the air when the propeller RPM is not synchronized between the engines on a multi-engine aircraft. Propeller synchronization was not yet developed in the First World War, and the Gotha produced this undulating noise. [Ref: Partridge (8th)]

WOODEN WONDER   See **Mossie**

WOOLWORTH CARRIER (Commonwealth Forces; WWII) — "Woolworth Carrier" was the nickname for a class of ship variously described as an "Escort Carrier" or a "Merchant Aircraft Carrier", a small aircraft carrier used primarily for convoy escort during the Second World War. The U-boat was the most serious threat to allied convoys. However, U-Boats could only travel quickly while surfaced, so aircraft patrols were very useful in keeping them submerged. It was very difficult for a slow-moving submerged submarine to stalk a convoy. Unfortunately, there weren't enough large aircraft carriers to go around, so the idea of the small escort carrier was born. These came to be known as Woolworth Carriers. (In the U.S. Navy they were often called "Jeep Carriers".)

Woolworth Carriers were usually American Lend-Lease vessels consigned to the British and were constructed from the hull of a merchant vessel; the ship's superstructure was removed to fit a flight deck and hangar deck. Most Woolworth Carriers were commissioned as warships, though some remained in the merchant marine and were crewed by merchant sailors. The air elements always belonged to the Fleet Air Arm.

Woolworth Carrier

They displaced between 11,000 and 15,000 tons, and carried about 18 fighter and patrol aircraft. Typically, Woolworth Carriers carried Grumman "Martlet" fighters (more commonly known as the "Wildcat") and Fairey "Swordfish" torpedo-bombers. (See also **Stringbag; Pusser Spitfire**)

The term Woolworth Carrier would seem to be a reference to the famous chain of department stores; just as Woolworths was a "discount store", so too was the Escort Carrier a "discount aircraft carrier"!

The RCN had no Woolworth carriers itself, though two Royal Navy escort carriers, HMS Puncher and HMS Nabob, were manned either totally, or in part, by Canadian sailors. HMS Puncher earned the unenviable nickname of the "Floating Coffin." HMS Nabob also had its problems, as it had a combined crew of British, Canadian and New Zealand sailors, all of whom were paid according to different pay scales. This led to resentment among the less well-paid Britons, though the Canadians and New Zealanders probably felt the British got their own back, because they all ate Royal Navy rations. (See also **Hurricat**) [Refs: Partridge (8th); Snowie]

> *Remember, taking off from a Woolworth Carrier is different from a fleet-sized carrier; they're smaller, so the roll and pitch is worse.*

WORKS AND BRICKS (some RCAF, originally RAF; since 1920's) — "Works and Bricks" was slang for the Air Ministry's Department of Works and Buildings, which was responsible for air base construction and maintenance. Though it was an RAF term, it lived on in the RCAF for a time. [Refs: Partridge(8th); Sargent]

WOP; WOP/AG (ie., "wopp"; "wopp-eh-jee") (RAF, RCAF; WWII) — WOP and WOP/AG (pronounced "wopp" and "wopp-eh-jee", respectively) were Second World War slang for "Wireless Operator" and for "Wireless Operator/Air Gunner". A Wireless Operator would today be termed a "Radio Operator", and was the aircraft crewmember responsible for airborne communications, an important task. The radios of the 1940's were temperamental, bulky, and based on tube technology. Communications were limited to the High Frequency range and much long-range communication was done with Morse code telegraphy. Wireless Operators were cross-trained as Air Gunners, to help in defending the aircraft from hostile fighters. These became known as the "Wireless Operator/Air Gunner", or "WOP/AG" (See also **Spider**) [Refs: Harvey; Partridge (8th)]

> *I'd like to be a wop a.g.*
> *I'd fly all over Germanee*
> *And blow the Huns to buggeree*
> *It's foolish but its fun!*

WRITE-OFF; TO WRITE OFF (General Usage since WWI) — In accounting, to "write-off" an inventory item is to reduce its book value to zero. In otherwords, when an item is deemed worthless it is "written off". So, when a pilot writes off an aircraft, the pilot has destroyed it, and that aircraft is becomes "a write off". The term is occasionally applied to people who are less than useful, as in *Ralph is a good pilot, but as an officer he's a write-off.* [Refs: Harvey; Voss]

 **X** RAY

X ORGANIZATION (Commonwealth POW's; WWII) — "X Organization" was code for the Allied prisoner's escape committee and its peripheral organizations, at a German POW camp during the Second World War. (See also **Kriegie**)

Alf is the head of the X Organization at this camp.

ANKEE

YANK (Universal, Commonwealth) — A "Yank" is an American (from "Yankee", a New Englander, though during the American civil war the term referred to people of the northern states). Yanks has been British slang since before the American Revolution and remains current slang today in the CF. However, one should use the term advisedly in referring to an American from south of the Mason-Dixon Line. [Ref: Partridge (8th)]

Those Yanks are sure noisy!

YEHUDI　　　See **Gremlin**

YELLOW NOSES; YELLOW-NOSE BASTARDS; YELLOW-NOSE COUNTRY (Allied Air forces; WWII) — "Yellow-Noses" and "Yellow-Nosed Bastards" were Luftwaffe fighter aircraft of the Second World War. The term derived from the fact that Axis air forces in Europe often used yellow as an identifying colour on the noses and wingtips of their fighter aircraft. Therefore, "Yellow-Nose Country" is enemy territory.

Keep your eyes open! We're in Yellow-Nose Country now!

YELLOW PERIL (RCAF; 1940 to 1960's) — "Yellow Peril" was the nickname for the North American "Harvard", the mainstay of the RCAF flying training program for over two decades. The term is not a disparaging comment about the Harvard, rather it is a comment on the perils it offered trainees. (The term "Yellow Peril" was borrowed from an old jingoistic catch-phrase warning of expansion of Asian races into Europe in the 1890's.) It was applied to most training aircraft because of the bright yellow paint on

Yellow Peril

"My present position is overhead Pool, Saskatchewan."

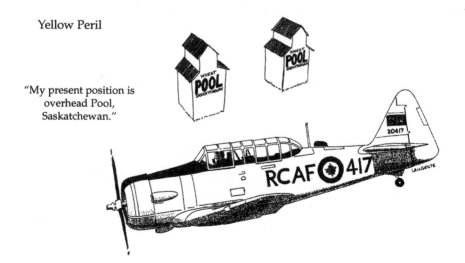

training aircraft. The Harvard, being the most common such aircraft, earned this sobriquet. Harvards were also flown by the Royal Canadian Navy, which likewise used a yellow paint scheme.

One of the most reliable training aircraft ever built, the Harvard was a two-place, single-engine propellor-driven aircraft. It bridged the gap between the gentle "initial" trainers of the day ("Tiger Moth" biplanes, and later, the De Havilland Canada "Chipmunk") and the more ferocious aircraft that the graduate military pilot could fly. The Yellow Peril was a common sight in the skies over the prairie provinces (where the RCAF preferred to conduct its flying training) from the Second World War to the mid-1960's. Eventually, the Harvard was retired in favour of the Canadair "Tutor" jet trainer. (See also **Tiger, Tute**) [Refs: Fletcher and MacPhail; Partridge (8th)]

Is that Joe's Yellow Peril on final approach?

YES SIR! YES SIR! THREE BAGS FULL, SIR! — "Yes Sir! Yes Sir! Three Bags Full, Sir!" is the mocking allusion to the act (or the pretence) of ready submission to authority. It derives from the nursery rhyme: *Baa, baa black sheep, have you any wool? Yes sir, Yes sir, three bags full!* [Ref: Partridge (8th)]

Q: *So what did you say to Sergeant Folkes?*
A: *Yes Sir! Yes Sir! Three Bags Full, Sir! What else could I say?!*

YING-YANG   See **Up the Ying Yang**

YUKE (RCAF, CF; 1960's) — "Yuke" is shorthand for the "Yukon", a military passenger and cargo aircraft produced by Canadair of Montreal. The "Yuke" developed from a 1957 RCAF request that Canadair develop a transport variant of the CL-28 Argus, then being developed as an anti-submarine patrol bomber. The Yukon, like the Argus, was a Canadian improvement and adaptation of the Bristol Britannia airliner. The Yukon had four turbo-prop engines and was pressurized. It became a common sight in the RCAF of the 1950's and 1960's, replacing the North Star transports in the strategic airlift role. The Yukon was itself replaced by the Boeing 707 in 1970. (See also **Argi; Boeing**)

We'll be taking a Yuke to Germany.

ULU

ZAP; ZAPPER; TO ZAP (CF; current, since at least early 1980's) — A "zap" or a "zapper" is a small sticker which bears the badge, motto or logo of a military unit, that is specifically left behind as a "calling card". The practice of "zapping" has become so widespread that the Canadian War Museum has even started collecting Canadian Forces unit "zappers".

Opinions vary about the social propriety of "zapping". To some, zapping is a challenging sport that expresses unit pride; the more inaccessible or outrageous the placement of the zap, the greater the accomplishment. Some flying units do not regard themselves as being "victims" of zappers and seem to "collect" zappers on their aircraft. Indeed, NATO fighter aircraft of the 1970's and 1980's in Europe became galleries for zappers. However, in more straight-laced organizations, finding a zap on an airplane is about as popular as finding a fly in one's soup. It is always the height of bad taste to zap things that would be defaced thereby, such as art or monuments or formal insignia. Still, aircraft are usually regarded as fair game, provided the zapper is discreet and no vents, antennae, or other components are interfered with.

Perhaps the most outrageous example of a zap occurred in the 1970's, when a US Navy "Orion" aircraft visited CFB Comox and its vertical stabilizer received - overnight, courtesy the Comox ground crew - a large Canadian Forces roundel. Reportedly, the American crew resisted for as long as possible the efforts of their superiors to have the offending roundel removed; the aircraft made several return visits over subsequent months, and still bore the Canadian badge!

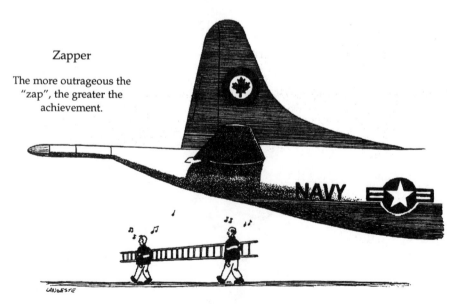

Zapper

The more outrageous the "zap", the greater the achievement.

Those Yanks have no sense of humour when it comes to zapping one of their airplanes!

ZEP (general usage; WWI) — "Zep" is short for "Zeppelin", the famous class of rigid, gas-filled airships named for their designer and builder, Count Otto von Zeppelin. Unlike its later cousin the "blimp", a Zeppelin had a metal superstructure covered in fabric that created its distinctive "sausage" shape. Within this metal superstructure were many large fabric gas bags, filled with lighter-than-air gas. Germany, unable to obtain safer helium gas, was forced to rely on highly flammable hydrogen for the Zeppelin's "gasbag". This made them very vulnerable to fire.

The Imperial German Air Service pioneered the use of rigid airships during the First World War. (The term "Zeppelin" was never current in the German language; in German it was the "Luftschiff".) "Zeps" were used in coastal patrol and more significantly, in night bombing. The first raid on British civilian targets occurred on the 19th of January, 1915 and continuing Zeppelin raids forced the RFC to withdraw fighter squadrons from France to protect England.

Clumsy and unweildy to fly accurately, Zeppelins were also difficult to destroy. A Zeppelin could easily outclimb a First World War fighter aircraft, simply by releasing ballast and letting the lighter-than-air hydrogen gas lift it. The service ceiling was as high as 16,000 feet. Furthermore, it was not enough to shoot at the Zeppelin; it had to be made to burn. However, once ignition occurred, total destruction was made certain by the flammable hydrogen within. The first zep ever destroyed (LZ37) was not, strictly speaking, "shot down". An RNAS Morane "Parasol" fighter flew above it and dropped a bomb on it! The last Zeppelin operations occurred in 1916. [Ref: Partridge (8th)]

Zeps are tough to shoot down, but when you get one, they really burn!

Zep

The Zepplin had an amazing rate of climb.

ZERO   See **Gremlin**

ZERO-ZERO (universal mil. aviation) — The words zero-zero have two connotations in military aviation.

(1)   First, **zero-zero** can be shorthand for thick fog, ie., zero visibility, and zero ceiling, as in: *the present weather conditions are zero-zero.*

Pilots of aircraft near an airport need information about current weather conditions. Aviators typically describe the "visibility" at an airport via a two-part message. The first part is the altitude of the cloud layer, in thousands of feet. The second part is the visibility on the ground, in miles. Thus, if the conditions are "3000 and 10", it means that the cloud layer is at 3000 feet above ground, and it is possible to see ten miles. In "zero-zero" conditions, on the other hand, no airplanes fly and even the birds walk.

(2)   The second connotation of the term **zero-zero** has to do with ejection seats, which are rated in terms of a two-digit code, as in: *The CF-104 has a zero-zero ejection seat.*

Not all ejection seats perform alike, some are extremely powerful and will catapult the occupant to safety in almost any flight condition. Others will only be effective if the aircraft exceeds certain minimum altitudes or airspeeds. Thus, they are "rated" in terms of two criteria: the minimum altitude above ground, and the minimum forward velocity, needed before the ejection seat will catapult the occupant to a height safe enough that the parachute has time to open.

For example, a "sixty-sixty" seat will only save the occupant if the aircraft exceeds sixty knots of airspeed, and exceeds sixty feet of altitude. An ejection seat described as "zero-zero" will catapult the occupant high enough to safely open the parachute, even when the aircraft has zero forward velocity, and is at zero altitude. In otherwords the crewmember can safely eject even while the aircraft is motionless on the ground!

ZIP; CF ZIP (CF, late 60's to early 70's) — "Zip" is a 1970's nickname for the CF-104 Starfighter, presumably for its high speed, as in: *My buddy is a Zip Driver in Cold Lake.* (See also **One-oh-Four, Widowmaker**) [Ref: Russell]

ZIPPERHEAD (CF; current) — A zipperhead is a soldier in the armoured corps. Apparently this term derives from a feature typical of an armoured corps soldier's physiognomy: scars on and about the head. The scars suggest zippers, apparently. Anyone inside a tank advancing rapidly across the countryside will have a job keeping their head from occasionally being knocked against the interior. So, they say you can tell an armoured corps soldier by the scars. Armoured corps soldiers are among those selected as "Tactical Observers". These soldiers fly as aircrew in tactical helicopter squadrons and use their knowledge of the land battle in aerial reconnaissance. (See also **LOH**)

The Tactical Observer I fly with is a zipperhead...

ZIZ, TO HAVE A (CF, though common in English-speaking air forces; since WWII) — To "have a ziz" is to have a nap or to fall asleep. Presumably the term comes from the cartoonists' practice of depicting a sleeping cartoon character by placing the letters "z-z-z" over the drawing of the sleeper. [Ref: Partridge (8th)]

I'm going to lie down and have a ziz...

ZOMBIE (Can; WWII) — "Zombie" was a derisive term for persons who were drafted into the Canadian Army late during the Second World War, but who never volunteered for overseas service. The usage is clearly borrowed from those Caribbean folk tales which spoke of dead men, made to walk and act as though they actually lived. The origins of the term are found in Canadian wartime politics.

Canada's armed forces relied on voluntary enrolment until late in 1944, and by then five Canadian divisions served in England and Europe - besides the home war establishment. However, in Northwest Europe the army suffered casualties at a rate faster than the voluntary recruiting system could reinforce it. Senior army commanders pressed Ottawa to impose compulsory service, the "draft", as all other combatant countries had done. However, Prime Minister Mackenzie King, mindful of the divisive effects that conscription had on national unity during the First World War, only partly acceded to this demand. Canadian men were finally subject to the draft (and only into the army), but, the government would still only commit volunteers to overseas combat service. The conscripts would stay home and protect Canada. In theory this would release Canada-based volunteers for active service, but in fact it did little to alleviate the desperate shortage of reinforcements. While 70,000 conscripted "zombies" remained at home and trained for a war that would never reach Canadian shores, army cooks and drivers in Europe were hastily diverted from the duties they were trained for, to become line infantrymen in brigades desperately short of troops. Unsurprisingly, the soldiers who served overseas, along with their comrades in the Navy and RCAF (which were all-volunteer services) tended to look upon zombies with great disdain. To distinguish volunteers from Zombies, the government issued the Canadian Volunteer Service Medal to all volunteers, who referred to the medal as the "Spam Medal". (See also **Spam Medal**)

On D-Day, several divisions of zombies marked time in Canada.

ZOOM (aviation, general) — Though more often used as a verbal "sound effect", the word "zoom" is also a legitimate aerodynamic term for a specific type of abrupt climb. A zoom (occasionally a "zoom climb") results solely from kinetic energy and an upward trajectory, rather than increased engine thrust. If the airplane is flying fast enough and the pilot pulls back on the controls, a climb results even if the engine is dead. A zoom climb cannot be sustained indefinitely because continued flight requires lift, produced by the wings and engine thrust. However, in an emergency, a "zoom" can gain the pilot a few feet of altitude, enough to bail out.

The aircraft's engine lost power, so the pilot zoomed and ejected.

ZOOMIE (CF current; mostly naval) — "Zoomie" is current naval slang for a member of the air force, probably because an aircraft "zooms". The term may be naval in origin, though perhaps it has other roots; in the Royal Australian Air Force of the Second World

War, the word "zoomer" referred to aircrew. [Refs: Elting; Partridge (8th)]

Welcome to HMCS Athabaskan; I'll take you to the Duty Zoomie.

ZULU ALERT (RCAF;1950's) — "Zulu Alert" was the 1950's RCAF code name for the highest degree of combat readiness. Interceptor aircraft on Zulu Alert were fuelled, armed, and ready to launch within minutes of the alarm sounding. (Zulu is the phonetic code word for the last letter of the alphabet: "Z". As such, it is often used to denote actions or situations that are in the last extreme.)

Throughout the 1950's the RCAF had Sabres on Zulu Alert, at bases in
France and Germany.

ZULU TIME (Universal military and aviation; current) — "Zulu Time" is the universal codeword for "Universal Coordinated Time", formerly known as "Greenwich Mean Time." Consequently, to ensure a common standard while coordinating activity across different time zones, Zulu Time is used. Thus, one speaks of the Time (Local) as opposed to the Time (Zulu), ie., 1800 versus "2300 hours Zulu".

When its 6:00 P.M. in Ottawa, its 2300 Zulu.

ZULU'D, TO BE — To be "zulu'd" is to be very, very inebriated. Zulu is the phonetic code word for "Z", the last letter of the alphabet, and is often used to denote extreme situations.

I'm afraid I got really zulu'd, last night.

ZWEI (Pronounced "zz-why") (RCAF, CF; 1960's) — "Zwei" is English-Canadian shorthand for *Zweibrucken*, the air base in Germany that was the home of Canada's No. 3 (Fighter) Wing from 1953 to 1969. 3 Wing flew the F-86 Sabre until 1960 when it was replaced by the CF-104 Starfighter. Zwei was closed in 1969 as part of the defence cuts of the Trudeau government, and was turned over to the United States Air Force.

If Baden is socked in, we'll have to land at Zwei.

PHONETIC ALPHABETS

A Phonetic Alphabet is a list of 26 codewords, each representing one letter of the alphabet. Phonetic alphabets are used in radio communications where there is a chance that one letter could be mistaken for another letter having a similar sound. For example, "B" can easily be mistaken for "D". Consequently each phonetic codeword is chosen for its distinctive sound. Many phonetic alphabets have been used over the years, though to 1945, Canadian forces used British codes. In 1957, the International Civil Aviation Organization alphabet was adopted.

	1914-1918	1939-1942	1942-1945	After 1957
A	Ack	Ack	Able	Alpha
B	Beer	Beer	Baker	Bravo
C	C	Charlie	Charlie	Charlie
D	Don	Don	Dog	Delta
E	E	Edward	Easy	Echo
F	F	Freddie	Fox	Foxtrot
G	G	George	George	Golf
H	H	Harry	How	Hotel
I	I	Ink	Item	India
J	J	Johnny	Jig	Juliet
K	K	King	King	Kilo
L	L	London	Love	Lima
M	Emma	Monkey	Mike	Mike
N	N	Nuts	Nun	November
O	O	Orange	Oboe	Oscar
P	Pip	Pip	Peter	Papa
Q	Q	Queen	Queen	Quebec
R	R	Robert	Roger	Romeo
S	Esses	Sugar	Sugar	Sierra
T	Toc	Toc	Tare	Tango
U	U	Uncle	Uncle	Uniform
V	Vic	Vic	Victor	Victor
W	W	William	William	Whiskey
X	X	X-Ray	X-Ray	X-Ray
Y	Y	Yorker	Yoke	Yankee
Z	Z	Zebra	Zebra	Zulu

FALCON CODES

The following Falcon Codes were reproduced from an unclassified Annex of a 1977 Operations Order produced by 405 Maritime Patrol Squadron at CFB Greenwood (courtesy Major Tom Sand), for use in maritime air and naval exercises at sea. The Annex also says:

1. **GENERAL**

Regrettably the Allied Naval Signal Book does not possess sufficient flexibility for Formation Commanders/Commanding Officers to address specific operational requirements; nor does it provide the means whereby pleasure or displeasure may be expressed. The Falcon Code that follows has been designed to fill the gap.

2. **AUTHORIZATION FOR USE**

The Squadron Commander or any Commanding Officer may transmit a single code number or multiple groups ... whenever the tactical situation dictates. Juniors may transmit to seniors with caution.

Code Number	Translation
Falcon 1:	You should at least try and give the impression that you know what you are doing.
Falcon 2:	If you think your next evolution is going to be equally disastrous please give me advance warning.
Falcon 3:	What you say is true but completely irrelevant.
Falcon 4:	You may not like the f—ing staff, but the staff likes f—ing you.
Falcon 5:	Report reason for foul up. (See also Falcon 6)
Falcon 6:	My excuse for the foul up is:
6a:	-lack of preparation
6b:	-Executive Officer's meeting
6c:	-fingertrouble
6d:	-was using the operations order for next exercise
6e:	-couldn't find target
6f:	-I can't read
6g:	-I've temporarily lost the bubble (translation: depth control in a submarine)
6h:	-the staff has turned in again
6i:	- (to be designated) ____

Falcon 7:	Your explanation:
7a:	-is unbelievable but I'll buy it.
7b:	-lacks a certain credibility
7c:	-is imaginative but not realistic

Falcon 8:   Please speak slowly and in English.

Falcon 9:   Let go of my ears, I know my job.

Falcon 10:   You are not going to believe my next command.

Falcon 11:   You're right, that last command was unbelievable.

Falcon 12:	If you think that was bad, wait until you see me:
12a:	-replenish at sea
12b:	-fire guns
12c:	-fire mortars
12d:	-fire missiles
12e:	-control aircraft
12f:	-launch chaff
12g:	-take charge
12h:	- (to be designated) _____

Falcon 13:   Move closer so that you may be identified.

Falcon 14:   Sailors may eventually rule the world, but don't count on a responsible job.

Falcon 15:   BUFF's (translation: Big Ugly Fat Fuckers)

Falcon 16:   GOYA (translation: get off your ass)

Falcon 17:   Swords and Medals on arrival if you please. (translation: wear your full dress uniform as in a Court-Martial)

Falcon 18:   See me on arrival; any dress will do.

Falcon 19:   Better never than late.

Falcon 20:   My intention was that you illuminate, not ram!

Falcon 21:   Give up now, try again later.

Falcon 22:   Happiness is a private ship.

Falcon 23:   You should go places; start immediately.

Falcon 24:   Why is it that you consistently push doors marked "pull".

Falcon 25:	Don't feel too proud of that last serial; you were being followed purely out of curiosity.
Falcon 26:	I know you believe you understood what you think I said, but I am not sure you realize that what you heard is not what I meant.
Falcon 27:	The resourcefulness of your reply astounds me.
Falcon 28:	The officer who drafted that reply deserves to be on my staff.
Falcon 29:	Strongly advise that you do not use braille on your next approach. (translation: don't touch my ship)
Falcon 30:	Why send a signal when you could have remained silent and have me suspect, rather than verify, that you are a boob?
Falcon 31:	The fact that I may be wrong has no bearing on the decision.
Falcon 32:	The final word that you have received should be treated as a firm maybe.
Falcon 33:	Things will remain much as they are, or they will change.
Falcon 34:	Pardon me, but I'm afraid you're making this evolution much simpler than it really is..
Falcon 35:	Regulations are a crutch for the weak, an excuse for the lazy, a benefit for the ignorant, a guide for the incompetent and are there to be broken by everybody else. You'd better stick to them.
Falcon 36:	Come, let us reason together before I lose mine.
Falcon 37:	Once upon a time there was a Sub-Lieutenant who was so dumb that even the other Sub- Lieutenants noticed.
Falcon 38:	Communications are the means whereby command is exercised. Speak to me, I need the exercise!
Falcon 39:	One more step to carefree electronic living!.
Falcon 40:	Mountain erected; see if you can find that missing molehill.
Falcon 41:	What you see is what you get.

Falcon 42:   You have established a precedent. Your PER (ie.,
                            Personnel Evaluation Report) has been suitably
                            downgraded.

Falcon 43:   If it feels good, do it! If it hurts, tough luck!

Falcon 44:   Your report/explanation has been received,with:
    44a: -Sympathy
    44b: -Incredulity
    44c: -Relief
    44d: -Satisfaction
    44e: -Amazement
    44f: -Admiration

Falcon 45:   Stay where you're to and I'll come where you're at.

Falcon 46:   Your last message is not understood, but don't bother to
                            explain.

Falcon 169:   Excuse me sir, but I think you have me confused with
                            someone who gives a damn.

BIBLIOGRAPHY

Alcorn and Souster	*From Hell to Breakfast*; Intruder Press, 39 Baby Point Road, Toronto, Ontario. 1980
Allen, H.R.	*Fighter Station Supreme*; Panther Books, Granada Publishing Ltd.; 8 Grafton Street, London W1X 3LA; 1985
Allison, Les	*Canadians in the Royal Air Force*; published by Les Allison; Roland, Manitoba, R0B 1T0, 1978
Beaver, Paul	*The British Aircraft Carrier* – (2nd Edition); Patrick Stephens Limited, Denington Estate, Wellingborough, Northants, NN8 2QD, England, 1982, 1984
Benet, William R.	*Benet's Reader's Encyclopedia* – (Third Edition); Harper & Row, Publishers Inc., 10 East 53rd Street, New York, NY 10022; 1948, 1955, 1965, 1987
Berrey and Van Den Bark	*The American Thesaurus of Slang* – Second Edition; Thomas Y. Crowell Company, New York, 1942, 1947, 1953
Bishop, Edward	*The Guinea Pig Club*; MacMillan & Co. Ltd., 1963
Bowyer, Chaz	*Pathfinders at War*; Ian Allen Ltd., Shepparton, Surrey. 1977
Bowyer, Chaz	*Royal Air Force*; The aircraft in service since 1918; Paintings by Michael Turner; Hamlyn Publishing Group Limited, Astronaut House, Feltham, Middlesex, England
Brickhill, Paul	*Reach for the Sky*; Collins (Fontana Books) London 1957
Brookes, A.J.	*Bomber Squadron at War*; Ian Allen Ltd., Shepparton, Surrey; U.K., 1983
Cacutt,	*Classics of the Air*; Marshall Cavendish Books Ltd., (Ed.Allez-Fernandez) 58 Old Compton Street, London, W1V 5PA; 1988

Campbell, Christopher   *Aces and Aircraft of World War 1*; Methuen Publications; 2330 Midland Avenue, Agincourt, Ontario; M1S 1P7; 1981

Carlson, S/L Don   *RCAF Padre*; published by D.G. Carlson, 64 Sherwood Crescent, Red Deer, Alberta, T4N 0A6 (Designed and Lithographed by Skytone Graphics, Red Deer)

Clostermann, Pierre   *The Big Show*; Chatto and Windus, London, 1951

Collins, Robert   *The Long and the Short and the Tall*; Western Producer Prairie Books, Saskatoon, Saskatchewan, 1986

Congdon, Philip   *Behind the Hangar Doors*; SONIK Books, Tarleton House, The Broadway, Woodhall Spa, Lincolnshire LN1 065Q, England, 1985

Conrad, Peter C.   *Training for Victory, The BCATP in the West*; Western Producer Prairie Books, Saskatoon, Saskatchewan; 1989

Cooper, Alan W.   *Beyond the Dams to the Tirpitz - The Later Operations of 617 Squadron*; William Kimber and Co. Limited; Godolphin House, 22a Queen Anne's Gate, London SW1H 9AE; 1983

Coote and Batchelor   *Winston Churchill's Maxims and Reflections*; Barnes and Noble Inc., New York, 1992

Dickson, Paul   *Words*; Delacorte Press, 1 Dag Hammarskjold Plaza, New York, N.Y. 10017, 1982

Elting, John R., et al   *A Dictionary of Soldier Talk*; Chas. Scribner's Sons, New York

Emmot, Norman   *One Foot on the Ground*; Lugus Publications, 48 Falcon Street, Toronto, Ontario M4S 2P5; 1992

Flanagan, Edward M.   *Before the Battle*; Presidio Press, 31 Pamaron Way, Novato California 94947; 1985

Fletcher and MacPhail   *Harvard! The North American Trainers in Canada*; DCF Flying Books; PO Box 8589; Dundas, Ontario, L9H 5G1; 1990

Freeman, Roger   *Experience of War: The British Airman*; Arms and Armour Press; Artillery House, Artillery Row; London, SW1P 1RT; 1989

Greer and Harold

Flying Clothing: The Story of Its Development; Airlife Publications (Shrewsbury) Ltd.; 7, St.John's Hill, Shrewsbury, England; 1979

Gunderson, Breian

P/O Prune...Dutiful But Dumb; article in *Airforce* Magazine, Volume 15, Number 2, July-August-September 1991

Halley, James J.

Squadrons of the Royal Air Force; Air Britain (Historians) Ltd.; 1 East Street, Tonbridge, Kent, England; 1980

Hampson, Bill

Canadian Flying Services-Emblems and Insignia 1914-1984; Published by Bill Hampson, 3128 Main Street, Vancouver, British Columbia, 1986

Harvey, J. Douglas

Boys, Bombs and Brussels Sprouts; McClelland and Stewart Limited, 25 Hollinger Road, Toronto, Ontario, M4B 3G2; 1981

James, John

The Paladins; Futura Publications, A Division of Macdonald and Company (Publishers) Ltd., Orbit House, 1 New Fetter Lane, London EC4A 1AR

Jones, R.V.

Most Secret War; British Scientific Intelligence 1939-1945; Coronet Books, Holder and Stoughton Ltd., 47 Bedford Square, London WC1 3DP; 1978

Jones, W.E.

Bomber Intelligence; Midland Counties Publications; 24 The Hollow, Earl Shilton, Leicester, England; 1983

Kostenuk and Griffin

RCAF Squadron Histories and Aircraft 1924-1968; National Museum of Man, National Museums of Canada; Samuel Stevens, Hakkert and Co., Toronto and Sarasota, 1977

Krisinger, Capt. Chris

In Operation Nickel Grass; (Article in *USAF Airpower Journal*, Spring 1989)

Lamb, Charles

To War in a Stringbag; Arrow Books Limited, 3 Fitzroy Square, London W1P 6JD, 1978

Lucas, Laddie

Flying Colours; Panther Books edition, Granada Publishing Ltd., 8 Grafton Street, London W1X 3LA, 1983

McGillivray, Don

The Edmonton Journal, November 30, 1991, *Second World War Words Revisited*

Messenger, Charles

Bomber Harris and the Strategic Bombing Offensive 1939-1945; St. Martin's Press, 175 Fifth Avenue, New York, N.Y. 10010, 1984

Milberry and Halliday

The Royal Canadian Air Force at War 1939-1945; CANAV Books, 51 Balsam Avenue, Toronto, Ontario; M4E 3B6, 1990

Milberry, Larry

Sixty Years; The RCAF and CF Air Command 1924-1984; CANAV Books, Toronto, 1984

Molson and Taylor

Canadian Aircraft since 1909; Putnam and Company Ltd., London; 1982

Neal/Rosher

Original Document in the possession of Carolyn Neal and Graham Rosher; Edmonton, Alberta

Nissen, with Cockerill

Winning the Radar War; St. Martin's Press, New York, NY. 1987

Partridge, Eric (FS)

A Dictionary of Forces Slang, 1939-1945; Secker and Warburg, London 1948

Partridge, Eric (8th)

A Dictionary of Slang and Unconventional English – (8th ed); Paul Beal; MacMillan Publishing Co., 866 Third Avenue, New York, NY 10022 1984

Peden, Murray

A Thousand Shall Fall; Canada's Wings Inc., Box 393, Stittsville, Canada K0A 3G0

Pettipas, Leo

Canadian Naval Aviation 1945-1968 - Second Edition; Winnipeg (Sea Fury) Chapter, Canadian Naval Air Group; 1990

Quill, Jeffrey

Spitfire; Arrow Books Limited, 17-21 Conway Street, London, W1P 6JD, 1985

Rawlings, John

Fighter Squadrons of the RAF and their Aircraft; (Revised and Updated), Crecy Books, 1993

Reed, Arthur

F-104 Starfighter; Ian Allen Ltd., Shepparton, Surrey, 1981

Rees, Nigel

Why Do We Say...?; Blandford Press, Artillery House, Artillery Row, London, SW1 P 1RT. 1987

Russell, E.C.

Customs and Traditions of the Canadian Armed Forces; Supply and Services Canada; Deneau and Greenberg Publishers Ltd., 1980

Sand, Major Tom	Letters to the author, 1985-1994
Sargent, J. William	*Sgt. Sargent's Trenton*; The Hangar Bookshelf, Box 1513 Belleville, Ont. K8N 5J2; 1985
Sharp, C. Martin and Bowyer, Michael J.F.	*Mosquito*; Faber and Faber Limited, 24 Russell Square, London WC1; 1967
Simpson, with Speak	*Concise Oxford Book of Proverbs* – 2nd Edition; Oxford University Press, Walton Street, Oxford, England OX2 6DP; 1992
Snowie, J Allen	*The Bonnie: HMCS Bonaventure*; Boston Mills Press, 132 Main Street, Erin, Ontario, N0B 1T0
Spick, Mike	*Fighter Pilot Tactics*; Stein and Day Publishers, Scarborough House, Briarcliff Manor, N.Y. 10510; 1983
Sutherland, BGen H.M.	Letters to the author, November 9th, 1993 and February 18, 1994
Terraine, John	*The Right of the Line, The Royal Air Force in the European War 1939-1945*; Hodder and Stoughton Limited, Mill Road, Dunton Green, Sevenoaks, Kent TN13 2YA; 1985
Welch, Col. John F.	*Van Sickle's Modern Airmanship* – (Fifth Edition); Van Nostrand Reinhold Company, 135 West 50th Street, New York, N.Y. 10020
Whitehouse, Arch	*Decisive Air Battles of the First World War*; Duell, Sloan and Pearce; N.Y. 1963
Williams, Eric	*The Wooden Horse* - (Revised Edition); William Collins Sons and Co. Ltd., St. James' Place, London, 1979
Winter, Denis	*The First of the Few - Fighter Pilots of the First World War*; Allen Lane, Penguin Books; 536 King's Road, London SW10 0UH and by The University of Georgia Press, Athens, Georgia, 30602; 1983
Yeager and Janos	*Yeager, An Autobiography*; Bantam Books Inc.; 666 Fifth Avenue, New York, NY, 10103; 1985 (p. 230)
Ziegler, Mary	*We Serve That Men May Fly, The Story of the RCAF Women's Division*; RCAF (W.D.) Association, Hamilton, Ontario, 1974

About the Author

Tom Langeste is a man of many parts. A native of Edmonton, he holds degrees in Commerce, Arts and Law from the University of Alberta. He currently practices law in his home town.

Tom is an aviator as well as a lawyer. While in high school he joined the Air Cadets where he earned his pilot's wings. He then became an aircraft technician in 418 (City of Edmonton) Squadron of the Air Reserves. Commissioned as an aerospace engineer in 1980, he was the Squadron's Engineer Officer until the Unit was disbanded.

Tom is also an author and illustrator. He began collecting items of air force slang some years ago and has put them together in this delightful book. His discerning eye, military service and sense of humour have enabled him to capture the essence of the air force experience in these pages.

The Canadian Institute of Strategic Studies

Chairman of the Board of Directors: Jean-Jacques Blais, QC, PC, BA, LLB
President: Don Macnamara, OMM, CD, MA
Executive Director: Alex Morrison, MSC, CD, MA
Associate Executive Director, Jim Hanson, CD, Eng Cert, MA, CET

The Canadian Institute of Strategic Studies provides the forum for, and is the vehicle to stimulate, the research, study, analysis and discussion of the strategic implications of major national and international issues, events and trends as they affect Canada and Canadians.

The CISS is currently working independently or in conjunction with related organizations in a variety of fields, including international peacekeeping; Canadian security and sovereignty; arms control and disarmament; Canada-US security cooperation; regional security studies; environmental issues; regional and global trade issues.

CISS publications include:

Free with membership:　The Canadian Strategic Forecast
Seminar proceedings
Strategic Datalinks
Strategic Profile Canada
The CISS Bulletin
Canadian Defence Quarterly
Peacekeeping and International Relations

By subscription:　The McNaughton Papers (*The* Canadian Journal of Strategic Studies)

The CISS is an independent, non-partisan, non-profit organization. For membership, seminar and publications information please contact:

The Canadian Institute of Strategic Studies
76 St. Clair Avenue West, Suite 502
Toronto, ON M4V 1N2
Tel: (416) 964-6632 Fax: (416) 964-5833